Sensing the Sacred i
Early Modern Cultu

MW00808483

This volume traces transformations in attitudes toward, ideas about, and experiences of religion and the senses in the medieval and early modern period. Broad in temporal and geographical scope, it challenges traditional notions of periodisation, highlighting continuities as well as change. Rather than focusing on individual senses, the volume's organisation emphasises the multisensoriality and embodied nature of religious practices and experiences, refusing easy distinctions between asceticism and excess. The senses were not passive, but rather active and reactive, responding to and initiating change. As the contributions in this collection demonstrate, in the pre-modern era, sensing the sacred was a complex, vexed, and constantly evolving process, shaped by individuals, environment, and religious change. The volume will be essential reading not only for scholars of religion and the senses, but for anyone interested in histories of medieval and early modern bodies, material culture, affects, and affect theory.

Robin Macdonald completed her PhD at the University of York and was a Postdoctoral Research Fellow at the ARC Centre of Excellence for the History of Emotions at the University of Western Australia.

Emilie K. M. Murphy is a Lecturer in Early Modern History at the University of York.

Elizabeth L. Swann is a Research Associate at the University of Cambridge. From September 2018, she will be Assistant Professor in Interdisciplinary Studies within the Department of English Studies, Durham University.

Sensing the Sacred in Medieval and Early Modern Culture

Edited by Robin Macdonald,
Emilie K. M. Murphy, and
Elizabeth L. Swann

Routledge
Taylor & Francis Group

LONDON AND NEW YORK

First published 2018 by Routledge

2 Park Square, Milton Park, Abingdon, Oxon OX14 4RN
605 Third Avenue, New York, NY 10017

Routledge is an imprint of the Taylor & Francis Group, an informa business

First issued in paperback 2022

Publisher's Note

The publisher has gone to great lengths to ensure the quality of this reprint but points out that some imperfections in the original copies may be apparent.

British Library Cataloguing-in-Publication Data
A catalogue record for this book is available from the British Library

Library of Congress Cataloging-in-Publication Data
Names: Macdonald, Robin, editor.
Title: Sensing the sacred in medieval and early modern culture / edited by Robin Macdonald, Emilie K.M. Murphy, and Elizabeth L. Swann.
Description: 1st [edition]. | New York : Routledge, 2018. | Includes bibliographical references and index.
Identifiers: LCCN 2017050482 (print) | LCCN 2018007384 (ebook) | ISBN 9781315608389 | ISBN 9781472454669 (alk. paper)
Subjects: LCSH: Senses and sensation—Religious aspects—History. | Human body—Religious aspects—History. | Civilization, Medieval.
Classification: LCC BL65.B63 (ebook) | LCC BL65.B63 S465 2018 (print) | DDC 248.2—dc23
LC record available at https://lccn.loc.gov/2017050482

ISBN: 978-1-472-45466-9 (hbk)
ISBN: 978-1-03-233910-8 (pbk)
DOI: 10.4324/9781315608389

Typeset in Sabon
by Keystroke, Neville Lodge, Tettenhall, Wolverhampton

Table of contents

Figures

Notes on contributors

John H. Arnold is Professor of Medieval History at the University of Cambridge. He has published on various aspects of medieval religion and culture, and on modern historiographical practice, and edited the *Oxford Handbook of Medieval Christianity* (2014).

Erin Lambert is Assistant Professor of History at the University of Virginia. She holds a PhD in early modern European history from the University of Wisconsin-Madison. Her recent book explores the interplay of body, community, and belief in the Reformation through two interconnected themes: theologies of the resurrection of the body and the practice of song.

Robin Macdonald was awarded her PhD at the University of York. She recently completed a postdoctoral research fellowship at the Australian Research Council Centre of Excellence for the History of Emotions at the University of Western Australia (project number CE110001011). Her research focuses on histories of encounter in seventeenth-century North America, letter writing, and the materiality of texts.

Joe Moshenska is Associate Professor of English at the University of Oxford and a fellow of University College. He is the author of *Feeling Pleasures: The Sense of Touch in Renaissance England* (Oxford University Press, 2014) and *A Stain in the Blood: The Remarkable Voyage of Sir Kenelm Digby* (William Heinemann, 2016). His monograph *Iconoclasm as Child's Play* is forthcoming from Stanford University Press.

Subha Mukherji is Senior Lecturer in English at the University of Cambridge, Fellow of Fitzwilliam College, and Principal Investigator on the ERC-funded interdisciplinary project, *Crossroads of Knowledge in Early Modern England: the Place of Literature*. She has published widely on law and literature in the Renaissance, early modern literature, Shakespeare, genre, literary epistemologies, and the poetics of space. She is currently writing a book provisionally entitled *'Full of doubt I stand': Questioning Knowledge in Early Modern Literature*.

Emilie K. M. Murphy is a Lecturer in Early Modern History at the University of York. Her research focuses on processes of religious change, identity formation, and cultural encounter for people living in Reformation England and for Anglophones in Counter-Reformation Europe. She has published several articles on the embodiment of religious expression through sounds, voice and language, and musical performance, and is currently completing her first monograph: *The Reformation of the Soundscape: Music and Piety in Early Modern England.*

Richard Newhauser is Professor of English and Medieval Studies, Arizona State University, Tempe. His research is focused on the history of the senses, the moral tradition in Western thought, and Middle English literature. He is the co-editor of *Pleasure and Danger in Perception*, special issue of The Senses & Society 5.1 (2010), and editor of *A Cultural History of the Senses in the Middle Ages* (Bloomsbury, 2014). His most recent contribution to sensory studies is "The Multisensoriality of Place and the Chaucerian Multisensual", in *The Five Senses in Medieval and Early Modern England*, ed. A. Kern-Stähler et al., Intersections 44 (Leiden and Boston, 2016), 199–218.

Michael Schoenfeldt is the John Knott Professor of English Literature at the University of Michigan. He is the author of *Prayer and Power: George Herbert and Renaissance Courtship* (University of Chicago Press, 1991), *Bodies and Selves in Early Modern England: Physiology and Inwardness in Spenser, Shakespeare, Herbert, and Milton* (Cambridge, 1999) and *The Cambridge Introduction to Shakespeare's Poetry* (2010). He is currently researching a book-length study of pain and pleasure in early modern England.

Abigail Shinn is a Lecturer in Early Modern Literature and Culture at Goldsmiths, University of London. Alongside Andrew Hadfield and Matthew Dimmock, she is the editor of the *Research Companion to Popular Culture in Early Modern England*. Her current book project *Conversion Narratives in Early Modern England: Tales of Turning* is forthcoming with Palgrave Macmillan.

Elizabeth L. Swann is a Research Associate on the European Research Council funded project Crossroads of Knowledge in Early Modern England: The Place of Literature, co-hosted by the Faculty of English and the Centre for Research in the Arts, Social Sciences, and Humanities at the University of Cambridge. From September 2018, she will be Assistant Professor in Interdisciplinary Studies in the Department of English Studies, Durham University. Her research investigates the relations between embodiment, affect, and epistemology in early modern literature and culture, with a particular focus on reformation theology and experimental philosophy. She is currently preparing for publication a monograph titled *Taste and Knowledge in Early Modern England: Honey Secrets.*

Bronwyn V. Wallace is Research Associate in the Department of English and Related Literature at the University of York, where she works on the AHRC-funded project 'Remembering the Reformation'.

C. M. Woolgar is Professor of History and Archival Studies at the University of Southampton. He has a long-standing interest in the history of the everyday. His publications include *The Senses in Late Medieval England* (Yale University Press, 2006) and *The Culture of Food in England, 1200–1500* (Yale University Press, 2016).

Acknowledgments

Many of the essays in this collection began as papers presented at an international conference, 'Sensing the Sacred: Religion and the Senses, 1300–1800', which took place at the University of York in 2013. The editors would like to thank the presenters and delegates for their contributions to the stimulating, cross-disciplinary discussions that were instrumental in shaping this collection. We would also like to thank the Centre for Renaissance and Early Modern Studies at the University of York, who hosted the conference and provided financial assistance. Special thanks are due to Sally Kingsley for administrative support. The Society for Renaissance Studies, the University of York Humanities Research Centre, the University of York Department of History, the University of York Centre for Eighteenth-Century Studies, the Royal History Society, and the Journal of Early Modern History all provided additional financial assistance, for which we are extremely grateful.

A number of scholars have supported this project, providing advice and encouragement: we are particularly grateful to Simon Ditchfield, Mark Jenner, Helen Smith, and Rachel Willie. We would also like to thank our respective colleagues at the ERC-funded project Crossroads of Knowledge: The Place of Literature in Early Modern England, co-hosted by the Faculty of English and CRASSH at The University of Cambridge; The Marco Institute for Medieval and Renaissance Studies at the University of Tennessee Knoxville; the ARC Centre of Excellence for the History of Emotions at the University of Western Australia; and the University of York. We are grateful to Lotte Reinbold who compiled the index.

Finally, we would like to thank our contributors for being part of this volume. It has been a privilege to work with them and we thank them for their commitment to the project.

Introduction: sensing the sacred

Robin Macdonald, Emilie K. M. Murphy,
and Elizabeth L. Swann

[God's] adoration is exprest by offices and sensible words; for it is man that beleeveth and praieth. . . I could hardly be made beleeve that the sight of our Crucifixes and pictures of that pittiful torment, that the ornaments and ceremonious motions in our Churches, that the voyces accomodated and suted to our devotions, and this stirring of our senses, doth not greatly inflame the peoples soules with a religious passion of wonderous beneficiall good.[1]

Writing in the aftermath of the European Reformations, Montaigne's insistence on the efficacy of devotional art, ecclesiastical ceremony, song, and 'sensible words', for rousing the souls of the people to a state of 'religious passion' stands both as a response to the recent waves of reformist iconoclasm in France and further afield, and as a recuperation of the senses in an essay characterised by extreme skepticism about their epistemological value. For the devout Catholic Montaigne, the impossibility of certain human knowledge – including sensory knowledge – leads to a fideistic conviction that religious belief must be founded not in the workings of the human intellect, but in faith alone.[2] Whilst Montaigne dismisses the evidentiary utility of the senses as a form of proof he retains a role for them in worship: 'the stirring of our senses', he implies, serves as a means of inciting the forms of pious affect that are at the root of true faith.

Montaigne's careful but vehement defence of the importance of sensory experience to the cultivation of religious devotion is at once exceptional – a product of Montaigne's brilliant, idiosyncratic mind – and entirely typical of a period which was profoundly concerned with the relationship between the physical life of the body, and the spiritual life of the soul. This was the case across denominational divides; given here in the translation by John Florio – a Protestant Italian religious refugee who made England his adopted home – Montaigne's words attest to the transnational and cross-confessional currency of such concerns. As the essays collected in this volume show, Protestant reformers of various stripes and the 'papists' they excoriated were equally concerned with negotiating – in their different ways – a place for sensation in the practice of religion. Montaigne's acknowledgement that 'it is man that beleeveth and praieth', for example, gestures towards the Calvinist doctrine of accommodation, according to which God clothes spiritual mysteries in physical form as a concession to human weakness.[3]

For medieval and early modern men and women, faith was characterised as much by embodied experience as by abstract theological dispute. As the theologian and religious historian David Morgan argues, sensation is integral to religious belief: 'belief happens as touching and seeing, hearing and tasting'. According to Morgan, whereas in the twenty-first century religious belief is usually conceived of as assent to propositional statements such as 'God exists', historically religious belief has been as much a matter of 'embodied forms of practice' as of 'the profession of creeds'.[4] Literary scholars, too, have recognised the intensely physical, passionate nature of faith in the early modern period, illuminating the ways in which physicality and spirituality, and ethics and affect, are entwined in the period's medical and devotional discourses.[5]

Nonetheless, it is important to acknowledge a tendency for medieval and early modern people to express an intense distrust of the senses and the pleasures they offer. The notion that the senses lead the believer away from God by encouraging indulgence in the sinful pleasures of the flesh is ubiquitous in the Western Christian tradition. In order to combat this perceived threat to spiritual integrity, a strong strand of asceticism developed, exemplified by the Church Fathers including Origen, St Jerome, and John Chrysostom, and which remained in play throughout the medieval and early modern periods. Thomas More, for example, famously wore a hair shirt under his luxurious clothes, and was said to practice other forms of self-mortification.[6] Whilst Protestant reformers denounced the extremes of asceticism, associating physical self-mortification with monastic hypocrisy and nugatory works, many retained a profound suspicion of sensory pleasure. The senses, then, were profoundly equivocal: both intrinsic to the experience of faith, and spiritually hazardous. As the English poet and devotional writer Richard Brathwaite put it, invoking Augustine, in his 1620 *Essaies upon the five senses*, the senses were '*windowes*' which open to all unbounded libertie', unobjectionable in themselves, but capable either of 'weale or woe: happy if rightly tempered; sinister, if without limit'.[7]

This collection covers an era of dramatic social, political, economic and technological change, and extreme religious turmoil. It traces transformations in attitudes to, ideas about, and experiences of the senses from eleventh-century debates about the real presence in continental Europe to late seventeenth-century missionaries proselytising in North America. As Wietse de Boer and Christine Göttler have recently suggested, such 'periods of profound cultural change' ensure that sensory experiences 'rise to the surface of observable historical reality'.[8] Indeed, in past decades much scholarship on the religious upheavals of the Reformations has described transitions between different forms of faith as characterised, in part, by sensory transformations. The shift from (medieval) Catholicism to (early modern) Protestantism has often been depicted as a move from a sensuous to a relatively austere form of religious faith. As the senses in this period were closely connected to the passions and affects (Thomas Wright, for example, famously described the 'amitie betwixt the passions and sense' in his 1601 treatise *The passions of the minde in general*) this putative shift is simultaneously described as a move away from an emotionally-charged, participatory form of religion, towards an intellectualised, individualised religion of the book.[9]

As numerous scholars have shown, the religious world of medieval Europe was profoundly material and sensory: Catholicism nurtured a vibrant culture of visual art, music, and architecture, and worship engaged the senses of smell (through the use of incense), touch (through practices such as kissing the pax board), and even taste (through the Eucharistic ritual).[10] According to revisionist historians such as Margaret Aston and Eamon Duffy, the Reformations were motivated in part by an iconoclastic distrust of such sensory abundance, resulting in the violent destruction of a richly affective form of worship and its replacement by an austere, intellectualised form of faith.[11] The endurance of this narrative in more recent work on religion and the senses is evident in Marcia Hall's introduction to the recent collection *The Sensuous in the Counter-Reformation Church*. In promoting the use of the senses (through visual imagery) to inspire religious devotion, Hall argues, 'Catholics recognized that emotion was a tool that Protestants renounced and that it could therefore be used effectively to woo the lapsed back to the Catholic fold'.[12]

Other scholars have presented reformist attitudes not as an outright rejection of the senses and affects, but rather as a change in emphasis. The Protestant suspicion of visual images, this argument runs, was compensated by a simultaneous (Lutheran) elevation of the status of audition, which drew on St Paul's insistence that 'faith cometh by hearing' (particularly the hearing of sermons).[13] Others highlight continuities between traditional and reformist approaches to the senses. Matthew Milner, for example, argues that 'reformers were still governed by traditional assumptions on sensory propriety and sensory theory'.[14] Simultaneously, there has been a move to explore the importance of the 'lower' senses of smell, touch, and taste to medieval and early modern piety. As Milner points out, 'sixteenth-century religion was more than eyes and ears; it was a full, synaesthetic experience'.[15]

In this volume, we build on the approach of scholars such as Milner, both in challenging the tendency to impose artificial divisions between the 'higher' and 'lower' senses, and in highlighting stability – as well as ruptures – in the role of the senses in medieval and early modern religion. In matters of religion, as elsewhere, scholars must resist constructing an easy antithesis between sensory abnegation and sensuous excess, and correspondingly between intellect and affect. As Richard Newhauser's and Joe Moshenska's essays variously suggest, severe asceticism and luxurious sensuality are not the only options available to the believer who wishes to regulate his or her senses for devotional ends. Neither do these two alternatives always have an adversarial relation. For medieval and early modern men and women alike, sensory pleasure and sensory self-denial existed in an ever-shifting dynamic, in some cases enhancing as well as diminishing the other, and mediated by the virtue of temperance. Similarly, the division of the human sensorium into the five clearly distinguished, hierarchically organised senses of sight, hearing, smell, taste, and touch has been historically influential.[16] A tendency to replicate this division in recent scholarship, however, has obscured both the complexity of sensory taxonomies in the period, and the complex, synaesthetic imbrications of the senses in the realm of human experience. Rather than focusing on hierarchies of the senses, the organisation of this volume stresses both collaborative and antagonistic interactions of the senses. Our collective emphasis on the multi-sensorial nature of embodied religious practices demonstrates the ways sixteenth- and seventeenth-century reformers engaged with, exploited, and transformed the prominence of corporeal experience in the Catholic tradition, as well as the ways that they challenged it.[17] In refusing to distinguish artificially between the senses – which often worked in tandem – and in rejecting a simplistic dichotomy between sensory and affective excess on the one hand, and intellectualised sensory asceticism on the other, we are able to present a more complex picture of the Reformations as characterised both by change and continuity.

The ambivalence of the senses – their dual status as agents of sanctity and iniquity – in medieval and early modern Western Christianity was further complicated by a widespread distinction between the physical senses and the spiritual senses, which originated with the Church Fathers and remained influential throughout the period in question here. As Paul Gavrilyuk and Sarah Coakley's edited collection *The Spiritual Senses: Perceiving God in Western Christianity* has shown, the precise nature of the spiritual senses, and their relation to the physical senses, is complex and variable: the tradition is modified and transformed as it is developed in the works of key authors such as Origen, Augustine, Aquinas, and Nicholas of Cusa.[18] Broadly speaking, however, the spiritual senses can be conceived of as analogous to the physical senses, but with two crucial differences: firstly, they are immaterial, and belong not to the body but to the spirit, soul, heart, or intellect, and secondly, they are capable of apprehending the divine. As such, the spiritual senses offered a form of perception supposedly purged of the physical body's sinful and self-indulgent appetites. In practice, however, a clear distinction between the physical and spiritual senses was difficult to maintain. For Brathwaite, they existed in a zero-sum relation: 'though the *eye* of my bodie allude to the *eye* of my soule', he writes, 'yet is the eye of my soule darkned by the eye of my bodie'.[19] Therefore the believer ought to cultivate the spiritual senses by regulating or denying the physical senses. For others, the physical and spiritual senses were more closely entwined, and existed as analogues, or on a continuum. Joseph Hall, for instance, writing in his 1679 *Contemplations upon the remarkable passages in the life of the holy Jesus,* explained that 'those two parts whereof we consist (the bodily, the spiritual) do in a sort partake of each other'.[20] For Hall, the physical and spiritual senses are inextricable.

Whilst the essays collected in this volume discuss the relation between the physical and spiritual senses at a number of points, the collective intention (*pace* Gavrilyuk and Coakley) is not to pin down or define the various permutations of this tradition. Rather, the contributions here seek to explore convergences between theories about the spiritual and physical senses and a range of other religious preoccupations, including (among other things) the formation of confessional identities, the construction of sacred space, and the nature of virtue. As we see in Subha Mukherji's essay, the distinction between the physical and spiritual senses casts considerable light on debates about the evidentiary value of the senses as a route to religious knowledge, including the experience of the divine.

In order to examine the ways learned ideas about the senses intersected with issues of urgent personal devotional concerns, Mukherji turns to the evidence provided by literature. It is frequently noted as a historiographical obstacle that evidence of sensory experience is hard to attain: sensation is inherently personal and ephemeral, and therefore elusive.[21] The present, moreover, cannot be taken as a reliable guide to the past: as anthropologists and historians agree, sensation is culturally and historically specific, and embodied practices and experiences can vary dramatically according to context.[22] In response to this perceived paucity of evidence, historians have tended to turn to prescriptive sources associated with elite intellectual cultures, such as medical and theological treatises, in order to understand the senses. As John Arnold argues in his contribution here, however, this is insufficient if we are to achieve a fuller understanding of the 'lived' practice of religion: faith as it is embedded in a wide range of material, intellectual, and social contexts.[23] As such, and as this volume attests, scholars must be prepared to explore unfamiliar and heterogeneous sources – including the literary – if they are to have any chance of recapturing the rich and diverse sensory world of medieval and early modern religious devotion.

The essays in this volume are highly interdisciplinary in approach, and draw on a wide variety of manuscript and printed source materials.[24] Sources include drama, poetry, and imaginative prose, as well as religious polemic and homily, psychological, medical, and didactic texts, personal and public epistles, and music. This broad range is significant, for it testifies simultaneously to the challenges and opportunities offered by sensory studies, and to the methodological underpinnings of this volume. In expanding the scope of enquiry in this way, the essays in this collection uncover a conception of religious experience as fundamentally dynamic and transactional. Taken collectively, they emphasise processes of sensing, rather than the senses as a reified object of investigation, thereby configuring sensation not merely as receptive, but as a potent agent of change.[25] In particular, essays by Christopher Woolgar, Emilie Murphy, and Erin Lambert examine how sacred objects and spaces are constituted through sensory interaction, developing a new notion of holiness as a process, occurring at the experiential intersection of subject and object.

Other essays in this collection follow their protagonists as they traverse confessional and experiential boundaries via the internal and external borders of Europe. Whilst the focus is predominantly on European cultures of sensing, we also consider encounters in the Americas. Although European colonisers attempted to impose their own sensory and religious perspectives and regimes on Indigenous cultures, these cultures inevitably also reciprocally influenced the ways in which Europeans perceived and experienced their own bodies and surroundings.[26] This could also be the case for armchair travellers, as Robin Macdonald's essay contends. Macdonald's focus on the materiality of birch bark letters that missionaries sent to friends, relatives, and colleagues back home highlights the extent to which texts themselves are material entities, and reading is an embodied, sensory activity.[27] Words and materiality, Macdonald argues, work together to create meanings. Macdonald's essay, and this volume as a whole, participates in, but also departs from, a series of recent cross-disciplinary 'turns' to (variously) the body, the visual, and material culture in medieval and early modern studies.[28] Such turns have been enormously productive, but they have also been hindered by a tendency to oppose a concrete world of things to an abstract realm of words.[29] Such a tendency goes against the grain of recent scholarship on the senses and early modern literature, which has emphasised the ability of certain modes of rhetorical language and literary form to encapsulate and precipitate sensory experience. For Holly Dugan, for example, 'metaphors can function as a historical archive of sensation', whilst Erika T. Lin argues the embodied and material performance dynamics of early modern theatre correspond to the sensory paradigms of religious ritual.[30] Building on such work, a number of contributors here – such as Abigail Shinn, Subha Mukherji, Bronwyn Wallace, and Elizabeth Swann – investigate the extent to which language is itself a sensory phenomenon, with the capacity to open a vista onto the experiential worlds of the past.

I: Prescription and practice

The essays in the opening section of this volume examine relationships between prescriptive and proscriptive literature on the senses, and sensory religious practices in the medieval period. The methodological and historiographical problems for investigating the sensory experiences of the medieval laity are foregrounded by John Arnold, who questions the utility of elite, learned medical sources for understanding ordinary men and women's sensory experience. Instead, Arnold suggests, scholars must attend to moments where the senses are addressed implicitly, in sources which invoke embodiment and affect more broadly. In particular, Arnold draws attention to the relationship between sensory metaphor, used to communicate experiences, and more essential claims about sensory knowledge (for instance, the contention that sin may literally enter through the senses). Citing examples from miracle stories, Arnold argues that the tension between sensory metaphors, the spiritual senses, and material reality remains 'productively unresolved' in narrative.

The second and third essays in this volume respond to Arnold's appeal to scholars to investigate a broader range of sensuous material, and to attend to the experiences of lay women and men. Richard Newhauser explores an instance of elite theory disseminated to the laity in the form of highly influential compendia on the vices and virtues by the Dominican priest and pastoral theologian William Peraldus. Newhauser's close reading of these significant, and yet understudied works offers an analysis of the ways in which devotional texts communicated knowledge about, and shaped experience of, the senses. In particular, he focuses on the role of high medieval pastoral theology in guiding and directing the senses of parishioners, and in so doing challenges the popular assumption that the repression of sensory pleasures was unanimously endorsed in the Middle Ages. For Peraldus, the 'correct' use of the senses could even be virtuous. Sacred contexts could be created through sensory perception, and (if performed with self-restraint) everyday activities such as eating and drinking could become imbued with devotional meaning. Therefore, Newhauser argues, it is temperance – not ascesis or denial – that should be viewed as central to the ethics of the senses in the medieval moral tradition.

Like Newhauser, Christopher Woolgar draws attention to the positive aspects of the senses in the Western medieval religious tradition. Using sources including monastic customaries and records from church councils and synods, Woolgar considers the material ways in which 'things' were made holy, exploring how the 'physical process of sensing' could consecrate objects or individuals. For instance, it was through the physical act of speaking the words of the liturgy (rather than the meaning of the words) that the bread and wine were transformed. Once objects became holy they could confer sacrality through other forms of physical contact, including seeing, touching, and kissing relics. There were, however, also grave concerns, particularly from the episcopacy, over the ways holiness might become lost, or polluted, through contact with the 'profane'. As Woolgar demonstrates, whilst theologians might debate the nature of holiness or the process of transubstantiation in intellectual terms, ordinary men and women were more interested in the practical, prophylactic, and salutary benefits of physical contact with holy objects.

II: Concord and conversion

Woolgar's focus on corporeal conversion and moments of liminal transition leads us into the second section of the volume. Moving forward to the early modern period, essays from Joe Moshenska and Abigail Shinn focus on the role of the senses in narratives of conversion in an age of extreme confessional disruption. Whilst acknowledging the conflicts and ruptures associated with conversion, Moshenska and Shinn also attend to moments of dialogue, concord, and constancy across confessional boundaries.

Through an analysis of the writings of Sir Kenelm Digby, Joe Moshenska discusses the neglected phenomenon of 'double conversion'. Digby, who was raised a Protestant, converted to Roman Catholicism before returning the Protestant faith. Since Christian tradition held that conversion was irrevocable, those who recanted (Digby included) risked accusations of insincerity. Moshenska's essay examines the ways in which Digby's writings responded to this risk. Digby's epistemological and theological interest in the senses, coupled with his constant re-writing of his life experiences, Moshenska argues, were intimately linked: indeed, Digby's writings can be viewed as a form of 'sensory autobiography'. In particular, Moshenska shows how Digby made use of the senses in his writing in order to assert continuities between his 'past and present sensing selves', thus challenging ideas of rupture traditionally associated with conversion. Though transformed by his religious experiences, he remained fundamentally unchanged. Moshenska leaves the reader with a final question, one which recurs throughout this volume: are the senses sites of purely subjective, individual experience, or can sensory experience be made communicable to others? Digby, Moshenska argues, insisted both to be the case.

Abigail Shinn's essay similarly complicates traditional understandings of early modern conversion narratives through an examination of the senses, and addresses the question of the communicability of individual sensory experiences. Shinn draws on a broad variety of Catholic and Protestant writings from seventeenth-century England and North America, a period in which conversion narratives flourished. While scholars often stress the antagonistic nature of conversion narratives, Shinn argues, the senses provided a significant 'cross-confessional trope', which provided a 'locus of spiritual transformation'. Although traditional historiography emphasises Protestant rejection of the senses, Shinn demonstrates that many characterised conversion in sensory terms. Conversely, although it might be tempting to exclusively associate Protestants with the 'distancing effects' of metaphor, Catholic converts also used figurative language. Sensory language, Shinn asserts, is thus employed by both Catholics and

Protestants in order to connect spiritual change with bodily metamorphosis. The language of the senses, moreover, is a powerful tool through which individual bodily experience can make visible to others that which is traditionally unseen, namely interior spiritual experience. The senses and sensory language, Shinn concludes, complicate and can even erase boundaries between the figurative and the corporeal.

III: Exile and encounter

Boundaries are key to the essays in the third section of this volume, which are united through the investigation of travel and encounter. Erin Lambert, Emilie Murphy, and Robin Macdonald all draw attention to the ways in which sensory experiences could shape, as well as traverse, boundaries – both geographical, as people moved through foreign lands, and imaginative, as individuals blurred the boundaries between bodies and texts. In so doing, all three authors explore how sensory experiences and sensuous actions played an active part in creating and shaping devotional spaces, places, and practices.

Lambert and Murphy demonstrate how attending to sound can enrich our understanding of two very different forms of exilic experience. Lambert investigates how Dutch reformed émigrés employed psalmody and liturgical gestures in order to create, and orient themselves within, particular places – notably, Austin Friars in London. Lambert reveals how hearing could prompt an embodied response from listeners, as demonstrated by the young refugee from the Low Countries who wept upon his arrival in Strasbourg when he heard fellow exiles singing in his own vernacular. Communal psalm-singing for those establishing Stranger churches during the reign of Edward VI also formed a vital way for exiles to carve out a place for themselves in London. Portable psalters were material marks of identity that were carried with individuals, and were sung from as they moved through the world, the object providing a sense of place as much as the act of psalm-singing itself. (There are significant parallels here with Robin Macdonald's essay, where the sensuous experience of objects, such as birch bark letters, provided the recipients with a physical reminder of the place of the text's origin.) Psalmody, Lambert reveals, united multifarious experiences of exile and for some anticipated a future home in heaven for the pious, figuring the entire earth itself as an exilic space.

Similarly focusing on auditory experience, Emilie Murphy explores the significance of musical sounds within English Catholic convents and seminaries founded in the Spanish Habsburg territories. Murphy attends to the uneasy reconciliation within the institutions of the positive and negative attributes of music. On the one hand, music was thought to effect physical and emotional changes in listeners, and held great power for the stirring up of devotion. Simultaneously, however, concerns over its improper use included anxieties over the voices of nuns triggering improper male fantasies about their singing bodies. Embodied responses to melodic sounds also facilitated connections to the divine, as Murphy shows in an analysis of the two poems written on the subject of bells by the English Catholic exile Richard Verstegan. By exploring the acoustic activities and boundaries of the convents and seminaries, Murphy challenges previous scholarship that has viewed these institutions in exile as unproblematically 'English'. She highlights the variety of cultural influences present, and the institutions' incorporation into local and international networks of piety. Musical performances, Murphy argues, formed part of a process of fashioning and communicating forms of identity. Communities were forged through the singing of harmonious music, which allowed English Catholics to locate themselves imaginatively and physically among their co-religionists on the continent and in England.

Connections between those at home and abroad are also vital to the final essay in this section. Robin Macdonald examines letters sent by missionaries – both men and women – from the French colony of New France to the metropole. Macdonald focuses on the materiality of letters, and in particular the ways in which form could elicit sensory responses from readers. Close attention is paid to two letters written on birch bark, rare survivals of a fragile material often used by missionaries. Missionary writings such as the Jesuits' *Relations* usually portray birch bark as a material used for writing in times of necessity (as a result of paper shortages or capture by hostile forces). Conversely, Macdonald argues that it was used deliberately – even when paper was available – owing to its particular sensory connotations. A letter's meaning, she further contends, could also be informed by the body of its bearer, blurring distinctions between bodies and texts. Indeed, whilst scholars have argued for the importance of embodied practices of reading and writing, little attention has been paid to the bodies of those who carried letters. Materiality, Macdonald concludes, had important implications for the storage and categorisation of sources, a point which scholars should attend to in order fully appreciate sources' meanings. Complementing Shinn's essay, which describes the senses as 'a powerful conversionary force' on the mission terrain, Macdonald stresses the probative function of the senses in demonstrating – to French readers of missionary relations – the apparent successes of the New France mission. All three essays in this section fulfil John Arnold's call for significant attention to be paid to embodiment and affect, a subject which is also taken up in the last section of the volume.

IV: Figuration and feeling

The final essays in this volume, from Bronwyn Wallace, Subha Mukherji, and Elizabeth Swann, are united by an interest both in the ways in which early modern authors responded to key 'sense' moments in scripture in their own works, and in the ways that such authors forged intimate links between devotional affects and literary forms. All are concerned, in varying ways, with a central tension in the relation between religion and the senses. On the one hand, faith is often described in terms which are vividly experiential, sensuous (or even sensual), and passionate. On the other hand, a long tradition in Christian thought defines faith as belief *beyond* the scope of sensory evidence; from this perspective, to require sensory proof is to reveal oneself as weak and wavering in faith. In all three essays, moreover, the resources of rhetoric and poetics are taken as instrumental not only in articulating, but also in probing and interrogating this fundamental tension.

Wallace's essay brings queer theory to bear on Southwell's interpretation, in his 1591 poem *Mary Magdalen's Funeral Tears*, of John 20's account of Mary Magdalen's encounter with the risen Christ. For Southwell, Mary's (frustrated) desire to touch Christ is simultaneously an expression of her faith (it is an outgrowth of her love of the divine), and an 'error of faith' (it is an over-investment in the corporeal). In his dilation on the encounter, Wallace argues, Southwell arrests the forward thrust of narrative temporality, opening up a space for the elaboration of Mary's passionate longing for the body of Christ. Southwell's exegetical-cum-poetic method shares with Mary an investment in the affective and erotic charge of deferral and delay. Scriptural collation, in particular, emerges both as a hermeneutical method, and as a means of 'suturing' the wound of Christ's prohibition of touch by bringing different scriptural moments into contact, thereby reconciling the figurative (spiritual) and literal (physical) meanings of the text.

Like Wallace, Mukherji is interested in the dynamic interplay between the immediacy of sense experience, and sensation that is deferred or denied. Mukherji is also deeply concerned with the relationship between literary form and religious faith, arguing that early modern drama is a neglected source for uncovering a 'lost' period in the long theological tradition of the spiritual senses. As in several essays within this volume, St Thomas plays an important role. Doubting Thomas's initial reluctance to believe in the truth of the resurrection stands for wavering faith: it is an inability to believe despite the sensory evidence available to him. This relation between tactile proof and faith, Mukherji shows, is also central to *The Winter's Tale*. In the course of the play, Mukherji argues, Leontes is taught to believe regardless of – or even against – sensory evidence. Leontes's reward for achieving this state of faith, however, is the sensory fulfilment offered by the apparent resurrection of his living, breathing wife. Mukherji interprets this irony as signalling the play's engagement with the theology of accommodation, according to which divine mysteries are made perceptible to our limited human capacities through divine generosity. In *A Midsummer Night's Dream*, this dynamic takes on a different aspect, as Bottom's account of his dream articulates a comedic version of the relation between sensation and faith.

In the final essay in this volume, Elizabeth Swann explores many of the issues raised by Wallace and Mukherji from a different perspective. Instead of examining the value and dangers of the human senses as a means of knowing the divine, Swann asks to what extent God himself can be said to sense humankind. Swann identifies a pervasive reformist tradition according to which early modern authors conceived of human virtue and vice in sensory terms. This tradition is concerned with God the father rather than with the incarnate son, and focuses heavily on the traditionally 'lower' senses of smell, touch, and taste. For early modern men and women, the experience of being perceived by God is equivalent to the experience of grace. For George Herbert, Swann argues, poetry plays an important role in maintaining the vital sensory relationship between humankind and God. Whilst early modern authors placed a high value on God's senses, however, the notion of an embodied deity was also potentially idolatrous. Swann argues that whereas reformist iconoclasm has conventionally been seen as a reaction against the sensuality of Catholic devotion, it was equally motivated by horror at the notion of an unfeeling God. Ending with the example of the Huguenot Guillaume Du Bartas's creation poem *The Divine weekes and works*, Swann shows how by focusing on ekphrastic descriptions of Adam's sense organs, Du Bartas redeems poetic imagery from such charges of idolatry.

For Montaigne – to return to the example with which this introduction opened – the 'stirring of our senses' enflamed religious passions. Ranging across a diverse spectrum of sources, the essays in this volume illuminate the complex, heterogeneous relations between religious faith, embodiment, and affect in medieval and early modern culture. While the senses were often conceived of as passive receptors for ecclesiastical or divine instruction, processes of sensing were also responsive and transformative, acting on and helping to shape specific practices and environments. In a period of immense social, economic, political, and religious upheaval, the ways in which people experienced religious faith – how they sensed the sacred – altered enormously. Our understanding of these changes, however, must be counterbalanced by an awareness and sensitivity towards the ways in which people used sensory experience as a site of resistance to, or a means of intervention in, broader historical developments. The experience of sensing the sacred could entail awe, submission, and humility. Moreover, individuals and communities used their senses actively to determine what counted as holy, to create particular kinds of sacred environment, to form and maintain a 'sense' of communal and confessional identity, and to forge personal connections with the divine.

Notes

1 Michel de Montaigne, 'An Apologie of Raymond Sebond', in *The essayes or morall, politike and millitarie discourses*, Book 2, chapter 12, trans. John Florio (London, 1603), Cc5r.

2 On Montaigne's 'skeptical fideism', see Terence Penelhum, *God and Skepticism: A Study in Skepticism and Fideism* (Dordrecht: D. Reidel, 1983), chapter 2. For an alternative view, see Manuel Bermúdez Vázquez, *The Skepticism of Michel de Montaigne* (Dordrecht: Springer, 2015), *International Archives of the History of Ideas* 24, especially 87–90.

3 On Calvinist accommodation and its precedents, see Jon Balserak, *Divinity Compromised: A Study of Divine Accommodation in the Thought of John Calvin* (Dordrecht: Springer, 2006). On other similarities in the thought of Calvin and Montaigne, see Lee Palmer Wandel, 'John Calvin and Michel de Montaigne on the Eye', in *Early Modern Eyes*, ed. Walter S. Melion and Lee Palmer Wandel, *Intersections: Interdisciplinary Studies in Early Modern Culture* (Leiden: Brill, 2010), 135–56.

4 See David Morgan, 'Introduction: The Matter of Belief', in *Religion and Material Culture: The Matter of Belief*, ed. David Morgan (London: Routledge, 2010), 1–3.

5 See, inter alia, Michael Schoenfeldt, *Bodies and Selves in Early Modern England: Physiology and Inwardness in Spenser, Shakespeare, Herbert, and Milton* (Cambridge: Cambridge University Press, 1999), especially chapters 2 and 5; Brian Cummings and Freya Sierhuis, ed., *Passions and Subjectivity in Early Modern Culture* (Farnham: Ashgate, 2013), especially the chapters in Part IV: Religion, Devotion, and Theology.

6 Seymour Baker House, 'More, Sir Thomas (1478–1535)', *Oxford Dictionary of National Biography*, Oxford University Press, 2004; online ed., Jan 2008 (http://www.oxforddnb.com/view/article/19191, accessed 11 March 2016).

7 Richard Brathwaite, *Essaies upon the five senses* (London, 1620), A3r.

8 Wietse de Boer and Christine Göttler, 'Introduction: The Sacred and the Senses in an Age of Reform', in *Religion and the Senses in Early Modern Europe*, ed. Wietse de Boer and Christine Göttler (Leiden: Brill, 2013), 3.

9 Thomas Wright, *The passions of the minde* (London, 1601), B7r.

10 See, for example, Eric Palazzo, 'Art and the Senses: Art and Liturgy in the Middle Ages', in *A Cultural History of the Senses in the Middle Ages*, ed. Richard G. Newhauser (London: Bloomsbury, 2014), 175–94.

11 Margaret Aston, *England's Iconoclasts: Laws Against Images* (Oxford: Clarendon Press, 1988), and Eamon Duffy, *The Stripping of the Altars: Traditional Religion in England, 1400–1580*, 2nd ed. (New Haven, CT: Yale University Press, 2005).

12 Marcia B. Hall, 'Introduction', in *The Sensuous in the Counter-Reformation Church*, ed. Marcia B. Hall and Tracy E. Cooper (Cambridge: Cambridge University Press, 2013), 2.

13 See, for example, Arnold Hunt, *The Art of Hearing: English Preachers and their Audiences, 1590–1640* (Cambridge: Cambridge University Press, 2011), especially 25.

14 Matthew Milner, *The Senses and the English Reformation* (Farnham: Ashgate, 2011), 4.

15 Ibid., 6. Until recently, scholars favoured the study of the so-called 'higher senses', vision and hearing. For recent scholarship on the 'lower senses', see Joe Moshenska, *Feeling Pleasures: The Sense of Touch in Renaissance England* (Oxford: Oxford University Press, 2014); Jonathan Reinarz, *Past Scents: Historical Perspectives on Smell* (Urbana: University of Illinois Press, 2014); Constance Classen, *The Deepest Sense: A Cultural History of Touch* (Urbana: University of Illinois Press, 2012); Holly Dugan, *The Ephemeral History of Perfume: Scent and Sense in Early Modern England* (Baltimore, MD: Johns Hopkins University Press, 2011); Elizabeth D. Harvey, ed. *Sensible Flesh: On Touch in Early Modern Culture* (Philadelphia: University of Pennsylvania Press, 2003).

16 On the hierarchy of five senses, see especially Louise Vinge, *The Five Senses: Studies in a Literary Tradition* (Lund: CWK Gleerup, 1975), especially 18 and 69; Constance Classen, *Worlds of Sense: Exploring the Senses in History and Across Cultures* (London: Routledge, 2003), 3–4; Susan Stewart, 'Remembering the Senses', in *Empire of the Senses: The Sensual Culture Reader*, ed. David Howes (Oxford: Berg, 2005), 59–69 (especially 61–62); Robert Jütte, *A History of the Senses: From Antiquity to Cyberspace* (Cambridge: Polity, 2005), 55–71.

17 See, for example, Susan C. Karant-Nunn, *The Reformation of Feeling: Shaping the Religious Emotions in Early Modern Germany* (Oxford: Oxford University Press, 2010); Nancy Bradley Warren, *The Embodied Word: Female Spiritualties, Contested Orthodoxies, and English Religious Cultures, 1350–1700* (Philadelphia: University of Pennsylvania Press, 2010); Christina Wald, *The Reformation of Romance: The Eucharist, Disguise, and Foreign Fashion in Early Modern Prose Fiction* (Berlin: De Gruyter, 2014).

18 Paul L. Gavrilyuk and Sarah Coakley, eds., *The Spiritual Senses: Perceiving God in Western Christianity* (Cambridge: Cambridge University Press, 2011).

19 Brathwaite, *Essaies*, A5r.

20 Joseph Hall, *Contemplations upon the remarkable passages in the life of the holy Jesus* (London, 1679), Hh3r.

21 As Holly Dugan and Lara Farina note, 'too ephemeral to persist in their original forms, the odors, flavors, textures, temperatures, and somatic pressures of the past appear destined to linger primarily through textual description'. Holly Dugan and Lara Farina, 'Intimate Senses/ Sensing Intimacy', *Postmedieval: A Journal of Medieval Cultural Studies* 3 (2012): 373–79 (at 374).

22 On sensing as a historically specific phenomenon, see Mark M. Smith, *Sensing the Past: Seeing, Hearing, Smelling, Tasting and Touching in History* (Berkeley: University of California Press, 2007), 3. See also Smith, 'Producing Sense, Consuming Sense, Making Sense: Perils and Prospects for Sensory History', *Journal of Social History* 40 (2007): 841–42. On the cultural specificity of sensing, see Constance Classen, 'Foundations for an Anthropology of the Senses', *International Social Science Journal* 49 (1997), 401–412. 'The fundamental premiss underlying the concept of an "anthropology of the senses"', Classen argues, 'is that sensory perception is a cultural, as well as a physical act' (at 401). See also David Howes, ed., *The Varieties of Sensory Experience: A Sourcebook in the Anthropology of the Senses* (Toronto: University of Toronto Press, 1991). For a penetrating critique of Smith's, Classen's, and Howes' approach which nonetheless affirms the historical specificity of the senses, see Mark S. R. Jenner 'Tasting Lichfield, Touching China: John Floyer's Senses', *The Historical Journal* 53 (2010): 669–70 and Jenner, 'Follow Your Nose? Smell, Smelling, and Their Histories', *The American Historical Review* 116 (2001): 348–51.

23 See also Sally M. Promey, *Sensational Religion: Sensory Cultures in Material Practice* (New Haven: Yale University Press, 2014), 1.

24 Another recent volume also offers a multi- and interdisciplinary approach to uncovering past sensory experience: See Simon Smith, Jackie Watson, and Amy Kenny, eds. *The Senses in Early Modern England, 1558–1660* (Manchester: Manchester University Press, 2015).

25 In the medieval period, for instance, the senses not only received information, but transmitted information outwards. See C. M. Woolgar, *The Senses in Late Medieval England* (New Haven: Yale University Press, 2006), 3.

26 Indigenous North American cultures of sensing during the early colonial period are difficult to analyse, since Europeans penned the majority of written

evidence. For a discussion of the senses in early America see, Peter Charles Hoffer's *Sensory Worlds in Early America* (Baltimore, MD: The Johns Hopkins University Press, 2003). On the Jesuits' use of the senses to convert Indigenous peoples in early Canada, see Muriel Clair, 'Entre vision et audition: la lumière dans les missions iroquoises du 17e siècle', *Anthropologie et Sociétés* 30 (2006): 71–92.

27 See, for example, Katharine A. Craik, *Reading Sensations in Early Modern England* (Basingstoke: Palgrave Macmillan, 2007); On women's embodied reading practices see, for example, Helen Smith, '"More swete vnto the eare / than holsome for ye mynde": Embodying Early Modern Women's Reading', *Huntingdon Library Quarterly* 73 (2010): 413–32.

28 See, for example, Sarah Kay and Miri Rubin, eds., *Framing Medieval Bodies* (Manchester: Manchester University Press, 1994); Peter Erickson and Clark Hulse, eds., *Early Modern Visual Culture: Representation, Race and Empire in Renaissance England* (Philadelphia: University of Pennsylvania Press, 2000) and Tara Hamling and Catherine Richardson, eds., *Everyday Objects: Medieval and Early Modern Material Culture and its Meanings* (Farnham: Ashgate, 2010).

29 Roger Chartier, for instance, argues that the form of a text works together with its written content to create meanings. See Chartier, 'Meaningful Forms', *Times Literary Supplement* (London), 6 October 1989, Issue 4514, *Liber* 1, 8.

30 Holly Dugan, *The Ephemeral History of Perfume: Scent and Sense in Early Modern England* (Baltimore: John Hopkins University Press, 2011), 5; Erika T. Lin, *Shakespeare and the Materiality of Performance* (Basingstoke: Palgrave Macmillan, 2012), chapter 2.

Part I
Prescription and practice

1   Problems of sensory history and the medieval laity

John H. Arnold

Christian thought in the Middle Ages always struggled with the question of the senses as the source of knowledge, pleasure, and desire. Heir to the Aristotelian principle that all knowledge begins in the senses as well as the Neoplatonic distrust of the body and its carnal modes of knowing, and itself committed to the principle that preternatural and supernatural sources of knowledge were available and meaningful, it was difficult for Christian thinkers to reconcile this classical legacy with its own physics and metaphysics.[1]

Gabrielle Spiegel presents the senses as a problem for medieval thinkers. In this essay, I want to suggest that they continue to present a problem, both methodological and interpretive, for modern medievalists. They are problematic, first, because the current history of the senses, particularly when applied to the study of religion, has lost track of some of its intellectual inheritance, leading to an unintended bias in focus; and, second, because how we think we can access the senses is often overly dependent on proscriptive sources, leading to a lack of full contextualisation. However, as I argue below, there are productive paths forward and these can be approached in part by recognising that the senses were a fundamental problem, particularly with regard to the faith of the ordinary laity in the later Middle Ages.

The historiographical problems

The current interest in sensory history and the history of the senses sits at a point where several different historiographical vectors intersect, and a focus on religion adds yet further lines to complicate the picture. However, these historiographies have different purposes, and current work is hampered by a failure to recognise that the underlying projects diverge. The most obvious inheritance comes from the work of the Annales School in the decades following 1980, where the project is to historicise both natural and cultural phenomena in order better to situate the changing nature of the human subject.[2] At their best, such histories reflect upon the history of affect, of what made people feel and do things at different times in the past, and are necessarily framed by an analysis of the wider political context. Thus, Alain Corbin's account of church bells across the period of the French Revolution tells us not only about how they sounded and what they meant, nor simply evokes their experience in that time and place, but also situates them within struggles for control. Corbin argues for both a changing sonic *habitus* (of what becomes aurally 'natural') and a more self-conscious political struggle over the soundscape of modern France. It should be noted, however, that not all works aim so high, some preferring simply to evoke or 'reconstruct' sensory experience in a particular period, often focusing on a particular sense. This 'evocative' project could be linked to a different, and much longer standing, inheritance, namely the study of 'lived religion' (*la religion vécue*). Much work on lived religion has been pleased similarly to reconstruct and make tangible the experience of faith in a particular moment in time, as a kind of exercise in rescuing that which is 'hidden from history'; though the best examples have again tried to move beyond evocation to something more analytical.[3]

The other main line of influence comes from the history of science and medicine, and its reconstruction of past understandings of the human body. Here the interest has been in how the senses and bodily sensory experience were explicitly understood and discussed in premodern times, a mode of analysis that is much closer to that of the history of ideas. Foundational medievalist work of this sort analyses the reception of Aristotelian theories of sight in the thirteenth century, attempting thus to understand the development of medieval thought, and, on occasion, to demonstrate its influence beyond the universities – for example, by arguing (as Michael Camille did most brilliantly) that it informed fundamental changes in gothic architecture.[4] One should note also that there is a particular subset to this more ideas-led approach, namely long-standing work in the field of theology which has studied the medieval notion of the 'spiritual senses', asking primarily whether or not they formed a 'coherent' system of productive thought.[5]

It is worth unpacking these inheritances because part of the problem with the 'sensory turn' – as manifest in the history of medieval religion in particular – is a tendency to take at least one interpretive step backwards in the midst of its other innovations. The different strands described in the preceding paragraphs, whilst not innately opposed, are not very closely attuned in their purposes or analytical frameworks: understanding how and why people were affected sensorily in a particular historical moment *may* be aided by reference to how the senses (or, as often, one particular sense) were understood to function, but it is not a clear or robust approach. It tends also to focus attention on specific discussions or evocations of the senses – moments at which sight or hearing or taste are explicitly evoked – but at the cost of thinking about moments at which the senses are implicitly addressed.

It is surely right to be wary of assuming that 'their' senses corresponded straightforwardly to 'ours', as Mark M. Smith has warned, and theories of sensory perception from a period can help us to avoid such essentialism.[6] But whilst contemporary ideas may allow us to understand some aspects of sensory *production* – the use of light in Gothic cathedrals, as analysed by Camille for example, or theories regarding the process by which the sound of preaching was imprinted on the 'inner' sense of hearing – it is problematical to assume that sensory *consumption* would be similarly informed and structured for all.[7] At the very least, it is clearly the case that theories based upon Aristotelian texts and Arabic learning largely developed in the University of Paris in the mid-thirteenth century were not immediately accessible to everyone in medieval Europe. Moreover, the theories had much more to say about the so-called 'higher' senses of sight and hearing than other forms of experience. For historians wishing to avoid the sin of projecting modern categories back into the medieval past, the existence of explicit discussion of, for example, extromission/ intromission theories of sight can be a welcome aid to avoiding ana- chronism; but that is not a tremendously secure methodology if one's project is to understand, for example, the experience of an ordinary member of the laity viewing the Eucharist at weekly mass, who may not have heard much about post-Aristotelian optical theory.

The latter project is much closer to the aims of the 'lived religion' inheritance, but the default tendency in recent medievalist work is to abandon the popular for the elite, perhaps unintentionally, and often without reflection. The desire to establish links between scientific theory and cultural practice tends to result in a focus on 'high' culture, with a tendency to assume that past experience can be reconstructed from elite didactic texts, which set out idealised religious sensations.[8] It is not wrong to focus on elite culture, and I am not arguing that elite cultures are hermetically separate from popular cultures – rather, that the former does not simply adumbrate or encompass the latter. But it is curious, in an area much indebted to the work of the Annales School and the legacy of *la religion vécue*, to find the issue of more general religious experience so quickly abandoned or problematically subsumed. In the desire to evoke fully and sympathetically the sensual experience of religion, guided by medieval texts and images steeped in theological and scientific tradition, there is a danger of mistaking ideology and pedagogy for the revelation of past reality. Thus, discussion of the senses, and the spiritual senses, is situated in time – by reference to theological discourse – but is not fully situated *historically*, as issues of social, cultural and political context fall out of the analysis.[9]

The issue is particularly acute with regard to medieval theological discussion of the 'inner' or 'spiritual' senses because of the importance of hierarchies within medieval discourses. The senses are themselves arranged in a hierarchy – often, though not always, with sight at the top – and they are understood to relate to a progression of modes of spiritual perception, where some direct (albeit 'inner') sensory experience of God is the eventual goal, whether in this life or the next. As Boyd Coolman explains, with regard to the theology of William of Auxerre in particular, but in a progression shared with various other thinkers, 'knowledge of God proceeds from an affirmation of creedal doctrines, through a deeper understanding of their meaning and coherence, to a direct and experiential perception of divine realities'.[10] This immediately links the senses to spiritual ability and discernment, where the ordinary lay person is rarely imagined to be particularly capable.[11] Lay people are required to affirm the creed, but are less often encouraged to delve into its mysteries. This is part of the problem for medieval theologians: not only were there different intellectual traditions regarding the physics and metaphysics of the senses, as outlined by Gabrielle Spiegel in the quotation at the head of this essay, but the implications of these traditions played out across a varied and spiritually unequal Christian people, ranging from those who were training themselves to ever greater spiritual acuity, to those who were thought to be spiritually dull – but all of whom nonetheless possessed physical senses.

The ordinary laity, then, presented a challenge for medieval Christian writers thinking about the senses; and in a different fashion continue to present a challenge to medievalists of sensory history, who need to think carefully about the purpose and scope of their analyses. If we wish to use sensory history to help us understand medieval religion, we must try to encompass not just 'religion' at its spiritual pinnacle, but the everyday religion of the laity. And we may find it useful, in regard to this project, to think about how 'the senses' were seen as a problem within the period, particularly with regard to the many.

The sensory problems of the laity

For all Christians, the senses were both an opportunity and a problem. They offered an opportunity, in that one could hope to interpret or commune with God's presence in the world through bodily experience, and perhaps hope also to connect with the divine through the 'inner' or 'spiritual' senses (understandings of the nature of these, and their relationship to the outer senses, wavered between metaphor, analogy, and some more innate and progressive connection, the outer leading to the inner). On the other hand, they were also a problem: it was through the senses that the body was bound to the sinful world and could be penetrated by temptation. The bodily senses might, moreover, mislead or misconstrue the spiritual benefit and truth of certain phenomena (most obviously, the Eucharist). For the ordinary lay person, these problems were seen as more severe, as they were not generally held to possess as securely the necessary skills of discernment and discipline that would protect them from exterior temptation, or, more importantly, allow them to read beyond the outer appearance of things. Theological discussion of the spiritual senses did not explicitly exclude any Christian. But such texts (from Augustine onwards) always framed sensory knowledge within a developmental hierarchy, presenting an ascent from a more basic to a more profound spiritual communion. In so doing, they implicitly constructed a spiritual elite, associated most clearly with those steeped in the necessary textual tradition and regulated way of life. Some (indeed, for some commentators, perhaps many) of the clergy would find themselves outside that elite; and, conversely, on rare occasion, a lay person might – most often with guidance from a supporting confessor – ascend to the more rarefied level.[12] Others might well ascend some way up the ladder of perception, even if not to the highest steps. Nonetheless, the overwhelming and default understanding was of lay people who were less sensorily gifted in regard to spirituality: more prone to being distracted by the sensory input of worldly things, and less able to develop their 'inner' senses to commune with God at a deeper level.

If we look then to where the senses appear explicitly with regard to the ordinary lay person in religious discourse, the most immediate area is as one of the frames by which the dangers of sin are communicated.[13] Handbooks advising confessors typically list sins of the 'five senses' alongside other schema such as the seven deadly sins, or sins against the ten commandments, and these tend to describe sensory experience as both acting upon and being acted upon by the physical world. Thus blasphemy (a sin of the tongue) is likened to wounding Christ; gazing lasciviously at people of the opposite sex acts physically on one's inner self; greed for food and drink (a sin of touch and smell) 'heats up' the sinner, potentially leading them to other temptations. The senses are here overwhelmingly presented as sites of danger, portals into the body that can ultimately harm the soul.

An element in the theological discourse on the spiritual senses lurks implicitly here – namely, the injunction to guard the outer senses so that the inner ones may prosper – but in pastoral instruction for the ordinary laity it is rarely made explicit until the late Middle Ages. The sermons of Federico Visconti, archbishop of Pisa (1254–77) are interesting in this regard, as at several points they gesture toward the importance of sensing 'properly' without quite addressing directly, for their lay audience, the notion of sensing 'spiritually'. Thus, for example, in a sermon given originally in the vernacular on the feast of St Stephen, Visconti elaborated on Matthew 5:8, 'Blessed are the clean of heart; they shall see God', by turning to Augustine, who had written (Visconti said) that 'In order to see God it is necessary to have eyes fit for contemplation, namely directed on high, and so that one can arrive at the state of contemplation' [*Oportet ut videns Deum habeat oculos sanos ut aspiciat, scilicet sursum, et ut aspectus perveniat*]. In fact, the closest passage in Augustine (from his commentary on the Sermon on the Mount, as the editors of Visconti's sermons point out) goes a little further, talking of how the properly 'cleansed' eye will be able to 'regard and contemplate its inner light: this indeed is the eye of the heart' [*mundatus oculus simplexque redditus aptus et idoneus erit ad intuendam et contemplandam interiorem lucem suam: iste enim oculus cordis est*]. Elsewhere, discussing listening (following the text of Matthew 13:9, 'He who has ears to hear, let him hear'), Visconti does mention the ears 'of the head' and the ears 'of the mind' [*aures mentis*], but the emphasis is again on being attentive to the sermon rather than developing a more elevated spiritual understanding.[14]

Sensory imagery is also frequently used in pastoral literature to convey examples and to explain theological points, as suitably direct and understandable metaphors for a wide audience. The thirteenth-century encyclopaedic text *Placides et Timeo*, for example, explains the co-creation of the body and the soul as being like the creation of a bell and the sound it contains. Similarly, the equal spiritual value of all souls, despite their social rank or bodily circumstances, is described as being like the light of a candle which burns equally brightly whether placed in an open or a closed lantern.[15] Archbishop Visconti explains in one sermon how faith without works is nothing, 'just as seeing in the dark is not seeing'.[16] To touch upon an area to which I shall return again below, the nature of the Eucharist – and particularly the question of how it was possible that the consecration and consumption of the host could be repeated endlessly in time and place without any diminution of Christ's body – was frequently explained through simple sensory metaphors, such as noting that many people can all hear the same voice, and can all see the light from the same candle.[17]

Sensory metaphor was also useful when warning of the dangers of sin and damnation, for it could make something beyond human lived experience both intellectually comprehensible and affectingly vivid. The *Book of Vices and Virtues* (c. 1375, but a close translation of a thirteenth-century French text) described what one would experience if, via inner mental reflection, one 'visited' Hell:

> Þere þou schalt see al þat herte hateþ and fleeþ: defaute of al goodnesse, and gret plente of al wikkednesse, brennynge fier, stynkynge brymston, foule stormes & tempestes, routynge ydousedeueles, hunger, þryst þat may neuere be staunched, many manere of turmentrye, wepynges, sorwes more þan any herte may þenke or any tunge may deuyse, and euere-more wiþ-outen ende lastynge.[18]

The images aim particularly at what is repellent to touch (fire), smell (brimstone), hearing (storms), sight (hideous devils having sex) and, at a slight stretch, taste (unassuageable hunger and thirst). The late medieval English vernacular text *Jacob's Well* similarly communicates the horrors of sin and damnation by expatiating on both the sensory elements of the body, and the reaction of those elements to negative sensory stimuli in order to evoke the never-ending labour of atonement for sin:

> But þis pytt, þi body, hath V entrees, þat arn þi V bodyly wyttes: þi sy3t, þin heryng, þi smellyng, þi mowth, þi towchyng. Be þise V entrees þe stremys of watyr, þat is, þe artycles of þe gret curse, entryn ofte tymes in-to þi pytt. . .[19]

On occasion the more positive corollary of the delights of salvation are similarly explained. In *The Book of Vices and Virtues*, for example, the positive state of 'soberness' (meaning overall spiritual balance and well-being, not just abstinence from alcohol) is evoked via clear images of things that are sensorily pleasing, leading to the 'grete swetnesse þat is in God'.[20]

As these examples begin to suggest, it is not always clear whether one is dealing in medieval religious texts with sensory *metaphor* – where sensory experience is presented as an immediately knowable phenomenon which can be used comparatively to communicate difficult theological arguments or concepts – or with more essential claims about sensory *knowledge*, where for example the real knowledge and experience of sin may literally enter through the senses. The issue is further complicated by the notion of the spiritual senses: although these are discussed explicitly in some theology, they may lurk – possibly not fully coherently – within some of the sensory images that appear purely metaphorical on first glance.[21] Do we, for example, take 'the grete sweteness þat is in God' to be a metaphor for something actually unknowable or directly incommunicable (namely, God's goodness and mercy), or to indicate an experience of the *spiritual* senses (that is, an inner, but actual, experience of sweetness)? Similar questions arise with regard to more clearly exterior sensory phenomena. Take, for example, church bells. The sound of bells was used metaphorically by various writers to describe preaching, and to indicate more broadly the reception of the word of God. But bells were also understood to tame the power of storms, and to frighten away the 'demons of the air' who were thought to promote social dissension.[22] Here, a much more literal meaning seems to be implied, as it would appear to be the physical action of sound that is involved in these protective effects – though this physical sensory element is also working in a spiritually 'real' fashion. Jean-Marie Fritz remarks that '[s]ound, by its immateriality, is the ideal image of the spiritual';[23] but one may also note that sound's curiously *material* efficacy is also part of its spiritual attraction – an invisible force, but a force nonetheless.

A rich example of some of the confusion of literal and spiritual meanings comes in a miracle story relating to St Privat, part of a set collated in the first half of the twelfth century by Aldebert III, bishop of Mende.[24] The dissolute son of a rich lord lost the power of both speech and hearing (by implication, as punishment for his sin). He went to Rome and to other famous shrines, hoping for a cure, but without avail. His father then led him to St Privat's shrine in the cathedral in Mende on the eve of the saint's feast day. At the cathedral many lights were burning, and, all through the night and without cease, the man pleaded to the saint for clemency. As dawn approached, and no improvement was perceptible, the father cried out bitterly. There was however still hope for his son:

> But behold now, as the day ascends, and the clergy sing the major mass . . . and then, with the clergy singing the angelic lauds [i.e. *Gloria in excelsis*], and the ill man's hand raised to heaven and his heart – doing that which his mouth could not – pounding to the majesty of heavenly gifts, he quickly began to tremble greatly, and collapsed to the ground, and vomited three gouts of blood.[25]

He was then helped up and – miraculously – his ears open and his tongue unbound, he regained a strong, clear voice with which he praised God and the saint. There is a pleasing congruence of imagery here: the day breaking – the light of the rising sun implied – and the welling up of music, breaking through the bonds that had tied tongue and ears; sound (the lauds) penetrating flesh (the heart beating), moving him bodily (the blood), and the cure prompting more sound (his clear, loud voice). To ask bluntly if the senses and phenomena here are spiritual, metaphorical or literal would clearly diminish the beauty of the story. But the point can be reversed: it is perhaps only through the power of narrative – its ability to keep disparate elements in play and in motion – that some of the tensions between the material, spiritual, literal and metaphorical can remain productively unresolved.

One might argue that my presumption that there is a problem to be addressed here is anachronistic, that one should instead recognise that all creation, for medieval people, had real spiritual meaning written into it as part of God's plan. Sensory experiences were thus simultaneously literal, metaphorical and spiritual; hence there is no need to arbitrate between them, and no difficulty to be solved. This is surely so; but my point is that it is successfully so only in certain modes of discourse, such as narrative – and where, as in the miracle story just noted, 'the senses' are not addressed explicitly, but are clearly fundamental to the effects of the story. Elsewhere, as in theological treatises specifically dedicated to such issues, medieval writers themselves attempted to delineate matters more clearly. With regard to the ordinary laity, my interest is not in the success or failure of the theological discourse, but the potential implications of the blurred boundaries between metaphor, the spiritual realm, and material reality. To communicate the spiritual via sensory imagery is a powerful strategy, but one which brings its own problems. Metaphor and allusion work, until and unless one's audience wants instantiation and

specificity; and then the very universality of the senses becomes a problem in itself. Are everybody's senses capable of perceiving the spiritual
element in the allusion (and if so, does that mean that they can gain direct
apprehension of the divine, without clerical assistance)? If *someone*
perceives the Eucharist as more than a piece of bread – for example, in a
Eucharistic miracle where it appears as a small boy or starts to bleed –
why doesn't everyone? As Caroline Walker Bynum notes, high medieval
theologians tended to explain the latter point by arguing that God has
effected a miracle on the eyes of the perceiver, rather than on the Host
itself: those 'seeing' the Host bleed are in fact doing so at two removes
(the Host is really Christ embodied, which appears to be bread, which
appears to those experiencing the miracle to be bleeding).[26] This
is theologically adept, but more than a little confusing within pastoral
discourse, where the point of miracles was usually to persuade the less
learned of the direct reality of spiritual things.

With the Eucharist in particular, the issue of the difference between
perception and reality is acute – indeed, one might say that belief in
Christ's presence in the bread and wine is *the* act of faith that stands at
the heart of later medieval Christianity. Various pastoral writers emphasised that one of the reasons that the Host appeared to the senses to be
just like bread was precisely because faith demands belief without proofs.
But miracles also seem to offer such proofs; and the metaphorical use of
sensory metaphors carries with it the possibility at least of suggesting that
the spiritually ineffable can be tugged into the corporeal realm of sensory
knowledge. Pastoral discourse on the Eucharist emphasised that God
could work all kinds of corporeal miracles (often by reference to various
biblical stories, such as Christ changing water into wine) and hence
that the real, material transformation of the Host should not be doubted.
At the same time, adapting earlier theological discussion of why that
transformation was not sensorily legible, priests emphasised that this was
an act of accommodation on God's part, to avoid horrifying the communicant. An extract from a poem written in the first half of the fourteenth
century by William of Shoreham, vicar of Chart in Kent, is exemplary in
this respect:

> For that colour, ne that savour / Ne beth nauȝt ther-inne Cryste / Thaȝ
> he ther-inne schewe hym / By hys myȝtefolle lyste [cleverness] / So
> couthe; / Ne myȝte elles bet be seȝe, / Ne beter yuȝred [chewed] inne
> mouth.
>   For ȝet he schewed hym in flesche, / Other ine blody thynge, /
> Hydous hyȝt were to the syȝte, / And to the cast wlatynge [revolting
> to sight], / And pyne [painful]; / Thanne hys hyt betere in fourme of
> brede, / And eke in forme of wyne.[27]

It is notable that, as in many other similar discussions of the Eucharist
for the laity, William does not attempt to turn to the philosophical (and

Aristotelian) distinction between the 'accidents' and the 'species' of the Host. Philosophical reflection or argument by the laity was not encouraged in this area: as Richard of Wetheringsett put it succinctly in his treatise for priests: 'this food is God and whoever denies this is a heretic . . . We are enjoined to believe. We are forbidden to discuss'.[28]

Affecting and policing the senses

I suggested earlier that one of the ways that the problems of the senses could be managed and contained – and perhaps particularly within pastoral discourse addressed to the laity – was via narrative, in its ability to distribute potentially conflicting elements across diegetic time and space. But probably the most important mode in which the relationship of the sensory and the spiritual was managed was via liturgy.[29] Eric Palazzo has provided very considerable insight into how the five senses were 'activated' by liturgy, and how the liturgical work of the mass in particular produced a 'synaesthetic' experience, in which the supernatural elements were evoked and then *embodied* via a fusion of sight, sound, and smells.[30] Palazzo's work, however, raises questions about how effectively all the elements of liturgy 'worked' for lay, rather than clerical, participants.

Not all parish churches would be able to produce such a successful, or sensorily rich, liturgical experience as, say, the cathedral church at the Easter mass. Take, for example, reports from Henri de Vezelay's visitations as archdeacon of thirty-one churches in Bayeux in 1267, at which various faults or lacks are noted regarding liturgical texts and objects. Vaucelles lacked a missal, whilst that at Varaville was 'old and difficult to read', a similar fault noted for the breviary at Banneville; Bretteville, Soliers, Tilly, Robehomme, and Emieville needed a psalter, and Colombelles 'lacked books'. A couple of places needed a chalice, though whether this was a total lack or to replace something considered worn out is unclear. At Cormelles-le-Royal the church was 'completely ruined', and similarly Petiville was noted for having a ruined chancel which was 'quite dangerous'. Croissonville had all necessary ornaments, but 'the church is old and quite dark'.[31] The visitation records of ninety churches in the archdeaconry of Totnes in 1342 give slightly greater detail regarding some faults: at North Bovey the chalice and missal had been stolen, the gradual was rotten and badly bound, the parish psalter was 'insufficient', and the images of the saints in the church were 'shameful and badly painted' (or possibly 'badly decorated') [*inhonestus et male depictus*], the cross also being *male depictus*.[32] At Widdecombe the books were falling apart, the nave roof leaked, the images were again *male depictus*, and the chancel was dark and badly roofed. At Lustleigh the chancel was also dark, plus a glass window was broken. At Hennock the chancel was extremely dark, a window was cracked, and when it rained the altar got wet.[33] In these visitations, the churches with problems were a small minority (perhaps between 5 and 10 percent of those in the diocese). But the problems were sometimes clearly serious, as at Tavistock where not only were the liturgical books deficient, but mass could not be celebrated when it was raining because of the disrepair to the chancel; and similarly, at Peaworthy where both the chalice and the pyx had been stolen – which presumably made it impossible to celebrate mass – and the nave roof was totally ruined.

My point here is not to suggest that the liturgy was not successfully celebrated in parishes; it clearly was. But 'successfully celebrated' indicates a range of potential outcomes, only some of which might achieve the kind of sensorily rapturous experience imagined in modern analysis. What could be achieved in some locales was much more limited via the available materials, setting, and audience (remembering that not all lay people attended mass regularly). Above all, as I have argued elsewhere, the sensorily rich and spiritually charged encounters aimed at – and sometimes achieved by – liturgical rituals need to be set in comparative context with other more quotidian lay experiences, such as frequently seeing simple wayside crosses or reciting the Ave Maria for various purposes.[34]

It is undoubtedly the case that liturgy aimed to bring together the sensory and the spiritual for all Christians, temporarily collapsing the more difficult issues which troubled theologians over the inner and outer senses, and working to produce spiritual affect through an embodied rather than a purely mental form of cognition. The archaeologist and theorist Yannis Hamilakis, in his important book on the senses, stunningly evokes the lived experience of liturgy. His focus in this passage is on medieval Byzantine Christianity, but many of his points can be related to western Christianity as well, particularly if one considers processional events as well as Sunday mass:

> Imagine being part of such context. How can you experientially isolate the visual from the tactile, the olfactory, the auditory? As you were moving through the church, the objects around you would be also changing. Your body and the icons would engage in a process of inter-animation: the space, the icons, the liturgical chants, the incense would elicit specific reactions from you; they would invite you to perform certain postures and gestures from crossing to kissing. As you moved closer to icons, your breathing and the breathing of your co-participants would make the flames from the kindles flicker. The changing lighting would thus activate the reflections from the glass, gold, or silver and make the figures on the icons move. At the same time, the whole space would resonate with chants, whereas extracts from liturgical hymns could even be found on the icons themselves, fusing yet again the visual and the aural. Humans, things, light, sound, smell, incense, smoke, all become elements of the 'flesh', as Merleau-Ponty would put it. This corporeal experience would reach its climax in another act of in-corporation – in the Eucharist.[35]

Where Palazzo emphasises synaesthesia, Hamilakis suggests something even more radical: that the usual understanding of 'the five senses' is only one way of thinking about the sensory, and that it is in fact a particular inheritance of western modernity, divorced from the sensory experiences in different cultures and periods (where, for example, speech or bodily posture may be understood as key senses).[36] To pursue further the kind of analysis which Hamilakis suggests, one might also reflect on how often the sensory experience of liturgy is a collective and communal phenomenon, particularly for the laity. The sensory stimuli trigger responses in individual bodies, but the affect thus produced is importantly communal: the experience of being part of the congregation, of coming together in friendship and charity (*caritas*) to open up collectively to a joint spiritual experience of viewing the Eucharist, and exchanging the kiss of peace at the end of the mass.

This suggests ways in which the simultaneous activation of what we tend to think of as different senses may be particularly powerful, and particularly suited at producing spiritual affect. A preacher might refer to an image – such as the crucified Christ – and evoke movement and tactility, as for example in a thirteenth-century Parisian sermon where the audience was invited to imagine that Christ was reaching out to embrace and kiss them. Or similarly, as in another of Archbishop Visconti's sermons, a preacher might ask the audience to think of themselves in Mary's place watching the unfolding horrors: 'And when the hour comes, you [Mary] will see the flesh, which was drawn from yourself, suspended on the cross, bruised, wounded and bleeding from five deep wounds, and hanged between thieves'.[37] The sound of the sermon, the visual stimulus of the crucifix, the activated memories of the Passion tale, the empathetic evocation of a mother's suffering, the sight of a broken and bleeding body, and an image of a very tactile encounter with all these – Visconti tells his audience that they should be 'pierced as with a sword' by the Passion – in a sermon delivered in the sensually rich environment of a wealthy church on a particular saint's day: all this works to forge a very strong and affective performance, where, as Hamilakis suggests, distinguishing between the 'different' sensory elements may not be the most useful analytical approach.

That we *do* however thus distinguish – that there is a schema of five senses that we have inherited in western Europe – is in part because of the medieval Church's attempt to grapple with the conflicted inheritance of Aristotelian and Platonic notions of worldly embodiment and spiritual transcendence. Hamilakis argues that the intellectual traditions that delimit and map the 'five' senses arose in large part in an attempt to control and assuage their otherwise unruly, unpredictable, and anarchic tendencies.[38] I would suggest that it is largely the fact that the ordinary laity were sensorily equipped but assumed usually to be lacking in spiritual discernment that particularly prompted both the elaboration of sensory spiritual affect and the development of pastoral discourses aimed at policing sensory experience – these then forming a major cornerstone in the development of that Western tradition. On the former point one notes, from the late twelfth century onwards, the increasing presence and sophistication of wall-paintings and other visual schema, the great explosion in preaching 'exempla' didactically aimed at a lay audience, and the increasing size and resonance of church bells, all of which sought to prompt an emotional, affective response from a lay audience.[39] None of this is solely lay rather than clerical; but the increasing scope and vitality of later medieval spiritual culture, as has long been recognised, rests upon the congruence of lay enthusiasm and material support, and the Church's desire to more effectively encourage and channel the spiritual aspirations of the laity.

The Church did not, however, embrace unfettered enthusiasm: there was also a policing of the senses. As the history of heresy makes all too apparent, it was not permissible for just anyone to preach or provide spiritual interpretation of worldly things. I noted above the prevalence of discussion of sin via the schema of the five senses. This was not only didactic – a means of explaining sin – but also a form of discipline, arranged within a pedagogic hierarchy. As sin was wont to enter all human beings via their senses, those senses must be managed, and pastoral discourse provided the means and the mode of instruction to attempt to control the bodily senses and – in some of the vernacular instruction of the late Middle Ages at least – to foster the inner, spiritual senses. There is something of a monastic model here, of course – advocating control of diet, speech, appetite, visual stimuli, the aural regularity of liturgical prayer – and some historians have indeed argued that, from perhaps the late twelfth century on, we start to see a 'monasticization' of the laity.[40] However, whilst the initial logic perhaps does come from the notion of the monastic rule, the pastoral texts – the theological *summae*, the sermon and exempla collections, confessors' manuals, and books of spiritual instruction addressed to those with the care of souls and latterly to the laity themselves – further elaborate a wider *regimen* for the management of sin, and to some degree for the development of spiritual ability.

Despite the increased focus that they display with regard to lay piety, these pastoral discourses continued to be predicated on the notion of a gulf between the spiritually adept elite and the vast majority of people. They hold out the possibility – as Catholic theology requires – of salvation for all, but present a 'never-ending work' (as *Jacob's Well* puts it) and a narrow path that only a few can fully achieve. All lay people have senses and thus can be addressed by these texts and practices; but developing sense experience into something spiritually meaningful requires further progress and a particular accomplishment, as individuals must work to make their senses discern things in a spiritually correct fashion. Within this circumscribed space there are many grades of ability, complications of experience, levels of discernment, and the like. In short, pastoral instruction is a *discourse* in a roughly Foucauldian sense, that draws upon the senses (among other things) in order to map, delimit, distribute, and give meaning to a range of positive and negative experience; and, with regard to the spiritual senses, to rarefy what we might call the spiritually sensing subject by emphasising the problems of false perception and the barriers to universal discernment.

As Brigitte Cazelles noted in her book on 'soundscape' in medieval France, a recurrent instruction for personal spiritual development was to remove oneself from the noise of the world in order to work on refining the inner senses. This sensory work depends upon a physical action (removing oneself from everyday concerns and needs), and maps out a kind of sensory hierarchy, placing vision over audition (in Cazelles's analysis), which

> thus corresponds to a social order that gives intellect priority over ignorance. The result is a distinction between, on the one hand, the mentally able members of society (a select community of thinkers each endowed with the power to read and reflect in silence) and, on the other hand, the unrefined masses.[41]

Here we can see that the understanding of the senses is similarly structured to the language of the emotions as deployed in pastoral discourse: as I have analysed elsewhere, a set of universal potentials (all Christian peoples being understood to have emotional responses *in potentia*) are deployed to produce moral affect, are coded as spiritually 'positive' and 'negative', are arrayed hierarchically in regard to spiritual discernment, and are a part of the manufacturing a particular kind of believing subject.[42] Thomas Lentes has discussed the devotional use of images in the later Middle Ages, arguing that we should not interpret late medieval 'private' worship of images as isolated from wider devotional practice. He notes that late medieval prayer books do not only instruct the lay reader *how* to look devoutly at an image, but what to *do* whilst engaged in such devotion, namely to pray and enact other moments of liturgy.[43] This element in pastoral discourse illustrates well the Foucauldian sense of 'power' I want to evoke here: one which instructs and shapes, rather than simply represses; but one which sits also in an uneven and unequal landscape of social, material, and cultural resources.

Conclusion

Here, in its entirety, is an *exemplum* – a little story for use by preachers – from a fourteenth-century southern French collection collated by an anonymous Sack Friar:

Exemplum against the ornamentation of women. I heard that a certain woman, against her husband's will, put makeup on her face. And when on a certain feast day she made herself up in this way, such that she looked like quite another woman, her husband asked her where his wife was. To which Portia said, 'Lord, sign yourself [with the cross] and commend yourself to God, for am I none other than Portia, your wife?' 'Truly you do not seem to be my wife, for my wife is usually brunette, and you are blond, she is usually pallid and you are ruddy-faced'. 'For God', said Portia, 'I am your wife!' Her husband said, 'If you are my wife, I will see if I can shift those adornments that I see on your face'. And using his robe as a scourer, he took her by the hair and began to scrub strongly at her cheeks until the blood ran. She, in truth, cried out 'Lord, I am your wife!' And thus, her being well scrubbed, he said 'Now I can see, because indeed you are Portia my wife!' – and thus he held his wife in check.[44]

This seems to me to be a sensory tale, although none of the five senses is explicitly cited. It is, firstly, about seeing and not seeing: about how surfaces can conceal the true nature of things. It is also interestingly vague about seeing 'through' those surfaces: we cannot be clear whether or not the husband 'sees through' the make-up from the very beginning, or whether, initially at least, Portia is like various other characters in medieval literature who are able to conceal themselves from even close friends and relatives with quite simple disguises. How we who hear or read the tale 'see' Portia herself is part of how the tale works as *narrative*, that is, as a movement from one situation to another that catches the audience up in the action. It is also a story about touch. It invites an embodied response from its audience, its female audience in particular: the putting on of makeup and the feeling of being adorned and painted; and then the experience of a particular kind of bodily suffering, as one's skin is scrubbed 'until the blood ran' – in the process of which, some further violence is done to one's presentation of one's self. Again, where the audience places itself – in whose skin – is dramatically complex; and, perhaps, depends upon each individual's past experience of violence, as perpetrator or victim.

There are three things to emphasise from the story of the made-up wife, by way of framing my conclusion. One is quite simply that if we look only at material which explicitly names one of the senses, we will miss much of what would actually tell us about the sensory worlds of the past, and will miss in particular various things that were likely to have *moved* people, through their sensory experiences. Religious historians are well-attuned to this point within the realm of liturgy, but should consider it in other contexts as well, where the ritualised structures and encoded meanings are less formalised. We need to think also of how the senses are activated not only by images, sounds, smells, and so forth, but also by texts which evoke an embodied imaginative response.[45] The second point is that when we look at how people are sensorily affected by cultural productions, we are likely to find a variety of responses, for although most human beings have much the same sensory makeup (barring accident and disability), their sensory experiences are not outside or beyond other 'positioning' factors such as gender, class, age, and so forth. This is again something that medieval sensory theory, such as Aristotelian optics, is unlikely to be able to supply us if we continue to use it as a preferred interpretive frame. And the third point is that within sensory encounters with the sacred we are likely to find fundamental issues of power and discipline: again, not only the explicit disciplining and training of the bodily and spiritual senses, but the use of sensory prompts and affective imagery to produce and shape moral subjects. I don't mean to suggest that this is all-encompassing or effortless: some women listening to the exemplum about Portia could no doubt resist internalising its multiple messages of subjection. But one suspects that it would not be that easy to shake off the unpleasantly effective – and, I would argue, affective – image of the rouged cheeks and bleeding skin (a sensory moment both visual and embodied).

I began this essay with Gabrielle Spiegel's astute summation of the tensions within the medieval understanding of the senses. But one could reframe the import of this: rather than saying that the bodily senses are a problem for medieval spirituality, one could argue that the inherent complexities and tensions within the senses (particularly as they ranged across a Christian community from the most learned and discerning, to the most 'simple' and worldly) formed a fertile problematic for the production of medieval 'religion' as a system of images, practices, and disciplines.[46] Theological abstractions are one part of that productive problematic, as they provide the discursive frame for explicit discussion on the topic, corralling the understanding of embodied reaction into the 'five senses' paradigm whilst elaborating also the more slippery notion of the inner or spiritual senses. However, a fully 'sensory history' that includes analysis of how the senses 'work' in regard to spiritual experience cannot rely only on this explicit discourse, and must not assume that it provides a transparent guide to the sensory 'consumption' of the greater part of the people. I would like to suggest that we could productively broaden this somewhat, to think harder about the notion of 'affect', where the main point for us historically is to understand how and why people were 'moved' by certain phenomena: moved bodily and cognitively, and indeed spiritually. In this line, we are not well-served if we think about that only via the 'five senses' paradigm, as focussed on discrete and individual human subjects, but should rather recognise that sensory history is one part of a wider set of issues, where questions of social class and status, emotions and disciplinary programmes, and the reach and address of cultural productions matter very considerably to both individual and collective experience.

Sensory history is proving to be a useful 'turn' in historiography; but it is clear that a focus on the 'senses' only makes sense – as it were – if also conducted in concert with analysis of other intersecting areas. These include the history of the emotions, a fully historicised understanding of embodiment (where the notion of a universalised and transhistorical 'human subject' is held at a critical distance for further inquiry), and, most of all, the analysis of different modes of subjectivity, power, and resistance. In all these ways, I would suggest once again that what we really need is not so much 'a history of the senses' – where the tendency is always to be pulled toward the specific viewpoint and arrangement of the senses found in a period's intellectual abstractions – but histories of *affect*.

Notes

1 Gabrielle M. Spiegel, 'Paradoxes of the Senses', in *Rethinking the Medieval Senses: Heritage, Fascinations, Frames,* ed. Stephen G. Nichols, Andreas Kablitz, and Alison Calhoun (Baltimore: Johns Hopkins University Press, 2008), 186.

2 Alain Corbin, *The Foul and the Fragrant: Odour and the French Social Imagination,* trans. Miriam L. Kochan (Cambridge, MA: Harvard University Press, 1986); idem, *Village Bells: The Culture of the Senses in the Nineteenth-Century French Countryside,* trans. Martin Thom (London: Papermac, 1999). As Mark Smith (see below) has noted, argument about the relative importance of different senses is found in earlier Annales work, particularly Lucien Febvre's suggestion in *The Problem of Unbelief in the Sixteenth Century: The Religion of Rabelais* (first published in French in 1942) that senses other than sight were more important in that era, and were then devalued in modernity; what is at stake in that analysis is therefore another element in the 'transition to modernity' debates. English translation by Beatrice Gottlieb (Cambridge, MA: Harvard University Press, 1982).

3 A recent evocation: Alec Ryrie, *Being Protestant in Reformation Britain* (Oxford: Oxford University Press, 2013). A classic analysis: William A. Christian, *Local Religion in Sixteenth-Century Spain* (Princeton, NJ: Princeton University Press, 1981).

4 Among many other publications, see Michael Camille, *Gothic Art: Visions and Revelations of the Medieval World* (London: Weidenfeld and Nicolson, 1996).

5 See Paul L. Gavrilyuk and Sarah Coakley, eds., *The Spiritual Senses: Perceiving God in Western Christianity* (Cambridge: Cambridge University Press, 2012); as the introduction to that collection sets out, there has been work on the spiritual senses since the 1930s.

6 Mark M. Smith, 'Producing Sense, Consuming Sense, Making Sense: Perils and Prospects for Sensory History', *Journal of Social History* 40 (2007): 841–58. For a nice attempt to nudge us away from assuming a transhistorical interpretation, in regard to medieval wall paintings, see Kate Giles, 'Seeing and Believing: Visuality and Space in Premodern England', *World Archaeology* 39 (2007): 105–21.

7 The useful distinction between production and consumption is made by Smith. See also his *Sensory History* (Oxford: Berg, 2007). For a very impressive attempt to combine both aspects, see Martin Roch, *L'intelligence d'un sens: Odeurs miraculeuses et odorat dans l'Occident du haut Moyen Age (V-VIII siècles)* (Turnhout: Brepols, 2009); assisted however by a focus on a period where evidence of 'reception' is essentially non-existent.

8 For example, Caroline Walker Bynum, *Christian Materiality: An Essay on Religion in Late Medieval Europe* (Cambridge, MA: MIT Press, 2011); Jean-Marie Fritz, *Paysages sonores du Moyen Age: Le versant épistémologique* (Paris: H. Champion, 2000); the essays in Nichols, Kablitz, and Calhoun, eds. *Rethinking the Medieval Senses.*

9 Thus Matthew Milner's important and thought-provoking *The Senses and the English Reformation* (Farnham: Ashgate, 2011) rather problematically takes the intellectual framework (presented as monovocally Aristotelian) and the idealisations of didactic works as too direct a guide to the lived experience of late medieval Christianity.

10 Boyd Taylor Coolman, *Knowing God by Experience: The Spiritual Senses in the Theology of William of Auxerre* (Washington, DC: Catholic University of America Press, 2004), 6. For an important discussion of how Aristotelian thought affected the understanding of the spiritual senses, see Boyd Taylor Coolman, 'Alexander of Hales', in *The Spiritual Senses*, ed. Gavriluyk and Coakley, 121–39.

11 On the intellectual disparagement of lay ability to 'believe' in any profound way, see Peter Biller, 'Oxen and She-Asses: Intellectuals and the Masses', in *The Oxford Handbook of Medieval Christianity*, ed. John H. Arnold (Oxford: Oxford University Press, 2014), 323–39.

12 One thinks particularly of various female mystics, but notes also the degree to which their claims to spiritual sensory ascendance could provoke concern; see Dyan Elliott, *Proving Woman: Female Spirituality and Inquisitional Culture in the Later Middle Ages* (Princeton, NJ: Princeton University Press, 2004).

13 Among various other writers, see further Milner, *The Senses and the English Reformation*, 53–62.

14 Nicole Bériou et al., eds., *Les sermons et la visite pastorale de Federico Visconti, archevêque de Pise (1253–1277)* (Rome: École française de Rome, 2001), 474, 530. In a further sermon on the same passage Visconti does mention the 'ears of the inner heart' (at 573) but the implication is again in regard to paying attention rather than developing a greater spiritual communion.

15 Claude A. Thomasset, ed., *Placides et Timéo, ou Li secrés as philosophes* (Paris: Librairie Droz, 1980), 119–22, 206–7; on the bell metaphor cf. Fritz, *Paysages sonores*, 49. This is an elite text, but written in the vernacular, framed as the instruction of young prince, and one can assume that the images and examples it provided were suitable for re-use in other pedagogic and pastoral contexts.

16 Bériou et al., eds., *Les sermons . . . Visconti*, 474.

17 Thus, for example, the early thirteenth-century pastoral work *Qui bene presunt presbiteri* by Richard of Wetheringsett (e.g. BL MS Eg. 655, f. 94r[a]), and the highly influential fourteenth-century pastoral work by William of Pagula, *Oculus sacerdotis* (e.g. BL MS Royal 6 E i, f. 31v). In the fifteenth-century *Pupilla oculi* (an adaptation of the *Oculus sacerdotis*), John de Burgo uses the slightly more complicated metaphor of a broken mirror producing multiple reflections (e.g. BL MS Royal 11 B X, f. 14v[b]).

18 *The Book of Vices and Virtues: A Fourteenth Century English Translation of the 'Somme le Roi' of Lorens d'Orléans*, ed. W. Nelson Francis, EETS o.s. 217 (London: Oxford University Press, 1942), 71.

19 *Jacob's Well: An Englisht Treatise on the Cleansing of Man's Conscience*, ed. Arthur Brandeis, EETS o.s. 115 (London: Kegan Paul, Trench, Trübner & Co., 1900), 1.

20 *The Book of Vices and Virtues*, ed. Francis, 279.

21 It should also be noted that influential and authoritative sources for the notion of the inner or spiritual senses, such as Augustine's writings (undoubtedly

influential on the Middle English texts discussed here), were not themselves fully coherent or systematic. See Matthew R. Lootens, 'Augustine', in *The Spiritual Senses*, ed. Gavrilyuk and Coakley, 56–70.

22 John H. Arnold and Caroline Goodson, 'Resounding Community: The History and Meaning of Medieval Church Bells', *Viator* 43 (2012): 99–130.

23 Fritz, *Paysages sonores*, 49. Several historians remark on the medieval 'belief' that sound was a physical thing; as anyone who has been in the vicinity of a large bell being struck – or stood next to a large bass amp at a gig – can attest, medieval people were right.

24 Clovis Brunel, *Les Miracles de Saint Privat; suivi des opuscils d'Aldebert III, eveque de Mende* (Paris, 1912), i-xix.

25 Brunel, *Miracles*, 13.

26 Caroline Walker Bynum, 'Seeing and Seeing Beyond: The Mass of St Gregory in the Fifteenth Century', in *The Mind's Eye: Art and Theological Argument in the Middle Ages*, ed. Jeffrey F Hamburger and Anne-Marie Bouché (Princeton, NJ: Princeton University Press, 2006), 208–40 (at 213).

27 Thomas Wright, ed., *The Religious Poems of William de Shoreham, Vicar of Chart-Sutton, in Kent, in the Reign of Edward II* (London, 1849), 26. See further John H. Arnold, 'The Materiality of Unbelief in Late Medieval England', in Sophie Page, ed. *The Unorthodox Imagination in Late Medieval Britain* (Manchester: Manchester University Press, 2010), 65–95; Jennifer Garrison, 'Mediated Piety: Eucharistic Theology and Lay Devotion in Robert Mannyng's *Handlyng Synne*', *Speculum* 85 (2010): 894–922.

28 BL MS Eg. 655, ff. 93v-94r: . . . iste cib[um] d[eu]s et qui negat hereticus est. . . . Credere iube[a]m[us]. Di[s]cut[er]e p[ro]hibe[a]m[us].

29 For a dazzling analysis of this for a very early period, see Georgia Frank, '"Taste and See": The Eucharist and the Eyes of Faith in the Fourth Century', *Church History* 70 (2001): 619–43.

30 See particularly Eric Palazzo, 'Art, Liturgy and the Five Senses in the Early Middle Ages', *Viator* 41 (2010): 25–56; idem, '*Missarum solemnia*: Eucharistic Rituals in the Middle Ages', in *The Oxford Handbook of Medieval Christianity*, ed. Arnold, 238–53; idem, *L'invention chrétienne des 5 sens dans la liturgie et l'art au Moyen Age* (Paris: Éditions du Cerf, 2014).

31 Leopold Delisle, ed., 'Visites pastorales de Maitre Henri de Vezelai, archdiacre de Hiémois et 1267 et 1268', *Bibliothèque de l'Ecole des Chartes* 54 (1893): 457–67.

32 George G. Coulton, ed., 'A Visitation of the Archdeaconry of Totnes in 1342', *English Historical Review* 26 (1911): 108–24. The complaint about images is repeated for Widdecombe, Bovey Tracey, Ipplepenne, Diptford, Dean Prior (where it is noted that the image of the Virgin lacked one hand), Cornworthy, Ashwater, and Peaworthy.

33 Ibid. Issues with roofs and windows are reported elsewhere: in five places the roof of the nave leaked, and the windows of three naves were broken or lacked all glass; in six places the chancel roof was a problem, and chancel windows similarly in nine churches.

34 See further Arnold, 'Belief and the Senses for the Medieval Laity', in *Les cinq sens au Moyen Age*, ed. Eric Palazzo (Paris: Cerf, 2016); Arnold, 'Materiality of Unbelief'.

35 Yannis Hamilakis, *Archaeology and the Senses: Human Experience, Memory, and Affect* (Cambridge: Cambridge University Press, 2013), 78.

36 On 'speech' as part of the medieval senses, see C. M. Woolgar, *The Senses in Late Medieval England* (New Haven, CT: Yale University Press, 2006), 84–116.

37 Sara Lipton, '"The Sweet Lean of His Head": Writing about Looking at the Crucifix in the High Middle Ages', *Speculum* 80 (2005): 1172–1208; Beriou,

ed., *Les sermons* . . . *Visconti*, 535 (sermon at church of St Peter-in-Chains, given originally in vernacular).

38 See particularly Hamilakis, *Archaeology and the Senses*, 55.

39 Note the increased use of bells to 'rouse' or 'kindle' piety in those *absent* from church when signalling the elevation of the Host, for example; Arnold and Goodson, 'Resounding community', 121–22.

40 André Vauchez, *The Laity in the Middle Ages*, trans. M. J. Schneider (Notre Dame, IN: University of Notre Dame Press, 1993), 72.

41 Brigitte Cazelles, *Soundscape in Early French Literature* (Turnhout: Brepols, 2005), 5–6.

42 John H. Arnold, 'Inside and Outside the Medieval Laity: Reflections on the History of the Emotions', in *European Religious Cultures*, ed. Miri E. Rubin (London: Institute of Historical Research, 2010), 107–30.

43 Thomas Lentes, '"As far as the eye can see . . .": Rituals of Gazing in the Late Middle Ages', in *The Mind's Eye*, ed. Hamburger and Bouché, 360–73.

44 Jean-Thiébaut Welter, 'Un recueil d'exempla du XIIIe siècle', *Etudes franciscaines* 30 (1913): 646–65; 31 (1914): 194–213, 312–20; story no. 219. See also no. 15, where the Virgin Mary tells a woman wearing make-up that she cannot see her face when it is thus adorned.

45 See similarly Patricia Cox Miller, 'Visceral Seeing: The Holy Body in Late Ancient Christianity', *Journal of Early Christian Studies* 12 (2004): 391–411.

46 Note the analysis of 'paradox' in fifteenth-century religious ideas about matter in Walker Bynum, *Christian Materiality*, although she is curiously uninterested in liturgical ritual or questions of cultural power and authority. For another, more specific but also highly subtle, analysis for a later period, see Nicky Hallett, *The Senses in Religious Communities 1600–1800: Early Modern 'Convents of Pleasure'* (Farnham: Ashgate, 2013).

2 *Virtus regens animam*: William Peraldus on guiding the pleasures of the senses

Richard Newhauser

Treatments of the virtue of temperance are not the setting in which some would expect to find ethical analyses of the five external senses in the Middle Ages. Considered from the perspective of a common, culturally regressive view of all things medieval, it might seem that treatises on ascesis, or particularly severe sermons, would be the more likely place for a focus on the ethics of the senses, types of literature, that is to say, in which one could anticipate that denunciations of sensory perception would flourish amid warnings about the dangers of not carefully guarding the senses. And in fact, ascetic considerations and homiletic reprimands do deliver on such expectations – but that is true whether these admonitions were composed in the European Middle Ages, the Italian Renaissance, or anywhere on the globe in the twenty-first century.[1] Nevertheless, in the contemporary popular imagination, an austere repression of sensory pleasure has been taken to accurately represent the position of sanctioned ideology in the Middle Ages in Europe, a controlling dogma that was only upended with the turn to the Italian Renaissance. The most recent and celebrated expression of this view is Stephen Greenblatt's *The Swerve*, where the resurgence of Burckhardtian historiography guides the depiction of the place of the sensory world in the millennium preceding the Italian quattrocento: 'something happened in the Renaissance, something that surged up against the constraints that centuries had constructed around curiosity, desire, individuality, sustained attention to the material world, the claims of the body'.[2] What one finds in Greenblatt's work, then, is a Middle Ages in which the senses served only to tempt humanity to the enjoyment of the beckoning material world, an allurement which was successfully quashed before that 'something' occurred. This claim is hardly new, though earlier and more scholarly statements of it were not as categorical in making the Italian Renaissance the decisive pivot to modernity. In his influential and controversial study of the late Middle Ages, Johan Huizinga, for example, also asserted that sensory enjoyment was considered sinful *per se* in the Middle Ages, but he then went on to stress that renaissance culture had not found a way of distinguishing between levels of acceptable or unacceptable pleasures. That separation, he felt, occurred only in the modern period, which he located in the eighteenth century, when Puritanism lost its intensity and anyone 'attempting to draw the dividing line between the higher and lower enjoyment of life according to the dictates of ethical consciousness would no longer separate art from sensuous enjoyment. . .'.[3] As John Parker and others have noted, Greenblatt's (and in some senses, even Huizinga's) narrow materialistic historiography flattens out the place of sensory pleasure to mean essentially a physical immoderation that was rejected wholesale by medieval Christianity in anxious warnings about the need to guard the senses, and then overcome in the Italian Renaissance to directly yield modernity.[4] It is a common view of the Middle Ages, one completed in the popular imagination by the view of a medieval 'counterculture' awash in sensuality, a bawdy age that lived out a permanent carnival of the senses as transgression against sanctioned authorities.

Medieval texts of moral theology dealing with moderation in its many varieties sound a much different note than one would expect from either of these stereotypes. Nowhere is there a better example of this more refined treatment of *temperantia* in the practical pastoral theology of the Late Middle Ages than in the influential, but still too often unexplored, works of William Peraldus (d. *c.* 1271).[5] The examination of Peraldus's *Compendium on the Vices*, and in particular the 'Tractatus de temperantia' in his *Compendium on the Virtues*, will demonstrate the importance to moral theologians of the moderation of sensory experience, not its ascetic denial. This emphasis on sensory restraint in understanding temperance is part of the inheritance and adaptation of Aristotelian thought by scholastic authors. Peraldus contributed to the ongoing process of adapting the Aristotelian tradition for late medieval Christian society by putting an Aristotelian-inflected notion of temperance and its sensory understanding at the disposal of generations of pastoral theologians and their congregations.

Peraldus may serve not only as a guide to the connection of temperance and the senses, especially in the pastoral literature of the late Middle Ages, but also as an author whose influential works demonstrate the wide variety of medieval conceptions of the senses and the way this diversity challenges presuppositions about the place of the senses in the Middle Ages. Born in Peyraud, France, William Peraldus (Guillaume Peyraut, Guilielmus Peraldus) probably studied at the university in Paris before entering the Dominican Order there and eventually becoming the prior of the Dominicans in Lyon. He wrote with such authority, and was accepted as such in his own time, that he is often referred to in contemporary manuscripts as the Archbishop (or suffragan) of that city, though he never held this office. As an active member of an order dedicated to preaching, he authored many sermons, and a large number of them have survived.[6] He also composed two important pedagogical texts that demonstrate his keen interest in the program of pastoral reform of the thirteenth century: *On Monastic Instruction* [*De eruditione religiosorum*] (*c.* 1260–1265), and *On the Education of Princes* [*De eruditione principum*] (*c.* 1265).[7]

But he was more widely known in the Middle Ages for his *Compendium on the Vices* [*Summa de vitiis*], which was completed about 1236 and sometimes circulated together with its companion volume, the *Compendium on the Virtues* [*Summa de virtutibus*] sometime after the latter work's completion before 1249.[8]

The compendia illustrate the importance of the literature of morality in Dominican instruction and the preparation of sermons, material which was meant to benefit above all the brothers who were carrying out the Order's specific tasks of hearing confession and, especially, preaching to the masses. Reform measures had been initiated at the Third Lateran Council (1178), but the specific tasks of preaching and hearing confession were set as the official duties of the clergy at the Fourth Lateran Council (1215–1216). These reform initiatives occurred in the period that saw the founding of the Dominican Order, as the Church leadership attempted to counteract the effects of a perceived indolence on the part of the secular clergy and monastic orders in educating the community of Christians, and of such heresies as that of the Albigensians in southern France, by making room for apostolic movements within legitimate Church authority that would reaffirm its power once more among the broad masses. But Peraldus's work on the vices became popular far beyond the Dominican Order because it served as a guide for all forms of instruction (in preaching, confession, and penance) at a time when pastoral work was emphasised by the Church as a way of promoting ecclesiastical self-reform and the simultaneous reform of society at all levels. The *Summa de vitiis* and the *Summa de virtutibus*, whether transmitted separately or together, grew to be some of the most successful tools for meeting the needs of the common members of the community in matters of moral education. Their popularity testifies to the importance of ethics as one of the most productive categories of conceptualisation in the later Middle Ages. The analysis of the vices and virtues that is so prevalent at the end of the medieval period is also a way of equating the individual with his or her moral identity. In their wider context, thus, in the way they encouraged and furthered the call to introspective examination of the conscience that forms the core of many sermons and self-examination in preparation for confession, Peraldus's compendia also had an important place in the development of ideas of the self in Western culture, a self conceived of as both a social and an ethical phenomenon.

From the time of its earliest dissemination, the *Compendium on the Vices* and its vision of individual and communal order in the task of overcoming the vices had a major impact on the moral tradition. It achieved a degree of popularity unmatched by any of its peers, such as the *Summa de bono* by Philip, chancellor of the Cathedral of Notre Dame (d. 1236); the *Summa de vitiis* by the Franciscan Johannes de Rupella (*c.* 1236); the *Summa de vitiis et virtutibus* by William of Auvergne, bishop of Paris (1228–1249); the Franciscan Servasanto da Faenza's *Liber de virtutibus et vitiis* (*c.* 1260); or the *Breviloquium de virtutibus antiquorum principum et philosophorum* by the Franciscan John of Wales (d. *c.* 1285).[9] A relatively limited number of copies of these works is still preserved – as the most popular of the group, John of Wales's text is extant in 153 copies – but Peraldus's *Compendium on the Vices* exists today in an extremely large number of manuscript copies – over 620 – either transmitted by itself or together with the author's treatment of the virtues, which is extant in about half as many copies as the *Compendium on the Vices*. These texts were also printed over twenty times before the late seventeenth century.[10] They served as the major inspiration for a very large number of Latin and vernacular compendia of ethics that extended far beyond the boundaries of the Order of Preachers, determining the form and content not only of many Latin treatises on the seven deadly sins and contrary virtues[11] for confessors and preachers, but also of just as many vernacular texts on the vices and virtues, including the *Fiore di virtù*,[12] the *Somme le roi*,[13] the *Spiegel der Sonden*,[14] Michel Beheim's *Büchlein von den sieben Todsünden*,[15] *The Book of Vices and Virtues*,[16] and many others. Their influence extended to a number of other genres, as well: encyclopaedias (such as Brunetto Latini's *Li livres dou tresor*),[17] or penitential manuals such as Heinrich von Langenstein's *Erchantnuzz der sund*,[18] or the work of poets like Dante Alighieri[19] and Geoffrey Chaucer.[20] The compendia were, in fact, so essential that by the fifteenth century, when Jean Gerson was chancellor of the University of Paris, he observed that the loss of all the books in the world could be tolerated if only Peraldus's *Summa de vitiis* and *Summa de virtutibus* would survive.[21]

Using the model of Aristotelian ethics, Peraldus posits an ideal amount of ardour as the virtuous mean between its sinful deficiency, the deadly vice of sloth, and its equally sinful excess, that he terms 'indiscreet fervour' (*indiscretus fervor*). In this critique of an excess of zeal in the asceticism and corporeal suffering that had been characteristic of the early saints, Peraldus also demonstrates his inheritance of what was expressed by twelfth-century authors as a 'new ideal of temperance and unostentation' in the monastery and, more generally, in twelfth-century spirituality and humanism.[22] When treating the sense of taste and the pleasures of food in his warnings against the extravagances of indiscreet fervour, Peraldus observes the following:

> We should know that we must very much fear taking excessive pleasure in the food we consume, for often one consumes too much delectable food and with too much zeal. Moreover, the consolation from delectable food sometimes prevents a person from receiving divine consolation. According to Bernard, divine consolation is extremely delicate, and it is not given to people who accept another [form of consolation]. But if someone is careful about how much and how eagerly he eats food, and gives thanks to the Creator for the created things he eats, he can consume as much food as is necessary to sustain his body not only without sin but even with merit. For God

has created food to be received with thanksgiving by the faithful, 1 Timothy 4[:3]. And to put it briefly, we should think of our body as a sick man who is eating; if he wants much that is not useful, it should be denied to him, but if he does not want what is useful, it should be forced on him.[23]

In this example, it is excess in the eagerness with which the appetite is quenched and a superfluity in the amount consumed to satisfy hunger that must be shunned, not delectable food *per se*, or even, in itself, the pleasure that accompanies eating. Overindulgence is to be avoided, as is its contrary, namely all slothful inactivity, but tasting with temperance not only sidesteps the commission of sin; it is, in fact, understood by Peraldus as a virtuous activity. The view of the external senses on display here is very different from one that sees them as invariably the five windows, portals, or water sluices that allow sin to flow into the corruptible body and contaminate the human soul.[24] The emphasis in Peraldus's examination lies not on padlocking the gateways to sensation, but on guiding the senses to reach a harmonious midpoint between excess and a harmful avoidance of sensory pleasure. As he further explains by appealing to auditory perception, disproportionate and unrelieved rigour in matters of the senses must be avoided if the pleasantness of virtue is to be achieved: 'It is the same with the strings of a harp: if they are tightened too little, they make a grating noise; if too much, they break; but if [done] moderately, they give a sweet sound'.[25]

Temperance, as it turns out, is so deeply involved in the actions of the senses that Peraldus partially defines the virtue in the context of sensory perception. The word 'temperance', he observes, is used in three ways: first, it designates a general sense of moderation regulating the action of all virtues and ensuring that they are not excessive or deficient but achieve the 'golden mean' of Aristotelian ethics; second, the term designates a virtue that restrains improper impulses of the mind. The third usage brings temperance into direct connection with the sensorium, for here:

> [T]emperance is spoken of as the virtue governing the soul (*virtus regens animam*) with respect to bodily pleasures or with respect to the pleasures of the five senses. The *Gloss* on Matthew 15: 'Temperance is the bridling of desire from those things that give temporary pleasure'. And Augustine says that temperance consists 'in restraining improper pleasures'.[26]

Temperance, thus, does not suppress sensory activity, but governs it by a process of edification expressed through the *Gloss*'s metaphoric language as bridling (*refrenatio*). Pastoral literature made frequent use of the metaphor: as a horse is controlled by a bridle, temperance guides the soul in matters of sensory perception. The goal for those engaged in the care of souls was to educate the Christian in applying the correct pressure of this bridle to guide the senses along a path of virtue.

Structurally, as well, the senses play a pivotal role in Peraldus's treatment of temperance. The treatise begins with introductory matters (chapters 1–4: the rationale for treating temperance after prudence in the examination of the cardinal virtues; the three ways in which the word 'temperance' is used; definitions of temperance according to Cicero, Macrobius, and Augustine; and a survey of biblical, classical, and medieval texts praising temperance). Next comes an examination of the parts of temperance according to Cicero (chapters 5–7: *continentia, clementia,* and *modestia*), and the rest of the treatise is taken up with an examination of the species of temperance distinguished by the external sense each species regulates (a principle announced in chapter 8):

> It should be noted that those parts of temperance which govern the mind in reference to the pleasures that exist according to taste and touch have been sufficiently noted and named: they are sobriety and restraint (*continentia*). Those parts which pertain to the pleasures that accord with sight and hearing and smell are not noted in this way, nor do they have special names.[27]

Taste is to be guided by sobriety (chapter 9), the analysis of which is divided into the variety of meanings of *sobrietas*; the commendation of sobriety adduced from nature, Scripture, and all of creation; and the number and kinds of effects of sobriety and the danger to human beings when it is missing. In the third category, Peraldus notes that sobriety is effective for health, long life, and bodily and spiritual enjoyment, and that moderation is to be practiced not just in the quantity of food and drink one indulges in, but in all circumstances. He develops five functions of sobriety, derived as virtuous opposites of Gregory the Great's five types of gluttony, namely, to avoid anticipating the time established for a meal, to avoid looking for luxurious foods, to avoid painstaking care in preparing foods, to bridle an excessive appetite for food and drink, and not to exceed the right portions at a meal.[28] Touch is to be guided by restraint (*continentia*; chapter 10). Its varieties include restraint in the soft touch of clothing, beds, oils, ointments, or bodily touching, of which there are two kinds: touching bodily members meant for reproduction, or touching the other bodily members. Temperance of all the aforementioned kinds is called *continentia,* but in sermons the term is used especially for the illicit pleasures of touch with respect to the bodily members used for reproduction, in which sense *continentia* is understood as abstinence from illicit sexual intercourse. The rest of this section of the treatise is devoted to the careful examination of sexual *continentia.* Continence is divided here into abstinence from illicit and licit sex, which has two varieties: *continentia virginalis,* for those who never had sex (chapter 11), and *continentia vidualis,* for those who had been married (chapter 12); clerical chastity (chapter 13); and married restraint, which is abstinence from illicit sex while practicing licit sex (*continentia coniugalis*; chapter 14).[29] Next follows a section in praise of marriage (chapter 15) that includes guidelines to contract marriage (chapter 16) and the practice of marital sex (chapter 17). Finally, in the last chapter temperance in sight, hearing, and smell is distinguished by the objects of these senses that should be perceived with self-discipline.

Peraldus's appeals to moderation in the activity of the senses vitiate notions commonly held today of medieval moral theologians' unrelieved campaign to curtail sensory pleasure. Challenges to such presuppositions can be found in Peraldus's discussion of the need for moderation included in a number of treatises on sins in the *Summa de vitiis*, but they take on sharper focus in the 'Treatise on Temperance' in his later *Compendium on the Virtues*. Here, too, Peraldus's analysis contests some common views on such basic aspects of the medieval sensorium as the hierarchy of the senses. The conception that humans have only five senses is purely arbitrary, but traditional in the West.[30] The paradigm of five external senses was inherited from antiquity, specifically from the classification of the senses by Aristotle (384–322 BCE) or Democritus (*c.* 460-*c.* 370 BCE),[31] with Cicero (106–43 BCE) as an important intermediary,[32] but this list was hardly as rigid as it is sometimes made out to be, and in all events it allowed for more multisensoriality than a static hierarchy might be taken to permit.[33] The influential monastic writer and papal advisor, Bernard of Clairvaux (1090–1153), gives a clear and schematic view of the five external senses, and one of their most frequently delineated hierarchies. In his *Sententiae*, a collection of Bernard's thoughts that may represent notes for later sermons, he states:

> There are five senses of the flesh, or the corporeal senses, by which the soul endows its body with sensation, namely, beginning from the inferior ones: touch, taste, smell, hearing, sight.[34]

This hierarchy, in which sight and hearing are considered 'superior' senses and taste and touch 'inferior', was repeated widely in the Middle Ages.[35] Yet, as a learned inheritance of antiquity, the five-sense taxonomy took some time to spread through medieval Europe,[36] and even when it was well established it could be supplemented and varied. Moreover, the list of the external or physical senses also coexisted with taxonomies of the spiritual senses[37] and classifications of the inner senses.[38]

More specifically, the hierarchical ordering explained by Bernard of Clairvaux is an inheritance of classical philosophy's notion that the value of sight and hearing derives from the fact that these senses occur at a distance from the object of perception. As Carolyn Korsmeyer has observed, 'in virtually all analyses of the senses in Western philosophy the distance between object and perceiver has been seen as a cognitive, moral, and aesthetic advantage'.[39] But with a changed context, the 'proximity' senses of touch and taste could be valued more than the 'distal' senses. Among the spiritual senses, the sense of taste could be more highly valued than sight or hearing – especially when it came to the taste of the Lord's sweetness (see Psalm 33:9).[40] In the medical field, taste was appreciated for its pedagogical value as the single sense that can teach each person perfectly about the various natures of things because we take a substance completely into ourselves when we taste it with the tongue.[41] As a diagnostic tool, tasting the bodily fluids of their patients served physicians as a more reliable guide to health than using most of their other senses; in a related fashion, a patient's experience of the feeling of pain was also considered especially useful in diagnosing illnesses.[42] Even on ethical grounds, the proximity senses could be appreciated more highly than sight or hearing. In Peraldus's 'Treatise on Temperance', proximity senses are valued because they do necessary service in preserving life: taste is a required element in eating, touch an essential part of reproduction. The other senses add to the quality of life, but are of less importance in its rudimentary maintenance. Basing his work on Aristotle's ethics and *libri naturales*, Peraldus observes that sight, hearing, and smell are activated at a distance from the object of perception, but taste and touch require proximity to that object:

> Whence the pleasures that occur through taste and touch are greater than those that occur through the other three senses. And the inclination to the actions and pleasures stimulated through these two senses is greater than that stimulated through the other three. And the vices that occur through the actions and pleasures of those two senses are more dangerous. Hence, the virtues that are contrary to these vices are more necessary and more noteworthy.[43]

This variation in what Bernard had presented as the hierarchy of the senses is a function of the context in which the senses are discussed. For pastoral theology, the immediacy of sensation and its possible allure had far more potential for the process of edifying the senses than a statement on vision as the superior sense. The possibility of sensory perception – especially the intensity of touch or taste – leading to sin provided the kind of pedagogical moment that invited pastoral authors to foreground the proximity senses when teaching how to cure the vices. For example, while Peraldus includes both sight (seeing women) and hearing (listening to lascivious songs) among the occasions that can lead to lust, as well as the sense of touch, he emphasises mainly the latter among the initial group of lust's remedies. If someone finds himself tempted by *luxuria*, in other words, he should put out this fire by dousing himself with cold water (either literally, or with the water of tears or the 'water' of corporeal discipline).[44] There is more complexity and variation in the choices of assigning positions in the medieval hierarchy of the senses than has at times been acknowledged.

Peraldus's view of temperance as a virtue with a special regard to regulating sensory experience demonstrates his inheritance of Aristotelian ethical thought. In the *Nicomachean Ethics*, Aristotle's treatment of temperance (*sophrosyne*) first excludes from consideration the pleasures of the intellect (or soul), such as ambition when it is gratified or the love of learning, and focuses on the pleasures of the body as the scope of this moral virtue.[45] More closely defined, the sphere of temperance is further distinguished by the sensory modalities it engages. Here, sight, hearing, and smell are excluded: Aristotle observes that those who are delighted by the pleasures of colours, or the sounds of music, or the odour of roses are not referred to as either temperate or profligate (the fault of excess related to temperance) through the use of these distal senses in themselves. What is left in the scope of sensory modalities proper to temperance are the proximity senses that human beings share with animals: those which are involved in the appetitive pleasures associated with eating and sex, namely taste and touch. And even more, touch plays the functionally decisive role in this distinction since, for Aristotle, the pleasure of eating is also essentially haptic. This is the background for his observation that a certain gourmet (*opsophagos*) wanted a neck that was longer than a crane's, showing that his pleasure came in the sensation of touch when he swallowed.[46] As John Sisko has noted, for Aristotle 'it is touch (in the gullet and the oesophagus) that plays the fundamental perceptual role in the bestial activity of feeding'.[47] Insofar as touch (and through it, taste) are senses that human beings have in common with animals, they are also senses of a lower order that potentially produce slavish behaviour. A profligate revelling in these senses is not characteristic of human beings, but of animals.[48] What makes temperance a moral virtue, then, is that by exercising it a human being demonstrates a conception of the self and the life worth leading that rises above that of animals. The action of temperance as a virtue is not the total rejection of the physical pleasures connected with nutrition and generation that humans have in common with animals, but it works to ensure that these pleasures are felt in the right way and to the right degree by human beings.[49]

The function of temperance in moderating touch remained a familiar element in the scholastic reception of Aristotelian thought on the cardinal virtue, though academic authors do not limit temperance to touch as, in essence, Aristotle had done. Albert the Great emphasises the haptic sense in defining temperance, which – along with prudence, fortitude, and justice – he defines as a civic virtue. He proposes what he terms a substantial reason to justify the number of four cardinal virtues, namely that the four of them together amount to what is required of good citizens.[50] These four necessary virtues include the habit in determining what is right about one's actions (prudence) and three varieties of carrying out the right actions in difficult and important matters, either in relation to others according to what is owed them by obligation (justice), or in relation to one's self. Of the latter, there are two types: one is when difficult matters, like war, are inflicted on us from external sources and we behave correctly (fortitude). The other concerns 'what is inherently pleasurable within our present life according to touch, as in taste, which is a kind of touch, and sexual desire. And the habit governing these matters is temperance'.[51] Thomas Aquinas also emphasised the sense of touch in understanding temperance when he justified the designation of the 'cardinal' virtues, not because they are general categories of virtue, but because of the particular scope Aristotle had given to each:

> And thus Aristotle more appropriately distinguished the virtues according to their objects or according to their subject matter. And according to this, the previously mentioned four virtues are not called 'principle' because they are general virtues but because their species are explained according to certain principles: . . .temperance is not concerned with just any kind of bridling, but only with desires for the pleasures of touch.[52]

The analysis of temperance in Aquinas's *Summa Theologiae* also depends closely on Aristotle's distinction of the scope of this virtue, arguing that temperance concerns desires for the greatest pleasures. Since pleasure results from a natural operation, the more natural the operation is, the greater the pleasure will be. For animals, the most natural operations are those that preserve the nature of the individual through food and drink and the nature of the species through the union of a male and a female. Thus, temperance is properly concerned with pleasures associated with food and drink and sexual pleasures, and these kinds of pleasures result from the sense of touch.[53]

While the Aristotelian tradition asserts that the proper scope of temperance is the sense of touch, Peraldus included both taste and touch as the focal points of temperance in his treatise on the virtue. Although he also observes that delectable food gives a brief pleasure as it passes through the throat,[54] he did not claim that the pleasure of taste is essentially haptic. He found a precedent for this in the same scholastic authors (and Dominicans) with whom he shared the study of Aristotle's writings. Moral theologians, such as Albert the Great and Thomas Aquinas, extended the scope of temperance to include the moderation of all the senses, even while they claimed to be following Aristotle in maintaining that the central sense modality implicated in temperance is touch. Albert notes that virtue can be exercised in other than the most extreme circumstances. Fortitude, for example, can be shown in situations less menacing than imminent mortal danger.

> And we can say in accordance with Aristotle that temperance exists in the highest degree and according to its greatest power in the

pleasure of touch concerning nourishment and sexual desire, but nevertheless it is also correctly exercised in other innate pleasures in accordance with the same habit. And this is in agreement with the words of Aristotle in many passages of the *Ethics*, as is evident to those who diligently examine that book.[55]

Similarly, in the *Summa Theologiae*, Aquinas includes under the aegis of temperance a number of virtues, or virtues understood in a broad sense, in which the sense of touch plays little or no role at all: for example, shamefastness (*verecundia*; question 144), honesty (*honestas*; question 145), clemency (*clementia*), and meekness (*mansuetudo*) (both addressed in question 157). Together, these parts of temperance demonstrate Aquinas's interest in extending the scope of virtuous moderation to matters beyond the sense modality that Aristotle had seen at the centre of temperance.[56]

Peraldus goes further in this direction, asserting the inclusion of the distal senses in the scope of temperance not just as a matter of theory, but by examining features of moderation in the activity of each of them. There is an order involved here which depends on the conventional hierarchy of the senses, in which the sense of sight has a higher position than hearing, and hearing a higher position than the sense of smell, and therefore 'it appears that sight is more dangerous than hearing unless it is restrained, and hearing more dangerous than smell'.[57] The control of sight involves restraint in merely glancing around idly, but also preventing oneself from looking at women, uncontrolled uses of vision that a number of passages in Ecclesiasticus warn about which are recommended for use by the preacher (unrestrained looking in general: Sirach 9:7, 9:8; looking at women: Sirach 9:3, 9:5, 25:28, 41:27). The combination of sight and hearing presents the danger of *vitium curiositatis*, which in no way implicates any and all intellectual inquiry – if nothing else, Peraldus's reading of the Aristotelian corpus demonstrates his own lively curiosity about any number of topics – but rather an inquisitiveness which expends itself in the useless knowledge of rumours about other people, on which Peraldus quotes Gregory the Great:

> 'Curiosity is a serious sin which, while it leads someone's mind to poke into his fellow human being's life, hides his own most inward qualities from him so that while he knows about others' affairs he does not know himself'. The same author: 'The more experienced the mind of the curious person is in someone else's merit, the more ignorant it is of itself'.[58]

The restraint of hearing is recommended in a number of areas, each supported by biblical passages or citations from authorities. These areas include the tempting sounds of musical instruments (Job 21:12–13, Isaiah 5:12; further supported by a brief exemplum: 'Antigonus, Alexander's teacher, broke his cithara and on top of that said: 'It is fitting that you rule already at your age, and it should be shameful that the pleasure of lust is dominant in the body of the royal authority").[59] Lascivious singing and casual conversations with women are also to be avoided (Sirach 9:4, 9:11), as is the sound of one's own singing voice (supported by a quotation attributed to Gregory: 'While one warbles with a fawning voice, the temperate life is abandoned').[60] But other forms of intemperate listening are also found to be in need of restraint: hearing about others' misfortunes (Sirach 28:28), and the recitation of one's own good qualities that flatterers customarily bring up. The avoidance of flatterers is supported by citations attributed to Seneca: 'If you have self-restraint, avoid flattery, and let being praised by sinners be just as disagreeable to you as being praised on account of sins'. And from the same source: 'The most difficult act of restraint is to reject the adulation of flatterers whose words enervate the mind with a certain pleasure'.[61] Finally, the sense of smell is to be tempered from sweet fragrances, while sinners should be reminded that one of the punishments in hell will be the smell of sulphur (Isaiah 3:24, 30:33; Psalm 10:7).

With all the care Peraldus takes in delineating restraint in activities of both the distal and the proximity senses, his goal in the 'Treatise on Temperance' is not to encourage an anxious guarding of the senses,[62] which is a static phenomenon, but rather an informed guidance of the senses, a progressive process of education that emphasises the value of moderation in sensory pleasures. Indeed, part of the conscious work of pastoral theologians following Peraldus – especially the generations of Dominicans who were trained by the study of his compendia on the vices and virtues – was to emphasise in their preaching the importance of edifying the senses.[63] Learning how to perceive as an aspect of the virtuous life was as significant for Peraldus as it had been for Aristotle, and this prominence can be seen not only in Peraldus's treatment of sight, hearing, and smell, but also in his analysis of the senses which afforded the greatest pleasures, taste and touch. In this way, he spends nearly as much time praising all aspects of marriage, including conjugal sexual relations, as he does lauding virginity.[64] This praise of the 'correct' use of the senses as virtuous actions had the effect of creating a sacral context for sensory perception, of imbuing the senses in a number of seemingly everyday situations – eating, drinking, sexual relations – with sacred meaning. The pastoral encouragement for every sensory act to participate in the divine as a part of the moral life was one more step in the process of edifying the senses. Peraldus, thus, also commends sobriety for its positive effects on health, resulting in long life, but also for the enjoyment of life:

> Chrysostom on the Epistle to the Hebrews: 'Nothing is so effective for health, nothing so effective for sharpening the senses, nothing chases away illness so much as moderation in a meal'. Likewise,

sobriety is efficacious for a long life; Sirach 37[:34]: *He who is temperate will prolong his life.* Likewise, sobriety is efficacious for enjoyment, both corporeal and spiritual; Sirach 31[:36]: *Wine drunken with moderation is the joy of the soul and the heart.*[65]

This is hardly a call for ascetic self-denial in the face of sensory pleasures that the Burckhardtian (or Greenblatt's neo-Burckhardtian) view of the Middle Ages would have us expect, but of course it corresponds perfectly with the task of preaching to the laity, especially in urban centres with their more cosmopolitan congregations, which was specific to the Dominican Order and necessitated its attention to all forms of cultural entertainment.[66] The Order of Preachers was ministering here to congregations for whom demands for ascesis would hardly have accorded with a life shaped by commerce and civic obligations. This process of reforming the interpretation of sensory data, of educating the senses in the ethics of moderation, was the great task Peraldus set for himself in his analysis of temperance. His success in these efforts makes it clear why, against common contemporary preconceptions, the treatment of temperance remained the most important context in which the ethics of the senses – always at the centre of the sensorium in the Middle Ages – is to be found in the medieval moral tradition.[67]

Notes

1 See the discussion of the call to guard the senses by the medieval preacher Geiler von Kaysersberg in Robert Jütte, *A History of the Senses: From Antiquity to Cyberspace*, trans. James Lynn (Malden, MA: Polity, 2005), 105. For an early Italian renaissance work that includes admonitions to control the senses, see Antonino Pierozzi, *Opera a ben vivere*, discussed in Theresa Flanigan, 'Disciplining the Tongue: Archbishop Antoninus, the *Opera a ben vivere*, and the Regulation of Women's Speech in Renaissance Florence', *Open Arts Journal* 4 (2014–2015): 41–60, available at: http://openartsjournal.org/issue-4/article-3/, accessed 15 July 2015; see also eadem, 'Art, Memory, and the Cultivation of Virtue: The Ethical Function of Images in Antoninus's *Opera a ben vivere*', *Gesta* 53 (2014): 175–95. The continuity of advice to guard the senses can be witnessed in contemporary, homiletically oriented presentations of what Buddha is said to have taught on sensory control: see, for example, 'Six Sense Organs', *Chinese Buddhist Encyclopedia*, available at: http://www.chinabuddhismencyclopedia.com/en/index.php/Six_sense_organs, accessed 15 July 2015: 'When seeing a form, hearing a sound, smelling a smell, tasting a taste, touching a thing, or thinking a thought, one does neither get caught up by any of the general features, nor does one become as if gripped, immersed, fixated, or captivated by any particular detail of this form, sound, smell, taste, touch, or mental state. . . . Since, if one leaves the senses of the eye, ear, nose, tongue, body, and mind uncontrolled, then evil detrimental states such as greed, lust, and discontent invade and dominate the mind!'
2 Stephen Greenblatt, *The Swerve: How the World Became Modern* (New York: Norton, 2011), 9–10.

3 Johan Huizinga, *The Autumn of the Middle Ages*, trans. Rodney J. Payton and Ulrich Mammitzsch (Chicago: The University of Chicago Press, 1996), 41. On the importance of Huizinga for the history of emotions in the Middle Ages, see Andrew Galloway, 'Petrarch's Pleasures, Chaucer's Revulsions, and the Aesthetics of Renunciation in Late-Medieval Culture', in *Answerable Style: The Idea of the Literary in Medieval England*, ed. Frank Grady and Andrew Galloway (Columbus: Ohio State University Press, 2013), 140–66, esp. 140–42.

4 John Parker, 'The Epicurean Middle Ages', *Exemplaria* 25 (2013): 324–29, here 326. See also Richard Newhauser, 'Sin, the Business of Pleasure, and the Pleasure of Reading: Exemplary Narratives and Other Forms of Sinful Pleasure in William Peraldus's *Summa de vitiis*', in *Pleasure in the Middle Ages*, ed. Naama Cohen-Hanegbi and Piroska Nagy, International Medieval Research, 24 (Turnhout: Brepols, 2017), 149–64.

5 Since the mid-1990s an increasing number of studies have been devoted to the study of Peraldus's works. For some examples, see the following: Richard Newhauser, 'Unerring Faith in the Pulpit: William Peraldus' *Tractatus de fide* in the *Summa de uirtutibus*', in *Fides Virtus: The Virtue of Faith from the Twelfth to the Early Sixteenth Century*, ed. Marco Forlivesi, Riccardo Quinto, and Silvana Vecchio, Archa Verbi. Yearbook for the Study of Medieval Theology. Subsidia, 12 (Münster: Aschendorff, 2014), 389–410; Richard Newhauser, 'The Capital Vices as Medieval Anthropology', in *Laster im Mittelalter / Vices in the Middle Ages*, ed. Ch. Flüeler and M. Rohde, Scrinium Friburgense / Veröffentlichungen des Mediävistischen Instituts der Universität Freiburg, 23 (Berlin: De Gruyter, 2009), 105–23; Petra Schulte, 'Einleitung', in *Strategies of Writing: Studies on Text and Trust in the Middle Ages*, ed. Petra Schulte, Marco Mostert, and Irene van Renswoude (Brepols: Turnhout, 2008), 1–12; Michiel Verweij, 'Princely Virtues or Virtues for Princes? William Peraldus and his *De eruditione principum*', in *Princely Virtues in the Middle Ages 1200–1500*, ed. István P. Bejczy and Cary J. Nederman, Disputatio, 9 (Turnhout: Brepols, 2007), 51–71; Michael Menzel, '"Historiarum armarium": Geschichtsexempla in Predigerhand', *Historisches Jahrbuch* 126 (2006): 1–23; Edwin D. Craun, '"It is a freletee of flessh": Excuses for Sin, Pastoral Rhetoric, and Moral Agency', in *In the Garden of Evil: The Vices and Culture in the Middle Ages*, ed. Richard Newhauser, Papers in Mediaeval Studies, 18 (Toronto: Pontifical Institute of Mediaeval Studies Press, 2005), 170–92; F. N. M. Diekstra, 'The Art of Denunciation: Medieval Moralists on Envy and Detraction', in ibid., 431–54; Louis-Jacques Bataillon, 'L'influence de Hugues de Saint-Cher', in *Hugues de Saint-Cher (†1263). Bibliste et théologien*, ed. Louis-Jacques Bataillon, Gilbert Dahan and Pierre-Marie Gy, Bibliothèque d'histoire culturelle du Moyen Age, 1 (Turnhout: Brepols, 2004), 497–502; István P. Bejczy, 'John of La Rochelle and William Peraldus on the Virtues and Vices', *Archivum Franciscanum Historicum* 97 (2004): 99–110; Peggy A. Knapp, 'The Words of the Parson's "vertuous sentence,"' in *Closure in the Canterbury Tales: The Role of the Parson's Tale*, ed. David Raybin and Linda Tarte Holley, Studies in Medieval Culture, 41 (Kalamazoo, MI: Medieval Institute Publications, 2000), 95–113; John Inglis, 'Aquinas's Replication of the Acquired Moral Virtues: Rethinking the Standard Philosophical Interpretation of Moral Virtue in Aquinas', *The Journal of Religious Ethics* 27 (1999): 3–27; Richard Newhauser, 'Jesus as the First Dominican? Reflections on a Sub-theme in the Exemplary Literature of Some Thirteenth-Century Preachers', in *Christ Among the Medieval Dominicans: Representations of Christ in the Texts and Images of the Order of Preachers*, ed. Kent Emery,

Jr. and Joseph Wawrykow, Notre Dame Conferences in Medieval Studies, 7 (Notre Dame, IN: University of Notre Dame Press, 1998), 238–55; David L. d'Avray, 'Christ in Dominican Marriage Preaching', in ibid., 271–82; Robert J. Schneider, 'Vincent of Beauvais, Dominican Author: From *compilatio* to *tractatus*', in *Lector et compilator: Vincent de Beauvais, frère prêcheur, un intellectuel et son milieu au XIIIe siècle*, ed. Serge Lusignan and Monique Paulmier-Foucart, Rencontres à Royaumont, 9 (Grâne: Editions Créaphis, 1997), 97–111; Edwin D. Craun, *Lies, Slander, and Obscenity in Medieval English Literature: Pastoral Rhetoric and the Deviant Speaker*, Cambridge Studies in Medieval Literature, 31 (Cambridge: Cambridge University Press, 1997), passim; Joan Heiges Blythe, 'Sins of the Tongue and Rhetorical Prudence in *Piers Plowman*', in *Literature and Religion in the Later Middle Ages: Philological Studies in Honor of Siegfried Wenzel*, ed. Richard G. Newhauser and John A. Alford, Medieval & Renaissance Texts & Studies, 118 (Binghamton, NY: Center for Medieval and Early Renaissance Studies, State University of New York at Binghamton, 1995), 119–42.

6 William Peraldus, *Sermones*, in *Guilelmi Alverni Episcopi Parisiensis . . . opera omnia*, 2 vols. (Paris, 1674), 2: 1–476.

7 *De eruditione principum* is available in digital format in the edition printed among the works of Thomas Aquinas at http://www.corpusthomisticum.org/xre0.html, accessed 21 January 2015.

8 For Peraldus's life and works, still essential is Antoine Dondaine, 'Guillaume Peyraut, vie et œuvres', *Archivum Fratrum Praedicatorum* 18 (1948): 162–236.

9 On these texts, see Richard Newhauser, *The Treatise on Vices and Virtues in Latin and the Vernacular*, Typologie des sources du moyen âge occidental, 68 (Turnhout: Brepols, 1993), 124–32.

10 On the transmission and printed editions, see Thomas Kaeppeli, *Scriptores Ordinis Praedicatorum Medii Aevi*, 4 vols. (Roma: Ad S. Sabinam; Istituto storico Domenicano, 1970–1993), no. 1622; Morton W. Bloomfield, Bertrand-Georges Guyot, Donald R. Howard, and Thyra B. Kabealo, *Incipits of Latin Works on the Virtues and Vices, 1100–1500 A.D.*, The Mediaeval Academy of America, Publication 88 (Cambridge, MA: The Mediaeval Academy of America, 1979), 1628, 5601, etc. The latter text is emended in Richard Newhauser and István Bejczy, *A Supplement to Morton W. Bloomfield et al., 'Incipits of Latin Works on the Virtues and Vices, 1100–1500 A.D.'*, Instrumenta Patristica et Mediaevalia, Research on the Inheritance of Early and Medieval Christianity, 50 (Turnhout: Brepols, 2008).

11 For the concept of the contrary virtues, formerly known as 'remedial virtues', see Richard Newhauser, 'Preaching the "Contrary Virtues,"' *Mediaeval Studies* 70 (2008): 135–62; reprint in *Classical and Medieval Literature Criticism*, 159, ed. L. J. Trudeau (Detroit: Gale, 2014), 266–81.

12 For editions of the *Fiore di virtù* see Newhauser, *The Treatise on Vices and Virtues in Latin and the Vernacular*, 38.

13 Frère Laurent, *La Somme le roi*, ed. Édith Brayer and Anne-Françoise Leurquin-Labie (Paris: Société des Anciens Textes Français, 2008).

14 *Die Spiegel der Sonden*, ed. Jacob Verdam, 2 vols. (Leiden: Brill, 1900–1901).

15 See William C. McDonald, 'Singing Sin: Michel Beheim's "Little Book of the Seven Deadly Sins," a German Pre-Reformation Religious Text for the Laity', in *Sin in Medieval and Early Modern Culture*, ed. Richard G. Newhauser and Susan J. Ridyard (York: York Medieval Press, in connection with Boydell & Brewer, 2012), 282–303. German adaptations of Peraldus began very early;

for a fragment of a translation preserved in a manuscript of the third quarter of the thirteenth-century, see Karin Schneider, 'Guilelmus Peraldus in früher deutscher Übersetzung', in *Fata Libellorum: Festschrift für Franzjosef Pensel zum 70. Geburtstag*, ed. Rudolf Bentzinger and Ulrich-Dieter Oppitz, Göppinger Arbeiten zur Germanistik, 648 (Göppingen: Kümmerle Verlag, 1999), 279–91. See also Gunhild Roth, 'Wilhelm Peraldus', *Die deutsche Literatur des Mittelalters: Verfasserlexikon*, 2nd ed. (Berlin: de Gruyter, 1999), 10:1116–29.

16 *The Book of Vices and Virtues: A Fourteenth Century English Translation of the 'Somme le Roi' of Lorens d'Orléans*, ed. W. Nelson Francis, EETS o.s. 217 (London: Oxford University Press, 1942).

17 Brunetto Latini, *Li livres dou tresor*, ed. Francis J. Carmody (Berkeley: University of California Press, 1948).

18 Klaus Wolf, '*Propter utilitatem populi: Durch nucz willen seines volkes*. Die 'staatstragende' Rezeption der 'Summa de vitiis' des Guilelmus Peraldus in der spätmittelalterlichen Wiener Schule', in *Laster im Mittelalter / Vices in the Middle Ages*, ed. Flüeler and Rohde, 187–99; Richard Newhauser, 'The Parson's Tale and Its Generic Affiliations', in *Closure in 'The Canterbury Tales'*, ed. Raybin and Holley, 45–76; reprint in Richard Newhauser, *Sin: Essays on the Moral Tradition in the Western Middle Ages*, Variorum Collected Studies Series, CS869 (Aldershot: Ashgate, 2007), essay IV.

19 Siegfried Wenzel, 'Dante's Rationale for the Seven Deadly Sins (*Purgatorio* XVII)', *Modern Language Review* 60 (1965): 529–33; reprint in Siegfried Wenzel, *Elucidations*, Synthema, 6 (Louvain: Peeters, 2010), 113–19.

20 Richard Newhauser, 'The Parson's Tale', in *Sources and Analogues of 'The Canterbury Tales'*, ed. Robert M. Correale and Mary Hamel, 2 vols., Chaucer Studies, 28 and 35 (Cambridge: D. S. Brewer, 2002–2005), 1: 529–613; Siegfried Wenzel, 'The Source of Chaucer's Seven Deadly Sins', *Traditio* 30 (1974): 351–78; Siegfried Wenzel, 'The Source for the *Remedia* of the Parson's Tale', *Traditio* 27 (1971): 433–53. On the reception of Peraldus's *summae*, see Newhauser, *The Treatise on Vices and Virtues in Latin and the Vernacular*, 127–30; Siegfried Wenzel, 'The Continuing Life of William Peraldus's *Summa vitiorum*', in *Ad litteram: Authoritative Texts and Their Medieval Readers*, ed. Mark. D. Jordan and Kent Emery, Jr., Notre Dame Conferences in Medieval Studies, 3 (Notre Dame, IN: University of Notre Dame Press, 1992), 135–63.

21 See Emile J. Arnould, *Le 'Manuel des Péchés': Étude de littérature religieuse anglo-normande* (Paris: Droz, 1940), 29n3.

22 Giles Constable, 'Moderation and Restraint in Ascetic Practices in the Middle Ages', in *From Athens to Chartres. Neoplatonism and Medieval Thought: Studies in Honour of Edouard Jeauneau*, ed. Haijo Jan Westra, Studien und Texte zur Geistesgeschichte des Mittelalters, 35 (Leiden: Brill, 1992), 315–27, here 326.

23 William Peraldus, *Summa de vitiis*, Tractatus de accidia, in Lyon, Bibliothèque municipale MS 678, f. 84rb (Paris, Bibliothèque Mazarine MS 794, f. 112ra–rb): 'Sciendum quod in cibis qui sumuntur ualde timenda est delectabilitas, quia frequenter nimis sumitur de cibis delectabilibus et cum nimio ardore. Preterea consolatio in cibis delectabilibus quandoque prohibet hominem a diuina consolatione. Secundum Bernardum nimis delicata est diuina consolatio que non datur admittentibus alienam. Sed si quis in cibis quos sumit in quantitate et in ardore caueat et Creatori de creatura eius quam sumit gratias agat, non solum absque peccato sed etiam meritorie potest sumere de cibis illis quantum necesse est ad sustentationem corporis sui. Deus enim *creauit cibos ad percipiendum cum gratiarum actione fidelibus*, <i> [*om.* MSS] ad

Thimotheum iiii. Vt breuiter dicam, sic deberemus habere corpus sicut eger comedit, cui multum uolenti inutilia sunt neganda, utilia uero etiam nolenti ingerenda'. For the passage from Bernard, cited frequently by scholastic authors, see Bernard of Clairvaux, *Sermones in adventu Domini*, 4.5, ed. Jean Leclercq and Henri M. Rochais, in *Opera*, 8 vols. (Rome: Editiones Cistercienses, 1957–1977), 4: 185. On the importance of moderation in maintaining good health in the works of later British pastoral writers, see Edwin D. Craun, 'Aristotle's Biology and Pastoral Ethics: John of Wales's *De Lingua* and British Pastoral Writing on the Tongue', *Traditio* 67 (2012): 277–303, here 287–88. On the physiological interests of moral theologians in thinking about sin, see Heather Webb, 'Cardiosensory Impulses in Late Medieval Spirituality', in *Rethinking the Medieval Senses. Heritage, Fascinations, Frames*, ed. Stephen G. Nichols, Andreas Kablitz, and Alison Calhoun (Baltimore: The Johns Hopkins University Press, 2008), 265–85, here 269, 273.

24 For an example of a text that adopts a metaphor begun in Late Antiquity in seeing the body as a city and the senses as gates or water sluices, see Sermon 34, titled *De quinque sensibus corporis*, in *Jacob's Well. An Englisht Treatise on the Cleansing of Man's Conscience*, ed. Arthur Brandeis, Part 1, EETS o.s. 115 (London: Kegan Paul, Trench, Trübner & Co., 1900), 216–22, here 217: 'þerfore, þe v watyr-gatys of 3oure pytt [i.e., the human body] arn 3oure v bodyly wyttes, as crisostom seyth, super Mat. in imperfecto, omilia xxxiiij'. The text was probably composed in the earlier fifteenth century in Suffolk. See Leo Carruthers, 'Where Did *Jacob's Well* Come From? The Provenance and Dialect of MS Salisbury Cathedral 103', *English Studies* 4 (1990): 335–40. On the manuscript, see Veronica O'Mara and Suzanne Paul, *A Repertorium of Middle English Prose Sermons*, 4 vols., Sermo, 1 (Turnhout: Brepols, 2007), 4: 2276–453.

25 William Peraldus, *Summa de vitiis*, Tractatus de accidia, in Lyon, Bibliothèque municipale MS 678, f. 84rb (Paris, Bibliothèque Mazarine MS 794, f. 112rb): 'Simile est de cordis cythare, que si parum tendantur, rauce sonant, si nimium, rumpuntur, si moderate, dulcem sonum reddunt'.

26 William Peraldus, *Summa de virtutibus*, 3.3.2, in Lyon, Bibliothèque municipale MS 678, f. 248va: 'Tercio dicitur temperantia virtus animam regens circa delectationes corporales siue circa delectationes quinque sensuum. Glossa super Mathei xv: 'Temperantia est refrenatio cupiditatis ab hiis que temporaliter delectant'. Et Augustinus dicit temperantiam esse 'in cohercendis delectationibus prauis''. For the citation from Matthew, see the gloss on Matthew 15:36 in *Glossa ordinaria*, in *Biblia latina cum Glossa ordinaria* (Strassburg: Adolph Rusch, for Anton Koberger at Nürnberg, 1480/81), vol. 4, 947v. For the quotation from Augustine, see *De Trinitate*, 14.9, ed. W. J. Mountain, 2 vols., CCSL 50–50A (Turnhout: Brepols, 1968), CCSL 50A, 439.

27 William Peraldus, *Summa de virtutibus*, 3.3.8, in Lyon, Bibliothèque municipale MS 678, f. 251va: 'Notandum ergo quod ille partes temperantie que regunt animum circa delectationes que sunt secundum gustum et tactum, satis sunt note et nominate, que sunt sobrietas et continentia. Ille autem partes que pertinent ad delectationes que sunt secundum visum et auditum et olfactum, non sunt ita note nec habent specialia nomina'.

28 Cf. Gregory the Great, *Moralia in Iob*, 30.18.60, ed. Marc Adriaen, 3 vols., CCSL 143, 143A, 143B (Turnhout: Brepols, 1979–1985), vol. 143B, 1531.

29 Peraldus frames his discussion in chapter 14 as a way of correcting the argument of those who condemn marriage, whom he explicitly names 'Cathars'. See David L. d'Avray, 'Some Franciscan Ideas About the Body', *Archivum Franciscanum Historicum* 84 (1991): 343–63, here 351.

30 Phillip Vannini, Dennis Waskul, and Simon Gottschalk, *The Senses in Self, Society, and Culture: A Sociology of the Senses* (London: Routledge, 2012), 6; C. M. Woolgar, *The Senses in Late Medieval England* (New Haven, CT: Yale University Press, 2006), 5–28; Constance Classen, *Worlds of Sense: Exploring the Senses in History and Across Cultures* (New York: Routledge, 1993).

31 Jütte, *A History of the Senses*, 61–71.

32 Peter Dronke, 'Les cinq sens chez Bernard Silvestre et Alain de Lille', *I cinque sensi / The Five Senses. Micrologus* 10 (2002): 1–14.

33 Holly Dugan and Lara Farina, 'Intimate Senses / Sensing Intimacy', *Postmedieval* 3 (2012): 373–79.

34 Bernard of Clairvaux, *Sententiae*, 3.73, ed. Jean Leclercq and Henri M. Rochais, in *Opera*, vol. 6.2, 108: 'Quinque enim sunt sensus animales vel corporales, quibus anima corpus suum sensificat, ut ab inferiori incipiam: tactus, gustus, odoratus, auditus, visus'.

35 Louise Vinge, *The Five Senses. Studies in a Literary Tradition*, Skrifter utgivna av Kungl. Humanistiska Vetenskapssamfundet i Lund, 72 (Lund: CWK Gleerup, 1975).

36 David Howes and Constance Classen, *Ways of Sensing: Understanding the Senses in Society* (London: Routledge, 2013), 67.

37 The spiritual senses were articulated at times as a system parallel to the external senses that was used to give expression to an encounter with the divine, as if they were the sense impressions of the 'eyes of the heart' or 'the tongue of faith', etc. See *The Spiritual Senses: Perceiving God in Western Christianity*, ed. Paul L. Gavrilyuk and Sarah Coakley (Cambridge: Cambridge University Press, 2011); Karl Rahner, 'La doctrine des 'sens spirituels' au Moyen-Age, en particulier chez saint Bonaventura', *Revue d'Ascétique et de Mystique* 14 (1933): 263–99, trans. David Morland as 'The Doctrine of the 'Spiritual Senses' in the Middle Ages', in Karl Rahner, *Theological Investigations* (Baltimore: Helicon Press, 1979), 16:104–34; Karl Rahner, 'Le début d'une doctrine des cinq sens spirituels chez Origène', *Revue d'Ascétique et de Mystique* 13 (1932): 113–45, trans. David Morland as 'The 'Spiritual Senses' According to Origen', in Rahner, *Theological Investigations*, 16: 81–103.

38 The 'inner (or internal) senses' could refer to the spiritual senses, as a way of contrasting them to the external or physical senses, but the phrase 'inner senses' was also used to designate the stages that were considered to be involved in the process leading from physical sensation by the external senses through perception to cognition. Here, too, these faculties of cognitive progression could be modeled on the five external senses, as Aristotle did. See Mary Carruthers, *The Book of Memory: A Study of Memory in Medieval Culture*, 2nd ed. (Cambridge: Cambridge University Press, 2008); Pavel Gregoric, *Aristotle on the Common Sense* (Oxford: Clarendon Press, 2007).

39 Carolyn Korsmeyer, *Making Sense of Taste: Food & Philosophy* (Ithaca, NY: Cornell University Press, 1999), 12.

40 Rachel Fulton, "Taste and See That the Lord is Sweet' (Ps. 33:9): The Flavor of God in the Monastic West', *Journal of Religion* 86 (2006): 169–204; Anne Astell, *Eating Beauty: The Eucharist and the Spiritual Arts of the Middles Ages* (Ithaca, NY: Cornell University Press, 2006), 3–4.

41 Faith Wallis, 'Medicine and the Senses: Feeling the Pulse, Smelling the Plague, and Listening for the Cure', in *A Cultural History of the Senses in the Middle Ages*, ed. Richard G. Newhauser, A Cultural History of the Senses, 2 (London: Bloomsbury, 2014), 133–52, here 147–49; Charles Burnett, 'Sapores Sunt Octo: The Medieval Latin Terminology For the Eight Flavors', *I cinque sensi / The Five Senses. Micrologus* 10 (2002): 99–112; Charles Burnett, 'The

Superiority of Taste', *Journal of the Warburg and Courtauld Institutes* 54 (1991): 230–38.

42 Esther Cohen, *The Modulated Scream: Pain in Late Medieval Culture* (Chicago: University of Chicago Press, 2010).

43 William Peraldus, *Summa de virtutibus*, 3.3.8, in Lyon, Bibliothèque municipale MS 678, f. 251vb: 'Vnde delectationes que sunt secundum gustum et tactum maiores sunt quam sunt secundum alios tres sensus. Et pronitas ad operationes et delectationes secundum illos duos sensus maior est quam secundum alios tres. Et uicia que sunt secundum operationes et delectationes illorum duorum sensuum magis sunt periculose. Ideo virtutes que sunt contra illa vicia magis sunt necessarie et magis note . . .'.

44 William Peraldus, *Summa de vitiis*, Tractatus de luxuria, in Lyon, Bibliothèque municipale MS 678, f. 25vb (Paris, Bibliothèque Mazarine MS 794, f. 22ra).

45 Aristotle, *The Nicomachean Ethics*, 3.10, trans. Harris Rackham, Loeb Classical Library 73, rev. ed. (Cambridge, MA: Harvard University Press, 1934), 172–75.

46 Aristotle, *Nic Eth*, 3.10, trans. Rackham, 176–77. A long neck was used to typify the glutton as late as Cesare Ripa's *Iconologia* (1603); see Silvana Vecchio, 'Gusto, piacere, peccato nella cultura medievale', in *L'infinita varietà del gusto: filosofia, arte e storia di un'idea dal Medioevo all'età moderna* (Padova: Il poligrafo, 2010), 27–39, here 33. For depictions of moderation in Nicholas Oresme's translation of the *Nicomachean Ethics*, see Claire R. Sherman, *Imaging Aristotle: Verbal and Visual Representation in Fourteenth-Century France* (Berkeley: University of California Press, 1995), 72–82.

47 John E. Sisko, 'Taste, Touch, and Temperance in *Nicomachean Ethics* 3.10', *Classical Quarterly* 53 (2003): 135–40, here 139. Cf. Charles M. Young, 'Aristotle on Temperance', *The Philosophical Review* 97 (1988): 521–42.

48 Aristotle, *Nic Eth*, 3.10, trans. Rackham, 178–79. For voluminous examples from antiquity of immoderate behavior in taste, depicted in the intemperate use of wine leading to drunkenness, see Hanneke Wilson, *Wine and Words in Classical Antiquity and the Middle Ages* (London: Duckworth, 2003), 77–113.

49 Gabriel Richardson Lear, *Happy Lives and the Highest Good. An Essay on Aristotle's Nicomachean Ethics* (Princeton, NJ: Princeton University Press, 2004), 165–66.

50 See István P. Bejczy, *The Cardinal Virtues in the Middle Ages: A Study in Western Moral Thought from the Fourth to the Fourteenth Centuries*, Brill's Studies in Intellectual History, 202 (Leiden: Brill, 2011), 212–13.

51 Albert the Great, *Commentarii in III Sententiarum*, 33.1. resp., in *Opera omnia*, ed. Auguste Borgnet, 38 vols. (Paris: Vivès, 1890–1899), 28: 607: '. . . in delectabili innato contemporaneo vitae secundum tactum, ut gustu secundum quod est tactus, et venereis. Et sic habitus regens est temperantia'. See Rollen Edward Houser, *The Cardinal Virtues: Aquinas, Albert, and Philip the Chancellor*, Mediaeval Sources in Translation, 39; Sources in Medieval Moral Teaching, 4 (Toronto: Pontifical Institute of Mediaeval Studies Press, 2004), 130.

52 Thomas Aquinas, *Sententia libri Ethicorum*, 2.8, in *Opera omnia iussu impensaque Leonis XIII P. M. edita*, vol. 1- (Roma: Ex Typographia Polyglotta S. C. de Propaganda Fide, 1882-), vol. 47; available online at http://www.corpusthomisticum.org/ctc02.html, accessed 12 May 2015: 'Et ideo convenientius Aristoteles virtutes distinxit secundum obiecta sive secundum materias. Et secundum hoc praedictae virtutes quatuor, non dicuntur principales quia sint generales sed quia species earum accipiuntur secundum quaedam principalia: . . . temperantia autem est non circa quamlibet refrenationem,

sed solum in concupiscentiis delectationis tactus'. See Bejczy, *The Cardinal Virtues*, 173.
53 Thomas Aquinas, *Summa theologiae*, 2a2ae.141.4.resp., in *Opera omnia iussu impensaque Leonis XIII P. M. edita*, vol. 1- (Roma: Ex Typographia Polyglotta S. C. de Propaganda Fide, 1882-), vol. 10; available online at http://www.corpusthomisticum.org/sth3141.html, accessed 12 May 2015. See Diana Fritz Cates, 'The Virtue of Temperance (IIa IIae, qq. 141–170)', in *The Ethics of Aquinas*, ed. Stephen J. Pope (Washington, DC: Georgetown University Press, 2002), 321–39, here 322.
54 William Peraldus, *Summa de virtutibus*, 3.3.9, in Lyon, Bibliothèque municipale MS 678, f. 252ra: 'Breuitate uero delectationis que non habetur, nisi in transitu cibi . . .'.
55 Albert the Great, *Comm. in III Sent.*, 33.1.ad 7 et 8, in *Opera*, ed. Borgnet, vol. 28, 608: 'Et possumus dicere secundum Aristotelem quod temperantia in maximo et secundum maximum suum posse est in delectabili tactus secundum alimentum et venereis, sed tamen bene se habet in aliis delectabilibus innatis secundum eumdem habitum. Et hoc consonat dictis Aristotelis in multis locis Ethicorum, sicut patet diligenter inspicientibus in libro illo'. See Houser, *The Cardinal Virtues*, 132.
56 See Houser, *The Cardinal Virtues*, 80.
57 William Peraldus, *Summa de virtutibus*, 3.3.18, in Lyon, Bibliothèque municipale MS 678, f. 260va: '. . . periculosior esse uidetur uisus nisi refrenetur quam auditus, et auditus quam olfactus'.
58 William Peraldus, *Summa de virtutibus*, 3.3.18, in Lyon, Bibliothèque municipale MS 678, f. 260vb: "Graue curiositatis est uitium, que dum cuiuslibet mentem ad inuestigandam uitam proximi exterius ducit, semper ei sua intima abscondit, ut aliena sciens, se nesciat'. Idem: 'Curiosi animus quanto peritus fuerit alieni meriti, tanto fit ignarus sui". For both citations from Gregory, see Gregory the Great, *Homiliae in Euangelia*, 2.36.4, ed. Raymond Étaix, CCSL 141 (Turnhout: Brepols, 1999), 335. On curiosity in the Middle Ages, see most recently Patricia Clare Ingham, *The Medieval New. Ambivalence in an Age of Innovation* (Philadelphia: University of Pennsylvania Press, 2015), 143–97, and specifically on sinful curiosity, Richard Newhauser, *Sin: Essays on the Moral Tradition in the Western Middle Ages*, essays XIII-XV, and Edward Peters, *Limits of Thought and Power in Medieval Europe*, Variorum Collected Studies Series, CS721 (Aldershot: Ashgate, 2001).
59 William Peraldus, *Summa de virtutibus*, 3.3.18, in Lyon, Bibliothèque municipale MS 678, f. 260vb: 'Antigonus pedagogus Alexandri cytharam eius fregit, adiecitque dicens: 'Etati tue iam regnare conuenit, pudeatque in corpore regni uoluptatem luxurie dominari". The passage is taken from John of Salisbury, *Policraticus*, 3.14, ed. K. S. B. Keats-Rohan, CCCM 118 (Turnhout: Brepols, 1993), 223.
60 William Peraldus, *Summa de virtutibus*, 3.3.18, in Lyon, Bibliothèque municipale MS 678, f. 260vb: 'Dum blanda uox queritur, sobria uita deseritur'. The quotation, also attributed to Gregory, is found in Caesarius of Heisterbach, *Dialogus miraculorum*, 4.8, ed. Joseph Strange, 2 vols. (Cologne, etc.: J. M. Heberle [H. Lempertz], 1851), 1: 180.
61 William Peraldus, *Summa de virtutibus*, 3.3.18, in Lyon, Bibliothèque municipale MS 678, f. 260vb: "Si continens es, adulationes euita, sitque tibi tam triste laudari a turpibus quam si laudari ob turpia'. Idem: 'Difficilimum opus continentie est assentationes adulatorum repellere, quorum sermones animum quadam uoluptate resoluunt". Both quotations are taken from Martin of Braga, *Formula uitae honestae*, 4, ed. Claude W. Barlow, in *Opera omnia*, Papers and Monographs of the American Academy in Rome, 12 (New Haven, CT: Yale University Press, 1950), 244.

62 Pierre Adnès, 'Garde des sens', in *Dictionnaire de spiritualité* 6 (Paris: Beauchesne et fils, 1967), 117–22.

63 On the importance of the edification of the senses, see Richard G. Newhauser, 'Introduction: The Sensual Middle Ages', in *A Cultural History of the Senses in the Middle Ages*, ed. Newhauser, 12–17; idem, 'Peter of Limoges, Optics, and the Science of the Senses', *The Senses & Society* 5 (2010): 28–44.

64 William Peraldus, *Summa de virtutibus*, 3.3.11, in Lyon, Bibliothèque municipale MS 678, ff. 253va-256vb: on virginity; ibid., 3.3.15–17, ff. 258va-260va: on praise of marriage, contracting marriage, and conjugal sex. The three circumstances in which conjugal sex is said to be meritorious are when sex leads to bearing children, when it is done as part of the obligations of marriage, and when it occurs so that one's spouse does not fall into the sin of lust.

65 William Peraldus, *Summa de virtutibus*, 3.3.9, in Lyon, Bibliothèque municipale MS 678, f. 252ra-rb: 'Chrisostomus super Epistolam ad Hebreos: 'Nihil salutem, nihil sensuum acumen operatur, nihil sic egritudinem fugat, sicut moderata refectio'. Item sobrietas ualet ad uite diuturnitatem; xxxvii Ecclesiastici: *Qui abstinens est, adiciet uitam.* Item sobrietas ualet ad iocunditatem et corporalem et spiritualem; Ecclesiastici xxxi: *Exultatio anime et corporis uinum moderate potatum*'. For the passage from John Chrysostom, see *Homiliae XXXIV in Epistolam ad Hebraeos*, 29.4, PG 63:206, 208; see also *Decretum magistri Gratiani*, pars 3 (De consecratione), dist. 5, can. 28, ed. Emil Friedberg, Corpus iuris canonici, 2 vols., 2nd ed. (Leipzig: Tauchnitz, 1879–1881), 1: 1419.

66 Still useful for the factors leading to the establishment of the mendicants is Herbert Grundmann, *Religiöse Bewegungen im Mittelalter. Untersuchungen über die geschichtlichen Zusammenhänge zwischen der Ketzerei, den Bettelorden und der religiösen Frauenbewegung im 12. und 13. Jahrhundert und über die geschichtlichen Grundlagen der deutschen Mystik*, Historische Studien, 267, 2nd ed. (Hildesheim: Olms, 1961).

67 On the central importance of ethical analysis for the medieval sensorium, see Woolgar, *The Senses in Late Medieval England*, 16–18.

3 What makes things holy? The senses and material culture in the later Middle Ages

C. M. Woolgar

A customary from the Benedictine Abbey of Bury St Edmunds, from the second half of the thirteenth century, sets out the punishments that a monk who had committed a serious offence might expect.[1] A series of actions isolated the monk, detaching him from things that were sacred, and from sensory aspects of life. In chapter, immediately after the president had noted the offence, the monk was to seek pardon. If that pardon was not given, the monk was straightaway to cover his face with his hood as far down as his mouth, or further, and he was to leave chapter in company with his master (the monk who had been allocated to take charge of him). He was to be taken to the church, between the pulpit and the great door of the choir. Here he was to sit on the great step throughout the day with his face covered to his mouth; if it was a great offence, he was also to sit there during every liturgical office, day and night, singing his psalter or crying and lamenting his crimes. His master was to ensure that whenever the convent processed from the choir, the monk was to lie prostrate on the floor, close to the door, with his head turned to the north, so that some of the monks could pass by his head, and some by his feet. The custom of the house was such and the scale of his crime so great that the convent might walk over his body and kick him if they wished.[2] After Compline, when members of the convent were aspersed, the monk was to lie prostrate in the church, and he was not to receive the holy water. He was never to be with the whole convent, except at night in the dormitory, and in summer, at the early afternoon sleep. The monk was to be excluded from all occasions when blessings were given. He was separated from anything that was holy, and – as far as possible within a community that was continually resanctifying itself through prayer and blessing, in a place that had been hallowed – he was cast out.

Religious practices have much to tell us about holy things and the processes by which they acquired, or lost, their sacred character. Typically, there is most information about this subject at points of transition, those moments at which holiness was acquired, lost, or suspended. The first focus of this essay is on these liminal events, especially the creation of the sacraments, and practices around baptism, death, burial, and canonisation – and, in the case of disobedient Bury monks, the ways in which they were separated from things holy.

How things became holy was both a theological question and a physical process. From antiquity onwards, theologians had debated consecration and the transformation made through the liturgy by which things became sacred. In the case of transubstantiation of the Eucharist, for example, there were a range of different, entrenched positions about what in fact happened, and a good deal of confusion. Ambrose of Milan (d. 397) maintained that the consecration of the bread and wine in the mass converted them into the body and blood of Christ, by divine action through the words of the priest; Augustine of Hippo (d. 430) and others following him believed that the elements remained unchanged, but that the process of sanctification added a divine grace to them. In the eleventh century, debates over the real presence in the elements of the mass divided churchmen between the symbolists, such as Berengar of Tours (d. 1088) – who held that Christ was only present figuratively – and realists, such as Lanfranc of Bec (d. 1089), who held that Christ was physically present. Berengar was made to abjure his beliefs and conform to the realist position, confessing at the Council of Rome in 1079 that the Holy Spirit, operating through the words of consecration spoken by the priest, converted the elements both to sacraments and to the physical body and blood of Christ.[3]

These theological debates have attracted a good deal of attention, but the physical process by which holiness was acquired, sustained and transmitted, has been examined less closely and is under-appreciated by historians. That transformation operated in ways medieval people would have understood as part of sensory perception. The monks of Bury had very different ideas about perception to those of the contemporary world. Perception was thought of as a two-way process, and one that was much more open and wide-ranging in its expectations of what might pass between perceiver and perceived than has commonly been the case in the West since the Enlightenment. As well as receiving information about the object of perception, other qualities might pass to the perceiver; and at the same time, qualities might pass the other way, from the individual to the person or object he or she perceived. These qualities might encompass a wide range of possibilities, but prominent among them were moral or spiritual qualities, such as good and evil. At the same time, the limits of life and the influence of perception on the body operated over a different timescale to present-day beliefs, from soon after conception, to well beyond death, to the Resurrection. Objects and the inanimate, then, might have an influence on those perceiving them – and on other objects with which they had contact – and vice versa.[4]

This was the normal pattern of sensation in the later Middle Ages. The way in which these qualities passed was by touch, or something closely akin to it: general proximity might be sufficient. From Aristotle onwards, the senses were believed to operate largely by a form of contact between the perceiver and the perceived. Medieval philosophy offered an explanation of the method of contact by means of *species* – that is (to take the example of sight), a series of images or similitudes replicated all the way between the eye and the thing perceived. Within the body, the *species* were then replicated from the sense organ to the brain. An identical process happened with touch, smell, taste, and hearing, with the sense organs receiving an impression of the item perceived. A common metaphor saw the senses as two-way gates. The *species* brought information and qualities to the body, and in the same manner the body's spirit, the spirit that animated the body's senses and movements, might convey its own qualities outside the body through further *species*.[5]

While the Middle Ages inherited from antiquity a notion of five senses – sight, smell, hearing, taste and touch – the two-way nature of perception made this a broader process. Speech, for example, was considered to be one of the senses of the mouth: taste was the receptive part, speech the outgoing part.[6] Speech was an ethical act: the speech of a good man might carry beneficence, whilst the speech of a bad man might convey the opposite. This conception of speech as a sense is especially important for a consideration of the ways in which things were made holy. We should not think that the sense or meaning of words was all that mattered, or all that might be conveyed; the sound was important too. When Thomas Flesshor, a Coventry Lollard, abjured his heresy in November 1511, he confirmed that he had 'spoken, affermed and holden divers articles, opynyons and erroures ageinst the feithe of all holy church and contrarie to the determynation of the same, to the evill sowding of the eres of well disposed cristen men'.[7] Evil was transmitted by the very sound of his words, just as holiness might pass through words of consecration. Individuals did not have to understand heresy to be guilty of it: simply hearing heretical words contaminated the individual, just as words of blessing or holy sound brought beneficence. This underlying breadth of qualities that passed by perception is paramount for understanding medieval life, especially given the moral outlook that characterised so much of it.

To return to the monk of Bury: his head was covered, certainly from the shame – that is implicit in his humiliation. But it was also covered for another reason, also implicit: his eyes were covered so that the negative influences that might come from the sight of a bad man would not pollute others (that is, the *species* that came from his eyes might not touch others). The Bury text says that he must always have his head covered, deeply ('profunde'), so that his face could not be seen, and this to avoid scandal ('Et hoc ad evitandum scandalum'). His mouth was not covered, but what he might say was closely limited: he was restricted to contrition, or to holy sound, saying psalms. He was also excluded from the beneficence that would come from the touch of holy water and from eating food that had been blessed.

The physicality of this separation from the holy brings the essay to its second focus, the ways in which holy objects were curated and disposed of. These were items of extraordinary power and a great deal of care and attention was given to looking after them. It is necessary here to consider a broad range of objects. Liturgy created holy items in an orthodox way, but others might acquire this characteristic by unofficial means. The same was true of the opposite process: pollution and desecration could occur through both official and unofficial means.

How do things become holy?

Consecration constituted the sacraments; it was used to create sacrality in objects and areas; and forms of the process were used on the living and on the dead. The process was conducted by consecrated individuals, in canonical orders – theoretically in an unbroken sequence stretching back to Christ and the apostles, or at least through the papacy as agent. Consecration occurred through the invocation of God, Christ and the saints by an individual in holy orders, that is, by one who had been consecrated himself. Consideration of this process in sensory terms is revealing. The ethical act of speech was used to consecrate individuals, who in turn then went on to consecrate others – touched by the words of holiness. Speech was also used to consecrate materials, especially the sacraments, that could then be used in the consecration of other things, by touching them, for example, through the use of holy water. In consequence, there was a chain of things holy, linked by the operation of touch.

How this was understood in detail and practice varied from place to place, and across time. For example, while practices for consecrating churches were similar over a wide area of Western Europe, processes of creating other kinds of spaces, such as cemeteries, as holy areas, were more disparate. Helen Gittos has demonstrated the importance of aspersion with holy water in English rites for consecrating cemeteries up to the eleventh century. At the same time, her research points to a later adoption on the Continent of separate rituals for hallowing a cemetery and to a much less elaborate liturgical procedure.[8]

The operation of the liturgy in practice was of great significance for understanding the creation and transmission of holiness.[9] Some of the most interesting evidence for how sacrality was transmitted arises when things went wrong. The customary of St Augustine's Abbey, Canterbury, from 1330–40, reviewed the preparation of the consecrated elements during mass. If there was negligence in speaking the words of consecration of bread or wine, for example, if the celebrant omitted all the form of their signification, or transposed words, or skipped over any word, it was considered to be a most grave sin, and the whole had to be started again from the beginning, from the words 'This is my body', or 'This is the chalice'. At the same time, however, there was doubt whether the omission of a minor word, such as 'enim', required one to start again.[10] Precision in speaking the words of consecration was important for their efficacy, and injunctions to say the liturgy correctly and exactly were made by long sequences of church councils and synods. Richard Poore's injunctions for his diocese of Salisbury, 1217×1219, required all priests to have a correct text of the mass according to the use of Salisbury so that the words could be said roundly and distinctly. There were similar provisions issued in the statutes for the dioceses of Winchester, probably 1224; Durham, 1228×1236; Worcester, 1240; York, 1241×1255; and Chichester, 1289.[11] The texts of the services were to be said without haste, without eliding words or skipping over them.

Lanfranc's *Monastic Constitutions*, for Christ Church Canterbury (but not for that house alone), from around 1077, point to other areas of negligence, where mishaps had occurred or other materials had touched consecrated elements:

> And if the body or blood of the Lord has fallen, or has been spilt, upon a stone or the earth or wood or mat or carpet or anything of that kind, the surface of the earth shall be taken up, that spot in the stone shall be scraped, and the part affected in the wood, matting, carpet or whatever it may be shall be cut out and thrown down the piscina [the drain in the church or sacristy, which leads directly into consecrated ground]. If the place where it fell cannot be accurately determined, and yet it is certain that it fell, a like taking up, scraping, cutting out, and secreting in the piscina shall be accomplished in and around the spot where it is thought most likely that the particle or drops fell.[12] . . .
>
> If the blood of the Lord shall have fallen upon the corporal or some other clean cloth, and it be quite certain where it fell, that part of the cloth shall be washed in a chalice and the water of the first washing shall be consumed by the brethren, and that of the two following washings shall be thrown down the piscina.[13]

Something similar can be seen in the process of the disposal of materials that had routinely – as opposed to inadvertently – touched the holy or consecrated elements. So, Lanfranc tells us, after anointing a dying monk, the priest who had performed the unction was to wash his hands, and the water was to be thrown into a fire or into the piscina.[14] In Cistercian practice, at the anointing of the sick, those cloths that had been used to wipe up the excess oil were afterwards to be burned in the piscina.[15] In the diocese of Winchester, in Peter des Roches's statutes of 1224, old corporal cloths (the cloths on which the host was placed), when worn out, were to be put in the place for relics in altars, or were to be burned in the presence of the archdeacon or his official.[16] In these cases, therefore, the touch of the holy item, the consecrated element, was sufficient to transmit sacrality to the item that it had been in contact with. Processes of disposal centred on arrangements that maintained these items, or the traces of them, in a holy environment. There was an understanding that objects, once they had become holy, continued to have this quality, and that holy matter generally could transmit holiness to anything that came into contact with it or was just even in close proximity.

This world was full of dangers and demons, engaged in a battle for souls that would only be concluded at the Last Judgement.[17] It was not just the living that needed protection: the dead required an eternal safeguard, too. The sacred was one of humankind's greatest supports in this long-lasting struggle. A defence for the dead was provided by burial in consecrated ground. On one level, the enclosure of the cemetery prevented material threats, such as disturbance by animals and other uncleanliness. Secular activities, such as markets, games, dancing, and so on, that might pollute the area from a spiritual perspective were excluded by episcopal statute. Further, physical touch with the sacred provided continuous spiritual protection: the cemetery was an area that was consecrated and then resanctified, through processions and services.[18] Other practices might protect the body in readiness for the Resurrection: in the treasury of Chichester Cathedral, there is a lead cross, with the words of papal absolution, granted to Godfrey (d. 1088), the second bishop of the see, which must have been buried with his body. Recovered from graves elsewhere are examples of texts and objects, such as papal bulls, which may have been held to give some form of protection in anticipation of the Last Judgement, as well as bearing witness at that point to the absolution of sins.[19] The same may also have been true of some other grave goods, such as fragments of crystal or the sapphires and other gems found in rings in episcopal burials.[20]

Especial care was taken to ensure the safety of the body from the moment of death until its committal in consecrated ground. The St Augustine's customary instructed the monastic chamberlain and his deputy on how to prepare the deceased monk's body for burial. They were not to use soiled cloths to wrap the head, the 'principal member of the human body, in which all the senses are active', as some did, saying 'That is good enough for the earth'. Rather, the body was to be buried in new clothing and footwear, which no one had ever worn – that is, without possibility of pollution – and the head was to be wrapped in a clean cloth (*sudarium*).[21] The unburied body was to be protected by the light of candles – light was one of the great beneficent forces in this world – and by sound. Sounds included the ringing of consecrated bells, which often had devotional inscriptions that they were effectively ringing out. Additionally, at no point between death and burial was the body of the monk to be without the protection of the psalms, continuously said by the brethren of the deceased monk.[22]

It was not only in the monasteries that these precautions were taken. In 1229, William of Blois, as Bishop of Worcester, forbade the singing of secular songs, dancing, and wrestling in houses where bodies lay unburied; nor was there to be dancing or wrestling near cemeteries at times when the offices were being sung: these were sounds and activities that had a diabolical inspiration.[23] Despite the protection that was offered by these measures, there was a paradox here: these practices safeguarded the dead, yet the corpse was itself a threat to the living. At St Augustine's there was another custom: those who had touched the corpse also had to be protected, and they were expected to bathe in a ritual manner before they next ministered at the altar.[24]

The significance of maintaining the holiness of consecrated ground lies behind the practice of burying outside these areas those who died excommunicate or as the result of suicide: their bodies were potential contaminants. Gratian's *Decretum* speaks of excommunication as exile from the Kingdom of God; effectively an excommunicated person had been given to the Devil.[25] If, by chance, those who had been excommunicated were buried in a cemetery, the decretals of Gregory IX advised that, 'because of the violence of their proximity' ('per eorum violentiam proprinquorum'), the cemetery had to be reconciled to holiness – this is the language of penance – by the aspersion of holy water, just as in the dedication of churches.[26] Suicide was a crime, inspired by the Devil. When a Dutchwoman called Abby drowned herself at Boston in Lincolnshire in 1375, the jury reported to the coroner that those on the other bank had implored her in the name of God not to destroy herself, but she, by the temptation of the Devil ('per temptacionem diaboli'), jumped in and drowned, unconfessed, before anyone could reach her.[27] A Northamptonshire coroner in 1340s and 1350s had followed a similar line of thought in setting apart suicides for burial, and instructed that their bodies be dragged to the landimere, that is, the parish boundary. In one instance, he ordered the uprooting of the tree – literally its eradication – from which a woman had hanged herself.[28] Evil might be transmitted in the same way as the holy, by touch, and it was important to obliterate any trace, and to remove a contaminated body as far as possible from the community.

The dead might also have a positive role, however. The saints, holy men and women generally, and those things associated with them, such as relics, could all help in the battle against evil. In the cult of relics, there were degrees of holiness, and therefore of effectiveness. Here, proximity or touch came to the fore. There was a long tradition of contact relics: contact could be brief, or maintained over a long period of time. Gregory of Tours (d. 594) tells us about the *brandea*, the cloths lowered by pilgrims onto the tomb of St Peter, which the devout pilgrim might then raise, soaked with divine power – and weighing more than when they were lowered.[29] Some tombs had openings (*foramina*) into which pilgrims might crawl to get especially close to their saint. Physical contact might come through the kissing of relics, and the ingestion of the special waters in which the relics had been washed or which contained dust from a saint's tomb.[30] In some instances, the mere sight of the reliquary was sufficient.[31]

The Church did not deny the efficacy of holiness and its consequences transmitted in this way, but it did attempt to manage them. Holiness had its own dangers: however beneficial holy items might be, uncontrolled use of them was undesirable and precautions had to be taken, as we shall see below. There were risks of sacrilege and desecration, actions that might let in the diabolical. The interests of the Church were therefore in keeping the holy as far as possible in ecclesiastical hands, and also in establishing itself as the arbiter of what was holy.

One way in which the Church set out to achieve closer control of the holy in the thirteenth century was through the institution of a more formal process of canonisation, reserving the creation of saints to the papacy. Before this period, the communal renown of an individual for miraculous works, especially the healing of the sick, was sufficient to establish sanctity. Pope Innocent III set in train a process that required a formal demonstration of the miracles and also, in a new development, an examination of the virtues of the supposed saint, that is, the quality of his or her life, faith, and works.[32] Canonisation, however, was formal recognition of something that had already happened, and the miracles examined as part of the process had already occurred. Miracles – recognised only by popular acclaim – had occurred in many instances where no process of canonisation was ever to take place. This was a reflection of an attitude of mind ingrained in popular belief, that holy people directly, or through items associated with them, might intervene to the benefit of those who sought their help – just as they had done before the Church intervened to establish a mechanism for the official recognition of cults. So, while the process, now framed by papal lawyers, set about establishing a formal arbitration of holiness and miracles, it ran in parallel with a more popular understanding of the holy and the operation of relics and miracles.

The canonisation process reveals the ways in which holy things might operate. Thomas Cantilupe, Bishop of Hereford, died in 1282. When the evidence for his sanctity was examined by a formal commission in 1307, witnesses were called to testify to his life, faith, habits, and conduct, and to his miracles, and to state how they knew these things. The witnesses responded to a series of interrogatories, which asked whether the miracles were 'above or against nature' ('supra vel contra natura'), that is, whether they were not part of the natural order and required divine intervention; and whether, in the working of the miracles, herbs or stones or other natural things had been used, or medicines, or whether incantations, superstition, or any deception had occurred.[33] It was therefore not only holy things that could have an effect that might appear miraculous; other things might do this too, in ways that could be recognised as part of the processes of sensation. Richard Kieckhefer comments in his *Magic in the Middle Ages* that 'One of the most puzzling questions was how incantations could have effect'[34] – but we may see them operating through the sense of speech, just as we can the words of the mass spoken by the priest. Sacrality was transmitted, in certain circumstances at least, by a physical process of sensing, and similar effects might be produced in other cases, by natural processes. From the Church's point of view, the distinction between the sacred and the profane was one of context. All words, both spoken and written, could have a transformative power; but circumstances and intent distinguished between liturgy on the one hand, and magic on the other.[35]

An example of the power of speech as a sense can be seen in baptism. The words of baptism, *in extremis*, could be used by anyone who had themselves been baptised: a process of sanctification had to have taken place at some point to create a link to the chain of holiness.[36] There was a good deal of episcopal concern about the process of lay baptism, including the exact form of words necessary to achieve this: Archbishop Pecham's constitutions of 1281 usefully gave the words in English and French, so that all might know them.[37] According to the statutes of Bishop Bitton for Bath and Wells, probably of 1258, the container which had been used to hold the water for a baptism in these circumstances was to be reserved to the Church or was to be burned; and the remaining water was to be poured into the fire or taken to the church and poured into the font – out of reverence for the sacrament.[38] A layman might thereby create something that was as holy as anything created liturgically by the clergy. The words had made the water holy, and that holiness had also come into contact with the container, necessitating careful arrangements for its custody or destruction. The power of the exact words was recognised as remarkable.

In the same way, the use of holy words in charms and inscribed on amulets – in direct contact with the body – was popularly believed to make them effective. The Dominican John Bromyard, writing his manual for preachers shortly before the Black Death, noted the deception that came from sorcery: those men were in error that carried around their necks, or in their purses, or bound or sewn into their clothing, objects inscribed with strange characters or unknown names – as if they were the names of God or the angels. One can assume from Bromyard's account, therefore, that those objects that were inscribed with holy names were effective, or might be so in some circumstances.[39] From private collections of relics, to reliquary jewels – such as the Middleham Jewel – worn on the body, charms and amulets provided protection through holy words, extending practice far beyond any official discourse about the holy.[40]

How were holy things to be kept and used?

Curating the sacred was a primary duty of the Church and its clergy. In cases where it was known that items would become holy, especial care was taken, for example, with the ingredients for wafers for the host. At St Augustine's, Canterbury, the wheat was to be chosen, grain by grain, and there was then an elaborate routine to be followed to protect against contamination. The wheat was to be milled carefully, so that it was not polluted in any way. In preparation for making the wafers, the subsacrist and his assistant were to wash their faces and hands, and to be dressed in albs, with amices; the board on which the flour was to be placed had to be exceptionally clean; and the servant who used the wafer iron was to wear gloves. The monks were to say the hours, the hours of the Virgin and the penitential psalms while the wafers were cooking; all others were to be silent.[41]

Yet there was a difficulty with some holy items in that they continued to behave – and decay – as material things.[42] Taking this into account, bishops legislated about the custody of the host. Archbishop John Pecham, in 1281, instructed that the wafers were to be made at least once, if not twice, a week, and that they were not to be kept beyond a fortnight lest there be any appearance of decay. Earlier injunctions, for instance those of Richard Poore for the diocese of Salisbury, 1217×19, had stipulated that the wafers should not be kept beyond a week. Each parish church was to have a tabernacle, with a lock, 'decent and honest', in which the host might be kept in a beautiful box with a linen lining.[43] Dignity was important, but so was maintaining the sacred in a way that prevented it from touching – or being touched by – other things, which might cause that sacrality to be transmitted further.

The tabernacles that appear in secular households that had their own chapels help us explore some of the other associations that came with liturgical equipment and the holy. The examples from elite households are more elaborate than those described among parish goods. The 1359 inventory of the possessions of Queen Isabella, made after her death, records a silver gilt and enamel tabernacle, with six pinnacles and crystal in the middle, with assorted jewels attached to it, for the Eucharist.[44] The presence of the crystal and jewels was not simply a question of their financial value: from their shine, they brought further beneficence as a source of light.[45] The construction and ornamentation of these and other holy objects was significant, serving not as superficial decoration, but as a contribution to the force of the object. In the 1388 inventory of the vestry of Westminster Abbey, all the patens listed had a sacred image – Christ in majesty, Christ in judgement, the Veronica – which would have carried a power of its own.[46] To add jewels and decoration of this kind to holy objects, or to place them near to them, enhanced the power of the holy. This was one reason that shrines attracted gifts of gold, silver and jewellery, and other holy objects were adorned in this way.[47]

There is little evidence in the late medieval period for the contribution of craftsmen to this enhanced sacrality, as opposed to that made by the intrinsic qualities of the jewels and precious metals; but there had earlier been a connection between at least some churchmen and the manufacture of religious artefacts in precious metals. Two eleventh-century Anglo-Saxon abbots, Mannig of Evesham (d. 1066) and Spearhafoc of Abingdon (*fl.* 1047–51), had been craftsmen, associated with work in precious metals; and the royal wardrobe had in 1300 a ring said to have been made by St Dunstan (d. 988), an object which can be traced in the royal household into the reign of Edward III. In Dunstan's case, the notion that he had been a craftsman was almost certainly a post-mortem addition to his reputation.[48]

The holy presented problems of curation, simply because of the scale and diversity of material that might be involved: anything might become holy. The overriding concern, however, was to achieve ecclesiastical control of these objects. Bishop Grosseteste instructed in 1239 that in the diocese of Lincoln the ornaments and holy vessels of the church should be in safe and honest custody, and not rest in the houses of the laity, nor in their custody, unless out of extreme need.[49] Testamentary practice was that sacred items, particularly those associated with the mass and the sacraments, and including vestments, were only to be bequeathed into contexts where they could be used legitimately for these purposes.[50] One of the consequences of this is that inventories of churches and the possessions of the clergy list large quantities of goods that had clearly been considered sacred, and which were kept because deconsecration was scarcely an option. Sometimes these accumulations cannot have received much sustained interest, other than continuing protection. Bishops' chambers must have had an element of the lumber room about them, with lots of sacred objects around, in chests and bags.[51] The privy wardrobe in the Tower of London, a great storehouse of the surplus goods of the Crown, inventoried under the keepership of John de Flete from 1325 onwards, had an array of liturgical goods, among them an entry for 'a case of various unknown relics'.[52]

Beyond the principal liturgical goods of the church and chapel, there was a whole range of items that might have an occasional and brief liturgical use and which then continued to have a sacred character. Many of these had an association with the lives of parishioners. The council of Winchester, in its canons of 1072 (reiterating those of Rouen of 1050), turned to the items accompanying baptism, particularly chrisom cloths and candles. The purpose of a chrisom cloth was to protect the oil of chrism that had been used to anoint the child's head, lest it rub off onto other things. The council of Winchester ruled that the chrisom cloth was not to be washed until the seventh day after it had been used, and then in church, over the font; both it and the candle used at this time were to remain in the church.[53] In Richard Poore's statutes for Salisbury, 1217×19, and for Durham, 1228×36, chrisom cloths were only to be used for church ornaments. Other church ornaments which had received a blessing were not to be turned to profane use.[54] Another set of statutes from the 1220s for an English diocese may suggest that these cloths had been brought to church by the family: its insistence that the *casule* in which the newly baptised were wrapped might not be taken from the church, nor out of reverence for the sacrament put to common use, suggests that there was a recurring problem and one that may have had its roots in a customary practice. Instructions, probably towards the mid-thirteenth century, from the diocese of Salisbury required nursing mothers to give the chrisom cloths to the church – and it was certainly practice by the sixteenth century that the cloth might either act as a shroud for an infant who had died close to birth, or that it should be offered by the mother to the church at her purification.[55] In 1229, Bishop William de Blois of Worcester was to point to a range of things beyond the chrisom cloths that might acquire a sacred character and were used both in the church and, clearly by some, out of it. Altar cloths, even those that had not been blessed, might not be used to decorate houses or marriage beds; candles blessed at the Purification might not be used for common purposes, although they could be liquified and reused.[56]

These examples show the demand for the holy in secular contexts and the laity's belief in the benefits of having these objects in their houses and possession, the countervailing position of the clergy notwithstanding. Beyond these items, a range of material moved in the opposite direction, coming into the church as gifts and offerings, thereby making a formal transition to sacrality. Prominent among these were domestic goods, or items associated with the events of the life course, given to the church. These items then took on a sacred character, and with it, something of the nature of a memorial. Robert Yislowe, rector of Onehouse in Suffolk, made his will on 13 September 1375, bequeathing a board cloth and two towels for use in the chancel, in honour of St John the Baptist.[57] Parishioners made gifts for those parts of the church for which they were responsible. Katherine French has documented a form of domestic piety: women's giving of gifts – gowns, curtains, textiles, veils, rings – in the diocese of Bath and Wells from after the Black Death until the end of the Middle Ages.[58] These goods sometimes had the character of heirlooms.[59] Simply placing them in the church may have brought to them a sacred character. Other objects, such as paternosters, were linked to the repeated sacred sound of prayer, which may have been sufficient in the opinion of some to make them holy. That they might then also be loaned out, for example, to assist at childbirth, speaks to the powers they might acquire. One of Katherine French's examples is of amber beads – perhaps a rosary – with this quality that were in the parish church of Netherbury in Wiltshire.[60] At the other end of the social scale, there were gifts of high-status items to form liturgical equipment, such as chalices. Sir John Neville, the son of Ralph, Earl of Westmorland, left instructions in 1449 that the standing cup of silver and gilt called 'ye Kateryne' be left to the church of Haltemprice in the East Riding of Yorkshire, to make a chalice.[61]

There is some opacity about whether gemstones and jewels should be considered as having powers or virtues in their own right, or whether they should be considered as invested with sacrality. From a medieval perspective, as a source of light, gemstones were of benefit to all who saw them, or came in contact with them. Beyond that, as catalogued by authors including the eleventh-century Marbode of Rennes, some stones were commonly believed to protect against thieves or sudden death, whilst others were considered to have innate sacred powers. On the other hand, some stones required consecration or episcopal intervention to recover powers that had been interrupted.[62]

Bishops had stones and jewels of this kind. Among the goods of John de Sandale, Bishop of Winchester, inventoried after his death in 1319 was a great ring with a crystal and a good sapphire – which was believed to be virtuous – surrounded by small rubies and emeralds, and enclosed in a copper box.[63] The Cantilupe enquiry had asked witnesses to distinguish the Bishop's own miracles from any in which stones, herbs and other natural things had been employed – without saying whether in fact those stones might have worked miracles themselves, but implying that they may have been involved. What was at issue here was establishing the Bishop's own powers, rather than the powers of things that might operate of their own accord or assist the Bishop in his work. It was therefore essential that the two should not be confused. Other items of jewellery, such as wedding rings and cramp rings (made from coins offered by the king on Good Friday, and valued for their medicinal properties), obtained powers from association with liturgical processes.[64]

Besides their direct use in the liturgy, holy items could be used in a range of other circumstances. In many of these, touch was the key component in bringing the holy directly to bear. For example, holy water might be employed to bring sanctity or beneficence. In a late twelfth-century case, a relation of Roger, son of Warin, who was possessed and who had threatened to eat his own wife and children, was taken to Lincoln Cathedral, where the saintly Bishop Hugh aspersed him and adjured the evil spirit to leave him. The man fell down, whereupon the bishop soaked him with holy water, in great quantity; immediately the man stood up and raised his hands to heaven, thanking God for curing him.[65] Yet it was not only the clergy who might use holy water as part of routines and rituals: the household ordinances of Henry VII, from c.1493, show it being used to impart sacrality to the King's bed after it had been made, by an esquire of the King's body – a body which had itself been sacralised at the anointing at the coronation.[66]

Consecration of an object did not ensure that it was used for virtuous purposes. Some people used holy elements for nefarious practices, for example, by secreting the host and then using it for magic. The fifteenth-century English translation of the *Alphabet of Tales*, following Caesarius of Heisterbach's twelfth-century collection of miraculous stories, tells of a woman whose bees kept dying. Others told her that to remedy this, she should take the sacrament and put it in her hive – so she surreptitiously took the host out of her mouth after it had been given to her by the priest, and placed it in her hive. The bees, however, recognised in the host their creator, and built a chapel for it in their hive.[67] One senses the nervousness of authorities about these possibilities in their injunctions for the safe custody of church goods. In order to guard against 'sortilegia' – sorcery – synodal statutes, such as those for Salisbury, 1217×19, and Chichester, 1245×52, required fonts to be covered and well kept, and for the oils, chrisom, and Eucharist to be kept under lock and key.[68] Even the clergy might be implicated in sorcery. In 1485, for example, Nicholas Barton, the rector of part of the church of Waddesdon, in Buckinghamshire, was accused of conjuring by the magic arts using a psalter and a key.[69] What is implicit in these cases, though, is that even misuse did not invalidate the sacred powers that might be inherent in the object. Indeed, in the case of the bees, when the woman showed the hive with its chapel to her priest there was joy and rejoicing, and she received the same sacrament in a proper manner.

Conclusion

Holiness appears to us as a spiritual quality above all others, but medieval men and women knew it too for its physical characteristics. They lived in a world where sacrality was directly linked to God, through Christ and his successors on earth, particularly the clergy. All holy items were connected by physical contact, in an unbroken chain (in theory at least), right back to the first days of the Church. Holiness passed down this chain, to individual or object, in a process that operated in the same way as, and as part of, sensory perception. It might embrace any being, alive or dead, or object, not just things that had been specifically consecrated, although the Church implemented patterns of control to keep the most obvious categories of sacred object in its custody and reserved to its own use, or to be used by others in defined circumstances. Almost anything might become holy by association with a holy person or object, or by touch, a category that included contact through any of the senses, including speech. People might gain benefit simply from seeing a holy object, such as the host. The same advantage might come from hearing sacred words, and objects that were frequently in the vicinity of holy sound would equally become holy.

The physical nature of holiness was apparent to most medieval people, even if it has been largely overlooked by historians. Theologians might debate the nature of holiness, or what happened in the miracle of transubstantiation; but most men and women were more interested in physical encounters with the holy that would allow its benefits to touch them and to protect them for eternity. There were no bounds to what might become holy, even if there were differences between ecclesiastical and lay approaches to the efficacy and agency of material objects. Ecclesiastical responses looked for control of the holy, for dignity and honour in the way holy items were looked after – and for the holy to be employed in defined ways, with theological support, for the benefit of the souls of parishioners in the eternal struggle against evil. The Church established official rites of consecration to create holiness, and did its best to avoid circumstances in which holy items were exposed to profanation. This control of holy items was essential to avoid their corruption or the misuse of their power. Implicit in these arrangements, however, was an acceptance by the Church of the physical process by which things became holy.

Secular society, particularly those members of it who spent a great deal of time in prayer, would not have found it difficult to see holiness in objects around them – or, indeed, to create it through, for example, the long usage of the sounds of pious prayer. Just as late medieval devotional texts ranged around household goods to recall divine truths from everyday objects as part of the process of meditation, any of those goods might in practice become holy in themselves.[70] That these objects might then be brought to churches for safekeeping, and for use in a wide range of secular contexts, speaks of a widespread reverence for the power of the holy and for the strength of unofficial religion. From the perspective of today's students of material culture, however, there may be nothing obvious to mark many of these objects as having a sacred character – the physical consequences of holiness may be invisible to us, but they were not to believers in the later Middle Ages. The holy was essential in the long journey towards eternal life: to be continually associated with it, to touch it, kept the powers of evil at bay, and it brought recurring benefits.

Notes

1 Antonia Gransden, ed., *The Customary of the Benedictine Abbey of Bury St Edmunds in Suffolk (from Harleian MS. 1005 in the British Museum)*, Henry Bradshaw Society, 99 (Chichester: Regnum Press, 1973), 82–3.
2 Lanfranc's Constitutions for Canterbury, which cover similar ground, are to us a little more humane, with the brothers saying to the offending monk in a low voice, as they passed, 'God have mercy on you': David Knowles, ed., *The Monastic Constitutions of Lanfranc*, revised by Christopher N. L. Brooke (Oxford: Oxford University Press, 2002), 150–51.
3 Edward J. Kilmartin, *The Eucharist in the West: History and Theology*, ed. Robert J. Daly (Collegeville, MN: The Liturgical Press, 2004), 67–78, 97–102; Eric Palazzo, *Liturgie et société au moyen âge* (Paris: Aubier, 2000), 33–4. See also Caroline Walker Bynum, *Christian Materiality: An Essay on Religion in Late Medieval Europe* (Cambridge, MA: MIT Press, 2011), 154–62.

4 C. M. Woolgar, *The Senses in Late Medieval England* (New Haven, CT: Yale University Press 2006), 5–62, 267–73; Béatrice Caseau, 'The Senses in Religion: Liturgy, Devotion, and Deprivation', in *A Cultural History of the Senses in the Middle Ages*, ed. Richard G. Newhauser (London: Bloomsbury Academic, 2014), 89–110.
5 Woolgar, *Senses in Late Medieval England*, 13.
6 Ibid., 84–116.
7 Shannon McSheffrey and Norman Tanner, eds., *Lollards of Coventry 1486–1522*, Camden fifth series, 23 (London: Cambridge University Press for the Royal Historical Society, 2003), 260.
8 Helen Gittos, *Liturgy, Architecture, and Sacred Places in Anglo-Saxon England* (Oxford: Oxford University Press, 2013), 19–54.
9 For an overview, see Palazzo, *Liturgie et société au moyen âge*.
10 Edward M. Thompson, ed., *Customary of the Benedictine Monasteries of Saint Augustine, Canterbury, and Saint Peter, Westminster*, Henry Bradshaw Society, 2 vols., 23 and 28 (London: Henry Bradshaw Society, 1902–1904) 1: 284.
11 For example, Frederick M. Powicke and Christopher R. Cheney, eds., *Councils and Synods with Other Documents Relating to the English Church. II A.D. 1205–1313*, 2 vols. (Oxford: Oxford University Press, 1964), 1: 79, 127, 300, 488; 2: 1085.
12 Knowles, *Monastic Constitutions of Lanfranc*, 134.
13 Ibid., 136.
14 Ibid., 178.
15 P. Bruno Griesser, 'Die "Ecclesiastica Officia Cisterciensis Ordinis" des Cod. 1711 von Trient', *Analecta Sacri Ordinis Cisterciensis* 12 (1956): 153–288 (at 256, 273–4).
16 Powicke and Cheney, *Councils and Synods II*, 1: 126.
17 Gerald R. Owst, *Literature and Pulpit in Medieval England: A Neglected Chapter in the History of English Letters and of the English People* (Cambridge: Cambridge University Press, 1933), 110–14.
18 Powicke and Cheney, *Councils and Synods II*, 1: 128, 172, 174, 297.
19 Elisabeth Okasha, 'The Lead Cross of Bishop Godfrey of Chichester', *Sussex Archaeological Collections* 134 (1996): 180–92; see also Elzbieta Dabrowska, 'Passeport pour l'au-delà: Essai sur la mentalité médiévale', *Le Moyen Âge* 111 (2005): 313–37.
20 David A. Hinton, *Gold and Gilt, Pots and Pins: Possessions and People in Medieval Britain* (Oxford: Oxford University Press, 2005), 165–66, 187–88; Roberta Gilchrist, 'Magic for the Dead? The Archaeology of Magic in Later Medieval Burials', *Medieval Archaeology* 52 (2008): 119–59.
21 Thompson, *Customary of . . . Saint Augustine, Canterbury, and Saint Peter, Westminster*, 1: 339–40: 'et involvunt capud, quod est principale membrum corporis humani, in quo vigent omnes sensus.'
22 Ibid., 1: 353.
23 Powicke and Cheney, *Councils and Synods II*, 1: 174, 601.
24 Thompson, *Customary of . . . Saint Augustine, Canterbury, and Saint Peter, Westminster*, 1: 361. For threats from the corpses of revenants, Stephen Gordon, 'Social Monsters and the Walking Dead in William of Newburgh's *Historia rerum Anglicarum*', *Journal of Medieval History* 41 (2015): 446–65.
25 Gratian, *Decretum*, Causa XI, Quaestio III, c. XI and c. XXI, in *Corpus iuris canonici*, ed. Emil Friedberg, 2 vols., 2nd ed. (Leipzig: Tauchnitz, 1881–1922) 1: cols. 646, 648–9.

26 Gregory IX, *Decretales*, lib. iii, tit. XL, cap. 7, in *Corpus iuris canonici*, ed. Friedberg, 2: col. 634.
27 Kew, The National Archives (TNA), JUST 2/78, rot. 2, m. 1r.
28 TNA, JUST 2/113, mm. 7r, 28r, 31r.
29 Discussed in Peter Brown, *The Cult of the Saints: Its Rise and Function in Latin Christianity* (Chicago: University of Chicago Press, 1981), 87–88; Walker Bynum, *Christian Materiality*, 131–45; Robert Bartlett, *Why Can the Dead Do Such Great Things? Saints and Worshippers from the Martyrs to the Reformation* (Princeton, NJ: Princeton University Press, 2013), 244–50.
30 Ronald C. Finucane, *Miracles and Pilgrims: Popular Beliefs in Medieval England*, 2nd ed. (Basingstoke: Macmillan, 1995), 89–90, 94; Bartlett, *Why Can the Dead Do Such Great Things?*, 248–49, 255–56.
31 For example, Brian Kemp, 'The Miracles of the Hand of St James', *Berkshire Archaeological Journal* 65 (1970): 1–19 (at 4).
32 André Vauchez, *Sainthood in the Later Middle Ages* (Cambridge: Cambridge University Press, 1997), 32–104.
33 The Vatican, Biblioteca Apostolica Vaticana (BAV), MS Vat. Lat. 4015, ff. 3r–4v: f. 4v, third article, 'Item tercio si dicta miracula fuerunt supra vel contra naturam'. . .; fifth article: 'Item quinto si in operacione dictorum miraculorum fuerunt apposite herbe vel lapides vel alique alie res naturales vel medicinales et si incantationes vel superstitiones vel fraudes alique intervenerunt in operatione ipsorum miraculorum'. For the process, Harriett Webster, 'Mediating Memory: Recalling and Recording the Miracles of St Thomas Cantilupe', *Journal of Medieval History* 41 (2015): 292–308. See also the discussion of marvels and miracles in Gordon, 'Social Monsters'.
34 Richard Kieckhefer, *Magic in the Middle Ages*, Rev. ed. (Cambridge: Cambridge University Press, 2000), 182.
35 See, for example, Florence Chave-Mahir, 'L'exorcisme des possédés, une parole efficace d'après quelques oeuvres doctrinales des VIe-XIIIe siècles', and Gábor Klaniczay, 'L'efficacité des mots dans les miracles, les visions, les incantations et les maléfices', in *Le pouvoir des mots au Moyen Âge*, ed. Nicole Bériou, Jean-Patrice Boudet, and Irène Rosier-Catach (Turnhout: Brepols, 2014), 305–26 and 327–47.
36 Gregory IX, *Decretales*, lib. iii, tit. XLII, cap. 4, in *Corpus iuris canonici*, ed. Friedberg, 2: cols. 646–47.
37 Powicke and Cheney, *Councils and Synods II*, 2: 896–7.
38 Ibid., 1: 589–90.
39 Don C. Skemer, *Binding Words: Textual Amulets in the Middle Ages* (University Park, PA: Pennsylvania State University Press, 2006); John Bromyard, *Summa predicantium* (Nuremberg: Anton Koberger, 1485), Sortilegium S xi, Art. ii: iii; and Art. iii: iiii.
40 Peter Murray Jones and Lea T. Olsan, 'Middleham Jewel: Ritual, Power, and Devotion', *Viator* 31 (2000): 249–90.
41 Thompson, *Customary of . . . Saint Augustine, Canterbury, and Saint Peter, Westminster*, 1: 119–20; also at Westminster Abbey: 2: 67.
42 Walker Bynum, *Christian Materiality*, 153–54.
43 Powicke and Cheney, *Councils and Synods II*, 1: 78; 2: 894–95, 1119–20.
44 TNA, E 101/393/4, f. 4r.
45 Martina Bagnoli, 'The Stuff of Heaven: Materials and Craftsmanship in Medieval Reliquaries', in *Treasures of Heaven: Saints, Relics, and Devotion in Medieval Europe*, ed. Martina Bagnoli et al. (New Haven, CT: Yale University Press, 2010), 136–47.
46 J. Wickham Legg, 'On an Inventory of the Vestry in Westminster Abbey, Taken in 1388', *Archaeologia* 52 (1890): 195–286 (at 202, 231–32). The images are

not all identified in 1388, but they are in the list of the same items in 1540: see 232, nn. a-f.

47 In 1307, for example, Cantilupe's shrine at Hereford was adorned with many silver and wax images, from the devotion of the people and by reason of the miracles that he had worked. Among the objects there were 65 gold necklaces, and 31 silver ones, 450 gold rings and 70 silver rings. BAV, MS Vat. Lat. 4015, ff. 74r-v.

48 Charles Reginald Dodwell, *Anglo-Saxon Art: A New Perspective* (Manchester: Manchester University Press, 1982), 48–55; John Blair, 'Spearhafoc (*fl.* 1047–1051), Abbot of Abingdon and Craftsman', in *Oxford Dictionary of National Biography*, ed. H.C.G. Matthew and B. Harrison, online edition, http://www. oxforddnb.com/view/article/49416 (accessed 30 August 2015); John Blair, 'Mannig [Wulfmær] (d. 1066), Abbot of Evesham and Craftsman', in *Oxford Dictionary of National Biography*, ed. H.C.G. Matthew and B. Harrison, online edition, http://www.oxforddnb.com/view/article/49414 (accessed 30 August 2015); Hinton, *Gold and Gilt*, 329, n. 146; Woolgar, *Senses in Late Medieval England*, 51–2; 289, n. 141.

49 Powicke and Cheney, *Councils and Synods II*, 1: 273.

50 C. M. Woolgar, ed., *Testamentary Records of the English and Welsh Episcopate 1200–1413: Wills, Executors' Accounts and Inventories, and the Probate Process*, Canterbury and York Society, 102 (Woodbridge: Boydell and Brewer, 2011), 73, 89, 102.

51 Ibid., 208–14.

52 London, BL Add. MS 60584, f. 11r: 'i cophino de diversis reliquiis ignotis sigillato sigillo domini Thome Donsflete'.

53 Dorothy Whitelock, Martin Brett, and Christopher N. L. Brooke, eds., *Councils and Synods with Other Documents Relating to the English Church I. A.D. 871–1204*, 2 vols. (Oxford: Oxford University Press, 1981) 2: 605.

54 Powicke and Cheney, *Councils and Synods II*, 1: 69–70.

55 Ibid, 1: 141, 512; *OED*, s.v. "chrisom."

56 Powicke and Cheney, *Councils and Synods II*, 1: 174.

57 Norfolk Record Office, Norwich Consistory Court Records, Will Register 1 Heydon (1370–82), ff. 102r-v.

58 Katherine L. French, *The Good Women of the Parish: Gender and Religion after the Black Death* (Philadelphia, PA: University of Pennsylvania Press, 2008), 17–49.

59 Roberta Gilchrist, *Medieval Life: Archaeology and the Life Course* (Woodbridge: Boydell and Brewer, 2012), 216–51.

60 French, *Good Women of the Parish*, 47.

61 James Raine, ed., *Testamenta Eboracensia II*, Surtees Society, 30 (London, 1855), 146–47.

62 Gervase of Tilbury, *Otia imperialia: Recreation for an Emperor*, eds. S.E. Banks and J.W. Binns (Oxford: Oxford University Press, 2002) 614–19; Hinton, *Gold and Gilt*, 187; Woolgar, *Senses in Late Medieval England*, 51–2.

63 Woolgar, *Testamentary Records of the English and Welsh Episcopate*, 212.

64 TNA, E 101/393/11, f. 61r; E 101/398/9, f. 23r; E 101/403/10, f. 34v.

65 H. Farmer, 'The Canonization of St Hugh of Lincoln', *Lincolnshire Architectural and Archaeological Society Reports and Papers* 6 (1956): 86–177 (at 98).

66 Anon., ed., *A Collection of Ordinances and Regulations for the Government of the Royal household . . .*, for the Society of Antiquaries (London, 1790), 121–2.

67 Mary MacLeod Banks, ed., *An Alphabet of Tales, an English 15th Century Translation of the Alphabetum Narrationum of Etienne de Besançon from*

Additional MS. 25,719 of the British Museum, 2 vols., EETS, o.s. 126–27 (London: Kegan Paul, Trench, Trübner & Co. 1904–1905), 2: 465.

68 Powicke and Cheney, *Councils and Synods II*, 1: 68, 453, echoing Lateran IV, cap. 20.

69 E.M. Elvey, ed., *The Courts of the Archdeaconry of Buckingham 1483–1523* (Buckinghamshire Record Society, 19; 1975), 23.

70 For example Anthony Ian Doyle, '"Lectulus noster floridus": An Allegory of the Penitent Soul', in *Literature and Religion in the Later Middle Ages: Philological Studies in Honor of Siegfried Wenzel*, ed. Richard G. Newhauser and John A. Alford (Binghamton, New York: Medieval and Renaissance Texts and Studies, 1995), 179–90.

Part II
Concord and conversion

4 Double conversion: the sensory autobiography of Sir Kenelm Digby

Joe Moshenska

I.

In 1630, Sir Kenelm Digby took Protestant Communion, publically renouncing his Roman Catholicism. Five years later, it became widely known that he had rejoined the faith into which he had been born. It was far from uncommon for individuals to convert more than once in the early modern period, whether this involved stages of progressive radicalisation, or, as in Digby's case, the return to a religious position previously occupied.[1] While double conversions of this sort may have been relatively frequent, they nonetheless present a challenge to certain central precepts of the conversion narratives integral to Christian tradition. In its most famous manifestations – St Paul on the road to Damascus, or St Augustine in the garden in Milan – conversion takes place in an instant of blinding clarity, and involves a change that is absolute and irreversible. A convert who later recants has two options: to dismiss the first conversion as merely superficial, and risk seeming flighty or insincere; or, alternately, to develop forms of narrative and self-understanding that construe the return to a position that one has previously occupied as the most decisive of transformations, and present the journey back to where one began as the journey that takes one furthest of all.

Double conversion, then, creates both specific challenges and certain opportunities for a coherent narrative of selfhood. It demands an account that can find room for transformation and discontinuity, while subsuming these moments of apparent rupture within a seamlessly integrated whole. In this essay, I argue that Digby responded to these challenges with particular acuity, and that he did so in part through a repeated invocation and exploration of sensory experience. Digby placed enormous weight upon the senses in both theological and epistemological contexts, and he rewrote his life experiences obsessively. These two aspects of his writings are, I argue, deeply interconnected: the exercise of the senses was integral to the way that he understood not only the workings of the world, but the internal consistency of his own life. Attending to the rewriting of sensory experience in Digby's oeuvre has significant implications for the way in which we understand the functioning of the senses in the early modern period, and the place of the senses in the enterprise of recounting a life. My argument has two parts. In the first, after explaining the context of Digby's religious transformations, I discuss the letters and devotional works that he wrote around the time of his reconversion, following the death of his wife. In these writings, I claim, his repeated and conventional avowal that piety can only be achieved by the utter renunciation of sensory experience and enjoyment is persistently undercut by a tacit acknowledgement that such sensuous pleasures are covertly perpetuated by being transposed onto a higher plane, even as they are seemingly renounced. In this way, Digby seeks to ensure the persistence and cohesion of his plurally converted self, which, like sensory experience, can both change utterly and remain the same. In the second part, I consider moments from Digby's philosophical magnum opus, the 1644 *Two Treatises* on the nature of body and soul, in which he vividly recreates sensory experiences that predated his original conversion. By evoking these earlier moments in the course of developing his philosophy of the senses, Digby thereby implies unbroken continuity between his past and present sensing selves, creating a seamless and cohesive sensory autobiography unperturbed by the ruptures attendant upon his double conversion.

II.

On 22 October 1635, James Howell wrote a letter to the Earl of Strafford, which he ended by updating the Earl on the latest spate of conversions to Roman Catholicism that had controversially taken place in courtly circles. 'Sir *Kenelm Digby* is gone over', Howell wrote, 'and Mr *Wat Montague* hath taken the portion his father intended him, and gone over an hot *Roman* to return no more'.[2] The conversion of Walter Montague was a sensation: as the son of the Earl of Manchester, his was a particularly high-profile and controversial apostasy, which provoked a public reply from his father, to which Lucius Cary, Viscount Falkland, appended a further reply in print.[3] At this fraught point in the mid-1630s, when it seemed to alarmed observers among the godly that the whole court was drifting back towards Rome and the King himself was rumoured to be leaning towards conversion, Montague's actions were particularly loaded.[4] By contrast, the 'going over' of Kenelm Digby seems to have provoked far less controversy or surprise. While Howell lumped them together, in fact the conversions of the two men would have seemed very different to contemporaries. Montague was abandoning the faith into which he had been born, and in which he had been raised by his illustrious father. Howell's prediction that he would 'return no more' proved prescient, and Montague ended his long and colourful life in 1677 as a committed Roman Catholic, in his position as Abbot of St Martin in Pontoise, twenty miles north of Paris. Digby, however, was not making a new and decisive change, but returning to a path that he had already trodden. His father, Everard, had been executed for his role in the Gunpowder Plot when Digby was a young boy, and he had been raised a Roman Catholic by his mother.[5] For Digby, unlike Montague, this was a reconversion, a return to a religious identity that had once been his.

While there has been abundant discussion of religious conversion in the early modern period in recent scholarship, Digby's has received only the briefest of mentions.[6] This is perhaps because reconversion itself prompts a degree of scepticism: if a person chooses to return to his or her original religion after a period of a few years, must this not suggest that the original conversion was superficial and insincere? This doubt was expressed in Digby's time, and is also evident in recent discussions. On 27 December 1630, the Venetian ambassador to England reported to the Doge and Senate that there had been talk of sending an ordinary ambassador to Spain: 'and many mention the name of Sir Kenelm Digby, who was at one time a pirate in the Mediterranean, and who let your Serenity's subjects feel the unlawful effects of his robberies. Moved by ambition he has recently abandoned the Catholic Faith and become a Protestant'.[7] Digby had spent 1628 in the Mediterranean as a privateer, culminating in a sea-battle with the Venetian vessels guarding the Turkish port of Scanderoon, and it was after his return that his conversion became public: no wonder the ambassador chalked it up to mere ambition.[8] The assumption has proven durable: more recently, we find the art historian Francis Haskell describing Digby as 'A Catholic convert (but had he ever *not* been a Catholic?). . .'[9] This tendency to describe Digby's original conversion as superficial is part of a long-standing inclination to dismiss him and his fellow court Catholics as generally frivolous and insubstantial: the great Victorian historian S.R. Gardiner insisted that 'The danger from Rome was less serious than it seemed. The bait held out by the papal clergy appealed to the low and more selfish side of human nature. Fantastic speculators like Sir Kenelm Digby, witty intriguers like Walter Montagu, brought no real strength to the cause that they espoused'.[10]

In the course of my work on Digby's correspondence, I have uncovered significant new evidence which demonstrates the sincerity and serious theological engagement that was involved both in his original conversion and in his reconversion, including his close relationship with Montague. Digby's double conversion was not an expression of base ambition or evidence of his insubstantiality: his original decision to abandon Roman Catholicism, and his subsequent return, were both the product of serious and highly deliberate thought. Nonetheless, it is necessary to recognise that both the fact and the occasion of Digby's reconversion rendered them ambiguous, both to his contemporaries and to later historians. If Digby's original conversion has been taken as a symptom of his insincerity, this is in part because his recantation seems on the surface to have been precipitated by personal trauma rather than religious principle. The event that apparently instigated Digby's reconversion was the death of his wife, Venetia, on 1 May 1633.[11] His immense grief was channelled into a concerted attempt to secure and shape her memory: he commissioned Anthony van Dyck to paint her on her deathbed, as well to produce a striking portrait of Digby himself in mourning garb; Ben Jonson and several of the prominent Sons of Ben, including Thomas May and Aurelian Townshend, wrote elegies in her memory; and Digby had a funeral monument erected in Christ Church, Newgate, that was later destroyed in the Great Fire of 1666.[12] He also penned a series of impassioned letters – to his sons, his brother John, his patron, the Secretary of State Sir John Coke, and various friends and relatives – in which he stressed Venetia's unimpeachable virtue and his own transformed, grieving self, and which were carefully copied for wide circulation. He also changed his demeanour and dress, with John Aubrey reporting that Digby wore 'a long mourning cloake, a high-crowned hat, look't like a Hermite, his beard unshorne, as signes of sorrowe for his beloved Wife'.[13] This outpouring of grief was subjected to a certain degree of scepticism at the time, and this has continued to be the case. Rumours began to circulate that Digby had poisoned his wife with wine made from a distillation of vipers – either deliberately, or as part of an unfortunate treatment for her complexion. Aubrey reported that Digby had 'retired in to Gresham College. . .to avoyd envy and scandall' following Venetia's death. Equally damaging rumours had earlier swirled around Venetia herself – Aubrey claimed that one nobleman, Richard, Earl of Dorset, 'kept [her] as his concubine' and even stated, implausibly, that she had borne him a child.[14] These facts and rumours made Digby's public and performative grief seem less an attempt to secure her reputation for piety and purity than a rearguard action against the gossip that threatened his wife's posthumous reputation and his own standing. Digby's way of mourning seems somewhat repellent to modern sensibilities: it is insistently public and histrionic rather than dignified and private; it is highly artificial and constructed rather than spontaneous and sincere; it emphasises the woe and the rampant subjectivity of the mourner rather than the personality of the mourned. It would be easy, but wrong, to dismiss Digby's actions in this way as a public-relations campaign, and to assume a division between authentic feeling and its inauthentic public performance that certainly did not exist in the seventeenth century.[15] They are better understood as a response to Digby's felt need to make public to others, and coherent to himself, the implications of his ongoing changes in his personal and religious conviction.

Even if we reject the complacent assumption that because Digby's mourning and his eventual reconversion were public they must necessarily be inauthentic, the structural vulnerability of his double conversion must still be recognised. This vulnerability is made clear by a letter written to Digby by Archbishop William Laud in 1636. It was never sent, apparently because Laud wrote it to dissuade Digby from re-converting, but then heard that the decision had already been made.[16] The letter was ultimately printed as the final item appended to the 1695 history of Laud's trial, and it allows us to reconstruct the reasons that Digby gave his friend the Archbishop for returning to Catholicism, which included serious doubts about the historical validity of the reformed church. Laud responds by stressing the inconsistency of reconversion as an act, and the objections to which it is structurally open. Digby, he observes, claims 'that you may preserve yourself in that Church [of Rome], without having your belief bound up in several particulars'. Laud, though, doubts that Roman Catholicism will really leave Digby's conscience as free as he claims, and asks 'doth that Church leave you free to believe, or not to believe, any thing determined by it? And did not your former Dislike arise from some things determined in and by that Church? And if so, what Freedom see you now, that you saw not then?'[17] Laud's final question is telling: because Digby had, at the point of his original conversion, acknowledged that the Roman Catholic Church determines certain points of belief and rejected it partly for that reason, it is difficult for him to distance himself from the reformed Church and justify his return on that same basis.

Digby answers the difficulties raised by Laud, and which are endemic to any reconversion, in part through the way in which he treats sensory experience. In some of Digby's writings from the mid-1630s, namely the letters written following Venetia's death and his *Conference with a Lady about Choice of Religion* (1638), his account of the senses vacillates. Sensory pleasure is described, on the one hand, as a transitory and debased aspect of human existence which must be overcome in the pursuit of spiritual purity and will finally be left behind by the immortal soul at the point of death. On the other hand, Digby repeatedly suggests that sensory pleasures are valuable in their own right, and that they can and will be retained and transformed, not abandoned, when higher states of piety and eventual immortality are achieved. This significant vacillation is one way in which Digby treats the problems of biographical disruption and continuity raised by his double conversion: it allows him to trace a trajectory for the pious self that incorporates apparently total transformation, while simultaneously suggesting that this change is less than total, and finally enables an assertion of continuity unaffected by contingent change.

Digby's *Conference with a Lady*, probably written in 1636, was almost certainly addressed to Francis Howard, Lady Purbeck, who had fled to France and resolved to change her religion to Roman Catholicism after being found guilty of adultery with Sir Robert Howard. The *Conference* is replete with fairly conventional denouncements of the body and the value of its material experiences. The soul, Digby insists, once 'released out of the body (which is like a darke prison to wall it in)' will attain to distinct and perfect knowledge: 'her conjunction here with resistent matter

was a burden and a clogge unto her'.[18] 'To avoid misery in the next life',
he claims, 'we must deny our senses the content and satisfaction that they
naturally desire in corporall things', and this involves 'withdrawing our
affections from sensible goods'.[19] Digby offers a lamenting description of
'a soule so disposed and wrought upon by the sensuall passions tyrannising
over it'.[20] These are standard sentiments, and they are not confessionally
specific: they would seem no more controversial to a reformed than to a
Catholic reader.

As the *Conference* develops, however, and Digby begins to justify the
specific and exclusive legitimacy of the Catholic Church, it becomes less
easy to dismiss the workings of the senses out of hand. He insists, against
what he describes as the Protestant scepticism towards the outward
dimensions of worship, that the effectual imprinting of Christ's doctrine
on the hearts of believers cannot be achieved through the pure inwardness of the soul. 'Now to have this compleately performed', he claims,
'it was to be done both by exteriour and interiour meanes; proportionable to the senses without, and to the soule within'.[21] Digby's account
of the historically assured validity of the Catholic Church relies upon the
'exteriour. . .meanes; proportionable to the senses without' having an
authority of their own. Or, more precisely, faith relies upon a specific form
of disjunction between spiritual and sensory experience: sensory experience
remains necessary precisely so that it can be confounded. The evidence of
miracles must be a scandal to the senses, and this in turn becomes evidence
that 'some inward and supernatural light be given her [the soul] to disperse
all the mistes that the senses rayse against the truth of the doctrine'.[22] In
order to make this point, Digby invokes the example of Doubting Thomas,
who 'would not believe his [Christ's] resurrection unless he saw him and
put his fingers into his wounds'.[23] In referring here to the sceptical disciple,
Digby endorses the bulk of Roman Catholic commentators who insisted
that Thomas did indeed probe the wounds inflicted at the Crucifixion,
and that this was a necessary step towards the acceptance of Christ's claim
that 'because thou hast seen me, thou hast believed: blessed are they that
have not seen, and yet have believed'.[24] Whereas, as Glenn Most points
out, many Protestant commentators worked hard to deny that Christ's
body had actually been subjected to touch in this moment, Digby asserts
that direct sensory experience must be undergone if it is to be overcome.[25]
Digby makes a similar point when describing 'the reall presence of Christs
body in the blessed Sacrament' as the point 'of the Romane doctrine
which [is] most repugnant to sense'.[26] Digby was much invested in these
questions at this point, having made extensive notes on the question of
communion under one species from February 1637 onwards.[27] Where
many Protestants ridiculed the standard Roman Catholic claim that
Christ's body and blood could be present beneath the apparently
unchanged sensory *species* of bread and wine, for Digby this scepticism
should not be answered by explaining its plausibility in philosophical

terms: rather its scandalous implausibility, its repugnance, should be accepted as the basis of the faith it demands. He argues for a specifically sensory corollary of the famous dictum attributed to Tertullian: *credo, quia impossibile est*. The initial and seemingly uncontroversial rejection of sensory experience in the *Conference*, then, gives way to something more complex: the mere fact that sensory experience *can* be rejected against its overwhelming persuasiveness is evidence for the guiding light of the Spirit. The fact that the believer should finally be led to accept a doctrine so repugnant to sense testifies not simply to the baseness and disposability of the senses, but to the constitutive necessity of the experience of their overcoming as the basis of Roman Catholic piety.

In this work, then, Digby does not dismiss sensory experience out of hand, as might first appear. He insists upon lingering with the senses precisely so that they might be overcome. This unstable dual impulse towards the dismissing and retaining of the senses as the basis of piety is of fundamental importance to the role of the senses in the early modern period. This unstable dynamic emerged as writers sought to avail themselves of the affective force and intimacy of the senses as a way of maintaining a relationship with God, but they could not do so without drifting into a dangerous position: a stress on the tempting dangers of the senses was a point of commonality between the differing ethical accounts provided by Platonic, Aristotelian, and Stoic ethics, while Christians who brought the senses too emphatically into the divine realm risked the excessive reification and concomitant diminution of the godhead. The tension between these impulses was acutely felt in the sixteenth and seventeenth centuries, and Digby was only one of many writers who developed subtle linguistic strategies through which a sensory piety might be disavowed and covertly perpetuated at once.[28] Digby develops similar techniques in a still more unstable and complex way in the letters that he wrote and had circulated amongst his friends following Venetia's death. Here too it is easy to find denunciations of sensory pleasure and a repeated insistence that the body must be entirely forgotten in order to assure the purity of the soul. In these letters, though, the status of sensory experience is particularly complicated by Digby's intensely affective emphasis on his encounter with the body of his freshly dead wife. Addressing his sons, he writes that:

> Her hair was tending to brown, yet shining wth a strange natural lustre and brightnesse; it was by many degrees softer than the softest that euer I saw, wch hath often brought into my consideration that the rules of Physiognomy many times fall out to be true for they direct to iudge of the mildnesse and gentlenesse of one's disposition by the softnesse and finenesse of their haire. Nothing can be imagined subtiler then hers was; I haue often had a handful of it in my hand, and haue scare perceiued I touched anything.[29]

Maximum softness, an extreme of sensory lustrousness, tends towards that which cannot be sensed: that which most merits or solicits touch is that which cannot finally be felt, which eludes feeling. This paradoxical dynamic is present elsewhere in the same letter: Venetia's flesh, he claims, 'was the tenderest, the softest and the finest graine of any that I ever looked upon; it was firm, and yet so gentle and smooth as it seemed to escape ones touch'.[30] Venetia's own body seems to be the quintessential object of sense, and by that very same token to exist beyond sense. A version of this paradox, moreover, migrates into Digby's description of his own spiritual state. 'My minde is now even with my body', he writes to his brother, 'for all the rebellions and faults it ever committed; these two tyrannize over one another by turnes. . .nothing but true vertue can keepe the beame even betweene these unsteady balances'.[31] This state is understood not, as we might expect, simply as the body capturing and weighing down the soul, but as a dual tyranny, in which acquiescing to solely spiritual concerns would be a suppression rather than a perfection of the self. He concludes that if God will allow him 'to take comforte and delight in spiritual objects. . .I may be happy even here; nay more happy than ye happiest sensuall man living'. This is not, though, simply because spiritual objects trump their sensory equivalents. He aspires to the condition of those who 'have enjoyed a kind of heaven here upon earth. . .And though ye worde voluptie be usually taken in ye worse sense, yet their condition may be fitly expressed by saying they lived in a most entire and full voluptuousnesse of spirit'.[32] While Digby's current turbulent state involves the painful and mutual tyrannising of the body and soul, he strives towards a condition in which sensory voluptuousness would be not forgotten or abandoned, but retained and redeemed by being elevated to a higher form.

Digby's refusal to leave behind the pleasures of the senses entirely is stated most emphatically in a reflection written on 23 June 1634, and which was circulated along with his letters. There, he claims that:

> when the end of time and motion shall setle all thinges in a state of rest and deliuer back unto each soule her own bodie, the senses shall also enjoy their delights; not by the use of their operations, which must cease when motion ceaseth, but by a redundance of the soul into them: the order of working in man being now inverted, when as att the first production the soul was belonging to the senses for all the impressions made in her, but then att the second the senses shall receive no impressions but from the soule, unto which they shall be perfectly subject. And all those good and naturall delights which in this life a man enjoyeth by meanes of his senses, he shall there enjoy infinitely more refined and perfectly by his soule.[33]

Here, most clearly, the anticipated transformation of sensory experience becomes a figure for Digby's own incipient reconversion – a total change

that is at the same time a reversion, and no change at all. The transformations that he has undergone by virtue of his double conversion will
be replayed on an apocalyptic scale. At the end of all things, the senses
will operate through the 'redundance' of the soul – that is, the soul's
overflowing and excess. This will represent the inversion of the human
compound of body and soul: where once the soul relied on the senses for
its impressions and experiences, now the soul will perfectly temper sensory
experience. Yet this later account of a 'full voluptuousnesse of spirit' is
all the more remarkable because it is so distant from the disavowals of
sensory experience and pleasure that Digby professes elsewhere. The
delights of the senses – or at least those that are good and natural – will
be retained in this higher state even as their basis is transformed, and
spiritual sensation will refine rather than simply transcend sensory
experience. This is a total sensory change in which the thoroughly mixed
status of the human, both sensate and ensouled, is not abandoned or
purified but merely reconfigured: a form of continuity that is achieved,
paradoxically, through thorough and absolute transformation, much like
the reconversion that Digby was soon to announce.

III.

By the beginning of the 1640s, Digby had moved from theological
discussion into the realms of physics and metaphysics, and was writing
his *Treatise on the Nature of Body*. In his *Observations* on Thomas
Browne's *Religio Medici*, written while imprisoned in 1642, Digby claimed
that he had produced a 'first draught' of his 'totall Survey of the whole
Science of *Bodyes*', covering 'neere two hundred sheets of paper'.[34] This
apparent shift in the focus of Digby's writings was, however, much less
absolute than it might seem: it is precisely his emphasis on the senses, and
the careful interweaving of sensory experiences that stress the unbroken
continuity of his own life, that form the connection between these stages
in Digby's authorial career. If the *Treatise. . .of Body* has received less
attention than it deserves then Digby himself is partly to blame, since he
described it in the preface to the *Two Treatises* as merely the 'proaemiall
part' of the work, and worries that it has grown 'so ample in respect of
the other' – that is, the *Treatise on the Soul* – 'which was the end of it,
and for whose sake I meddled in it'.[35] John Henry claims on this basis that
it is 'quite evident' that the entire work 'was written to provide a
philosophical basis on which to erect a new eschatology', and Digby's
account of the nature of body has been generally overlooked by those who
have explored his religious commitments.[36] In the *Treatise. . .of Body*
Digby develops an unusual and original account of the senses, and rather
than drawing a strict line between his theological and epistemological
concerns, we might instead see the senses as the bridge between them.
Digby's account is unusual in two ways: the first, which I cannot explore

in detail here, concerns the intellectual traditions on which he draws and seeks to amalgamate. Digby engages closely with the differing atomist and mechanist accounts of the senses developed by Hobbes, Gassendi, and Descartes – all of whom he knew personally – but, unlike many exponents of the New Philosophies who contrasted their accounts vociferously with Aristotle and his followers, Digby sought to reconcile Aristotelianism and mechanised materialism in idiosyncratic fashion.[37] The second, and scarcely less striking difference, concerns the range of examples upon which Digby draws when developing this philosophically hybrid account of sensation. In deploying an array of outlandish examples, he departs from writers such as Descartes, who emphasised everyday, quotidian forms of sensory experience and sought to reconfigure them.[38] When Descartes described himself sitting before the fire and watching a ball of wax metamorphose in the second of his *Meditations on First Philosophy*, the rhetorical force of this most famous of philosophical fables arises precisely from the everydayness of the scene: Descartes need not even leave his hearth to shatter the secure basis of sensory reality, and any reader can easily envisage and imaginatively inhabit the scene that he describes.[39] In drawing upon examples from his own idiosyncratic and exotic experiences, Digby proceeds very differently, and his procedure, I would argue, is closely connected with the techniques developed in his theological writings in the 1630s, where discussions of the senses were deployed to manage the combination of rupture and underlying continuity occasioned by his double conversion.

The *Treatise. . .of Body* is studded with striking and vivid anecdotes, drawn from tales that Digby has heard but especially from his own past experiences, which are used to reinforce his philosophical points. Nowhere is this more ostentatious than in his account of the senses. This is not so unusual in itself, but the episodes from his earlier life upon which Digby chooses to focus, and the particular experiences that he selects, are remarkable. As a young man, in the early 1620s, Digby made a Grand Tour through France and into Italy. He lived in Tuscany for two years before he was summoned to Madrid in 1623 by his powerful relative John Digby, the Earl of Bristol, who was embroiled in the negotiations to marry the future Charles I, then Prince of Wales, to the Spanish Infanta. Digby arrived in Madrid shortly after Charles and Buckingham made their remarkable and ill-advised trip to the city, incognito and in disguise, and was able to observe these events from close quarters. He returned to England with Charles, and was named a gentleman of the Prince's privy chamber. It was a few years later – at the end of 1627, by which point England was at war with both France and Spain – that Digby undertook his privateering voyage into the Mediterranean, and it was following his return from this voyage that the Venetian ambassador reported his initial conversion, as we saw above.[40]

When Digby discusses the workings of the senses in his *Treatise. . .of Body*, he turns repeatedly to experiences from this earlier period in his life: the time spent in Spain with Charles, and his year in the Mediterranean. This begins even before he arrives at the detailed account of the senses in this work, when he is arguing near the outset for the corporeity of light. Digby acknowledges that 'among all corporeall thinges, [light] seemeth to ayme rightest at a spirituall nature, and to come neerest unto it', and anticipates objections to his arguments for 'the corporeity of this subtle thing, that so queintly playeth with our eyes'.[41] But, he insists, just because an entity seems akin to a spirit, this does not mitigate or reduce its fundamental physicality, and to make this point he shifts between the senses, from vision to olfaction:

> When they that are curious in perfumes, will have their chamber filled with a good sent in a hoat season, that agreeth not with burning perfumes, and therefore make some odoriferous water be blowne about it by their servants mouthes that are dexterous in that Ministery, (as is used in Spaine in the summer time;) every one that seeth it done, though on a suddaine the water be lost to his eyes and touch, and is onely discernable by his nose; yet he is well satisfyed that the sent which recreateth him, is the very water he saw in the glasse extremely dilated by the forcible sprouting of it out from the servants mouth, and will by litle and litle fall downe and become againe palpable water as it was before; and therefore doubteth not but it is still water whiles it hangeth in the ayre divided into litle atomes.[42]

The argument is quite cogent and straightforward: we accept that water can be rarefied and distributed through the air without any change in its atomic constitution, and no one would argue that water becomes spirit, so why can the same not be true of light?[43] The basis for this argument, however, is deliberately made both cosmopolitan and amusing, for it is located in Spain, a place which Digby offhandedly reminds the reader that he had experienced first-hand, and it depends on a particularly odd Spanish custom, whereby a servant is transformed into a sort of primitive air-freshener. Rather than reducing everyday phenomena to fundamental physical facts, Digby dwells with the most eclectic experiences of the senses, and insists that they can be of philosophical import in illuminating the material constitution of reality.

In this moment Digby draws the senses close together and implicitly argues for their shared material basis by drifting from an account of vision to one of scent; when he turns in greater detail to the senses he continues both his synaesthetic claims, and the type of anecdote through which he supports them. He prepares to illustrate the manner in which 'one sense will oftentimes supply the want of an other' with a strikingly blunt claim: 'I have seene one, who could discerne soundes with his eyes'.[44] This claim turns out to be less astounding than it initially appears, but only just. The man in question is 'a noble man of great quality that I knew in Spaine, the yonger brother of the Constable of Castile', who 'was borne deafe; so deafe, that if a gunne were shott off close by his eare, he could not heare it'. The young man was eventually taught to understand and to speak by a priest: 'after strange patience, constancy and paines; he brought the yong Lord to speake as distinctly as any man whosoever; and to understand so perfectly what others said that he would not loose a word in a whole dayes conversation'. Acknowledging that the overcoming of these great obstacles to speech might be difficult for his readers to credit, Digby writes that:

> The priest who by his booke and art, occasioned this discourse, I am told is still alive, and in the service of the Prince of Carignan, where he continueth (with some that have neede of his paines) the same employment as he did with the Constables Brother: with whom I have often discoursed, whiles I wayted upon the Prince of Wales (now our gratious Soveraigne) in Spaine. And I doubt not but his majesty remembreth all I have said of him and much more: for his majesty was very curious to observe and enquire into the utmost of it.[45]

What is notable here, once again, is that Digby's account both tends towards unusual and marginal rather than everyday sensory experiences, and that he again locates such experiences in Spain. Here he is much more precise, detailing not only the kind of sense experiences involved, as was the case with the perfume-breathing servants, but specific individuals – most importantly, Charles himself. Writing in the midst of civil war, at the time of his own imprisonment, Digby looks back to earlier halcyon days, when he enjoyed easy intimacy with the future monarch, and they could concern themselves with sensory curiosities, not the violent struggles of politics and religion. By vividly re-imagining the events of the 1620s in the 1640s, however, Digby not only draws an unspoken contrast with his own embattled present, but implicitly claims that his own identity and experiences have proceeded in unbroken continuity since that point: so immediate are the memories of that time, before his double conversion, that he appears as the same man who once experienced the sensory wonders of Spain, and the *Treatise. . .of Body* becomes an argument for Digby's own biographical continuity even as it presents a general account of the senses and their workings. The same is very much true of the reminiscences of his Mediterranean voyage. In discussing the sense of touch, Digby makes the general point that 'severall men of differing constitutions, do frame different notions of the same thinges'. He first makes the general observations that 'the same liquor is sweete to some mens taste; which to an others appeareth bitter: one man taketh that for a purfume; which to an other, is an offensiue smell'. To make the same point in relation to the fluctuating experiences of touch, he then observes that in the Turkesh bathes; (where there are many degrees of heate in divers roomes, through all which the same person useth to passe, and to stay a while in euery one of them, both att his entrance and going out, to season his body by degrees, for the contrary excesse he his going unto) that seemeth chilly cold att his returne; which appeared melting hoat att his going in; as I my selfe have often made experience in those countries.[46]

Digby's account is very different from the ways in which experiences from far-flung locales were typically treated by seventeenth century natural philosophers. An illuminating contrast can be drawn with the writings of Robert Boyle, whom Digby knew personally and provided with alchemical manuscripts.[47] When Boyle's argument requires knowledge of an exotic or inaccessible place, he disavows any responsibility for experiencing it directly in order to provide a reliable interpretation. In his discussion of the temperature of the undersea regions, Boyle writes that 'I do not pretend to have visited the bottom of the sea; [and] none of the naturalists whose writings I have yet met with, have been there any more than I'.[48] In response to this difficulty, as Stephen Shapin notes, Boyle 'sought reliable testimony wherever he could', and carefully sifted and assessed its reliability, performing his expertise and sceptical discernment in the process.[49] Digby refused to maintain a stance of refined withdrawal in his own writings (and, while he may never have visited the bottom of the sea, he had enjoyed night swimming off the island of Zante, and 'found the water warmer than att any time in England').[50] Where Boyle admitted that he had not experienced these distant phenomena for himself and then developed strategies by which he – and his reader – could nonetheless assess them, Digby insisted that he had undergone a range of sensory experiences of a sort that the reader was unlikely to replicate. The mixture of sensory vividness of description and exoticism of location makes a different sort of claim on the reader's credulity. The fluctuating and relative experiences of heat and cold are commonplace enough, easily identifiable by the reader; but the location of the experience through which Digby illustrates these everyday shifts are calculatedly alien and exotic. He draws upon an emphatically personal reservoir of sensory experiences: 'as I my selfe haue often made experience in those countries'. Readers are asked both to believe that such experiences took place as described, and accept that they could never experience them for themselves. When Digby proceeds to treat the sense of hearing, he similarly draws upon the experiences of his Mediterranean voyage: his expedition is rewritten in retrospect as an excursion into new sensory as well as geographical regions. Arguing for the materiality of sounds, Digby considers the violent physical effects that they can have, and recalls that

after a fight I once had with some galleasses and Galliones in the roade of Scanderone (which was a very hoat one for the time, and a scarce credible number of pieces of ordinance were shott from my fleete) the English Consull of that place coming afterwardes aboard my shippe, tould me that the report of our gunnes, had, during all the time of the fight, shaken the drinking glasses that stood upon shelues in his house; and had splitte the paper windowes all about; and had spoyled and cracked all the egges that his pigeons were then sitting upon: which losse, he lamented exceedingly.[51]

A decade and a half after this battle was fought, Digby cannot resist a passing brag regarding the 'scarce credible' prowess of the artillery under his command. He breezily reminds the reader of his naval triumph, while shifting the focus away from the more obvious havoc that his guns created among the French and Venetian ships towards intriguing forms of collateral damage – the cracked eggs of carrier pigeons, a communication network for which Scanderoon was famous.[52] The cannons that his crews fired did obvious and decisive damage to the vessels of their foes, but the sounds that they made were so great that they acquired a physical force of their own, akin to a hurtling projectile but on a much smaller scale, that did more delicate and incidental damage to the crystalline glassware and frail eggshells belonging to the English consul. The cumulative effect of these examples is to ground Digby's account of the shared material basis of the senses in a series of evoked instances, with multiple effects. They delight and engage the reader; they remind the reader that Digby himself is a remarkable and atypical sensory agent, a man who has had the opportunity to exercise his senses in far-flung locales, and derived philosophical significance from what he has sensed there; and they implicitly suggest that the author, the Kenelm Digby who writes his *Two Treatises* at the beginning of the 1640s, is the same extraordinary sensory agent who underwent them in the 1620s. In this way, his descriptions silently elide the transformations of Digby's double conversions, and present the reader with a smooth and seamlessly integrated account of his life and the sensory experiences that he has undergone.

IV.

In the letters, theological writings, and philosophical treatises written in the decade and a half following his original conversion, then, Kenelm Digby turned repeatedly to the nature and basis of the senses in order to manage the challenges to the coherence of his individual life that a double conversion – a decisive return to a religious position previously occupied, as a matter of choice rather than birth – presented to him. In closing, I would like to argue that we can usefully understand the role of the senses in his writings by considering them as forms of sensory autobiography. I adapt this term from the notion of 'sensory biography', which has been important in contemporary anthropological writings, but has as yet had little impact in literary and historical studies.[53] The phrase was, to my knowledge, first used by Nadia Seremetakis in her discussion of 'perceptual memory as a cultural form', which is 'encased and embodied out there in a dispersed surround of created things, surfaces, depths and densities that give back refractions of our own sensory biographies'.[54] There is a deliberate tension in her description between a notion of possession – '*our* sensory biographies', which might be ours alone to define and relate – and a notion of dispersal, in which these biographies emerge only through transformative encounter, and can never be individually defined and demarcated. The multiplicity and complexity of this understanding was taken as a guiding orientation by Robert Desjarlais, in his book *Sensory Biographies*, an account of the Yolmo *Wa* population of Nepal, which, by focusing on the role of the senses in the telling of individual life stories, sought to identify patterns and emphases in Yolmo culture rather than arguing for a unified sensory regime, concluding that 'Sensory engagements are as much intersubjective processes as they are personal ones'.[55]

Kenelm Digby's sensory autobiography, I have argued, emerged in part from the tension between two imperatives: to argue that all sensing functions on a material basis, and to develop a coherent account of his own individual development, which elided in various ways the challenging transformations of his double conversion. He was able to turn to the senses as a coherent response to these challenges in part because they are common to all humans, even as their exercise is deeply individual to each. The senses are a privileged site for continuing to think through the implications of human commonality and human difference, and this general point can in large part explain the growth of studies surrounding the senses across disciplines in recent years: Digby is of interest because he grasped this issue so clearly, and responded to it so acutely. The notion of sensory autobiography is helpful precisely because it contains *in nuce* the central question raised by the senses themselves in the early modern period: are the senses the basis of an individual life story, those memories and experiences that can be related but not truly shared, just as Digby's readers could not travel to Scanderoon or Algiers and feel or listen for themselves? Or are the senses precisely the route by which the lives of others and their stories can be made available, rendered vivid? Digby for his part insisted that his sensory experiences – whether of his recently deceased wife or of the Mediterranean Sea – were both vividly accessible, and irreducibly his and his alone, both transformed utterly and entirely unchanged by his double conversion.

Notes

1 Multiple conversion in this period has been relatively little studied as a phenomenon in its own right. For an exception see Alison Shell, 'Multiple Religious Conversion and the *Menippean* Self: the Case of Richard Carpenter', in *Catholicism and Anti-Catholicism in Seventeenth-Century Texts*, ed. Arthur K. Marotti (Basingstoke: Macmillan, 1999), 154–97.

2 *The Earl of Strafforde's Letters and Dispatches*, ed. William Lowler (London, 1739), 1.474. Emphases in the original. The news was almost certainly broken with Digby's approval, if not at his direction, since he and Howell were life-long friends. There are a series of letters to Digby in Howell's *Epistolae Ho-Elianae*, and in Digby's late work on the so-called 'Powder of Sympathy', it was Howell's wounded hand that he claims to have cured from a distance with his amazing invention.

3 See Michael Foster, 'Walter Montague, Courtier, Diplomat and Abbot, 1603–77 – I', *The Downside Review* 96 (1978): 85–102, 95–8; Richard W. Serjeantson, 'Elizabeth Cary and the Great Tew Circle', in *The Literary Career and Legacy of Elizabeth Cary, 1613–1680*, ed. Heather Wolfe (New York: Palgrave Macmillan, 2007), 165–82.

4 See Philip Hughes, 'The Conversion of Charles I', *The Clergy Review* 8 (1934): 113–25; 114–16; Gordon Albion, *Charles I and the Court of Rome* (Louvain: Bureaux du Recueil, Bibliotheque de l'Université, 1935), 193–215; Elfriede Dubois, 'Conversions a la Cour de la Reine Henriette-Marie', in *La Conversion au XVIIe Siecle: Actes du XIIe Colloque de Marseille* (Marseille: CMR, 1983), 201–208; Caroline Hibbard, *Charles I and the Popish Plot* (Chapel Hill: University of North Carolina Press, 1983).

5 For Everard Digby's trial and execution see Mark Nicholls, *Investigating Gunpowder Plot* (Manchester: Manchester University Press, 1991), 19–20, 34, 42, 52–57; Antonia Fraser, *The Gunpowder Plot: Terror & Faith in 1605* (London: Weidenfeld & Nicolson, 1996), 225–26, 229–32.

6 For brief discussions of Digby in the context of conversion see Anthony Milton, *Catholic and Reformed: The Roman and Protestant Churches in English Protestant Thought, 1600–1640* (Cambridge: Cambridge University Press, 1995), 84, 233–34; Michael C. Questier, *Conversion, Politics and Religion in England, 1580–1625* (Cambridge: Cambridge University Press, 1996),182n62; Molly Murray, *The Poetics of Conversion in Early Modern English Literature* (Cambridge: Cambridge University Press, 2009), 114–15, 121; passim for an excellent account of the impact and expressive implications of conversion.

7 Giovanni Soranzo to the Doge and Senate of Venice, 27 December 1630, *Calendar of State Papers and Manuscripts, Relating to English Affairs, Existing in the Archives and Collections of Venice, and in Other Libraries of Northern Italy, Volume 22: 1629–1632*, ed. Allen B. Hinds (London: Longman, Roberts, and Green, 1919), 452.

8 I discuss these events, and the literary dimensions of Digby's voyage, in detail in '"Spencerus isthic conditur": Kenelm Digby's Transcription of William Alabaster', *Spenser Studies* 27 (2012): 315–28, and in 'Sir Kenelm Digby's Interruptions: Piracy and Lived Romance in the 1620s', *Studies in Philology* 113 (2016): 424–483.

9 Francis Haskell, *The King's Pictures: The Formation and Dispersal of the Collections of Charles I and his Courtiers*, ed. Karen Serres (New Haven, CT: Yale University Press, 2013), 7.

10 Samuel R. Gardiner, *History of England, 1603–42* (London: Longmans, Green, 1889–93), 8.231. For Gardiner's wider tendency to distinguish Protestant men of character as agents of historical change from others who were irrelevant to it see John S. A. Adamson, 'Eminent Victorians: S.R. Gardiner and the Liberal as Hero', *The Historical Journal* 33 (1990): 641–57.

11 For an account of Venetia's death which recognises but ultimately overstates its significance to Digby's later intellectual output see Bruce Janacek, 'Catholic Natural Philosophy: Alchemy and the Revivification of Sir Kenelm Digby', in

Rethinking the Scientific Revolution, ed. Margaret J. Osler (Cambridge: Cambridge University Press, 2000), 89–118.

12 The fullest discussion of these events, though unevenly reliable, are the essays collected in *Death, Passion and Politics: Van Dyck's Portraits of Venetia Stanley and George Digby*, ed. Ann Sumner (London: Dulwich Picture Gallery, 1995). The poems by Jonson and others are contained in British Library MS Additional 30259. For the funeral monument see Brian *Burch*, 'Sir Kenelm *Digby* and *Christchurch, Newgate* Street', *Guildhall Miscellany* 2 (1964): 248–56.

13 John Aubrey, *Brief Lives*, ed. John Buchanan-Brown (London: Penguin, 2000), 113.

14 Aubrey, *Brief Lives*, ed. Buchanan-Brown, 113.

15 I am grateful to my student, Ted Tregear, for discussion of this point.

16 This is made clear by a note written on the surviving copy of the letter in the library of the Society of Antiquaries, London.

17 *The History of the Troubles and Tryal of the Most Reverend Father in God, and blessed martyr, William Laud. . .and some other things relating to the history* (London, 1695), 614.

18 Kenelm Digby, *A Conference with a Lady about Choice of Religion* (Paris, 1638), 20–21.

19 Ibid., 37.

20 Ibid., 66.

21 Ibid., 79.

22 Ibid., 85.

23 Ibid., 102.

24 John 20:29, King James Version.

25 Glenn Most, *Doubting Thomas* (Cambridge, MA: Harvard University Press, 2005), esp. 145. Elsewhere, though, I have argued that Most overstates the Protestant minimization of Thomas's touch, and explored the enduring role of Doubting Thomas in cross-confessional seventeenth century writing: see *Feeling Pleasures: The Sense of Touch in Renaissance England* (Oxford: Oxford University Press, 2014), 75–7, 81–2.

26 Digby, *A Conference with a Lady*, 102.

27 These notes are in BL MS Add 41846, ff.166–8.

28 For further discussion see my article, '"A sensible touching, feeling and groping": Metaphor and Sensory Experience in the English Reformation', in *Passions and Subjectivity in Early Modern Culture*, ed. Brian Cummings and Freya Sierhuis (Farnham: Ashgate, 2013), 183–99, and *Feeling Pleasures*, chapters 1–2.

29 Kenelm Digby to Kenelm, John and George Digby, 18 May 1633, in 'A New Digby Letter-Book: "In Praise of Venetia,"' ed. Vittorio Gabrieli, *National Library of Wales Journal* 9 (1955): 129–30.

30 'A New Digby Letter-Book', 130.

31 Kenelm Digby to John Digby, 24 June 1633, in 'A New Digby Letter-Book', ed. Gabrieli, 143.

32 'A New Digby Letter-Book', 145.

33 'A New Digby Letter-Book', 101.

34 Kenelm Digby, *Observations Upon Religio Medici* (London, 1643), 11.

35 Kenelm Digby, *Two treatises in the one of which the nature of bodies, in the other, the nature of mans soule is looked into in way of discovery of the immortality of reasonable soules* (Paris, 1644), unpaginated preface.

36 John Henry, 'Atomism and Eschatology: Catholicism and Natural Philosophy in the Interregnum', *The British Journal for the History of Science* 15 (1982): 211–239 (at 225).

37 See Christa Mercer, 'The Vitality and Importance of Early Modern Aristotelianism', in *The Rise of Modern Philosophy: The Tension Between the New and Traditional Philosophies from Machiavelli to Leibniz*, ed. Tom Sorrell (Oxford: Clarendon Press, 1993), 33–67 (at 62–66).

38 See Ann Wilbur Mackenzie, 'The Reconfiguration of Sensory Experience', in *Reason, Will and Sensation: Studies in Descartes's Metaphysics*, ed. John Cottingham (Oxford: Clarendon, 1994), 251–72.

39 On the rhetorical basis of this scene see Michel Foucault, 'My Body, This Paper, This Fire', trans. Geoff Bennington, *The Oxford Literary Review* 4 (1979): 9–28.

40 I discuss these events in significantly more detail in 'Sir Kenelm Digby's Interruptions'.

41 Digby, *Two Treatises*, 39, 45.

42 Ibid., 48.

43 For the wider debates in this period regarding the corporeality of light see David Park, *The Fire Within the Eye: A Historical Essay on the Nature and Meaning of Light* (Princeton, NJ: Princeton University Press, 1997), chapter 6.

44 Digby, *Two Treatises*, 253.

45 Ibid., 258.

46 Ibid., 243. See my discussion in *Feeling Pleasures*, 211.

47 For their connections see Lawrence M. Principe, *The Aspiring Adept: Robert Boyle and His Alchemical Quest* (Princeton, NJ: Princeton University Press, 1998), 167.

48 Robert Boyle, 'Of the Temperature of the Submarine Regions', in *The Works of the Honourable Robert Boyle*, ed. Thomas Birch (London, 1744), 3. 342–49; 342.

49 Stephen Shapin, *A Social History of Truth: Civility and Science in Seventeenth-Century England* (Chicago: University of Chicago Press, 1994), 260.

50 Kenelm Digby, *Journal of a Voyage into the Mediterranean*, ed. John Bruce (London: J.B. Nichols and Sons, 1868), 58.

51 Digby, *Two Treatises*, 251.

52 For the fame of Scanderoon's carrier pigeons see 'Part of a Letter from William Biddulph, from Aleppo', in Samuel Purchas, *Hakluytus Posthumus or Purchas His Pilgrimes* (Glasgow: James MacLehose and Sons, 1905–7), 8.260; James Mather, *Pashas: Traders and Travellers in the Islamic World* (New Haven, CT: Yale University Press, 2009), 19.

53 I am grateful to Mark Jenner for first alerting me to the notion of sensory biography.

54 C. Nadia Seremetakis, 'Implications', in *The Senses Still: Perception and Memory as Material Culture in Modernity*, ed. C. Nadia Seremetakis (Chicago: University of Chicago Press, 1994), 123–45 (at 129).

55 Robert Desjarlais, *Sensory Biographies: Lives and Deaths Among Nepal's Yolmo Buddhists* (Berkeley: University of California Press, 2003), 341–43.

5 The senses and the seventeenth-century English conversion narrative

Abigail Shinn

The conversion narrative, a text which recounts a process of confessional change or spiritual awakening, is recognised as being one of the most dynamic literary forms associated with early modern religious culture. Growing out of the turmoil of the post-Reformation English church as well as the emergence of divergent Protestant sects in the Civil War period, the early modern conversion narrative is often equated with spiritual autobiography, although the parameters of autobiography in this period are by no means uncontested.[1] The work of Kathleen Lynch, Bruce Hindmarsh, Patricia Caldwell, and Michael Questier has done much to illuminate our understanding of the form's prevalence and complexity, and the genre is frequently allied to the Protestant literary tradition and the religious writings of John Bunyan.[2]

Variously read as 'an act of self-interpretation' or the result of combined political and religious motivations, conversion narratives are often composed by men and women to offer proof of a change in confession or spiritual awakening.[3] Crucially, they are also designed to provoke further change on the part of the reader; converts frequently attest to their hopes that their individual story will inspire others to join their faith. Many of these texts consequently rely upon patterns of religious experience, typified by a movement from despair to comfort, that are replicated within religious communities in order to form a pathway to conversion that can be followed by future members of a congregation.[4] They are produced by both Protestant and Catholic believers and can be found in print and manuscript. The result of a rhetorically literate culture, conversion narratives also rely upon a number of commonplace figures and tropes in order to add substance to what is, in effect, an invisible and unquantifiable spiritual change.[5] One of the most prevalent of these commonplaces is the use of the senses and sensory experience as a locus for spiritual transformation. The senses are repeatedly invoked by converts as liminal conduits between the earthly and the divine, but this is also accompanied by the use of sensory metaphors which succeed in producing a similar effect while ostensibly bypassing the body.

Scholars have come to recognise that early modern religious experience is overwhelmingly mediated by sensory discourses and practices, and that despite the Protestant emphasis upon language and the whitewashing of churches after the Reformation, often framed as a shift from the eyes to the ears, religion continued to be a full synaesthetic experience for believers.[6] Richard Brathwaite argues in his *Essaies vpon the Fiue Senses* (1620) that the senses are the conduits through which the Devil reached the believer: 'the *fiue Sences*. . .be those *fiue gates*, by which the world doth besiege vs, the Deuill doth tempt vs, and the flesh ensnare vs'.[7] Similarly, converts often describe moments of demonic or divine intercession that are enacted via the senses. The senses are simultaneously identified as instrumental agents in an ongoing dialogue with supernatural forces, and reactive conduits which provoke movement on the part of the believer. The sensate language of the body thereby provides a powerful system of comparison which can concretise and reify that which is invisible to others, a phenomenon allied to the doctrine of accommodation (the notion that God adapts divine truths in order to make them accessible to the limited comprehension of fallen humanity).[8]

In this chapter, I explore how the senses and sensory metaphor are harnessed by both Protestant and Catholic converts in order to ally their spiritual change to corporeal systems of exchange and metamorphosis. While we might expect Protestant converts to be more likely to employ the distancing effects of metaphor in order to avoid charges of sensuality, Catholic converts also utilise metaphor. Furthermore, Protestants are not always averse to the sensory when describing their conversion experiences. Central to the use of sensory language as a bridge between the divine and the bodily, however, is the capacity of such language to erase any distinction between the literal and the figural.[9] This is a phenomenon that Nigel Smith identifies as a crucial component of the prophetic tenor of radical Protestant conversion narratives, but the conflation of the literal and figurative at the level of sensation is present in a discursive range of conversion texts from different faiths and sects.[10] The indistinct boundaries of corporeal and metaphorical sensing thus allow the convert to harness both the symbolic and physiological power of sensation, even when wielding a rhetorical trope.

Examining both Catholic and Protestant narratives, as well as more diverse sources for attitudes to conversion, including rhetoric manuals and religious treatises, I will demonstrate that despite the early modern period's adversarial culture of conversion, the senses act as an important cross-confessional trope for writers across a range of literary modes. The texts that form the basis of my study span the length of the seventeenth century (one of the richest periods for the circulation of conversion narratives, particularly in print) in order to determine the persistent and pervasive role played by the senses in shaping a language of conversion during this period.[11] I will begin by exploring the relationship between the soul and sensation, and then move on to a number of examples of converts who cite the senses as transformative loci for their experiences. This will necessitate an examination of the distinction between the corporeal senses, and the inner spiritual senses, which were often used to search the believer for the truth of their salvation. Finally, I will consider the role played by sensory metaphor in shaping and elucidating the process of conversion. Such is the cliché of the believer who has 'seen the light' or 'heard the voice of God' that the role of sensory language in conversion texts has frequently been overlooked. My aim in this essay is to argue that sensory language in fact occupies a complex position at the edge of literal and figurative bodies and plays a central role in the fashioning of the new convert into a believable and persuasive entity.

The soul and sensation

The immortal soul was the cornerstone of Christian theology and its effect upon the mortal concerns of the flesh prior to death was a preoccupation of religious, medical, and literary writing.[12] Michael Schoenfeldt has persuasively argued that for early moderns 'bodily condition, subjective state, and psychological character are. . .fully imbricated' and that a sense of self can only be understood in relation to the body.[13] Schoenfeldt also notes that Galenic medicine maintained that the behaviour of the soul depended on the temperature of the body, so that 'the purportedly immaterial subject is constituted as a profoundly material substance'.[14] The soul, like the body, could therefore be affected by changes in environment and diet. As William Vaughan claims in his *Directions for Health* (1600), 'there is a great concord betwixt the bodies qualities and the soules affections', a link explored by the nonconformist minister Richard Baxter in his posthumously published *Reliquiae Baxterianae* (1696) when he equates copious sweating with the purging of sin.[15] An individual could also be described as being soul-sick, as is the case with the sixteenth-century Spaniard and Protestant backslider Francis Spira. Falling ill after he renounces his Protestantism, he is sent to Padua and examined by eminent physicians who can find nothing wrong with him. Spira ascribes his illness to his apostasy claiming '*neither potions, plaisters, nor drugs . . .can helpe a fainting soul cast downe with sense of sinne, and the wrath of God*'.[16] Such a reading of Spira's sickness was possible because people believed that the soul could only be perceived through the workings of the body, as Helkiah Crooke notes in the *Microcosmographia* (1615):

> [. . .] the knowledge of the soule cannot be made manifest but onely by her operations, which also seeing she doth not performe without the helpe of corporall organs, there is a necessity imposed, that wee also vnderstand the exact composition of the body.[17]

It is essential for people to understand the body if they wish to understand the soul, although, following the Fall, this knowledge can only be limited in scope.[18] Consequently, when the convert gestures, weeps, sweats, and senses, the condition of their body can be directly related to the state of their soul.

Both influenced by the environment and assessed via the constitution of the body, the soul also operated as an instrument of consumption comparable to the mouth and digestive system. In *A Christian Love-Letter* (1606), a Protestant named John Swynnerton recounts his frustration that the object of his affection has been converted to Catholicism by a 'little booke', using language which connects reading to the ingestion of Popish poison which fails to sate the hunger of the consumer:[19]

> [. . .] to haue your soule (after such sort) to be fed, or rather feasted and not fed, or rather filled, and not feasted: but to speak more properly, neither fed, nor feasted, nor filled, but flatly poisoned with such Italian drugs, with such superstitious and Antichristian confections, as in the said booke. [20]

Swynnerton's focus on the soul being 'neither fed, nor feasted, nor filled' but poisoned, indicates that the consumption of Catholic writing is an empty gesture which gives only the appearance of nourishment. In this case, the site of literary ingestion is the soul rather than the stomach, indicating the extent to which the soul was understood to function in ways comparable to bodily systems.

The soul also played a fundamental role in shaping theories of sensation in the early modern period. This was because the seat of sensation was commonly located in the soul, although writers often disagreed about precisely where the soul itself was situated. Aristotle argues that the soul resides in the heart and when summarising the opinions of his predecessors in the *De Anima* he states that beings that have a soul can be distinguished from those that do not by their capacity for sense perception and their ability to instigate movement.[21] Sensation was thereby intrinsically connected to the presence of the soul. Furthermore, Aristotle argues that movement on the part of the soul often derives from sensory processes: 'the most obvious way in which one might say that the soul is moved . . .would be by the objects of perception'.[22] The soul was therefore reactive to sensory systems. Crooke, following Galen, argues that 'the Brain is the common instrument of Sensation or the organ of all the senses' and that 'it [the brain] is the instrument by which the *Sensatiue Soule* perceiueth all sensible qualities, yea distinguisheth and iudgeth of them'.[23] The Galenic model locates the soul in the brain and thus connects sensation to this organ, rather than the heart. Whether centred on the heart or the brain, however, the resulting connection between body and soul in a heuristic economy presided over by the perceptive faculties influences the way that the sensate or 'feeling' soul is articulated by converts. If the state of the body can affect the state of the soul and vice versa, then converts' analogies between the two are not simply metaphorical; rather they reflect a genuine sense of interchange.

The Church of England clergyman and lexicographer Robert Cawdray in his *Treasvrie or Storehovse of Similes* (1600), a rhetoric manual which is structured as a commonplace book, articulates the belief that the soul itself feels in much the same way as the flesh in an entry under the title *Feeling of Faith*:

> And altogether like as the disposition of the body followeth the qualitie and temperature of the ayre, Elements and exercises, to which wee giue our selues: Euen so according to the places where we liue, and the nourishment that wee there take, is the estate of our soules and consciences. But bee it that water is sometime hote, and sometime colde, and that it chaunge his qualities, sometimes one way, sometimes an other, yet it is alwaies water; Euen so the man that is elect, after his regeneration, is always faithfull, howsoeuer in that he is the child of *Adam*, he bee sometimes enclined to euill, and that his Faith be not alwayes accompanied with the like zeale and affection. For oftentimes it commeth to passe, that we feele Iesus Christ to stirre and mooue himselfe in vs, and by and by after, wee haue no manner of Feeling at all: But therefore hee ceaseth not to dwell in vs, no more then our soules doo dwell in our bodies when we sleepe, although in sleeping, wee neither Feele them, nor any of their operations.[24]

Cawdray argues that election does not guarantee that the convert will be impervious to temptation. Much as the body alters along with the temperature and quality of its environment, the soul is subject to reverberations in its complexion once the first zeal and enthusiasm which accompanies conversion has passed. Cawdray emphasises, however, that despite the potential for the soul to incline towards evil, the groundwork of election remains constant, albeit fluid: 'it is alwaies water'. The sensate soul will sometimes fail to feel the movement of Christ, but this is not a sign that the believer has been abandoned, only that the initial tempest has passed. Cawdray compares this process to the quietude of the soul in sleep when 'wee neither Feele them, nor any of their operations'. In this way, the soul was frequently described by converts as 'feeling' in a similar way to the body and feeling most acutely at the moment of conversion. As the former Catholic priest and Protestant convert Richard Sheldon notes in his *Motives* (1612): 'I sensibly feele (in such sort as the soule can feele) my vnderstanding and soule, as it were a new inlightned, illustrated, conforted, and encouraged by a new change and translation out of the shadow of darknesse, into the Kingdome of Gods beloued sonne Iesus'.[25] Following his conversion Sheldon *feels* that his soul now basks in the light of divinity, an incidence of the commonplace of conversion or revelation being figured as a movement from darkness to light which links the metaphor to the 'felt' experience of the soul. This is qualified, however, by Sheldon's observation that he sensibly feels 'in such sort as the soule can feele', implying that the feeling soul is by no means easy to observe and that its sensations do not directly correspond to embodied sensation.

The soul's ability to feel is also linked to its preparation prior to conversion, particularly in Protestant texts interested in the workings of humiliation. As the Scottish minister Arthur Morton notes in *The Touch-Stone of Conversion* (1647), in response to the question '*What be the marks that go before faith?*', 'the Lord. . .works in them that. . .ground-work of humiliation in the soule, and consequently a very sensible change, a work indeed painfull, & not joyous for the present'.[26] A 'sensible change' accompanied by pain (albeit only in the present), stands for Morton as a sign, a 'mark', for a coming conversion: the soul must sense the 'work' of God before it can begin the long road to salvation.

Sensing conversion

The soul is thus understood as a locus for sensory perception and fully implicated in the workings and environment of the body. When the convert's spiritual complexion changed it is felt in the soul as an – often-painful – sensate experience. The feeling soul therefore provides the background to conversion texts which articulate instances of powerful revelatory experience which occur at the threshold to the body – the senses.

Tobie Matthew, the son of the archbishop of York who converted to Catholicism while travelling in Italy in 1605, describes an Augustinian moment of auditory influence in his autobiography:

> Every day there passed once, and sometimes oftener, under my window, near a certain hour, a procession of little boys, singing the litanies of our B. Lady And I know not by what chance, or rather Providence of Almighty God, the tune of that sweet verse, *Sancta Maria, Ora pro nobis*, came so often in at mine ears, and contented me so much that at length my tongue took it up; not indeed as a prayer (such was my misfortune at that time; for it is a misery to have been, at any time, other than our B. Lady's most humble servant) but as a song, whose ditty fell not unpleasingly to that air, and so when I found myself alone, my usual entertainment would be to sing *Sancta Maria, Ora pro nobis*, in the tune of those babes and suckling's, who showed forth her praise. These would ordinarily fall out to be the last words before my sleep, and the first after it and though I pronounced them, at that time, but like a parrot, yet those words made me grow into some few thoughts; and I considered now and then what hurt

there might be, in desiring the Mother of God to pray for us; and at least I was enured thereby to pronounce them, not long after, as I now do.[27]

Matthew's parrot-like repetition of a phrase from the litany of the blessed virgin – albeit as song rather than prayer – precipitates his conversion experience. The cumulative effect of hearing it sung every day by 'little boys' while he was in Naples ensures that he cannot get the prayer out of his head and eventually his 'tongue took it up'. He proceeds to sing *Sancta Maria, Ora pro nobis* – 'Holy Mother pray for us' – before going to sleep and upon awakening, his ritual both reminiscent of Compline, the final church service for Catholics at the end of the day, and the Angelus prayer's traditional recitation at morning, midday and the end of the day (the Angelus, like the litany of the blessed virgin, includes the phrase *Sancta Maria, Ora pro nobis* but with the inclusion of 'mother of God': 'Sancta Maria, Mater Dei, ora pro nobis'). This has a clear antecedent in Augustine's conversion in the garden in Milan, as recounted in his *Confessions*, where he hears disembodied voices, either of 'a boy or a girl', reciting the phrase 'pick up and read' (*tolle lege, tolle lege*), which he interprets as a 'divine command. . .to open the book [the Bible] and read the first chapter I might find'.[28] For Matthew, divine intercession comes through the ear in a similar manner to Augustine, but this providential act of hearing leads to the daily verbal repetition of a prayer which initially parodies Catholic practice before affecting a fundamental spiritual change. Matthew's experience thereby charts a trajectory from hearing to singing, from the passive reception of the senses to an active participation in Catholic liturgy, which *creates* rather than simply expresses a change in faith. This is an instance of the unconscious reception of the divine via the senses that reverses the typical framing of Catholicism as the religion of the eye and Protestantism as the religion of the ear.

The view that the ear was a conduit for God's grace was a commonly held belief, as articulated by the clergyman Stephen Egerton in his treatise *The Boring of the Eare* (1623): 'to hear. . .is to attend with the eare, to receiue with the heart, to conuert in the life and conuersation, else our sinfull soules can neuer be healed'.[29] For Egerton, the ear is the link to the heart and thereby the primary site for conversion in life and conversation. The figuration of the ear as a conduit to the soul or the heart, Jennifer Rae McDermott argues, both responded to and appropriated 'medical language of permeability, fluidity, and invasion', particularly following the discovery of the Eustachian tube, the thin corridor connecting the ear and the throat.[30] This discovery provides an interesting medical parallel with Matthew's shift from hearing the litany to singing it to himself, as the Eustachian tube allows liquids and other soluble substances to be conveyed into the interior of the body via firstly the ear and then secondly the throat. Matthew's auditory revelation thereby references both the commonplace that grace can enter the soul via the senses and the anatomical understanding of the ear as a permeable orifice which connects the outside world to the depths of the body's interior.

In *A further Account of the progreß of the Gospel Amongst the Indians In New England* (1660), the Protestant missionary John Eliot's description of the conversion of the native Algonquian-speaking peoples repeatedly uses the word 'heard' and 'hearing' in order to highlight how the reading aloud of scripture precipitates religious change.[31] In the narrative of a convert called Anthony, Anthony routinely uses the phrase 'I heard' before recounting an episode from the Bible or quoting scripture.[32] The implication is that at this point in his conversion he could not read English and was therefore reliant upon Eliot and his fellow missionaries for his auditory exposure to the word of God. Anthony's narrative, like those of the other Algonquins in the collection, is framed as an oral confession made in front of the missionary church elders. Early on he states that 'I hope Christ hath taught mee his Word; Oh let him (my Lord!) help mee to speak it'.[33] Like Matthew, Anthony therefore moves from the auditory consumption of God's grace to vocalising his newly converted state, a transition which is potentially also marked by his increasing ability to both understand and speak English. This is an instance of cross-confessional parity between Catholic and Protestant narratives at the level of sensation, even if what the two converts hear falls along confessional lines: Matthew's change of heart is prompted by hearing a Catholic litany, while Anthony is inspired by hearing scripture spoken aloud. This is also evidence of two narratives related to spaces outside of England harnessing the senses as a powerful conversionary force. The permeability of the senses ensures that the possibility of metamorphosis is always present within the structures of the human body regardless of geography, religion, or race.

The senses' position at the threshold to the soul ensured that converts were acutely aware of the power of sense perception to alter their spiritual makeup. They also had an important role to play in judicial systems of proof, as signs or marks of proof were understood, in the words of the schoolmaster Richard Sherry, to be those occurrences which 'come vnder the sences of men'.[34] The importance of the organs of sense perception for religious feeling was, however, a source of contention for early moderns, with some arguing that reliance upon the senses for proof of the divine was tantamount to a failure to trust in God. The writer Thomas Browne in his *Religio Medici* (1643) argues that the proof offered by the senses undercuts the 'greater blessing' offered by blind faith:

> I desire to exercise my faith in the difficultest point, for to credit ordinary and visible objects is not faith, but perswasion. Some believe the better for seeing Christ his Sepulchre, and when they have seene the Red Sea, doubt not of the miracle. Now contrarily I blesse my selfe,

and am thankefull that I lived not in the dayes of miracles, that I never saw Christ nor his Disciples; I would not have beene one of those Israelites that passed the Red Sea, nor one of Christs Patients, on whom he wrought his wonders; then had my faith been thrust upon me, nor should I enjoy that greater blessing pronounced to all that believe & saw not. 'Tis an easie and necessary beliefe to credit what our eye and sense hath examined [. . .][35]

Browne reads the information gathered by the embodied senses as a persuasive force, but argues that faith itself should be blind: 'to credit ordinary and visible objects is not faith, but perswasion'. He goes so far as to argue that he is glad that he does not live in the time of Jesus as to do so would lessen 'that greater blessing pronounced to all that believe & saw not'.

In contrast to the physical organs of sense perception, which could overwhelm or distract the believer from the dictates of true faith, the spiritual or inner senses were often afforded greater weight in religious discourse. Augustine in Book X of the *Confessions* outlines the role of the spiritual or inner senses and pledges to 'rise above' the physical sense perceptions shared with 'the horse and mule'.[36] When asking what it is that he loves about God, Augustine outlines two fields of sensory awareness, one exterior and one interior:

[. . .] when I love you, what do I love? It is not physical beauty nor temporal glory nor the brightness of light dear to earthly eyes, nor the sweet melodies of all kinds of songs, nor the gentle odour of flowers or ointments and perfumes, nor manna or honey, nor limbs welcoming the embraces of the flesh; it is not these I love when I love my God. Yet there is a light I love, and a food, and a kind of embrace of my inner man, where my soul is floodlit by light which space cannot contain, where there is sound that time cannot seize, where there is a perfume which no breeze disperses, where there is a taste for food no amounting of eating can lessen, and where there is a bond of union that no satiety can part. That is what I love when I love my God.[37]

It is not the wonders of earthly sense perception which inspire Augustine's love, but rather the senses of the 'inner man'. For Augustine, the interior senses are inexhaustible counterparts to the limited physical senses; they have no boundaries and will never be sated. The inner senses, which inspire the love of the believer by providing proof of God's glory, have the potential to be harnessed by men and women when searching themselves for the signs of sin and faith. There is consequently a distinction to be made between relying upon the physical senses for proof of the presence of God (a tendency that Browne warns against) and harnessing the inner senses as a heuristic aid when trying to ascertain one's status as a believer (a method recommended by a number of early modern authors).

It was this latter understanding of the spiritual senses that inspired the personal reflection advocated in conversion texts such as *The Sound Beleever. Or, a Treatise of Evangelicall Conversion* (1645) by the Massachusetts minister Thomas Shepard. Shepard aligns proof of faith with the capacity of the spiritual senses to perceive the marks of sin, figured here as marks or tokens of plague:

> I shall hereafter prove that there can be no faith without sense of sinne and misery, and now there can be no sense of sinne without a precedent sight or conviction of sin; no man can feele sin, unlesse he first see it; what the ey sees not, the heart rues not. . .As a man that hath the plague not knowing the disease, he hopes to live; but when he sees the spots and tokens of death, upon his wrist, now he cryes out, because convinced that the plague of the Lord is upon him; so when men see some one or more speciall sins break out, now they are convinced of their lamentable condition. [38]

Sight has to precede a 'sense of sin' as sin cannot be 'felt' unless it is first seen by the eye of the believer. In this instance, the metaphor of disease or plague produces a powerful justification for the power of sight as a spiritual sense and it is the spiritual senses that provide the catalyst for fundamental change: an internal recognition of the boils and pustules left by sin guarantees metamorphosis. This sentiment is echoed in Morton's *Touch-Stone of Conversion* (1647) when he argues that 'it behoves every man to use all deligence to make his calling and election sure, to get clear evidence of his interest in and union with the Lord Jesus Christ'.[39] Morton goes on to make a clear distinction between the clumsiness of the 'naturall eye' versus the probing subtlety of the 'inner eye' in this process of evidence gathering:

> Concerning thy sinfulnesse and corruptions: try if thou doest see and perceive them, if thou be convinced of them, and they be discovered unto thee; and not onely those grosser ones which a naturall eye may perceive; but try if thou seest thy inward, spirituall, subtile, and most secret corruptions, as thy hypocrisie, infidelitie, spirituall idolatrie, a whoring of thy heart, &c. for then mayest thou comfort thy self, that the Lord hath performed that his promise, in some measure toward thee.[40]

If the penitent sinner recognises their inner corruptions in this fashion and is 'earnest with the Lord', then 'according to his promise, he would circumcise thy heart, and cause thee to love him with the whole heart'.[41] A successful application of sensate probing to the incorporeal soul will lead to the oldest mark or token of conversion – circumcision – although in this instance as an interiorised proof realised through the inner senses rather than a bodily process.

Sensory perception is therefore not only a point of entry to both the body and the soul, but also the means by which the convert can garner proof of their religious condition. The spiritual senses which are employed to search the interior of the convert are simultaneously connected to and detached from the bodily organs of sense perception. Their use by converts highlights how the invisible processes of religious change are frequently understood via corporeal systems, but also how central the language of sensation (both physical and spiritual) is to the early modern culture of conversion more generally.

Sensory metaphor

As well as the physical and spiritual senses acting as transformative entry points and tools for religious self-examination, there is a long tradition of using sensory language in religious meditative practice. This is emphasised in Brathwaite's *Essaies vpon the Fiue Senses* when Brathwaite directs the senses towards the body of Christ:

> [. . .] I haue tyed my selfe to my spouse in all my *Sences*; being *He*, that ministers refreshment to all my *Sences*. If I *eye* any thing, it shall be my Sauiours crosse; if I *heare* any thing, it shall be my Sauiours praise; if I *touch* any thing, it shall be my Sauiours wounds; if I *taste* any thing, it shall be my Sauiours *comforts*; if I *smell* any thing, it shall be my Sauiours oyntments.[42]

Brathwaite seems to here be ruminating on the spiritual senses, but he does not identify them as such, instead conflating the physical and the inner senses in order to argue that the five forms of sensory perception should be trained solely upon Christ. This indeterminacy is achieved because of the variety of senses harnessed in the excerpt. While it is plausible that Brathwaite can '*eye*' Christ on the cross (in the form of a crucifix or painting) and '*heare*' his praise using his physical senses, he would have to use the spiritual senses in order to touch Christ's wounds, smell his ointment or taste his '*comforts*'. Brathwaite's overlaying of embodied sense and spiritual sense privileges the senses as a conduit to God, particularly when focusing upon the crucified body of Christ as a meditative object. This elision of the distinction between the literal and the figural, between the embodied and the imagined at the level of sensation, allies the Christian with the bodily hermeneutics of doubting Thomas as he probes Christ's wounds. This urge to '*touch*', '*taste*', '*eye*' '*heare*', and '*smell*' the absent body of the saviour is founded upon a desire to tangibly witness his suffering and sacrifice. This form of spiritual sense is not directed primarily at self-reflection or self-discovery, however, but rather moves outwards to both manifest and explore an embodied Christ.[43] For Brathwaite, the senses operate simultaneously on a bodily and spiritual plane, thereby providing a focus for spiritual animation and meditation.

The potential for the physical and spiritual senses to overlap in this manner is also reflected in the difficulty associated with distinguishing the spiritual senses from sensory metaphor. Spiritual perception is often differentiated from sensory metaphor via an emphasis on the closely ana-logous relationship between physical and spiritual sensation. In contrast, sensory metaphor does not rely upon a close relationship to the corporeal sensorium.[44] This difference, however, does not preclude the possibility of the spiritual senses merging with metaphor as any binary opposition between felt experience and literary construct has the potential to collapse in the same manner that Brathwaite merges the spiritual and physi-cal senses for meditative ends. This ensures that the distinction between physical, spiritual, and metaphorical sensing is often indeterminate rather than absolute. This indeterminacy allows converts to wield sensory metaphor as a rhetorical form which nonetheless remains connected to both corporeal perception and spiritual sensation.

Sensory metaphor ostensibly bypasses the body while providing an evocative means of reifying an invisible alteration in religious sensibility. This can take various forms in conversion narratives but frequently a change in the senses is directly connected to spiritual metamorphosis. For example, believers might describe their conversion as a change in taste or appetite – from gluttony or excess to a more discerning palate. This was the case for John Forent, a former Carmelite friar who converted to Protestantism, whose story is recounted in *The Voluntarie Conversion* (1604):

> I will now swallow no more of those bitter-sweete baites, which haue so long time abused my taste, as now appeareth by this contrarie heauenly sauour. I desire in the company of the Children of God, to feede on liuing bread in the house of the Lord. The Onions, Leekes and Garlike of *AEgypt*, haue seemed most odious and stinking to me, since I tasted the celestiall *Manna*, which the heauens haue rained downe vpon vs.[45]

Forent's claim to have fed on spiritual food in the form of Manna plays on the punning potential of heavenly 'sauour' and heavenly saviour, a Eucharistic image of perpetual nourishment which will ensure that the convert, like the Israelites during the flight out of Egypt, never goes hungry, and also, one imagines, have sweeter smelling breath. Heavenly feeding, Forent envisages, will bring him into a community of the saved who reside in the 'house of the Lord'. This also reinforces the trope of Eucharistic sustenance, but situates the consumption of 'living bread' within the context of Protestant congregation and community. No longer abusing his taste with the bitterness of onions, leeks, and garlic, Forent charts his movement from Catholicism to Protestantism along the same path as the Israelites fleeing Egypt, but realises this change through a shift in palate.

The senses could also be used to emphasise the convert's position within an unbroken line of believers, mirroring the role of sensory experience in the chain of consecration applied to sacred objects such as relics and the host by Catholics. For example, the multiple convert William Alabaster, following his initial conversion to Catholicism, uses the sense of touch to place himself in a consecutive line of converts including St Augustine and St Paul:

> [. . .] that excellent and famed Doctour . . .Saint Augustine, what syghes and sorrowes, what afflictions of mynde what aboundance of teares what vehemency of prayer he gave hym, which the Saint hymselfe describeth most excellently in his bookes of Confessions. And the lyke our Saviour bestowed (or rather much more) upon St Augustines Master, the greatest persecutor then, but afterwards, Doctor, Apostle and Martir, St *Paul* when he opened his eyes from Judaisme to Christiansme. . . wherof I thanke the same God our saviour I had my parte also after when yt pleased his Devine Maiestie to touch me with the same finger of mercy that he had donn to them.[46]

Alabaster maps his own response to conversion, in the form of copious weeping, onto the experiences of two of the most famous converts in the Christian tradition, and claims that this is evidence of how he too has been 'touched' by the 'finger' of God. In drawing a link firstly between himself and St Augustine, and then further back in time to the Biblical figure of St Paul, Alabaster imagines his tears as a form of religious inheritance. This is an inheritance which is achieved via God's touch, ensuring that the sensory metaphor conveys an image of proximity and tactility which validates Alabaster's claim that he is part of an illustrious lineage of converts. As touch was one of the senses most commonly associated with the Catholic reverence for sacred objects, particularly those connected with saints, Alabaster's use of the metaphor also places him squarely within the Catholic sensorium.[47]

The inactive or smothered senses also operates as a metaphor for tepid religious feeling. As the French Protestant convert and former Capuchin John Colleij states in a collection of narratives published in 1601:

> [. . .] those who hitherto haue beene wrapped vp in the palpable darknesse of errour and ignorance, and luld a sleepe vnder the shadow of the wings of that strumpet, hauing ben drunke with the wine of her idolatry, may now awake out of that profound sleepe, and slumber of death, to taste how little soeuer it be of the sauourous fruite of life, and drinke onely a glasse of the delicious waters of the fountaines of

immortalitie, which streame from the house of God, into the assembly of the elect [. . .][48]

Colleij's description of error as a 'palpable darknesse' paradoxically locates blindness in a tangible absence of light, thereby linking the loss of one sense with the heightening of another. The synesthetic combination of sightlessness with touch imagines the unbeliever suffocating in the smothering shadows of their ignorance, before awakening to the sensory delight of election. For Colleij, it is an awakening of the sense of taste in particular which ends the slumber of error, as 'sauourous fruite' and 'delicious waters', which represent the fountain of life and immortality, are starkly contrasted with the drunken sensory deprivation of idolatry.

Similarly, in *Zacheus Converted* (1631), the Protestant writer John Wilson argues that the reading of scripture will awaken those who slumber in darkness, precipitating a forceful, and bodily, intercession by God:

> Many grow slugglish, drowsie, and luke-warme: Now the words of the wise and their writings, are like goads and nailes fastened to the spirits of men, which might quicken them up unto their duties, & their lines being spirituall and sparkling, might set their hearts a burning within them, with a holy zeale for God and his Glory. . .Some hee draggeth as by the haire of the head painfully; others he leades as by the hand gently.[49]

Varying degrees of sensory awareness precipitate this vivid image of the power of God's intercession on the behalf of the convert – a violent jerking out of complacency or a gentle shepherding onto the right path. The Word can act like nails hammered into the soul and the sluggish and drowsy of spirit can expect to be hauled physically into the realm of the elect. The implication is that those whose slumber is shallow require less stimulation to precipitate action.

Conclusion

The instruments of sense perception provide a conduit through which heavenly or demonic forces can affect the constitution of the believer's soul. Converts also understand that their physical senses have a counterpart in the spiritual senses which can be used to search their inner self for proof of their election. The thresholds to the body and soul, however, can also be harnessed as powerful metaphors which help to substantiate any change in the convert's spiritual condition. The importance of the senses and sensory language for converts and their witnesses, both Protestant and Catholic, therefore lies in the way sensate experience brings the divine into the purview of corporeal sensation: the sensing convert looks to the transformative margins of the body in order to add fleshly weight to the intangible. The prevalence of sensory language in these texts also attests to the burden of proof carried by Christian converts who, without recourse to the physical mark of circumcision, have few means by which to proclaim their changed status. While the body is doubtless a locus for anxieties about humankind's sinful nature, its thresholds nonetheless prove invaluable for converts who wish to provide evidence for a metamorphosis which is both unseen and silent.

Notes

1 Kathleen Lynch and Brooke Conti, in particular, have sought to critique spiritual autobiography as a coherent genre. Lynch looks to 'reanimate the aspects of language that constitute social action' by placing Protestant autobiography in the Anglophone world within the context of networks of congregation, community, the print trade, and an emerging scientific empiricism. Conti identifies texts concerned primarily with religious controversy as an important site for autobiographical reflection. Kathleen Lynch, *Protestant Autobiography in the Seventeenth-Century Anglophone World* (Oxford: Oxford University Press, 2012), 12–26; Brooke Conti, *Confessions of Faith in Early Modern England* (Philadelphia: University of Pennsylvania Press, 2014), 2–17.

2 Lynch, *Protestant Autobiography*; D. Bruce Hindmarsh, *The Evangelical Conversion Narrative: Spiritual Autobiography in Early Modern England* (Oxford: Oxford University Press, 2005); Patricia Caldwell, *The Puritan Conversion Narrative: The Beginnings of American Expression* (Cambridge: Cambridge University Press, 2009, first ed. 1983); Michael Questier, *Conversion, Politics and Religion in England, 1580–1625* (Cambridge: Cambridge University Press, 1996). Hindmarsh argues that Bunyan's *Grace Abounding to the Chief of Sinners* (1666) and the *Pilgrim's Progress* (1678) 'helped to establish the form of the conversion narrative', *The Evangelical Conversion Narrative*, 51. Molly Murray's work has also highlighted how the early modern culture of conversion influenced poetic style, *The Poetics of Conversion in Early Modern English Literature: Verse and Change from Donne to Dryden* (Cambridge: Cambridge University Press, 2009).

3 Hindmarsh, *The Evangelical Conversion Narrative*, 6; Questier, *Conversion, Politics and Religion in England*, 3.

4 Conversion texts which follow a particular narrative pathway in this manner tend to belong to radical Protestant sects and are associated with congregation building. See for example, Vavasor Powell, *Sprituall Experiences, of Sundry Beleevers* (London, 1653) and John Rogers, *Ohel or Beth-shemesh: A Tabernacle for the Sun* (London, 1653).

5 The work of Brian Vickers has emphasised the importance of figures and tropes for the expressive power of rhetoric, *In Defence of Rhetoric*, 2nd ed. (Oxford: Clarendon Press, 2002), 294–339.

6 Matthew Milner, *The Senses and the English Reformation* (Farnham: Ashgate, 2011), 6. On the medieval senses and the cultural framing of perception, see C. M. Woolgar, *The Senses in Late Medieval England* (New Haven, CT: Yale University Press, 2006).

7 Richard Brathwaite, *Essaies vpon the Fiue Senses, with a pithie one vpon Detraction. Continued With Sundry Christian Resolues, full of passion and deuotion, purposely composed for the zealously-disposed*, 2nd ed. (London, 1620), E1ʳ.

8 Joad Raymond points out that 'accommodation means that language is *neither* figurative *nor* literal', *Milton's Angels: The Early Modern Imagination* (Oxford: Oxford University Press, 2010), 177.

9 As Joe Moshenska argues, Protestant writers frequently elided any distinction between the literal and figural when harnessing the senses as this allowed English reformers to retain a role for the senses in devotional practice while distancing themselves from the carnality of popery. See Moshenska '"A Sensible Touching, Feeling and Groping": Metaphor and Sensory Experience in the English Reformation', in *Passions and Subjectivity in Early Modern Culture*, ed. Brian Cummings and Freya Sierhuis (Farnham: Ashgate, 2013), 183–199 (at 184).

10 Nigel Smith, *Perfection Proclaimed: Language and Literature in English Radical Religion 1640–1660* (Oxford: Clarendon Press, 1989), 24.

11 Hindmarsh dates the rise of the Evangelical conversion narrative to the mid seventeenth-century, *The Evangelical Conversion Narrative*, 2.

12 The writer who represents the apogee of this preoccupation is John Donne. See Ramie Targoff, *John Donne: Body and Soul* (Chicago, IL: Chicago University Press, 2008).

13 Michael C. Schoenfeldt, *Bodies and Selves in Early Modern England: Physiology and Inwardness in Spenser, Shakespeare, Herbert, and Milton* (Cambridge: Cambridge University Press, 1999), 1.

14 Schoenfeldt, *Bodies and Selves*, 10. Fernando Vidal notes that the dualism resulting from the distinction made between the organic soul, which was connected to the flesh, and the intellective soul, which was immortal, meant that any discussion of psychology in the sixteenth-century, what he terms a 'project in the making', looked to the body, *The Sciences of the Soul: The Early Modern Origins of Psychology*, trans. Saskia Brown (Chicago, IL: University of Chicago Press, 2011), 25.

15 William Vaughan, *Naturall and Artificial Directions for Health* (London, 1600), E2ᵛ. Richard Baxter, *Reliquiae Baxterianae: or Mr Richard Baxter's Narrative of the Most Memorable Passages of his Life and Times*, ed. Matthew Sylvester (London, 1696), C2ʳ.

16 Nathaniel Bacon, *A Relation of the Fearefvll Estate of Francis Spira, in the yeare, 1548* (London, 1638), B9ᵛ. Spira's sickness led to him becoming a curiosity and 'multitudes of all sorts' (B10ʳ) came to see him and marvel at the physical manifestation of his despair. For a compelling examination of conversion as a cure for the diseased soul and its relationship to both embodied rhetoric and the experience of imagined sensation, see Helen Smith, 'Metaphor, Conversion and Cure in Early Modern England', *Renaissance Quarterly* 67 (2014): 473–502. An example of a convert who figures their conversion as a cure is the Catholic convert Benjamin Carier who suffered ongoing illness which led to him visiting Spa where 'I found myselfe rather worse then better. . .therefore I resolved that it was hightime for me to setle my thoughts vpon another world [. . .]', *A Carrier to a King* (St. Omer, 1635), A4ᵛ. On Carier's illness and the 'providential' role played by ill health for converts in general, see Questier, 'Crypto-Catholicism, Anti-Calvinism and Conversion at the Jacobean Court: The Enigma of Benjamin Carier', 57–64. Similarly, the puritan convert Rose Thurgood describes her sin as a 'foul disease' and a 'wound'; this is followed immediately by an account of her 'sister Farnam[s]' 'Fever' and sickness, so that sin and bodily illness are conflated. She also distinguishes between the 'stone in the heart' that is her sin and 'the stone in the kidneyes', an act of differentiation which frames the metaphor in bodily terms, 'A Lecture of Repentance', *Scripture Women: Rose Thurgood, 'A Lecture*

of Repentance' & *Cicely Johnson, 'Fanatical Reveries'*, ed. Naomi Baker (Nottingham: Trent Editions, 2005), 1–27 (at 11–12).

17 Helkiah Crooke, *Microcosmographia: A Description of the body of man* (London, 1615), Iii6[r].

18 After the Reformation, the Fall was central to Protestant theology and the soul was identified as a spiritual organ which encompassed both the potential and the danger of human knowledge. Consequently, Protestant congregations were warned to be skeptical about knowledge of the soul garnered through religious experience. Nonetheless, moments of revelation thought to signal the condition of the soul became a central part of the process of testimony advocated by the churches in the New England colony, Sarah Rivett, *The Science of the Soul in Colonial New England* (Williamsburg, VA: University of North Carolina Press, 2011), 3–4.

19 John Swynnerton, *A Christian Love-Letter: Sent particularly to K. T. a Gentlewoman mis-styled a Catholicke, but generallie intended to all of the Romish Religion, to labour their conuersion to the true faith of Christ Iesus* (London, 1606), B1[r]. The little book is later identified as '*A quarten of reasons of catholicke Religion, with as many briefe reasons of refusall, collected and composed by T. Hill*', B3[v].

20 Swynnerton, *A Christian Love-Letter*, B1[r]

21 Aristotle, *De anima (On the Soul)*, trans. Hugh Lawson-Tancred (London: Penguin, 1986), 132.

22 Aristotle, *De anima*, trans. Lawson-Tancred, 140.

23 Crooke, *Microcosmographia*, Ggg4 v.

24 Robert Cawdray, *A Treasvrie or Storehovse of Similes: Both pleasaunt, delightfull, and profitable, for all estates of men in generall. Newly collected into Heads and Common places* (London, 1600), Nn3[v]-Nn4[r].

25 Richard Sheldon, *The Motives of Richard Sheldon Pr. for his iust, voluntary, and free renouncing of Communion with the Bishop of Rome, Paul the 5 and his Church* (London, 1612), *4[v].

26 Arthur Morton, *The Touch-Stone of Conversion. Or, Marks of true Faith. Wherein The Impenitent Sinner is rowsed. The True Beleever discovered. And The Doubting Saint resolved. By that Excellent Man of God now in Heaven, Mr Arthur Morton Scotch Man* (London, 1647), B4[v]-B5[r].

27 Tobie Matthew, *A True Historical Relation of the Conversion of Sir Tobie Matthew to the Holy Catholic Faith; with the Antecedents and Consequences Thereof*, ed. Arnold H. Mathew (London: Burns & Oates, 1904), 14.

28 Saint Augustine, *Confessions*, trans. Henry Chadwick (Oxford: Oxford University Press, 2008), 152–53. Matthew's conversion story was originally directed to Dame Mary Gage, a Benedictine nun from the prominent recusant family. It remained in manuscript until 1795 with Matthew exhorting his readers to keep 'it wholly to yourself' (1). In his autobiography, Matthew repeatedly invokes Augustine as a model and he was the first translator of Augustine's *Confessions* into English, see Lynch, *Protestant Autobiography*, 31.

29 Stephen Egerton, *The Boring of the Eare Contayning a plaine and profitable Discourse by way of Dialogue. . .* (London, 1623), A4[r].

30 Jennifer Rae McDermott, '"The Melodie of Heaven": Sermonizing the Open Ear In Early Modern England', in *Religion and the Senses in Early Modern Europe*, ed. Weistse de Boer and Christine Göttler (Leiden: Brill, 2012), 177–98 (at 180). For a useful discussion of how the ear was thought to communicate to the soul and the primacy of hearing above the other senses, see Bruce R. Smith, *The Acoustic World of Early Modern England: Attending to the O-Factor* (Chicago, IL: University of Chicago Press, 1999), 103–106.

31 John Eliot, *A further Account of the progreß of the Gospel Amongst the Indians In New England: Being a Relation of the Confessions made by several Indians. . .in order to their admission into Church-fellowship* (London, 1660), C4^r.

32 Eliot, *A further Account of the progreß. . .*, C4^v.

33 Eliot, *A further Account of the progreß. . .*, C1^r.

34 Richard Sherry, *A treatise of Schemes & Tropes* (London, 1550), E7^v.

35 Thomas Browne, *A true and full coppy of that which was most imperfectly and Surreptitiously printed before under the name of Religio Medici* (London, 1643), B3^r-B3^v.

36 Augustine, *Confessions*, trans. Chadwick, 185.

37 Augustine, *Confessions*, trans. Chadwick, 183.

38 Thomas Shepard, *The Sound Beleever. Or, a Treatise of Evangelicall Conversion. Discovering the work of Christs Spirit, in reconciling of a sinner to God* (London, 1645), B4^r- B5^v.

39 Morton, *The Touch-Stone of Conversion*, A4^v-A5^r.

40 Morton, *The Touch-Stone of Conversion*, B8^v- B9^r.

41 Morton, *The Touch-Stone of Conversion*, I2^v.

42 Brathwaite, *Essaies vpon the Fiue Senses*, E4^r-E4^v.

43 On Christ's body as a space in which social identity was negotiated in the medieval period see Sarah Beckwith, *Christ's Body: Identity, Culture and Society in Late Medieval Writings* (London: Routledge, 1993), 22–44.

44 Paul L. Gavrilyuk and Sarah Coakley, 'Introduction', in *The Spiritual Senses: Perceiving God in Western Christianity*, ed. Gavrilyuk and Coakley (Cambridge: Cambridge University Press, 2012), 1–19 (at 6).

45 Anon, *The Voluntarie Conversion, and Severall Recantations, of foure great learned men, professed Fryers in sundry Monasteries of Fraunce, From the Errovrs of Idolatrie and Poperie, to the true religion established in the Reformed Church* (London, 1604), C3^r.

46 William Alabaster, *Unpublished Works by William Alabaster 1568–1640*, ed. Dana F. Sutton (Salzburg: Salzburg University, 1997), 114–15.

47 See Woolgar, *The Senses in Late Medieval England*, 42.

48 Anon, *Eight learned personages lately conuerted (in the Realme of France) from papistrie, to the Churches reformed: hauing aduisedly and holily set downe the reasons that moued them thereunto*, trans. by W. B (London, 1601), K3^r.

49 John Wilson, *Zacheus Converted: Or the Rich Publicans Repentance Restitution. In which the Mysteries of the Doctrine of Conversion, are sweetly laid open and applyed for the establishing of the weakest* (London, 1631), A7^v-A10^v.

Part III
Exile and encounter

6   Hearing exile and homecoming in the Dutch Stranger church

Erin Lambert

> I will make the nations your heritage, and the ends of the earth your possession.
>
> Psalm 2:8

> Even the sparrow finds a home, and the swallow a nest for herself. . . Blessed are the men whose strength is in thee, and in whose heart are the highways to Zion.
>
> Psalm 84:1 and 5

> How shall we sing the Lord's song in a foreign land?
>
> Psalm 137:4[1]

For many sixteenth-century Christians, the words of these psalms had particular resonance. As confessional conflicts mounted in the middle decades of the century, growing numbers of Europeans found themselves in danger when their understanding of Christianity differed from their rulers'. While some chose to conform and others died for their faith, thousands became exiles.[2] They left behind home, family, and work, and took to the roads and seas in search of a place where they might safely practice their faith. We find evidence of the presence of religious exiles in cities scattered throughout Europe: Geneva, Strasbourg, Frankfurt, Emden, London, and many others.[3] No matter where they found themselves, they faced the challenge of beginning new lives and building communities in lands that were not their own.

The sound of psalm-singing was a thread that connected many of these experiences of exile. A young refugee who arrived in Strasbourg from the Low Countries around 1545, for example, wrote that he wept when he first heard the exiles there singing in the vernacular.[4] Listening to many voices raised together in his own language brought to a strange place the sounds of the home to which he could not return. Those voices also provided a sign that he had found the company of friends who shared his faith as well as his loss. For others, the singing of psalms made audible their solidarity in the face of hostile circumstances. Enduring persecution in France, Huguenots sang together in secretive gatherings even if it was too dangerous to meet with a preacher.[5] For them, the sound of communal song signified resistance: in the midst of persecution, they raised their voices as one. And for Jan Utenhove (1516–66), a Dutch exile in London, the Psalms similarly provided proof that God had the power to overcome any enemy that might threaten the faithful. Singing or listening to the Psalms, he wrote, was a comfort to those lost in the woods or at sea.[6] His people had been expelled from their fatherland, but no matter where they went, they might sing the words that comforted David in his suffering.[7] If they listened carefully, they would find assurance that God would one day gather his followers from all corners of the earth.[8]

In songs sung in a foreign land, Utenhove found a means of building a community with his fellow exiles in London.[9] He therefore translated many of the Psalms into Dutch to meet the needs of the growing numbers of refugees from the Low Countries who came to the city during the reign of Edward VI. Like Utenhove, many of them had left their homes on the continent as the persecution of evangelicals intensified under the rule of Charles V.[10] They joined an established community of Dutch immigrants who had come to England in search of economic opportunity.[11] In London, the foreigners became known as the Stranger church, a name that articulated their place in the city and, as we shall see, evoked their complex relationship with the wider world. In 1550, their community gained official recognition as Edward issued letters patent, which granted to the Stranger church the nave of the abandoned monastery of Austin Friars.[12] There, they were permitted to worship in their native language and to develop their own liturgy. Each week, members of the community gathered to listen to sermons and sing the Psalms from the metrical psalters that Utenhove prepared for them.[13]

Through an examination of the sounds of the liturgy and psalm-singing, this essay explores the ways in which the Strangers carved out a place for themselves in London.[14] As such, it joins a growing body of scholarship attuned to the importance of song and aurality in the course of the Reformation and in the formation of early modern communities more broadly.[15] As a number of scholars have shown, the sense of hearing was fundamental to the dissemination of information in the early modern period. Sixteenth-century communities were filled with the sound of gossip, and many heard the news from a town crier as merchants' voices advertised their wares in the marketplace.[16] In a world of limited literacy, reading often took place aloud.[17] As a result, for many early modern Europeans, texts were conceived not only as printed or written objects, but as sound. For scholars, sermons, liturgies, broadsheets, proclamations, and other sources that evoke such acts of speech can provide access to that aural world. So too can records of acts of song. In a society in which oral communication was essential, song had particular significance. The sound of singing voices accompanied work and provided entertainment at home. In church, song had long offered praise and instruction. In the sixteenth century, it took on other purposes as well: the sound of song came to convey the differences between one form of Christianity and another, as Utenhove recognised when he began to translate the Psalms in the early 1550s.[18]

Robin Leaver has investigated the evolution of Utenhove's psalters, their role in the Strangers' weekly worship, and their relationship with the repertory of English liturgies and metrical psalms that took shape even as the Strangers built their community in London.[19] This essay takes a different approach: it attends to the sensory experiences evoked by the psalters as physical objects, and it examines the Strangers' psalm-singing in concert with the gestures, spoken words, and material culture of the liturgy. In this way, it also explores how we might reconstruct sensory experiences in the absence of individuals' accounts of them: prescriptive texts such as psalters, liturgies, and theological treatises are virtually the only surviving sources from the Edwardian Stranger community.[20] Through these sources, this essay re-envisions the Strangers' acts of singing and listening as practices of place-making and community-building. After attending to the ways in which the Stranger community and its psalmody were shaped by exile, I explore the use of psalms, spoken words, and liturgical spaces as modes of boundary-making in the Strangers' discipline. Through the sound of many voices raised together as one, a group of individuals became a community and claimed their London church as a place of their own, and more specifically, as the place of the elect. Against this background, the sonic and material aspects of the Lord's Supper emerge as ways of envisioning the exiles' true home in heaven. In the face of growing uncertainty in the 1550s, sound united the Stranger church on a shared path through the world. And ultimately, this essay suggests, the sound of the Strangers' worship redefined 'exile' and 'home' themselves.

Community in exile

The London Stranger community was, by its nature, shaped by migration. By the time the community received its charter, the experience of exile was familiar to growing numbers of Reformed Christians. The challenges of exile, for example, guided John Calvin's conception of the true Christian church. In his *Institutes of the Christian Religion* (1559), Calvin outlined a Christian community that might take shape no matter where the faithful found themselves; that fellowship was to be defined by the true preaching of the Word and the administration of the Sacraments.[21] The Christian community, in other words, was bound by no earthly geography. It could be constructed in any place, and it might be rebuilt again and again, no matter how many times its members were displaced or dispersed.

Such transience was familiar to the leaders of the Stranger church, who had already endured multiple migrations before their arrival in England.

Like others who fled or were expelled from their homes, they faced an ever-shifting geography with little other than word of mouth to guide them. A purported safe haven might thus prove dangerous; a place that had provided temporary refuge might at any time become hostile.[22] As a result, as the Strangers' leaders had found, exile was not simply a single journey from home to a strange place, but an on-going migration. Years of travel on the continent shaped their approach to their newfound community in London. Much like Calvin, Johannes a Lasco (1499–1560), who was named the superintendent of the London exiles, defined the church as a fellowship of the elect called together from throughout the earth, and marked by the preaching of the Word and the enactment of the sacraments.[23] In London, he began to write an ordinance for the Stranger church, which put this understanding of Christianity into practice.[24] At the outset, Lasco identified devotion and sensory experiences as central elements of the life of the true Christian community, which was to take shape through the sound of preaching and the gestures of the liturgy.

Lasco suggested that those practices were also to be of use to other Christians facing the challenge of building a community anew. He intended his Latin liturgy, which he completed some time before it appeared in print in 1555, to serve as a model for exilic communities throughout Europe, even as it guided the Strangers' own practices.[25] In order to meet the day-to-day needs of the London congregation, one of the ministers, Marten Micron (1523–1559), produced a vernacular liturgy based on Lasco's text.[26] For all who gathered in Austin Friars, the liturgy was to provide a common bond. Over the course of time, its rhythms were to become familiar, structuring each week and guiding the course of each member's life from baptism to burial. Through the words, sounds, and gestures of the liturgy, lives that had been redefined by exile were to find new patterns, and individuals with a range of experiences were to become a tight-knit community.

The liturgies of Micron and Lasco confirm that the Psalms were to play a vital role in that community: the church order incorporated congregational song into each Sunday's service and called for psalm-singing to mark key occasions in the Christian's life, such as baptism and marriage.[27] Utenhove's psalm settings thus complemented Lasco and Micron's work, providing evidence of the aural culture of the Stranger community. Like the Strangers' other liturgical, devotional, and theological texts, Utenhove's psalters were published by printers who were themselves members of the community.[28] Although no copies of his first editions are extant, references indicate that Utenhove's initial collections, consisting of ten and twenty-five metrical psalms respectively, appeared in 1551.[29] The earliest of his surviving psalm publications, a pamphlet containing settings of Psalms 23, 101, 115, and 128, appeared in 1552.[30]

While the texts of Lasco and Micron reveal much about the Strangers' ecclesiology, the physical attributes of Utenhove's pamphlet and the sounds it evokes carry us more deeply into the community's sense of its place in the world. His edition of four psalms was a visual and tactile reminder of its readers' status as exiles. Like Lasco and Micron's theological texts, and like the psalters that Utenhove later published, that pamphlet was printed in a small octavo format. As Utenhove noted in one of his subsequent publications, this consistent size made it possible to bind all of the texts that a Christian needed into a single volume.[31] In this light, it is notable that the sole surviving copy of Utenhove's pamphlet is bound together with Micron's treatise on the Eucharist and a copy of the catechism. The small size of the volume ensured that no matter where its reader went, all that was necessary for the practice of his or her faith might be held in the palm of the hand.[32] In a community shaped by migration, the Strangers' books emphasised portability. They could be hidden or carried easily in a pocket. The Strangers' books, in other words, themselves provided sensory evidence of the uncertainty that exiles faced: at any moment, one might endure another expulsion and a new journey.

At the same time, those books, through which the Strangers might continue their devotions even if they were forced to migrate once more, also signified the endurance of their faith despite any forces that might disrupt it. The familiar pages of a psalter or the catechism might be turned in any place, even if one found oneself in a new or hostile territory. Thus, even as the Strangers' books were markers of transience, they also fostered the formation of enduring communal bonds. Sung in unison, Utenhove's psalm settings joined together many different voices: male and female, young and old. Guided by melody and rhythm, they declaimed the text together as one, and the sound of their song incorporated diverse individuals into a single community. For new arrivals, adding one's voice to the chorus built and strengthened ties to that fellowship.[33] Like a young exile in Strasbourg, Utenhove recognised that in a world in which much was uncertain, the sound of many voices joined together provided assurance that one was not alone.

For listeners attuned to the musical culture of the sixteenth-century Low Countries, psalm-singing might also bring familiarity to a strange place. In some of his psalm-settings, Utenhove adapted texts from the *Souterliedekens*, a Dutch psalter first published in 1540 and widely used among evangelicals in the early years of reform in the Low Countries.[34] For the Strangers, to whom the *Souterliedekens* were likely familiar, Utenhove's metrical psalms would have called to mind memories of their communities on the continent. By singing the psalms together in their native language, the Strangers' raised voices made their new church of Austin Friars sound more like their former homes. At the same time, the melodies Utenhove employed in many of his psalm settings emphasised his community's commonality with other exilic congregations. In some cases, he chose to use melodies that had become familiar to him in Strasbourg; in later translations, he increasingly drew upon the work of

Clément Marot, basing metrical patterns on the French psalter or incor-porating its melodies.[35] Utenhove's 1552 edition of four psalms, for example, included three melodies drawn from Strasbourg psalters and one from Geneva.[36] Musical borrowings, as a result, evoked the Stranger congregation's place within a broader network of exilic communities: even if members found themselves in search of a safe haven on the continent, they might find much that was familiar.

As the Strangers gathered together in Austin Friars, their metrical psalms thus provided multiple clues to the nature of their community. As material objects, the psalters from which they sang underscored both uncertainty and endurance. The melodies that resonated in the nave were reminders of what they had lost, even as they brought familiarity to a new place. The sound of many voices singing together made evident the bonds that they were forging together in London, even as their psalters ensured that they could build a community anew no matter where they might travel. The Strangers' psalters, as a result, reveal the centrality of exile to their identity. So too, their metrical psalms can attune us to the ways in which the sensory experience of devotion was interconnected with the formation of a community.

Hearing boundaries

The sounds and gestures of the Strangers' liturgy enable us to reconstruct that process of community building. The ways in which the Strangers employed sensory experiences to articulate their community's boundaries and mark the individual's membership within their fellowship emerge in instructions for the use of the liturgical space of Austin Friars. Throughout Micron's vernacular liturgy, rituals at each stage of the Christian's life employ the physical orientation of one member to others in order to emphasise passages in and out of the community. When children were baptised into the Stranger church, for example, their parents stood with them in the centre of the congregation so that the entire community might witness their introduction.[37] Similarly, during a funeral, the congregation was instructed to surround the body that was to be buried.[38] At key moments in the Christian life, therefore, membership in the community was articulated by the individual's orientation to the congregation, signifying inclusion at baptism and departure at the graveside. The actions of the liturgy made movement across the community's boundaries visible.

Such spatial relationships were especially vital to the Strangers' practice of discipline, which was of particular importance to the life of the community. As in other Reformed communities, the Strangers demarcated the boundaries between their community and the world at large.[39] Only those who lived in accordance with the Strangers' discipline, for example, were permitted to be married or receive the Lord's Supper in Austin Friars. The four disciplinary rituals included in Micron's vernacular liturgy thus outlined processes of excommunication and reconciliation for those who transgressed the Stranger community's moral boundaries. The first was a private procedure to be conducted in the presence of the ministers and elders, through which the Strangers' leaders sought to educate members about the nature of their transgressions and entreated them to reconcile themselves with the community. For those whose offense had affected the entire congregation, or who could not be brought back into the fold through these private admonitions, the liturgy also included three public rituals: a ceremony of penitence, a service in which the unrepentant were excommunicated, and a ritual to welcome the repentant back to the community.[40]

Through sight and sound, each of those public liturgies emphasised the interaction of the penitent, the minister, and the congregation within the liturgical space of Austin Friars. In the first of the public rituals, members who committed an offense against the community and subsequently demonstrated heartfelt repentance to the elders were to be reconciled with their congregation. As the fallen member expressed remorse to the whole community, he or she stood in sight of the entire congregation. The preacher stood with the repentant member in the centre, and he reminded all present that the forgiveness of a single sinner demonstrated that all Christians stood upon the shoulders of Christ, and all were members of his flock.[41] The preacher's words implied that Christ, too, was spiritually present within their gathering. After a series of prayers of thanks for God's forgiveness, the penitent reaffirmed his or her submission to the community's discipline, and one of the leaders pronounced absolution 'not only on earth, but also in heaven'.[42] In combination with his spoken words, the Strangers' arrangement within liturgical space emphasised the individual's continued membership in the community. For the penitent, being surrounded by the community was proof of the potential for forgiveness, as well a reminder of the moral standards to which members were expected to conform.

Standing and speaking together in Austin Friars, the Strangers made visible and audible the ties that bound their community in London. As the preacher's reference to forgiveness in heaven and on earth hints, their gathering within that space also signified their status as the elect who would one day be assembled at the right hand of Christ. In the liturgy of excommunication, through which those who refused to repent were expelled from the congregation, Micron used the image of this heavenly fellowship to describe both the formation and fragmentation of the Christian community on earth. Through excommunication, the impenitent sinner was utterly cast off from the congregation, in a decision taken by the full group of elders and deacons. Once again, the liturgy emphasised the close bonds that the Strangers had built through the practice of discipline in London. To remove a member from the community, Micron stated, was to cut off a piece of the living body of Christ.[43] By speaking the words of prayers and admonitions, the preacher amputated a rotten limb from the body of the faithful.[44] The excommunicated member faced the damnation of both body and soul, and was shut out of the eternal life promised to the Christian community. The ritual of excommunication further marked the continuity of the earthly and heavenly communities that the penitential liturgy had evoked; what was bound and unbound on earth, the liturgy repeatedly pronounced, was joined and severed in heaven.[45]

The sounds and gestures of the liturgy suggested, therefore, that the Strangers' fellowship was to be eternal. Implicitly, the Strangers' liturgy also recognised Austin Friars as a place belonging to a community of true Christians alone. Even though their congregation's members had lost their homelands, they had found their way to the place of the elect. In the ceremony through which they welcomed a reformed excommunicant back to the congregation, the Strangers articulated understandings of departure and return that were not oriented to any earthly place, but instead, to that elect fellowship itself. Although the excommunicant had been severed from the community like a diseased limb, the preacher reminded his congregation, the ritual incorporated the repentant back into the body that was already whole in heaven. The penitent swore an oath of contrition, and the preacher pronounced that because the repentant member visibly returned to the community on earth, he was a member of that heavenly community in the sight of God.[46] Echoing the ritual of excommunication, the preacher once again reminded the congregation that what Christians bound on earth, they also built in heaven; sin was thus forgiven both in their earthly community and in its heavenly counterpart.[47]

Finally, as they did at the close of every liturgical occasion, the congregation raised their voices together. To mark the penitent's return to the fold, they sang the words of Psalm 103 – the same psalm that the liturgy called for them to sing beside the graves of the dead:

> Bless the Lord, O my soul, and forget not all his benefits . . . who satisfies you with good as long as you live, so that your youth is renewed like the eagle's. The Lord works vindication and justice for all who are oppressed. He made known his ways to Moses, his acts to the people of Israel. . . .As far as the east is from the west, so far does he remove our transgressions from us.[48]

The words of the psalm are filled with promises of forgiveness and images of renewal appropriate to the ritual of reconciliation. The melody to which the Strangers sang those words, however, recalled a different story: Utenhove paired the words of Psalm 103 with a melody borrowed from a setting of Psalm 137 familiar in exilic communities on the continent.[49] The borrowed melody bore with it connotations of lament: Psalm 137 expressed the Israelites' sorrow beside the rivers of Babylon. As the

Strangers welcomed a member back to their gathering, their raised voices thus blended the text's promise of return and renewal with a lament for a lost homeland. The words of the psalm were placed in tension with its musical setting, so that the aural experience of hearing its melody undercut its celebratory text. Sung and heard in the context of the ritual of reconciliation, the psalm setting transformed exile's meaning: true exile, the liturgy as a whole implied, was separation from the elect on earth and in heaven. At the same time, as the penitent returned to the community of the elect, the sound of the congregation's song implied their commonality with the wandering Israelites, who remained under God's protection even in their captivity. As long as they were among those who shared their faith, the Strangers were home.

Through the sound of psalm-singing and their orientation to liturgical space, the Strangers claimed Austin Friars as the place of the elect and defined departure and return in relation to that community itself. In this light, exile was not defined by the loss of an earthly place; instead, expulsion was recast as separation from one's fellows, and homecoming was in reunion with them. Although each of the Strangers had left his or her home behind, the sights and sounds of the liturgy cast their newly founded congregation as the true place of the faithful.

Envisioning heaven

As sung and spoken words repeatedly called upon the congregation to look to a future in heaven, the disciplinary liturgies also emphasised the Strangers' shared presence in the exilic space of Austin Friars as a mode of imagining a place far beyond it. In the Liturgy of the Lord's Supper that the Strangers practiced in London, objects and sounds similarly enacted a process of picturing through which they envisioned the heavenly community of the elect. As the Liturgy of the Supper invoked the senses of hearing, sight, touch, and implicitly, taste, it constructed an image of the Stranger community's ultimate home. As Micron noted, the Eucharistic liturgy was a public profession of the Strangers' pledge to follow the example of Christ, and it made the nature of their faith visible to any who encountered them. In advance of the day on which they received the Supper as members of that fellowship, each person made a public confession of his or her faith to the ministers and elders. When all who were thus prepared to receive the Supper had assembled, the minister explained the significance of their membership in that community. Those who were prepared to receive the Supper, he reminded them, were members of a community 'in which [God's] voice was openly heard in the Gospel of Christ'.[50] One who was truly a Christian, and fortunate enough to live in a place where a true Christian community was gathered, was to devote him- or herself fully to that community. Those who received the Supper in Austin Friars, then, had been called to live as Strangers in the name of Christ.[51]

Like the disciplinary rituals, the Supper emphasised the community's distinctness from the wider world by evoking multiple sensory experiences. With the entire community gathered together in Austin Friars, the congregation's leaders prepared an ordinary table for the Supper, doing away with altars, candles, bells, and vestments.[52] The setting of the Supper marked the Strangers' separation from the practices of the traditional church. Instead of a space perfumed by incense, lit by candles, and resonating with the sound of bells, the Strangers' Supper was structured by everyday objects and the sound of human voices speaking and singing in the vernacular. The replacement of an altar with a table was among the most striking departures from the traditional liturgy, and it became a visual sign of the Stranger community's bonds.[53] To gather at a table for food and drink, Micron explained, was a universal sign of peace and unity. As the Strangers' table imitated that of the Apostles at the Last Supper, they bore witness to the love that bound their community and recognised that their fellowship foreshadowed the assembly of the elect in heaven.[54] Their gathering in Austin Friars, in other words, was intended to make visible a community apart from all others, just as the disciplinary liturgies had done. In order to define that community's separation from the world around them, Micron's instructions for the Supper further emphasised the visual symbolism of everyday objects – things in keeping with the Strangers' rejection of idolatry, but which might also be gathered from an ordinary home. The liturgy called for the table to be covered with a linen cloth. In the middle were placed four goblets and three tin plates, the largest of which held ordinary white bread.[55] As with Utenhove's pocket-sized psalters, the liturgy focused not on any particular location or specialised ritual objects, but on items that could be assembled in any place that a few of the faithful might gather. No matter where they travelled, the practice of the Supper remained constant – and so too might the earthly community of the elect.

The Supper formally began as the ministers, elders, and deacons were seated around the table and invoked God's presence among their gathering. The leaders passed plates of bread and cups of wine from one to the next, their gestures underscoring the bonds among them as they ate and drank.[56] In turn, members of the congregation took their place at the table, first men and then women, until all had received the Supper. As they gathered around that table, the Strangers experienced a constant stream of sound. From the pulpit, the preacher's voice resounded over their gathering, reminding them once more of the significance of their fellowship and the sacrament they were to receive. So too, he called upon God to look down upon them from heaven.[57] As the Strangers ate the bread that signified the body of Christ, their minister read to them from the book of John – words that described Christ as the bread of heaven that was to feed the faithful, and which promised mansions for those who followed God's commandments.[58] As they looked around the table at one another, the preacher's voice reminded them, they were to see the community of the elect that was to be gathered in heaven beside Abraham, Isaac, and Jacob – the fellowship that was to live in those mansions.[59]

Through the actions of the Supper, Micron's liturgy continued, the faithful themselves became the heavenly bread, the body of Christ. As they tasted the bread and listened to their preacher, the Strangers were to consider the process of the elect community's formation. Like a loaf of bread, the true Christian community could be made only through the milling and mixing of many disparate members:

> Just as no bread can be made unless many grains are gathered together and broken with the mill, so let us think that we cannot be a bread of the Lord unless we are gathered together as members of a body under the head of Christ . . . Just as one must purify the milled grains to have pure bread, so must we also sift out the coarse grit through the use of Christian discipline, if we wish to be a pure bread in the sight of Christ.[60]

Through the practice of discipline and the hearing of the Word, the Strangers' souls were to be purified and unified like those grains, and kneaded and shaped until they became more like Christ:

> Just as the broken and purified grains must be unified in a dough with water in order to make bread of them, so must we have life-giving water poured into us in order to be a bread of God . . . Just as the dough must be worked to the form of bread, and placed in a fiery oven to be baked, so must we also be worked to the image of Christ our whole lives long, so that his deeds may be seen more and more in us each day.[61]

As the Strangers ate together around the table, the words they heard thus transformed the physical objects of the Supper into images of the Christian life. By seeing, hearing, and tasting, they were to mould themselves into the bread of heaven – the body of Christ and the fellowship of the elect.

Finally, at the conclusion of the Supper, the Strangers raised their voices to claim heaven as the true home of those whose lives had been so moulded. As they prepared to leave the shelter of Austin Friars for the busy streets of London, they sang Psalm 23's promises of a place beside still waters, a table laden with food, protection even unto death, and an eternal dwelling place in God's house.[62] Whether around the table or as they made their way through the world, their voices gave thanks for God's presence among them and made the strength of their community audible. As with the disciplinary liturgies, ritual gestures and the sound of human voices claimed Austin Friars as the Strangers' own. Most importantly, however, the acts of passing a plate, eating bread, and listening to a preacher's voice cast the congregation gathered around the table as the people of heaven. For individuals who had lost so much that was familiar, their gathering around a table signified that those whose voices were joined together in Austin Friars were forever a community, bound together as fundamentally as the particles of flour in their bread, no matter what befell them on earth.

Conclusion

The Strangers' understanding of their community sheds new light on the well-known migration on which they embarked in 1553, when England became unsafe for evangelicals after the accession of Mary I.[63] By the time of Edward's death, the number of Dutch exiles in London had grown so large that not all could travel together. Their community, as a result, had to be divided. While hundreds of Strangers remained in England, a smaller group of 175 sailed for Denmark in September 1553. Soon, they too were separated as a storm blew them off course and onto the shores of Norway. When the group reached their destination in Denmark weeks later, they immediately came into conflict with local Lutheran leaders over their Eucharistic theology. The exiles were expelled and set sail once again. Lasco and Utenhove took one group to Emden, where the former had been instrumental to reforms during his earlier stay there. The others travelled to northern Germany and attempted to find refuge in Wismar, Lübeck, and Hamburg. Again and again, they refused to submit to local doctrines, and their efforts resulted in conflict and expulsion.

Finally, the Strangers were reunited in Emden in 1554, where they once again found a place of safety in which they could build their community anew. As the sounds and objects that structured their liturgy reveal, however, the particular location in which they established that community was ultimately of little importance. Throughout their journey, they had borne their liturgy and their psalters with them – objects that marked them as migrants, but also ensured that they carried all that they truly needed to practice their faith. No matter where they found themselves, the sound of voices singing the Psalms and reading the Word had the power to build a community and define a new space as their own. As they journeyed, those sounds provided assurance that heaven was the ultimate destination for the elect, no matter how much they might be forced to wander on earth.

In those psalms, we hear the anthem of the Strangers' own exile. As they moved through the world, they sang in a place of their own making – indeed, a space carved out by the sound of song and the practice of their faith. The resonance of voices in an empty cloister and the sight of members gathered around a table defined Austin Friars as their own, and promised that no matter what befell them, they were forever bound to their true community. And ultimately, as the Strangers faced separation and were forced to leave yet another haven behind, those psalms promised them a home unlike any they could find on earth.

Raised together, their voices separate exile from any political geography, and they reshape our understanding of its objective. Those sounds demonstrate that exile entailed much more than travel from one place to another. Instead, the story of the Strangers' expulsion was defined by what they carried with them. Exile, their liturgy and psalms reveal, entailed not only the loss of a home, but a continuous journey towards it – a journey endured with the familiar weight of a psalter in the hand and guided by practices that could make any place their own until they reached the true home of the elect in heaven. Most broadly, then, the sounds of the Strangers' worship expose modes through which we can better understand the Reformation's reshaping of sacred space. Singing together, they attune us not only to the physical settings of worship, but to the ways in which sacred spaces were imagined and enacted, seen and touched, and above all, heard.

Notes

1 These psalm quotations are selected from early editions of the Strangers' metrical psalters. See Jan Utenhove, 25. *Psalmen end andere ghesanghen diemen in de Duydtsche Ghemeynte te Londen, was ghebruyckende* (Emden, 1557), 5–6, 34–35 and idem., *Andere 26. psalme[n] Dauidis* (Emden, 1559), 58. All biblical quotes in English are from the Revised Standard Version.

2 On conversion, see Benjamin J. Kaplan, *Divided by Faith: Religious Conflict and the Practice of Toleration in Early Modern Europe* (Cambridge, MA: Harvard University Press, 2009), chapter 10, and David M. Luebke et. al., eds., *Conversion and the Politics of Religion in Early Modern Germany* (New York: Berghahn Books, 2012); on martyrdom, see Brad S. Gregory, *Salvation at Stake: Christian Martyrdom in Early Modern Europe* (Cambridge, MA: Harvard University Press, 1999).

3 On exile in the Reformation, see Heiko A. Oberman, *John Calvin and the Reformation of the Refugees*, with an introduction by Peter A. Dykema (Geneva: Droz, 2009), Ole Peter Grell, *Brethren in Christ: A Calvinist Network in Reformation Europe* (Cambridge: Cambridge University Press, 2011), and most relevant to this chapter, Bernard Cottret, *Terre d'exil: l'Angleterre et ses réfugiés français et wallons, de la Réforme à la revocation de l'édit de Nantes, 1550 1700* (Paris: Aubier, 1985), Andrew Pettegree, *Foreign Protestant Communities in Sixteenth-Century London* (Oxford: Clarendon Press, 1986) and idem., *Emden and the Dutch Revolt: Exile and the Development of Reformed Protestantism* (Oxford: Clarendon Press, 1992).

4 Alfred Erichson, ed., *L'Église française de Strasbourg au seizième siècle d'aprés des documents inédits* (Strasbourg: Librairie C.F. Schmidt, 1886), 21.

5 Barbara B. Diefendorf, 'The Huguenot Psalter and the Faith of French Protestants in the Sixteenth Century', in *Culture and Identity in Early Modern Europe (1500–1800): Essays in Honor of Natalie Zemon Davis*, ed. Barbara B. Diefendorf and Carla Hesse (Ann Arbor: University of Michigan Press, 1993), 42.

6 Jan Utenhove, *Hondert Psalmen Dauids Mitsgaders het ghesangk Marie, t' ghesangk Zacharie, t' ghesangk Simeons, de thien Geboden, de artikels des Gheloofs, t' ghebed des Heeren* (London, 1561), 97v.
7 Ibid, 4v–5r.
8 Utenhove, *Hondert Psalmen*, 100r; see also Utenhove's extensive list of the benefits of reading or singing the psalms, 3v–5v.
9 On psalmody in sixteenth–century England, see Robin A. Leaver, *Goostly Psalms and Spirituall Songes: English and Dutch Metrical Psalms from Coverdale to Utenhove, 1535–1566* (Oxford: Clarendon Press, 1991).
10 On the Reformation in the Low Countries, see Alastair Duke, *Reformation and Revolt in the Low Countries* (London: Hambledon Continuum, 2003). For a biography of Utenhove, see Fredrik Pijper, *Jan Utenhove: Zijn Leven en Zijne Werken* (Leiden: A.H. Adriani, 1883).
11 On the multiple reasons for migration in early modern Europe, see Randolph Vigne and Charles Littleton, eds., *From Strangers to Citizens: The Integration of Immigrant Communities in Britain, Ireland, and Colonial America, 1550–1750* (Portland: Sussex Academic Press, 2001).
12 Initially, the French and Dutch exile congregations shared Austin Friars, but they quickly outgrew the space and conflicted over its use. The French moved to a new space and left Austin Friars to the Dutch. Pettegree, *Foreign Protestant Communities*, 36–37.
13 For an edition of the Strangers' vernacular liturgy, see Marten Micron, *De Christlicke Ordinancien der Nederlantscher Ghemeinten te Londen (1554)*, ed. with an introduction by W. F. Dankbaar, *Kerkhistorische Studien VII* (The Hague: M. Nijhoff, 1956).
14 On the complexities of space and place, see Yi-Fu Tuan, *Space and Place: The Perspective of Experience* (Minneapolis: University of Minnesota Press, 1977; repr., 2003).
15 On music's role in a range of confessional experiences of the Reformation, see Christopher Boyd Brown, *Singing the Gospel: Lutheran Hymns and the Success of the Reformation* (Cambridge, MA: Harvard University Press, 2005); Alexander J. Fisher, *Music and Religious Identity in Counter-Reformation Augsburg, 1580–1630* (Aldershot: Ashgate, 2004); idem., *Music, Piety, and Propaganda: The Soundscapes of Counter-Reformation Bavaria* (Oxford: Oxford University Press, 2014); Joseph Herl, *Worship Wars in Early Lutheranism: Choir, Congregation, and Three Centuries of Conflict* (Oxford: Oxford University Press, 2004); Emilie K. M. Murphy, 'Music and Catholic Culture in Post-Reformation Lancashire: Piety, Protest and Conversion', *British Catholic History* 32 (2015): 492–525; Rebecca Wagner Oettinger, *Music as Propaganda in the German Reformation* (Aldershot: Ashgate, 2001); and Jonathan Willis, *Church Music and Protestantism in Post-Reformation England: Discourses, Sites, and Identities* (Farnham: Ashgate, 2013).
16 Eric Wilson, 'Plagues, Fairs and Street Cries: Sounding Out Society and Space in Early Modern London', *Modern Language Studies* 25 (1995): 1–42.
17 Robert W. Scribner, 'Oral Culture and the Diffusion of Reformation Ideas', in *Popular Culture and Popular Movements in Reformation Germany* (London: Hambledon Press, 1987), 49–69. Also see Alison Shell, *Oral Culture and Catholicism in Early Modern England* (Cambridge: Cambridge University Press, 2007).
18 See above, n. 15, as well as Andrew Pettegree, *Reformation and the Culture of Persuasion* (Cambridge: Cambridge University Press, 2005), 40–75.
19 *Goostly Psalmes*, especially chapters 3 and 5.
20 The only formal record of the daily life of the congregation before their Marian exile is a membership register; no consistory records survive. Apart from a few

letters, which largely detail the interaction of the Strangers' leaders with English reformers, printed texts provide the only sources for this period. Notably, many of these survive only in editions printed after the Strangers' flight to the continent, and can only be presumed to record practices that were already in place in London. Pettegree, *Foreign Protestant Communities*, 46.

21 John Calvin, *Institutio Christianae Religionis*, in *Corpus Reformatorum: Ioannis Calvini Opera Quae Supersunt Omnia*, (Braunschweig: Schwetschke, 1864), 30: 4.1.9.

22 Lee Palmer Wandel, 'Exile in the Reformation', in *Space and Self in Early Modern European Culture*, ed. David Warren Sabean and Malina Stefanovska (Toronto, ON: University of Toronto Press, 2012), 202.

23 Jaroslav Pelikan and Valerie Hotchkiss, eds., *Creeds and Confessions of Faith in the Christian Tradition*, 4 vols. (New Haven: Yale University Press, 2003), 2:559. For biographies of Lasco, see Henning P. Jürgens, *Johannes a Lasco in Ostfriesland* (Tübingen: J.C.B. Mohr, 2002), and Judith Becker, *Gemeindeordnung and Kirchenzucht: Johannes a Lascos Kirchenordnung für London (1555) und die reformierte Konfessionsbildung* (Leiden: Brill, 2007).

24 Although Lasco began to write the church order in London, it was not completed and published until 1555. See Michael S. Springer, *Restoring Christ's Church: John a Lasco and the* Forma ac Ratio (Aldershot: Ashgate, 2007). On the French translations, see Leaver, *Goostly Psalmes*, 153–54. For Lasco's text, see *Forma ac ratio tota ecclesiastici ministerij, in peregrinorum, potissimum uero Germanorum Ecclesia instituta Londini in Anglia, per pientissimum principem Angliae [et]c* (n.p.: n.d.); also in *Joannis a Lasco Opera tam edita quam inedita duobus voluminibus comprehensa*, ed. Abraham Kuyper, 2 vols. (Amsterdam: Muller, 1866), 2:1–283.

25 Springer, *Restoring Christ's Church*, 7.

26 Micron, *Christlicke Ordinancien*.

27 For a summary, see Leaver, *Goostly Psalmes*, 170–73.

28 On Dutch printers in London, see Pettegree, *Foreign Protestant Communities*, 84–96, as well as Elizabeth Evenden, 'The Fleeing Dutchmen?: The Influence of Dutch Immigrants upon the Print Shop of John Day', in *John Foxe at Home and Abroad*, ed. D. M. Loades, 63–78 (Aldershot: Ashgate, 2004).

29 Leaver, *Goostly Psalmes*, 160.

30 Jan Utenhove, [*Psalmen 23, 101, 115, 128*] (London, 1552).

31 Jan Utenhove, *LXIIII Psalmen en[d] ander ghesangen, diemen in de Duytsche Ghemeynte te Londen was ghebruyckende* (Emden: Gellius Ctematius, 1561), f. 1v.

32 Utenhove, [*Psalmen 23, 101, 115, 128*]; Martin Micron, *Een claer bewijs, van het recht gebruyck des Nachtmaels Christi, ende wat men van de Misse houden sal* (London, 1552); and idem., *De cleyne catechismus, oft kinder leere, der Duytscher ghemeynte, die te Londen is* (London, 1552). The *Sammelband* containing these three texts is held in the Special Collections of the library of the University of Amsterdam, OK 72-5.

33 On the power of congregational song, see Fisher, *Music, Piety, and Propaganda*, 32–34.

34 Leaver, *Goostly Psalmes*, 160 and 163. Utenhove's sources have been a matter of debate. In addition to Leaver, see Samuel Jan Lenselink, *De Nederlandse psalmberijmingen in de 16e eeuw van de Souterliedekens tot Datheen met hun voorgangers in Duitsland en Frankrijk* (Assen: Van Gorcum, 1959). Lenselink's attempts to cite specific songbooks as sources for Utenhove have increasingly come under scrutiny. For example, see Leaver, *Goostly Psalmes*, 163.

35 Leaver, *Goostly Psalmes*, 163.

36 Ibid., 168–69.

37 Micron, *Christlicke Ordinancien*, 73–74.
38 Ibid., 151–52.
39 Scholars have recently begun to rethink the role of discipline in Reformed communities. Most often, discipline is cast as a mechanism of social control, which created the austerity typically associated with the Reformed. See, for example, Raymond A. Mentzer, ed., *Sin and the Calvinists: Morals, Control, and Consistory in the Reformed Tradition* (Kirksville, MO: Sixteenth Century Journal Publishers, 1994). More recently, Heiko Oberman has suggested instead that discipline played a vital role in the construction of communal bonds. See *John Calvin and the Reformation of the Refugees*.
40 Micron, *Christlicke Ordinancien*, 112–40. On Lasco's formulation of the Strangers' discipline, see Springer, *Restoring Christ's Church*, chapter 6.
41 Micron, *Christlicke Ordinancien*, 116–17.
42 Ibid., 121.
43 Ibid., 125.
44 Ibid., 127–28.
45 Ibid., 124.
46 Ibid., 134–35.
47 Ibid., 135.
48 Psalm 103:2, 5–7, 12; Micron, *Christlicke Ordinancien*, 135.
49 Like many other sixteenth-century songwriters, Utenhove used the process of contrafacture, in which a new text was applied to a pre-existing melody. As Rebecca Wagner Oettinger has demonstrated, the borrowed melody brought with it references to its original setting. See *Music as Propaganda*. On Dutch contrafacture more specifically, see Louis Peter Grijp, *Het Nederlandse lied in de Gouden Eeuw: Het mechanisme van de contrafactuur* (Amsterdam: P.J. Meertens-Instituut, 1991).
50 Micron, *Christlicke Ordinancien*, 83.
51 Ibid., 83.
52 Ibid., 80.
53 On the shift from altar to table and the transformation of Reformed liturgical space, see Lee Palmer Wandel, *The Eucharist in the Reformation: Incarnation and Liturgy* (Cambridge: Cambridge University Press, 2006), 167.
54 Micron, *Christlicke Ordinancien*, 81.
55 Ibid., 95.
56 Ibid., 101.
57 Ibid., 96.
58 Micron indicates John 6 and 13–15. Ibid., 102.
59 Ibid., 103.
60 Ibid., 104. '. . . ghelyck gheen broot wesen can, dan doer veel granen t'samen vergadert ende met de moelen ghebroken: so laet ons ooc dincken, dat wy niet connen een broot des Heeren wesen . . . ghelyckmen de ghemalen granen suyueren moet om suyuer broot te hebben: so moeten wy ooc het grof gruys, doer t'ghebruyck der Christelicker straffen, wtseften, ist dat wye en suyuer broot in t'gesichte Christi willen wesen'.
61 Ibid., 104–105. '. . .gheylyckerwyse als de ghebroken ende ghesuyuerde granen in een deech met water vereenicht moeten wesen, om broot daer af te maken: also moeten wy, om een broot Gods te wesen, leuendichmakende water in ons ghegoten hebben. . .ghelyck dat deech gewrocht moet wesen tot een forme des broots, ende in een vierighen houen ghedaen, op dat het ghebacken werde, also moeten wy ooc ons gansche leuen lanck gewracht werden tot het voerbeelt Christi: so dat syn gedaente in ons daghelicx meer ende meer ghesien mach werden'.
62 Ibid., 105; for Utenhove's psalm text, see *LXIIII Psalmen*, 7v.

63 For a primary account of that journey, see Jan Utenhove, *Simplex et fidelis narratio de institvta ac demvm dissipata Belgarum, aliorumque peregrinarum in Anglia, Ecclesia: et potissimum de susceptis postreà illius nomine itineribus,* in *Bibliotheca Reformatoria Neerlandica,* ed. S. Cramer and F. Pijper (The Hague: M. Nijhoff, 1912), 9:39–40. For scholarly studies, see Frederick A. Norwood, 'The London Dutch Refugees in Search of a Home, 1553–1554', *The American Historical Review* 58 (1952): 64–72 and Andrew Pettegree, *Marian Protestantism: Six Studies* (Aldershot: Ashgate, 1996), 55–85, and most recently, Erin Lambert, *Singing the Resurrection: Body, Community, and Belief in Reformation Europe* (New York: Oxford University Press, 2017).

7 A sense of place: hearing English Catholicism in the Spanish Habsburg territories, 1568–1659

Emilie K. M. Murphy

I.

In recent years, scholars have at last started to listen to the past.[1] Historical research on the acoustic, aural, and musical aspects of earlier societies is currently being produced with increasing momentum, and this has provided a wealth of insight into the experiences of historical men and women.[2] In this essay I utilise this methodology to uncover the experiences of English Catholic men and women who lived on the continent. Studies of English Catholics have traditionally neglected the experiences of their continental compatriots and co-religionists. John Bossy's seminal work marked English Catholics off from the 'Catholicisms of the continent' and subsequent discussion generally remained insular.[3] In the last few years, scholars have demonstrated the value of looking beyond England's borders. For example, in her work on English exiles in sixteenth-century Paris, Katy Gibbons firmly rejects the view that English Catholics were isolated and introverted, by placing English Catholic experience in the context of wider European religious and political tensions.[4] Recent work on English Catholic exile convents also firmly integrates the experiences of English Catholics within Europe.[5]

Drawing on this burgeoning research, I ask what music can tell us about the ways English Catholics in the Spanish Habsburg territories from 1568 to 1659 cultivated a 'sense of place' in exile.[6] I focus on five religious institutions founded in the Spanish Habsburg territories during this period: the Benedictine convent of Our Lady of the Assumption in Brussels (founded 1598); the Augustinian convent of St Monica's in Louvain (founded 1609); the double monastery of the Syon Abbey Bridgettines that settled in Lisbon in 1594; the seminary college of St Omer, which was established for the education of English Catholic boys in 1593; and the Royal English College in Valladolid (founded 1589). I explore these communities in order to witness, or rather 'hear', in new ways the manifold musical interactions that they had with other English Catholics, their co-religionists on the continent, and those at home.

The notion that the bond between English Catholics and their nation was irrevocably severed when they were exiled to the continent (even temporarily) – as implicit, for instance in Richard Helgerson's *Forms of Nationhood* – has been firmly rejected by Mark Netzloff in his analysis of Catholic polemical texts.[7] Other scholars have also been quick to emphasise a sense of English 'nationalism' within the exile community, but in contrast to Netzloff's nuanced approach, which recognises that 'Englishness' is not a 'stable or monolithic entity', we have been told that English Catholics did not share communal relationships with their continental co-religionists;[8] that seminaries and convents were 'stridently English' in their orientation and composition;[9] and even that 'nunneries functioned in effect as little self-enclosed Englands that shut out foreign cultures around them'.[10] The most recent surveyor of such literature has disparaged this 'apparent obsession with ethnic exclusiveness', and blamed scholars for their over-reliance on the available source material such as pamphlets and other printed polemic with an explicit agenda.[11] A potentially misleading picture has been painted, skewing our understanding of 'English' exile identities by obscuring other priorities and activities, such as musical performances that helped to secure patronage, which blurred national and cultural lines.

In asking what 'hearing' English Catholicism can tell us about the way communities constructed their relationships, this essay stands as a corrective to scholarship that either presumes exiles had little connection with England, or that they remained unproblematically 'English'. Instead, I highlight various examples of multicultural influences present in the communities, and the transnational exchanges between them. I call attention to the daily musical rhythm of the institutions, including established practices, musical training, and the local and international interactions with such sounds. From this I argue that aural engagement played a significant, if not vital, role in supporting English Catholic exiles' 'sense of place' on the continent, showing how the aural environment could prompt a multifaceted sensory response from its listeners, which was critical to experiencing the sacred.

I am concerned with the music that nuns made, as well as the reactions of those outside of the convents to the sounds produced within the convent walls. Hearing was not isolated from the other senses, and in this period noises were believed to have significant powers. As the Oxford scholar John Case asserted in 1588:

> Music. . .has God for a father, Nature for a mother; it has a divine quality whereby the mind, the image of God, is wondrously delighted. It is a physical and natural thing, by which not only the ears of men, but the sense of all beings, as it were, are comforted in a way which is beyond speech or thought.[12]

Music had the power to effect physical and emotional changes in hearers, both curing illnesses and comforting at times of distress.[13] Music could be harmful as well as beneficial: as Jonathan Willis has highlighted, the human mind was regarded 'as stable as a weathercock when it came to the buffeting effects of music, swinging in accordance with the mood of a particular melody'.[14] Accordingly, a person's relationship with music had to be carefully controlled and monitored.

This tension was manifest in the seemingly contradictory advice from the Bible and church fathers, epitomised in Saint Augustine's attempt to reconcile both the positive and negative attributes of music in an uneasy synthesis:

> I realise that when they are sung these sacred words stir my mind to greater religious fervour and kindle in me a more ardent flame of piety than they would if they were not sung. . . But I ought not to allow my mind be paralysed by the gratification of my senses, which often leads it astray.[15]

This power extended beyond music to other melodious sounds. For example bells were blessed and consecrated with devotional messages so that when they were rung their sounds would banish demons, and prevent bad weather.[16] It was also thought that ringing unconsecrated bells might attract the devil.[17] Due to the physical properties sound could convey, Murray Schafer's observation that 'hearing is a way of touching at a distance' seems particularly pertinent as continental English Catholics used music to bring themselves closer to their co-religionists back in England.[18]

II.

Music (including song, chant, and the ringing of bells) was ever-present in convents and seminaries on the continent. Fundamental to the daily rhythm of the institutions was the call to choir with the ringing of bells for the performance of the divine office. From the institutions' foundation, the regulations for these performances were set out explicitly in the rule books and constitutions. As well as specifying when and where music should be used, these texts were also clear about the proper way communities should sing. In the *Lisbon Rule* from 1607 for the Bridgettine community of Syon, the directions reflected concerns about music's power over men and women's physical bodies, specifying that 'when ye sing, see ye sing nothing but what is appointed to be sung in the book: and that which is not written to be sung, let it not be sung'.[19] Curtailing the scope of the nuns' singing in this way was intended to curb the power that music had to gratify the senses, which might lead the mind astray. This was expanded upon, albeit more positively, in the *Lisbon Additions* of the same year, where it was emphasised:

> [A]ll singing ought to bee the office of the Divine praise, and the fruit of the labour. . . not only of them that do sing the psalms, but also of them that do hear them. . . The singing of all shall bee grave simple plain and modest: not broken, high or clamorous but with all humility and devotion.[20]

Rigorous standards were vital; the experience for listeners was as important as for the singers, and the music was not to be high or clamorous, which might have a negative and distracting effect. The music was to be simple, and divine, in order to ensure that those hearing had their devotions enhanced by the music as much as those performing.

Singing in the choir was first and foremost an act of prayer, and such a critical part of monastic life that, on occasion, discounts were offered on the dowries of potential nuns with musical skills and beautiful singing voices.[21] Particularly musical nuns were singled out within the convent chronicles by name. At St Monica's in Louvain, the chronicler recorded the professions of Sister Anne Evans who had 'learnt in the world to play upon the virginals [and] was since become so skilful upon the organ', Sister Lioba Morgan who 'was also very skilful in prick-song',[22] and Sister Mary Skidmore who was able to enter St Monica's in part 'because she could play on the organs'.[23] Similarly, men with a calling to the priesthood who demonstrated musical ability might be shown leniency if other qualities were lacking. This is clear in the record made in the diaries of the English college of Douay (founded by William Allen in 1568) after the entrance of John Worthington on 5 January 1607:

> And he desires to become a priest if he can now obtain the knowledge for that office, for he can only understand Latin and at the most, write it. But he is a skilful musician, both in singing and at the organ. And so he is received into the College that he may at the same time help our choir and instruct others in this art, while he performs his studies.[24]

Musical leaders like Worthington were important for ensuring high musical standards. In the convents, this was the responsibility of the nun elected 'Chantress'. Musical expertise was essential for this position, and formed the basis of their election. The Chantress instructed the choir and was also responsible for appointing the best singers. As the constitutions for St Monica's explained: 'when two are to sing together, she shall be careful to appoint two such as have voices that will best agree one with another, that there be no discord'. The constitutions also made clear that the Chantress 'shall also be very careful that. . . it be done in such a manner that it might stir one up to devotion'.[25]

The daily performance of music was vital to the lives of those within the institutions, although musical practice within the communities was diverse, and a product of the experiences of its individual members.[26] Within the convents, musical practices were also affected by the ecclesiastical authorities' implementation of enclosure. The provisions of enclosure were first asserted in the papal bull *Periculoso* in 1298 and were unambiguously reaffirmed at the Council of Trent. In the twenty-fifth session in December 1563 it was announced:

> [T]he enclosure of nuns be restored wherever it has been violated. . . No nun shall after her profession be permitted to go out of the monastery, even for a brief period under any pretext whatever, except for a lawful reason to be approved by the bishop.[27]

The physical boundaries of the convents were clearly demarcated from the surrounding landscape by high walls. This was essential for the institutions' definition as explicitly sacred spaces, and acted as protection, as Trent decreed, from 'the rapacity and other crimes of evil men'.[28] Yet sounds could carry beyond the convent walls, and Trent also raised a series of questions over the compatibility of music with enclosure. As we have seen, music's ability to gratify the senses and arouse moral deviance, as much as devotion, was a serious concern – especially with regard to female religious. This anxiety was present before Trent; in 1446, for example, the City Fathers of Florence sheltered the nuns from the 'corrupting influence of secular music' by barring heraldic civic musicians from playing within fifty yards of any convent.[29]

Walls also divided the convents on the inside and separated the easily accessible public church from the nuns' church, which was part of the internal, cloistered space of the convent. Interactions between these spaces were strictly aural. Heard but not seen, from the choir the nuns followed the public religious ceremonies; they listened to the words of the priest, sang their parts in the office and sang in unison with the local community. Concerns over musical performance also extended to the performance of sacred music by the nuns: as Silvia Evangelisti explains, 'even when hidden in their choir or behind the curtains of their parlours, singing nuns might be heard by outsiders, triggering fantasies about their forbidden bodies'.[30] The Tridentine response, as implemented by the episcopacy, was often to discourage more elaborate forms of music. And yet, despite several laws banning nuns from playing instruments and singing for outsiders (except sacred music related to religious subjects or episodes related to the lives of saints) it is clear that a more flexible approach, permitting various kinds of performances, prevailed.

The evidence for these more diverse musical occasions is found in surviving music books, the employment of musicians, records of instruments, and accounts of specific musical performances. This documentation demonstrates that despite concerns, it was important for the sounds from the convents to be heard beyond their walls. This was partially due to patronage, as musical performances advertised both the convents and seminaries as beacons of 'English' devotion, which attracted English lay exiles. The convents and seminaries simultaneously appealed to the local laity, who were attracted to the foundations as exemplars of Counter-Reformation zeal. The style of the music they heard was also a poignant amalgamation; the institutions contained English men and women, and, as we shall see, they seem to have generally preferred using English musicians as teachers and performers. At the same time, as Andrew Cichy has shown, the institutions used continental repertoire in their liturgical functions. To hear 'English Catholicism' in the Spanish Habsburg territories, then, was to hear 'a meeting point between English Catholics and the musical fruits of the Counter-Reformation'.[31] The convents and seminaries stood defiant on the continent, in the face of established Church of England, and consequently, they were incorporated into networks of transnational piety.

Influence from continental Catholics and from England was facilitated in part by the employment of musicians. The jubilee of Margaret Clement at Louvain in 1606 was marked by an entire week of musical festivities; musicians were loaned from the Archducal chapel itself to support the music-making, with volunteers from the local burghers performing alongside them.[32] Similarly, in 1599 the clothing ceremony of the first eight postulants at the Benedictine convent in Brussels was conducted in the presence of the entire court of the Archdukes, as well as the Archbishop of Mechelen and the papal nuncio.[33] Musicians employed by the Archdukes Albert and Isabella included several English Catholic exiles, including Peter Philips and John Bull. At St Omer, the Annual Letter of 1653 provides evidence that music and dancing were still being taught at the College and that despite the troubled years of the interregnum, they maintained 'two skilled singing masters brought from England'.[34] St Monica's and the Brussels Benedictines also employed permanent musicians during this period, namely the English Catholic exiles John Bolt and Richard Dering.

Instruments were fundamental to the acoustic environment of the institutions; John Bolt is recorded as having instructed the nuns of St Monica's on the organ as well as in voice, and it is possible that Dering did the same in Brussels.[35] Instruments were provided in abundance at St Omer, and Giles Schondonch, the rector from 1600 to 1617, left written instructions listing the variety of musical instruments befitting particular situations. For the reception of guests and persons of distinction, 'the broken consort' was the most 'delightful', and instruments should include 'the bass viol, or viol de gamba; the lute, or wanting this, the orpharion; the treble viol, the cither, the flute; add the tenor violin and the bassoon for effectiveness and charm'.[36] Wind instruments should be used 'especially for church services, for the reception of persons of high rank and for the theatre'. Schondonch also detailed the variety of wind instruments available to the scholars, including the hautbois, recorder, the sackbut and the cornet. The organ and harpsichord were identified as 'suitable and pleasing for church music'.[37]

With such lavish provision, it should be no surprise that music was renowned at St Omer.[38] Music was important to the college for inspiring the devotion of the scholars, and this piety was displayed prominently during musical entertainments for guests. As the Apostolic Nuncio, Guido Bentivoglio recorded in his letter to Cardinal Scipione Borghese after his visit in 1609:

> I returned soon after dinner to inspect the Seminary more carefully, and was entertained by the scholars with vocal and instrumental music, in which they are instructed so as to increase in them a spirit of devotion. . . [A]fter supper I was again treated with sacred music, to my infinite delight.[39]

Music was also vital for the edification of the local laity, and for building relationships with St Omer's citizens. The scholars' duty in this regard was fulfilled, as the Nuncio noted that the 'city shows itself very favourable to the College'.[40] When the boys left St Omer, it was either for a career in the priesthood, or to return to England in order to support the faith of their beleaguered community as laymen. The importance placed on musical training, and the frequency of musical recreation and performances, suggests that for either of the paths they chose, music was fundamental for their preparation.[41]

Musical recreation also occurred in the convents. For example, according to both her contemporary biographer, Sister Shirley, and the chronicler of the convent, Mary Copley, Mother Margaret Clement of St Monica's sung a 'Dutch ditty' before her death in May 1612.[42] The particular song Clement performed has proved impossible to identify, but Shirley recorded that it was 'from the exceeding Joy & Jubilation of her hart [she] sang a devout song of Jesus which made of the Elders to weep that sat near her'.[43] That this song was a 'Dutch ditty' highlights the outside influences that were present within the institutions. The Clement family had lived in exile in the Low Countries since the accession of Elizabeth, when Margaret was about nineteen. She would therefore have been very familiar with Dutch music, and brought this influence into the convent of St Monica's, when she joined as a founding member in 1609.

In a similar way, the majority of the other nuns who had grown up in England would have brought popular English songs with them to the continent. This is evident from the ex-Syon brother Thomas Robinson's 1622 'exposé' of the Bridgettine community. After Robinson left the community, he penned an assault on its many alleged failings, and its scandalous use of music:

> [W]ell doe they [the nuns] manifest the abundance of idleness that is in them, when at sundry times playing upon their instruments for their fathers [confessor's] recreation, they sing him ribaldrous Songs and jigs, as that of Bonny Nell, and such other obscene and scurrilous Ballads, as would make a *chaste ear to glow* at the hearing of them, and which I would scarce have believed would have proceeded out of their mouths, had I not heard them *with my own ears*.[44]

Sources such as this made the English populace aware of England's Catholic exiles whilst simultaneously denouncing them, and Robinson did so very specifically by criticising their ears. Robinson highlighted the chastity of his own ears, and solidified his role as the 'earwitness' of the event, by inferring how *un*chaste the nuns' ears were, as ears were often linked with the female genitals during this period (a point I will return to later).[45] Keith Botelho has drawn attention to the way that 'earwitnessing' was a vital form of proof during this period, and Robinson used this strategy to underline his trustworthiness.[46] He would scarcely have believed what he had witnessed, if he had not 'heard them', with his own chaste, and reliable ears.

The Bridgettines were soon aware of Robinson's text, as is evident from a manuscript letter that survives in the British Library:

> About the first of December 1622, Syon had a full notice and sight of a most slanderous printed libel, sett forth by one Thomas Robinson against them: but because they then understand that it bine published divers months before it came to there knowledge and no doubt to the grief of their parents and friends whose remedy and comfort they were bound to procure with all possible speed.[47]

The community made sure to respond to Robinson point-by-point, including his attack on music:

> And though these Nuns as others of this country singe or have music sometimes at their grates, yet that these ever sung Bonny Nell, or any immodest tunes or ditty, it is only his false tongue which doth affirm it.[48]

The nuns' response confirmed Syon's use of recreational music with the retort that it was no different to the behaviour of other religious communities. They also attempted to restore their reputation for chastity by denouncing Robinson's 'false tongue'. Tongues, in a similar way to music, were also viewed as extremely unstable during the period: as Carla Mazzio has argued, quoting the words of Erasmus, the tongue was 'an ambivalent Organ'.[49] As the organ of speech and singing, the tongue was also associated with the ear, and with hearing. As George Webbe stated in *The Arraignment of an Unruly Tongue* (1619) 'they [who] imitate the poyson of the Adder in their Tongue; so they have the deafenesse of the Adder in their Eare'.[50] By condemning Robinson's tongue, then, the nuns were also implicitly casting doubt on his ability to hear clearly.

Syon's indignant response in order to protect their reputation was partially due to their reliance on patronage, because the relationships that the communities held locally and internationally were often forged by musical performances. The principal income for the English convents and seminaries came from the support of longstanding patrons of high status. As a result of their exile, the communities were reliant on the many sporadic gifts they received in exchange for specific acts. For example, individual directions to pray for the souls of deceased, usually during vespers and matins, were recorded in benefactors' books for the communities. Several are extant, and the money secured and recorded in these accounts represents an economy of song, whereby musical performances were part of a cycle of economic transactions. This is exemplified by the following extract from the year 1624–5 in the benefactor's book of St Monica's:

> In primis received of Mr Standford to *pray for his soul* 20
> Item received of Mr Bannister to *pray for his wife* 60
> Item received of Mrs Copley *to pray for her brother* 40
> Item received from Mrs Cooke *a legacy* left us by her husband 200
> Somma 320.[51]

Singing prayers from the choir attracted potential new benefactors by arousing their devotions at the services they attended, and in turn they made payments and legacies for the communities to pray for their souls, the cycle thereby beginning again.

The importance of the economy of song to the communities is particularly conspicuous when things go wrong, as a series of incidents from the Brussels Benedictine convent demonstrates. The strife started simmering from the early 1620s, and from 1628 to 1632 the convent was in a state of 'open warfare'.[52] The disputes in the convent were related to the rivalries that fragmented English Catholics between Jesuits and seculars during the period, which began soon after the arrival of the first Jesuits to England in the 1580s and were to last until well into the seventeenth century. Put briefly, Catholic loyalties were divided between the secular clergy (those without a Rule) and the Jesuits. Both at home and abroad there were frequent arguments between the two factions over strategies for the Mission and tactics to be adopted by Catholics in England.[53] This split was explosively paralleled in the Brussels convent, and catalysed controversies that had a devastating effect on the community, which was not in agreement over the choice of confessor. Although from 1599 the secular priest Robert Chambers was the community's official spiritual director, the abbess Mary Percy had made the decision to allow some of the nuns to have an English Jesuit confessor. In 1628 Chambers died and the Archbishop of Mechelen, Jacobus Boonen, appointed Anthony Champney (then Vice-Rector at Douay) as confessor to the Brussels community. This was a controversial choice: Champney had been involved in the anti-Jesuit movement, and was one of thirteen priests who had signed the protestation of allegiance to Queen Elizabeth in 1603. By 1631, two clear factions in the convent had emerged: a pro-Jesuit group led by Mary Vavasour, and the rest led by the abbess, Mary Percy, and her prioress Agatha Wiseman. The following events serve to underline my point that music was a fundamental form of expression for the nuns, as well as vital for generating patronage, and therefore critical for their survival.

Within a haphazard collection of documents relating to the community in the Archive of the Archdiocese of Mechelen is an extremely revealing letter to Archbishop Boonen from 1632. The letter is in the hand of Agatha Wiseman and endorsed in the margins and at the end by various nuns of her faction.[54] The letter is fourteen pages long, and contains twenty-eight points describing a series of violent events that had occurred at the convent since the Archbishop and papal nuncio's last visit in February of that year. This visit was supposed to have put an end to the unrest in the convent, as permission had been granted to the Appellants, the Jesuit faction, to receive a Father of the Society six times a year. However, when the time came to elect new officers 'the Appellants made there a mutiny'. The group surrounding Mary Vavasour cried out that they would not surrender their places and offices: 'that the said convent had confirmed them, and that they would maintain their right'. From then on, conflict was 'made daily in the places where the convent meet but especially in the choir'. It began on Saturday in the first week of Lent, when:

D[ame]. Martha [Colford] began her office of chantress, but D. Aurea [James, pro-Jesuit] would perforce intone the psalms with her, w[hi]ch she did in extraordinary and unaccustomed tunes of purpose (as it may seem) to – make a discord, see that one part of the religious following the Chantress, and the other part D. Aurea, there was made

an unsupportable discord and confusion, to the great scandale of
those who were in the church.

Musical terminology such as 'discord' frequently translated into other
categories of expression during the period; in particular, it was often used,
as it still is today, to describe disrupted social and political relations. The
use of 'discord' twice here emphasised the situation: the discord was both
a metaphor and an acoustic reality, as the two factions battled for power
through clashing simultaneous psalm-tunes.

The conflicts in the choir steadily worsened: the letter explained
how on March 12 the two chantresses appointed rival nuns to sing from
the martyrology, with the result that the nuns physically fought over the
book. In an attempt to prevent similar embarrassment, later that day, 'at
the high masse my Lady [Abbess Mary Percy] to prevent contentions
ordained that the tract (which is ordinarily sung by 2 or 3 religious to each
verse who are appointed by the chantress) should be sung by all the religious together'. The resulting violent fall-out led to the Abbess physically
intervening as she commanded the nuns 'not to strive so at masse' and in
the process 'received a blow on the face' from the pro-Jesuit Mary Phillips.

The fisticuffs in the choir stalls did not cease and on Sunday 14 March
at Matins the letter described how similar factional rivalry resulted in 'the
religious laying aside for a time the divine office they betook themselves
to chiding and striving together in the choir'. The letter explained how
the sounds of the nuns' dispute were 'to the scandal of the people in the
church', as they listened to the nuns snatching books from one another
and pushing each other to the ground. The violence continued, and on
26 March the community had to take a dramatic step: 'we have bin forced
to shut the choir door, and to say our office in private, rather than by
irreverence in the church to offend god and scandalize those that come
thither'. The fact that the nuns were prepared to cut themselves off from
the local community in this way indicates that the problems were so severe
that they were willing to risk their livelihoods: as previously discussed,
the community relied on their performance in the choir to generate patronage. It was this that prompted the desperate prioress, Wiseman, to
write the letter to the Archbishop.

It is clear that the nuns' reputation was greatly damaged, as stories of
the divided convent were soon circulating in manuscript.[55] These troubles
had a devastating effect on professions to the convent, which plummeted
during the years of strife. Only one sister, Elizabeth Sunley, joined the
community between 1628 and 1637, in stark contrast to the immediately
preceding years between 1618 and 1627, when twenty-eight new choir
nuns and lay sisters were professed.[56] Between 1638–1652 only one other
nun, Grace Bake, was professed and 1652 marked a resolution to the
conflicts when Mary Vavasour was elected abbess after the death of Alexia

Blanchard. Normal musical practice and provision was restored, the economy of song gained momentum again, and the 'discord' was over.[57]

III.

Alongside the devotion aroused by the performance of sacred music and the divine office, bells were critical in demarcating the aural boundaries of the communities.[58] Of especial importance to Catholic communities was the Ave or Angelus Bell, which according to the constitutions from St Monica's was rung every day after Compline: 'they shall ring the Ave bell three times, and every time ring it thrice'.[59] At every peal the *Ave Maria* was said, and in between the Angelus devotion in memory of the incarnation. Bells were audible to individuals beyond the convent and seminary walls, as their echoes across the landscape were intended to summon the faithful hearers to prayer. The sound of bells prompted a significant response from one listener in particular. In 1601, when English Catholic exile Richard Verstegan was based in Antwerp, working as a publisher and intelligence agent for the superiors of the English mission, he composed two poetic 'expositions of the Ave bell', and published them within his *Odes in imitation of the Seaven Penitential Psalms* (1601), which were dedicated to the English Benedictine convent in Brussels, to be performed with their 'sweet voices and virginals'.[60]

Verstegan had strong ties to the Brussels community through a mutual Catholic friend, Gabriel Colford. Colford's arrival on the continent in 1593 was noted in a letter from Verstegan to Robert Persons, and by 1595 the authorities were soon aware that, like Verstegan, Colford was involved in the illicit English Catholic book-trade.[61] By 1600, Colford had a close relationship with Verstegan, and Verstegan paid the account for Colford's purchases at the Plantin House printing press in Antwerp.[62] In the following years, Colford was intimately linked with the convent: his daughter Martha entered in 1609, he was also one of the house's translators, and by 1629 the community noted that he had transcribed the convent's statutes for them.[63] In the dedication of his *Odes* to the community, Verstegan explained how he had already 'communicated them with a friend' who had encouraged him to publish them: 'And now hauing yeilded unto the one, and aduentured the other, I knew no better way then to make dedication of them unto your selues'.[64] Based on their mutual acquaintance it could well be that Verstegan dedicated the *Odes* to the community on Colford's insistence; perhaps Colford and Verstegan had visited the convent together and heard the community's Ave bells ringing across Brussels's soundscape. Written in the first person, sounds permeate Verstegan's poems, and prompt multifaceted sensory responses that are vital for stirring memories. Verstegan's sensuous language is explicitly intended to arouse devotion, and the aural and metrical aspects of his poetry demonstrate the way that the sound of the poetry itself could invoke a sense of time and place.

In the two poems, sounds provoke specific physical and emotional responses: as we hear in the opening line of his first poem, an Ave bell was the 'the Chaser of my sence-detayning slumber'. The sounds then stimulate memory, as Verstegan explains in the second stanza: 'For sounds and sights are messengers assigned / To bring lost memory unto the mind'.[65] The memory in this instance was the message that the Angel Gabriel had brought to Mary, and the sound of Gabriel's voice is repeatedly referenced, which Verstegan imagines due to the sound of the bell: 'whereof an Angels voice the message brought / As metals noise renewed it to my thought'.[66] This notion of imagined sounds prompted by real sounds recurs in the second poem, where the 'bel reneweth to our eares / The sound of ioy now twyce before exprest'. The recollection, as Verstegan explains, is in honour of 'The contemplation of the mystery / Of the subjected state of heavens king / And the revival of the memory / That three times, thrice a day the bell doth ring'. Verstegan also highlights the chastity of Mary in distinctly aural terms. In the first poem 'her chaste ears. . . could no noise receive', and he emphasises the sacredness of sound itself: it was Mary's ears that 'conceived first' with the sound of the Angel's voice.[67] The poem ends with the birth of Jesus, which was heralded by the sound of trumpets: 'The Angels trumps did sound the heavens peace'.[68]

In the second poem, Verstegan emphasises how bells' punctuation of the day provokes thoughts on life's transience. He calls on those who hear the midday bell to remember the sacrifice of Jesus, to examine their consciences and remember their own personal sins.[69] In the last stanzas, at the end of the day, the bells served to remind those listening of the end of life on earth and the importance of living well in order to die well.[70] Together, Verstegan's poems testify to the ability of sounds, particularly bells, to move listeners to further devotion by recalling key events in Christian history and precepts of Christian doctrine. Moreover, in the second poem these memories and devotional acts are intimately linked with the passage of time, with the repeated references to the hours of the day and the course of life. The sensory and temporal rhythms of devotion are enhanced by the metrical regularity of Verstegan's verse, and by his extensive use of repetition throughout. Nearly every stanza contains multiple uses of the same words, for example in the eighth stanza of the first poem where love begins and ends the first three lines, beginning and completing the cycle ready for it to start again:

Love first bred grief and grief did pittie moue,
And pittie sought the way to woork redresse,
And kynde redresse the true effect of loue.[71]

In combining the rhetorical tropes including enumeratio (the division of a subject into causes and effects) and anadiplosis (the repetition of a word or clause at the end of one line at the beginning of the next line), Verstegan invokes a specific, liturgical sense of time as circular.

From the outset Verstegan explicitly emphasises the aurality of his verses, referring to them as 'ditties' and making plain that they were intended for performance with the nuns' 'sweet voices' and their virginals. This gives the poetry a sense of dual temporality. The sound of the bells recalls the past, prompting an imagined remembrance of Gabriel's voice as he spoke to the Virgin Mary in Nazareth, and at the same time the verses are designed to be heard in the present moment as they are performed by the nuns. This was evidently effective, and Verstegan's *Odes* were popular in England as well as on the continent and circulated widely even among Protestants. For example, Verstegan's poetic imitations of the seven penitential psalms were included anonymously in Elizabeth Grymeston's *Miscellanea, Meditations, Memoratives* (first printed 1604), and then in 1620 Martin Peerson's *Private Musicke*, which included a musical setting of 'Our Blessed Lady's Lullaby'.[72]

Verstegan's meditations on the Ave bell demonstrate both the imaginative ways that Catholics forged an individual relationship with Christ, and the communality of such interactions for those within earshot. For readers in England, the imagined sounds of the bells prompted by Verstegan's poetry, as well as the sounds of the meditative poetry itself as it was read aloud, would have bound Catholics together and consolidated the community of hearers. On the continent, as their Catholic faith instructed them, those that heard the bells sounding from the institutions will have cast their minds to the nuns and seminarians at prayer, and were united with them during their private devotions. Forged through both real and imagined sounds, communal relationships between English Catholics both at home and abroad, as well as the local international laity, were unavoidable, and indeed desirable. These relationships are underlined in the final part of this essay, where I explore the events and devotions surrounding a damaged statue of the Virgin Mary at the English College in Valladolid.

IV.

In the summer of 1596, the Spanish port of Cadiz was raided by English and Dutch soldiers under the dual command of Lord Charles Howard of Effingham and Robert Devereux the earl of Essex. In the carnage, a statue of the Virgin Mary with the Christ child was attacked: dragged along the streets, beaten and mutilated. The figure of Christ was cut out of the Virgin's arms and her face disfigured. The statue was discovered abandoned in the wreckage left by the soldiers in the plaza and was claimed by Martin de Padilla, secretary of state and war to Philip II, where it was sent to Madrid and placed in his private chapel. A few years later, hearing of the wounded Madonna, the scholars at the English College at Valladolid signed a petition claiming it was more appropriate that 'the English Catholics should disclaim the injuries which the English heretics have inflicted upon our Lady, and should serve and revere the image abused by them'.[73] The petition was successful, and in September 1600 the image was carried in procession from Madrid to Valladolid.

Although scholars such as Peter Davidson have argued that the statue became 'the image of England self-wounded by the ignorance and blindness of her children', this should not overshadow the multi-national and multi-cultural aspects of the festivities surrounding the arrival of the statue to Valladolid, which attracted the devotion and attention of several nations within this cosmopolitan city as well as the local Spanish laity.[74] According to the surviving contemporary account penned in Spanish by Antonio Ortiz, when Philip III and his consort Margarita arrived at the College ready for the festivities to celebrate the arrival of the Vulnerata, they were greeted by the students who:

> above in the quire sang *Te Deum laudamus*, in their accustomed Ecclesiastical Music which contented so much. . . [T]he Duke of Lerma and other noble men that came with the king; thought the singers had been procured from abroad, but understanding that it was the ordinary music of the College, and only the students, received double contentment to hear it. . .[75]

It was important for the College to emphasise that it was their own students singing for the monarchs: their Englishness was emphasised alongside their musical prowess. As well as music for the liturgy, the students also performed for the Spanish monarchs when they entered the Great Hall: 'the Musicians in the other room adjoining, divided only with a curtain, began to play upon their vials and virginals a very grave and pleasant song of eight parts'.[76] Music supported the College's assimilation within the city, as the students 'integrated Spanish identity into English music'.[77] This is explicit when the English students, giving thanks for the Spanish monarchs' 'favour and protection' also 'began a sweet and artificial song made after their country [England's] manner of musicke and the ditty in Spanish to the purpose'. Hearing English Catholicism on this occasion, then, was to hear purposeful hybrid of English music with Spanish words, and 'the English musicke with the Spanish ditty gave extraordinary contentment to all'.[78]

The *Vulnerata* quickly became fundamental to the musical tradition and devotions of the College. In the College archives are the *Diario de Costumbres*, a collection of documents that reveal a vivid picture of College life from 1600–1731. Among the documents are the details of 'What is observed in devotion to and veneration of the statue of Our Lady, Saint Mary Vulnerata'. These included the directions that:

> A Mass of our Lady will be said all through the year at 10am and 11am of which notice will be given by ringing the bell at full swing, and at this Mass, *the statue of Our Lady will be exposed to view.*

The Mass at 10am will be said from Easter to St Michael's, and that at 11am from St Michael's to Easter and on all Saturdays *the statue will be exposed to view* after the Mass.

Every Saturday the Salve will be sung, in winter at four o'clock in the afternoon, in summer at six, and *the statue will be unveiled.*

On Christmas Day, Easter and Whit Sundays, the nine feasts of Our Lady, the feasts of the Apostles and the Evangelists and on others marked on the College lists as feasts with Mass, vespers and antiphon, on the eve, at winter at four o'clock in the afternoon, in the summer at five, an antiphon will be sung with instrumental accompaniment, and on that day itself, there will be High Mass and vespers, and on these three occasions *the statue will be unveiled,* as it will also be on all feasts of Our Lady during the Masses said at the High Altar.[79]

Especially important was the visibility of the Virgin, which as the instructions repeatedly stressed should be 'exposed to view' or 'unveiled' during the devotions. This indicates the importance of viewing the *Vulnerata* whilst singing the liturgy and during musical performances at feasts. It was imperative for the students to contemplate the wounds of the Madonna in order to heighten their religious experience. From these rituals, there is a strong sense in which the singing of the masses was a form of reparation for the violent touch of the iconoclasts, and acted as a form of musical healing. Similar devotional behaviour was occurring among the Catholic community in England; as Alexandra Walsham has argued, disfigured shrines were regarded as symbols of the embattled Roman faith and enhanced the devotion of the beleaguered laity.[80] The *Vulnerata* was the visible witness of suffering, and this made her almost like a relic: she had been touched, she was to be seen, and the music performed would have been heard. All the senses of the faithful individual were to be aroused by the regular performance of this communal devotion.

The impact of these rituals was significant and boosted missionary zeal, whilst attracting the devotions of the local people, both Spanish and English alike. Moreover, as Anne Cruz has argued, the festivity and the devotions of the *Vulnerata* placed the College in a strategic position in international politics, and at the centre of Spanish society, as the ceremonies of Valladolid made a great impression on the local community.[81] For example, the Spanish noblewoman Luisa de Carvajal took an especial interest in the plight of the English and was 'transfixed' by the *Vulnerata.* Her letters revealed that 'since it is just a few steps away from home, I present myself before her every day even if I am very sick'.[82] The festivities at the college need therefore to be contextualised not only within the atmosphere of persecution and propaganda, but also in terms of border-crossing between cultures and languages which were critical to Catholic life in exile during this period.

V.

By listening to the past experiences of English Catholics on the continent, it is clear that exiled men and women must not be investigated in isolation from their continental co-religionists, nor from their Catholic compatriots in England. With the economy of song, the English convents and seminaries were linked through public piety and patronage. The local Spanish and Dutch communities were attracted to the institutions as centres of devotion, which were advertised by music and in turn inspired donation and support. Music facilitated connections between individuals, which could be discordant as much as harmonious (as we saw in the Brussels convent). Music also fostered links to the divine, and the ability of sounds to prompt a multifaceted sensory and devotional response from the listening laity is evident in Richard Verstegan's poetry dedicated to the English Benedictine nuns at Brussels. The way that music allowed people to sense the sacred was also clear at Valladolid, where the significance of singing, seeing, hearing, and touch was epitomised through devotion to the *Vulnerata,* and as the ceremonies demonstrated, the way English Catholic exiles enhanced the sense of their own national identity was complex. Musical performances often blurred national and cultural lines, as we saw in Valladolid, where the seminarians performed 'English' music with the text of a local Spanish 'ditty'. Another form of national expression was through the image of a wounded Mary, and yet at the same time the image was utilised by local and international visitors to the community, who adopted the image for their own devotional needs and political ends. The English seminaries and convents have been described as inhabiting 'a liminal position – geographically separate from the families and English Catholic population they served and culturally distinct from the neighbourhoods in which they were situated'.[83] And yet, rather than 'seemingly dislocated pockets of resistance to the Protestant Church and state', the convents and seminaries were specifically located, and their sense of place defined by what they heard.[84] By sensing the sacred through sounds, English Catholics were spiritually and physically located amongst their co-religionists both at home and abroad.

Notes

Thanks to audiences at the University of Konstanz and University College Dublin for their helpful questions and comments on earlier versions of this essay.

1 See, for example, Mark M. Smith, ed., *Hearing History: A Reader* (Athens: University of Georgia Press, 2004).
2 See, for example, Christopher Marsh, *Music and Society in Early Modern England* (Cambridge: Cambridge University Press, 2013), Jonathan P. Willis,

Church Music and Protestantism in post-Reformation England: Discourses, Sites and Identities (Farnham: Ashgate, 2010).

3 John Bossy, *English Catholic Community, 1570–1850* (London: Darton, Longman & Todd, 1975), 6.

4 Katy Gibbons, *English Catholic Exiles in Late Sixteenth-Century Paris* (Woodbridge: Boydell Press for the Royal Historical Society, 2011).

5 See Caroline Bowden and James Kelly, eds., *The English Convents in Exile, 1600–1800: Communities, Culture and Identity* (Burlington, VT: Ashgate, 2013), James E. Kelly and Susan Royal, eds., *Early Modern English Catholicism: Identity, Memory and Counter-Reformation* (Leiden: Brill, 2016), Laurence Lux-Sterritt, *English Benedictine Nuns in Exile in the Seventeenth Century: Living Spirituality* (Manchester: Manchester University Press, 2017).

6 For more on theories of 'senses of place' and space from the field of historical geography, a good starting point is Yi-Fu Tuan, *Space and Place: The Perspective of Experience* (Minneapolis: University of Minnesota Press, 1977). In 1568 the first Catholic seminary, the English College in Douay, was founded by William Allen. In 1659 the *Treaty of the Pyrenees* was signed to mark the end of the Franco-Spanish war, as part of this treaty the County of Artois was annexed and St Omer became part of France.

7 Richard Helgerson, *Forms of Nationhood: the Elizabethan Writing of England* (Chicago: University of Chicago Press, 1992), Mark Netzloff, 'The English Colleges and the English Nation: Allen, Persons, Verstegan, and Diasporic Nationalism', in *Catholic Culture in Early Modern England*, ed. Ronald Corthell et al. (Notre Dame, IN: University of Notre Dame Press, 2007), 236–60.

8 Netzloff, 'The English Colleges', 237; Lisa McClain, *Lest We Be Damned: Practical Innovation and Lived Experience Among Catholics in Protestant England, 1559–1642* (New York: Routledge, 2004), 234.

9 Claire Walker, *Gender and Politics in Early Modern Europe: English Convents in France and the Low Countries* (New York: Palgrave Macmillan, 2003), 38.

10 Christopher Highley, *Catholics Writing the Nation in Early Modern Britain and Ireland* (Oxford: Oxford University Press, 2008), 183.

11 Geert H. Janssen, 'The Exile Experience', in *The Ashgate Research Companion to the Counter Reformation*, ed. Alexandra Bamji, Geert H. Janssen, and Mary Laven (Aldershot: Ashgate, 2013), 73–90 (at 84).

12 Cited in Linda Phyllis Austern, '"Tis Nature's Voice": Music, Natural Philosophy and the Hidden World in Seventeenth-Century England', in *Music Theory and the Natural Order, from the Renaissance to the Early Twentieth Century*, ed. Suzannah Clark and Alexander Reading (Cambridge: Cambridge University Press, 2001), 30–67 (at 1).

13 For music and medicine, see Penelope Gouk, 'Raising Spirits and Restoring Souls: Early Modern Medical Explanations for Music's Effects' in *Hearing Cultures: Essays on Sound, Listening and Modernity*, ed. Veit Erlmann (Oxford: Berg, 2004), 87–105.

14 Willis, *Church Music*, 26.

15 Augustine, *Confessions*, 10.33, trans. R.S. Pine-Coffin (London: Penguin, 1961), 238.

16 Alexander J. Fisher, 'Bells and Apotropaic Magic in Post-Tridentine Germany', paper delivered at *For Whom the Bell Tolls. Sound, Time, and Acoustic Communication in the Early Modern World*, University of Konstanz, Institute of Advanced Study, 16 January 2015. For the first book to deal explicitly with bells from the perspective of cultural history, see Alain Corbin, *Village Bells: Sound and Meaning in the 19th-century French Countryside*, trans. Martin

Thom (New York: Colombia University Press, 1998). John Arnold and Caroline Goodson have also discussed this for the medieval period, see 'Resounding Community: The History and Meaning of Medieval Church Bells', *Viator* 43 (2012): 99–130.

17 Fisher, 'Bells and Apotropaic Magic'.

18 R. Murray Schafer, 'Soundscapes and Earwitnesses', in Smith, ed., *Hearing History*, 3–9 (at 9). This also relates to Aristotle's description of all the senses, including sound, as forms of touch or contact – for Aristotle 'sound. . . is generated by an impact', and 'there seems to be a sort of parallelism between what is acute or grave to hearing and what is sharp or blunt to touch'. *De Anima*, book 2, chapter 8. From 'The Internet Classics Archive', accessed 28 October 2015. http://classics.mit.edu/Aristotle/soul.2.ii.html.

19 All spelling for this source has been modernised to ease reading. Lisbon Rule (1607) and Additions (1607), ed. James Hogg, *The Birgittine Legislation for Syon Abbey Lisbon* (Salzburg, 1991), 19.

20 *The Birgittine Legislation*, 99.

21 See Sylvia Evangelisti, *Nuns: A History of Convent Life* (Oxford: Oxford University Press, 2007), 113.

22 Douai Abbey, Berks. St. Monica's Louvain [hereafter DAB St. Monica's] MS. C2 Chronicle, 1548–1837, 469. This chronicle was edited, and published as *The Chronicle of the English Augustinian Canonesses Regular of the Lateran at St Monica's in Louvain*, ed. Adam Hamilton, 2 vols. (London: Sands, 1906). Prick-song means 'pricked song' i.e. noted down, marked on a page. Lioba could therefore read music.

23 DAB St. Monica's MS. C2 Chronicle, 89.

24 E.H. Burton and T.L. Williams, eds., *The Douay College Diaries 1598- 1654 Vol. 1*, Catholic Record Society Record Series, 10 (1911), 344–45.

25 DAB St. Monica's MS. E5 Constitutions, Ancient Customs & Ceremonies AD 1609, ff. 55–56.

26 For the only published work on music in the English convents, see Andrew Cichy, 'Parlour, Court and Cloister: Musical Culture in English Convents during the Seventeenth Century', in *English Convents in Exile*, ed. Bowden and Kelly, 175–90 (at 187).

27 Norman P. Tanner S.J., ed., *Decrees of the Ecumenical Councils*, 2 vols. (London: Sheed & Ward, 1990), 2: 778.

28 Ibid.

29 Cited in Sharon T. Strocchia, *Nuns and Nunneries in Renaissance Florence* (Baltimore: Johns Hopkins University Press, 2009), 173.

30 Evangelisti, *Nuns*, 114.

31 Cichy, 'Parlour, Court and Cloister', 61.

32 'Life of Mother Margaret Clement', in *The Troubles of Our Catholic Forefathers Related by Themselves*, ed. John Morris, 3 vols. (London: Burns and Oates, 1872–1877), 1: 40–42.

33 SP 12/273/49.

34 These Letters, normally printed for each year, were compilations made at Rome from the digests sent by each provincial superior deriving from the letters written to him every year from each of the colleges. Cited in William H. McCabe, 'Music and Dance on a 17th-Century College Stage', *The Musical Quarterly* 24 (1938): 313–22 (at 321).

35 DAB St. Monica's MS. C2 Chronicle, 466.

36 Schondonch's inventory from Louvain Univ. Lib. MS. D. 321 (160), 29–30. Copied in McCabe, 'Music and Dance', 314–15. A 'broken consort' was a term used to describe a musical ensemble that featured instruments from more than one family, e.g. strings and wind.

37 Ibid.
38 Whitehead and Leech, 'In Paradise and Among Angels'.
39 Henry Foley, ed., *Records of the English Province of the Society of Jesus: Historic Facts Illustrative of the Labours and Sufferings of its Members in the Sixteenth and Seventeenth Centuries*, 7 vols. (London: Burns and Oates, 1875–1883), 7: pt. 2, 1152–55.
40 Ibid.
41 This training likely supported the type of music that was used by lay-Catholics for their own household piety, and their wider communities. See Emilie K. M. Murphy, 'Adoramus te Christe: Music and Post-Reformation English Catholic Domestic Piety', in *Religion and the Household*, ed. Alexandra Walsham et al. (Woodbridge: Boydell and Brewer, 2014), 242–55; 'Music and Catholic Culture in Post-Reformation Lancashire: Piety, Protest and Conversion', *British Catholic History* 33 (2015): 492–525; 'Musical self-fashioning and the 'theatre of death' in late Elizabethan and Jacobean England', *Renaissance Studies* 30 (2016): 410–429.
42 *The Chronicle of the English Augustinian Canonesses*, vol. 1, 99. Copley (prof. 1612 d.1669) has been identified as the first scribe of the Chronicle, whose hand is present from pages 1–621, the years 1535–1660. See Victoria Van Hyning, 'Naming Names: Chroniclers, Scribes and Editors of St Monica's Convent, Louvain, 1631–1906', in *The English Convents in Exile*, ed. Bowden and Kelly, 71–86.
43 DAB St. Monica's MS. Q1 Life of our Most Reverent Mother Margrit Clement, 1628, f. 140.
44 My emphasis. Thomas Robinson, *Anatomy of the English Nunnery at Lisbon in Portugall* (London, 1622), 13.
45 For links between ears (and mouths) and genitals, see Carla Mazzio, 'Sins of the Tongue in Early Modern England', *Modern Language Studies* 28 (1998): 93–124.
46 Keith Botelho, *Renaissance Earwitnesses: Rumor and Early Modern Masculinity* (New York: Palgrave Macmillan, 2009).
47 BL. Add. MS. 21203, f.42v.
48 BL. Add. MS. 21203, f.49.
49 Mazzio, 'Sins of the Tongue in Early Modern England', 93.
50 George Webbe, *The Arraignment of an unruly tongue...* (London, 1619), 90–91. This drew upon the story of Eve's fall, which was represented in Psalm 58.4.5 (as Webbe annotated at the side of the page), 'They are like the deafe Adder which stoppeth her eare, and will not hearken to the voyce of the Charmer, charming never so expertly'.
51 DAB St. Monica's MS. P1 Benefactor's Book, 1609–1627, unfoliated. Emphasis in original.
52 Peter Guilday, *The English Catholic Refugees on the Continent 1558–1795*, vol. 1, *The English Colleges and Convents in the Catholic Low Countries, 1558–1795* (London: Longmans, 1914), 259. For more on this conflict, see Emilie K. M. Murphy, 'Language and Power in an English Convent in Exile, c.1621-c.1631', *The Historical Journal* (Forthcoming, 2018), doi: 10.1017/S0018246X17000437.
53 An outline of these affairs has been astutely summarised in James Kelly, 'Kinship and Religious Politics among Catholic families in England, 1570-1640', *History* 94 (2009): 328–43.
54 Mechelen, Archief van het aartsbisdom Mechelen, doos 4: Regulieren Brussel, Engelse Nonnen, 12/2, unfoliated.
55 BL. Add. MS. 18393, 16. From the beginning of the crisis the nuns were concerned over their reputations abroad. See for example, Potentiana Deacon

[in Brussels] to the Archbishop of Mechelen [Jacobus Boonen], 13 December [1622] and others in Archief van het aartsbisdom Mechelen, Mechelen, Belgium, Regulieren Brussel, Engelse Nonnen, Doos 12/1, unfoliated. See also boxes 12/2, 12/3 and 12/4, all uncatalogued and unfoliated.

56 Information from the Who Were the Nuns? Database, accessed 23 March 2015. wwtn.history.qmul.ac.uk.

57 My sincere thanks to Jaime Goodrich for allowing me to mine her expertise on the Brussels Benedictine community, and for helpful comments on a draft of this chapter.

58 As Ben Kaplan has emphasised, 'church bells were the voices of local communities. Just as their sound carried to all within earshot, so it expressed the feelings and served the needs of the same. It proclaimed their unity as a Christian community'. In *Divided by Faith: Religious Conflict and the Practice of Toleration in Early Modern Europe* (Cambridge, MA: Harvard University Press, 2007), 50.

59 DAB St. Monica's MS. E5 Constitutions, f. 38.

60 Richard Verstegan, *Odes in imitation of the Seaven Penitential Psalmes* (Antwerp, 1601), A2. Paul Arblaster has argued that Verstegan was alluding to the Brussels community in the dedication of the *Odes* to 'the vertuous ladies and gentlewomen readers of these ditties'. See *Antwerp and the World: Richard Verstegan and the International Culture of the Catholic Reformation* (Louvain: Louvain University Press, 2004), 80–84.

61 Anthony G. Petti, ed., *The Letters and Dispatches of Richard Verstegan, 1550–1640* (London: Publications of the Catholic Record Society, 1959), 155. Colford was cited in a warrant from 12 November 1595 from Sir Thomas Fleming to the Solicitor General: 'There is one Gabriel Colford lately apprehended, that brought certain seditious books from beyond the seas into the realm, being a most lewd person, as wee do understand, and one that is emploied for the fugitives beyond the seas in messages hither into the realm'. See SP. 12 / 2 / 21, f.40.

62 Petti, *Letters and Dispatches*, 155–57.

63 Cited in Jaime Goodrich, 'Nuns and Community-Centred Writing: The Benedictine Rule and Brussels Statutes', *The Huntington Library Quarterly* 77 (2014): 287–303 (at 289).

64 Verstegan, *Odes*, unpaginated preface (A2r).

65 Ibid., 98.

66 Ibid.

67 Ibid.

68 Ibid., 101.

69 Ibid., 103.

70 Ibid., 104.

71 Ibid., 99.

72 Elizabeth Grymeston, *Miscelanea, Meditations, Memoratiues* (London, 1604), Fr-Hr; Martin Peerson, *Private Musicke: Or the First book of ayres and dialogues,* (London, 1620), Dv-D2r.

73 Cited in Michael E. Williams, *St Alban's College, Valladolid: Four Centuries of English Catholic Presence in Spain* (London: C Hurst, 1986), 61–62.

74 Peter Davidson, 'Recusant Catholic Spaces in Early Modern England', in *Catholic Culture in Early Modern England*, ed. Ronald Corthell et al, 19–51 (at 25).

75 Antonio Ortiz, *A relation of the solemnitie wherewith the Catholike princes K. Philip III and Quene Margret were receyued in the Inglish Colledge of Valladolid the 22. of August. 1600. Written in Spanish by Don Ant. Ortiz and*

translated by Frauncis Riuers and dedicated to the right honorable the Lord Chamberlayne (Antwerp, 1601), 17.

76 Ortiz, *A relation of the solemnitie*, 39.

77 Andrew Cichy, '"How Shall We Sing the Song of the Lord in a Strange Land?" English Catholic Music after the Reformation to 1700: A Study of Institutions in Continental Europe' (Unpublished PhD Thesis, University of Oxford, 2014), 116.

78 Ibid.

79 My emphasis. Cited in Williams, *St Alban's College Valladolid*, 240–241.

80 Alexandra Walsham, *The Reformation of the Landscape: Religion, Identity, and Memory in Early Modern Britain and Ireland* (Oxford: Oxford University Press, 2011), 173.

81 Anne J. Cruz, 'Vindicating the *Vulnerata*: Cadiz and the Circulation of Religious Imagery as Weapons of War', in *Material and Symbolic Circulation between Spain and England, 1554–1604*, ed. Anne J. Cruz (Aldershot: Ashgate, 2008), 39–60.

82 Glyn Redworth, *The She-Apostle: The Extraordinary Life and Death of Luisa de Carvajal* (Oxford, Oxford University Press, 2008), 84.

83 Walker, *Gender and Politics*, 174.

84 Ibid.

8 Sensing sacred missives: birch bark letters from seventeenth-century missions in New France

Robin Macdonald

I.

Amongst the papers of the Jesuit historian Camille de Rochemonteix (now held at the Archives des jésuites au Canada) is a letter penned in 1894 by Henri Omont, archivist and philologist at the Bibliothèque nationale in Paris.[1] 'Your work on the missions in the Americas', Omont wrote, 'will without a doubt prompt your interest in two very fragile documents which you will permit me to signal to you'.[2] These documents were two letters, 'written on birch bark [*écorce de bouleau*]': the first, penned in 1647 by Jesuit missionary Father Joseph Poncet from his posting at the Wendat mission in New France to Dom Claude Martin in Paris, and the second, composed in 1676 by a group of Indigenous girls and young women at the Ursuline seminary of Quebec and sent to Monsieur Charles Sain, *receveur général des finances* in Bourges.[3] Rochemonteix's reply is no longer extant, but presumably Omont's letter piqued his interest, for in December of the same year, he received a second letter. This missive was from one 'A. Prempain' and included transcriptions of the birch bark letters.[4] Although Prempain had managed to fully transcribe the second letter, he had only deciphered a few words of the first. After listing the phrases he had been able to make out, he explained:

> This is all one can glean that *makes any sense*. The low-quality ink has worn away and one can only decipher a few words here and there. To be able to read them, one needs good light and instruments. Monsieur Omont tells me that there is only one way to glean information from what remains of this artefact [*monument*]. Pick out the words that one can just about read, just about guess. . . lay them out one by one on paper, leaving gaps between them, [and] then with the help of these words, construct [*construire*] sentences that will fit around them, and that *make sense*. This very tiring work would take a long time; and then, where would the authenticity be of a letter constructed [*fabriqué*] in this way[?][5]

Although Prempain conceded that it was possible to construct logical sentences that '[made] *sense*', he challenged the authenticity of this approach. The letter alone, he implied, had little historical meaning, except as a tangible '*monument*' of the New France mission.

Prempain's letter raises important questions about the ways in which archivists and historians have catalogued and studied materials relating to the New France mission. For what reasons, for instance, do certain documents appear in edited collections, whilst others remain in manuscript alone? In this case, the letters' unusual material form – that is, that they were birch bark letters – seems to have informed their storage and categorisation. Although they were written almost thirty years apart (in 1647 and 1676, respectively), they were stored together in a double wooden frame, which opens like a book (see Fig. 8.1).[6] This storage solution was implemented soon after the letters' acquisition by the Bibliothèque nationale (when Omont wrote to Rochemonteix in 1894, they were still 'at the framer's [shop]').[7] The frame protected these 'fragile documents' (Omont's words) from careless researchers who might damage them, but it also ensured that they were stored in a manner more suited to display than study: encased in glass, they could be looked at, but not touched.[8] That neither of these letters was included in any of the expansive, late-nineteenth-century edited source collections relating to the New France mission implies that the editors of these collections understood texts and objects to be in separate conceptual categories.[9] Since many historians rely on these collections for research, the birch bark letters stored in Paris have been largely passed over in historical analyses.[10] By contrast, this chapter foregrounds letters written on birch bark and argues that their physical form – the reason for their relative exclusion from historiographical accounts – was integral to the ways in which they were sensed and understood.

In recent years, scholars have become attuned to the ways in which the materiality of texts of all kinds, including letters, can shape their meanings.[11] Reading is now understood to be an embodied practice. Readers' physical experiences can affect their understandings of texts and vice versa.[12] Scholars of religion, too, have fruitfully examined complex entanglements of bodies and texts. Julia Boss's analysis of the Manuscript of 1652 (a book containing diverse accounts of the lives and deaths of the 'North American Martyrs') provides an evocative examination of the ways in which holy figures could be embodied by the manuscripts describing their lives. Some hagiographic texts, Boss reminds us, were written in blood, and were thus literal fusions of body and manuscript. In a colony with very few relics, texts not only authenticated sacred objects, but could simultaneously become them, functioning as 'physical site[s] of saintly holiness'.[13] The circulation and collective reading of these texts, moreover, could create 'imagined' Catholic communities, connecting people on both sides of the Atlantic.[14]

For early modern Europeans, birch bark letters were rare artefacts, and objects made from this material could often be found in cabinets of

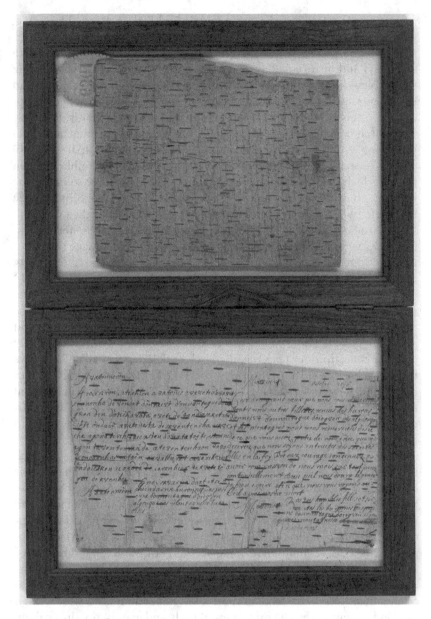

Figure 8.1 Birch bark letters in storage frame. Poncet's letter to Martin, 1647 (top), Indigenous seminarians' letter to Sain, 1676 (bottom)

Source: Bibliothèque nationale de France.

curiosities.[15] Any examination of their meanings must therefore consider early modern European cultures of collecting, which were facilitated by the invasion and colonisation of the Americas and elsewhere. Owing to Jesuit missionaries' sophisticated communication networks and privileged access to specimens and curiosities, they were often involved in conveying these objects to Europe.[16] Practices of collecting were also rhetorically significant in printed relations of exploration and colonisation. As Neil Kenny has argued, sixteenth- and seventeenth-century travel narratives frequently presented themselves as 'collections', and included lists of 'real' objects, as well as information '*recueilli*' (gathered/collected) by travellers.[17] Readers' engagements with early modern missionary letters were therefore shaped not only by hagiographic traditions, but by early modern collecting practices. Why write a letter on birch bark (rather than paper) if not to stimulate the sensory curiosity of its recipient?

This essay draws together and builds upon historiographies of both mission narratives and cultures of collecting in order to analyse the ways in which readers in France sensed the letters that arrived from the New France mission. Rather than focusing solely on 'making [narrative] sense' of texts (as Prempain sought to do in the letter with which I began this chapter), I argue that a letter's discourse – and, by extension, missionary discourse – was supported not only by its materiality, but also by the sensory experiences of its authors, bearers, and readers. Since there is no direct evidence of the ways in which birch bark letters were read – and sensed – in the seventeenth century, I begin with a brief examination of the rhetorical functions of letters' materiality in printed missionary accounts. This is followed by a discussion of the ways in which bodies, particularly those of letter bearers, were entangled with the objects they carried, co-creating meanings. In order to examine readers' experiences of birch bark letters, the final section draws together examples of reader reception. Birch bark letters, I argue, were sensory synecdoches – little pieces of New France – that enabled their recipients to sense, experience, and gain a feeling of ownership over the colony, without ever leaving the metropole.[18]

II.

The materiality of letters was rhetorically important in narratives of the New France mission.[19] Letters or parts of letters were often printed in the Jesuits' *Relations*, annual accounts of missionary activity published in Paris between 1632 and 1673. The *Relations* were composed by the mission superior in Quebec, using letters he had received from missionaries in the field, before being sent to Paris for further editing and publication.[20] Although few birch bark letters survive today, references to this type of missive can be found in a variety of missionary documents. As well as birch bark, these sources detail a number of other paper substitutes (including gunpowder wrapping paper) that were used when paper was in short supply – one of the many hardships and privations described by missionaries in the field.[21]

Descriptions of the conditions in which all kinds of letters were composed were intended to shape their readers' experiences. A series of fragments that appeared in the *Relation* of 1660–1661, for instance, gave detailed descriptions of the dire conditions of several Frenchmen held captive in villages of the Haudenosaunee.[22] A young soldier, François Hertel, who was being held prisoner in a Mohawk village, was the author of one of these fragments. Hertel had been tortured, and his hands and fingers had been burned and mutilated.[23] 'My Father', he wrote to Jesuit Father Simon Le Moine:

> [. . .] bless the hand that writes to you, which has had one finger burnt in a Calumet as reparation to the Majesty of God, whom I have offended. The other hand has a thumb cut off, - but do not tell my poor Mother.[24]

Another Frenchman, a fellow captive of Hertel, opened his letter to Le Moine in a similar fashion: 'I have scarcely any fingers left', he wrote, 'so do not be surprised that I write so badly'.[25] The men's bodily suffering was confirmed by their letters, which were poorly penned and grubby.

Although these might appear to be highly personal evocations of hardship, they clearly conform to contemporary standards of hagiographic writing. Indeed, there are similarities between these letters and a letter written a number of years earlier (1644) by Jesuit missionary Father Francesco-Giuseppe Bressani, when he too had been a captive of the Haudenosaunee. '*The letter is badly written*', Bressani wrote,

> *and quite soiled, because, in addition to other inconveniences, he who writes it only has one finger on his right hand; and it is difficult to avoid staining the paper with the blood which flows from his wounds, not yet healed; he uses arquebus powder for ink and the earth for a table.*[26]

This letter, which was printed in Bressani's *Breve Relatione* (1653), is not simply about the trials of letter writing in inhospitable environments; it is filled with the rich symbolism of martyrdom. But the missionary carefully manipulated hagiographic tropes. Unlike some holy texts, the account was not deliberately written in blood, but was inadvertently 'soiled'. Rather than representing his blood as a symbol of his passion for the faith, the missionary portrayed it as worldly and unclean. Paradoxically, this display of humility only served to confirm the missionary author's saintliness. All of the above letters appeared in print, but their meanings were shaped by descriptions of their soiled materiality. Readers of the printed

Relations were encouraged to imagine receipt of these letters – stained and physically repellent – in order to elicit empathetic, sensory responses.

III.

Since the only means of sending letters was on board the ships that brought supplies to the colony and returned to France with trade goods, letters from New France were infrequent and subject to the hazards of the crossing.[27] Letter writers ran the risk of their correspondence being lost during the long transatlantic voyage; ships could be wrecked in storms or captured by enemy vessels. Furthermore, the messengers who carried these letters could be robbed or simply lose the letters out of carelessness.[28] Choosing a reliable letter bearer was therefore important.

When possible, missionaries placed their letters in the care of trusted missionary colleagues, who often had first-hand knowledge of the events described therein. This knowledge enabled them to verbally supplement a missive's written content.[29] But missionary authors also recognised the benefits of sending their letters with Indigenous travellers.[30] The 1636 *Relation*, for instance, included a fragment of a letter written by Fathers Charles Garnier and Pierre Chastellain. '*The bearers [porteurs] of this*', they wrote, '*will tell you, better than we can, the name of the place where they met us*'.[31] The letter's authors here rely on the knowledge of Indigenous letter bearers to correctly pass on (and pronounce) the name of the place where the missive was written. Additionally, the printed *Relation* presents the text of the letter in italics (as was often the case with printed letters or letter fragments included in these accounts), signaling the letter's existence as an object simultaneously part of – and separate from – the *Relation* itself.[32] The letter's text was important, but so too was its materiality.

When Francesco-Giuseppe Bressani returned to France in 1650, he carried a letter by Mother Marie de l'Incarnation, the first superior of the Ursuline seminary at Quebec, to her son Claude Martin.[33] Marie's letter included a description of Bressani's body, which was presented as an object of awe-inspiring curiosity that could be investigated using the senses. 'You will see a living Martyr', she wrote, 'of whose sufferings you have heard, especially of his captivity in the country of the Iroquois'.[34] This was an opportunity, Marie implied, for Claude to acquire visual proof of the sacrifices made in New France for the holy faith, sacrifices which he had – up until this point – only heard about in texts, such as the *Relations*. (Hearing had connotations of unreliability here: the word 'bruit' could imply 'rumour').[35] The missionary's body – and his evident physical suffering on the mission – thus authenticated textual and reported missionary discourse. Claude's visual experiences, Marie's letter implied, would confirm the reports he had heard. But his 'investigation' of Bressani's body had to be a covert one. 'Without seeming to', Marie urged her son, 'look at his [Bressani's] hands; you will see them mutilated, and almost without one finger which is whole'.[36] Marie's warning to Claude that his observation of Bressani had to be discreet implied a need to respect the missionary's holy person. Indigenous individuals taken to Europe (often against their will) were, in contrast, frequently 'displayed' in port towns and at court.[37] Many Europeans viewed these people as objects of study, like those that could be seen in cabinets of curiosity.[38] What one could and could not *be seen* to investigate, therefore, depended on who was the object of investigation.

The letter described above was one of Marie's shorter letters to Claude; we might speculate that she believed the missionary's body needed little additional explanation, except an initial guide to interpretation. Two weeks previously, she had written to her son to inform him that she had sent a letter with each of the missionaries who was returning to France that winter. 'Please receive these saintly figures', she implored him, 'as though they were *living Martyrs*, who have undertaken [spiritual] works, and suffered incredible hardships [*croix incroïables*] for those who have not experienced the Huron mission'.[39] Missionary bodies, Marie implied, were to be exalted because of the 'incredible hardships' that they had experienced, hardships that other Europeans could only imagine. Jesuit priests would have prepared for deployment using Ignatius of Loyola's *Spiritual Exercises*.[40] In an oft-quoted passage in the fifth exercise of the first week (the 'meditation on hell'), the exercitant is required to imagine himself in the 'length, breadth, and depth of hell' through guided meditation on each of the five senses.[41] But French missionaries in Canada recognised the limitations of this preparation. In Canada, Jesuit missionary Father Jacques Bruyas stated, 'One must expect to have all his senses martyred daily'.[42] After five years on the mission terrain he wryly conceded that there was 'a great difference between meditating on the [C]anada mission in one's oratory, and finding oneself Exercising the duties of a [C]anadian missionary'.[43] Mother Cécile de Sainte-Croix, an Ursuline nun who travelled to New France in 1639 as part of the first group of nuns to settle in the colony, shared Bruyas's sentiment. 'It has often crossed my mind', she wrote, with some humour, to the superior of the convent at Dieppe, 'that experiencing the hardships of the sea is a very different thing from only hearing about them'.[44] Imagining New France, these accounts implied, was no substitute for being there.

While missionary bodies provided living examples of missionary discourse, however, these bodies were simultaneously authorised by the texts they carried. Marie's instruction, 'Please receive these saintly figures', is evocative of the letters of authentication that accompanied and legitimised relics. Two days after Marie sent her letter describing 'these saintly figures', the nun sent Claude relics of the Canadian martyrs, accompanied by another letter. 'It is by the Reverend Father Bonnin', she wrote, 'faithful witness to the sufferings of our Saintly Martyrs that

I send you their relics'.[45] In this account Bonnin was the authenticator; he legitimised the relics and, if necessary, could provide testimony as to their origins. The missionary's authority to do so was simultaneously established by the letter he carried. Missionary letter bearers, then, were not only intermediaries between correspondents, but co-created meanings with the objects they delivered.

In some cases, the bodily *absence* of a letter bearer could be rhetorically significant. Writing to Father Barthélemy Vimont from Wendake in 1640, Father Jérome Lalemant told the superior of the death of Joseph Chihouatenhoua, a pious convert. 'I was preparing to write to Your Reverence for the last time in this current year, by the hand of Joseph Chihouatenhoua, our good Christian: and now the same paper of which he should have been the bearer is used to carry to Your Reverence news of his death'.[46] Joseph Chihouatenhoua was regarded by the missionaries as an exemplary convert. In Lalemant's account, the letter recounting his death is styled as an almost-contact relic (it was the paper he *almost* carried). 'No doubt this death', Lalemant asserted, 'although sudden for this good and excellent Christian, did not take him unprepared', for not only was he 'continually in the grace of God', but he had also commended his soul to God that very morning, as was his custom.[47] Lalemant wrote that on the afternoon of his death, Joseph had gone to the woods 'to cut some sticks of Cedar to finish the canoe which was to carry him to Kébec' (with the missionary's letter).[48] The unfinished task signified a life cut short, a journey not taken, a letter undelivered. In Lalemant's narrative, texts and bodies intertwined. Whilst accounts of missionary captivity stress the haptic contact of authors with their letters, what strikes the reader here is the *absence* of contact with the letter's subject. In a colony in which there were not yet any martyrs (the first 'martyrdom' was not recorded until two years later, in 1642), the evocation of the sacred in everyday, bodily actions (as described in missionary texts) was vitally important for the establishment of a Catholic culture.[49]

IV.

The birch bark letters with which I opened this essay performed dual functions: on the one hand, they related the events of the mission, and on the other, they were 'curiosities', small pieces of the colony sent in recompense for financial and spiritual support. The recipients of both letters were important advocates of the New France mission. As the son of Marie de l'Incarnation, Claude Martin had a personal interest in the colony and was acquainted with a number of its missionaries, including Joseph-Antoine Poncet de la Rivière (known as Joseph Poncet), who wrote him a birch bark letter in 1647 from Wendake.[50] Claude would also become the editor of Marie de l'Incarnation's *Vie* after her death in 1672, and his editorial work would ensure his mother's place as one of the most well-known chroniclers of the New France mission.[51] The recipient of the second letter, the *receveur général* Charles Sain, was also a staunch supporter of the mission. He was the principal benefactor of a small chapel in the Ursuline church that was dedicated to the Child Jesus on 29 November 1671.[52] Over the years Sain sent numerous adornments for the chapel: paintings, gilded candlesticks, gilded figures of the Child Jesus made from wax and wood, gilded vases, bouquets, hangings, dye for making tapestries, and ornamental candlesticks.[53]

The birch bark letter sent to Sain in 1676 was likely a recompense for these benefactions. Written in the Wendat language with a French parallel translation on the same piece of bark (see Fig. 8.2),[54] the letter identified its authors as 'very humble servants the Hurons, Gaspesians, the Onondaga, the Cayuga, Algonquins, Montagnais, and Odawa'.[55] Although in a single hand, it is clear that the letter was intended to be viewed as a collective effort, and the young women asked their correspondent to 'Take courage: continue to have compassion for us. [And] in particular pray continually to God that he gives us the grace to believe well so that we can see you in heaven after our death'.[56] Writing letters, as Fay Bound Alberti argues, was a social undertaking that engaged author and correspondent in 'a relationship of obligation and expectation'.[57] The birch bark letter written to Sain was no different. The 'gift' of this object was presumably

Figure 8.2 Indigenous seminarians' letter to Sain, 1676.

Source: Bibliothèque nationale de France

intended to foster a sense of connection between the *receveur général* and the seminary's pupils. The affective words used in this short note of thanks were likely meant to encourage Sain to continue making donations to the seminary ('continue to have compassion for us'), and – of course – to prompt him to pray for the mission's success ('pray continually to God that he give us the grace to believe well'). In response for his generosity, Sain was given not only gratitude (as expressed in the letter's content), but a material recompense, in the form of the birch bark letter.

Sain's letter was thus imbued with spiritual meaning, but it was also a 'curiosity'. Owing to missionaries' privileged access to the 'wonder' of the so-called New World (and their extensive correspondence networks), they often supplied rare specimens to correspondents in France.[58] In 1687, Jesuit missionary Father Thierry Beschefer sent 'Pieces of bark on which figures have been marked by teeth' to the French collector, Cabart de Villermont.[59] Birch bark biting is an Indigenous art form, but Beschefer neglected to describe the intricate designs that would likely have adorned the bark (these may have been human figures, animals, or flora).[60] In contrast to the supposedly holy touch of suffering Jesuits, the human contact with these objects may have been viewed by Europeans as animalistic, since the Indigenous peoples of the Americas were widely – and erroneously – believed to be cannibals. As Constance Classen and David Howes have argued, the 'actual uses' of objects were unimportant; their principal function was to 'confirm Western representations of non-Western cultures and serve as a springboard for the Western imagination'.[61] Furthermore, teeth played an important role in missionary rhetoric. In accounts of torture they were often used to 'crush' fingers or to tear out nails.[62] Like contact relics, the pieces of bark received by Villermont enabled him to touch – by extension and without danger – the bodies of those who had made the incisions.[63]

In this context, birch bark letters might be viewed as pieces of the 'rude' North American landscape, 'tamed' by the inclusion of writing, one of the supposedly civilised traits that missionaries believed set Europeans apart from those they regarded as 'barbarians'.[64] In 1635, for example, Jesuit missionary Father Jean de Brébeuf described the practice of learning Indigenous languages through writing on birch bark. 'All the French who are here have eagerly applied themselves to it', he enthused, 'reviving the ancient usage of writing on birch bark, for want of paper'.[65] Although Jesuit rhetoric here styled material shortage as a (European) cultural renaissance, however, Indigenous people in North America had long used birch bark as a support for scribal production.[66]

Like the birch bark itself, the inclusion of text from the Wendat language in Sain's letter also lent this 'curiosity' an air of authenticity. Without the assistance of the French translation, the *receveur général* would not have understood the meaning of the words written on the letter. The principal purpose of the Wendat text, therefore, seems to have been to emphasise that the letter had been composed by Indigenous seminarians. But the inclusion of these 'novel' words might also have prompted new sensory experiences for the reader or listener.

Since there is no textual evidence of Sain's responses to the letters he received, it is helpful to briefly consider some comparative examples. Writing to Mother Marie-Gillette Roland, a sister of the Visitation, on 4 September 1640, Marie de l'Incarnation greeted her in Anishinâbemowin (a language Marie would have known as 'Algonquin').[67] 'I received great consolation reading your letter', Marie wrote. She continued:

> Ni-Misens, cri8ek 8asa 8apicha entaien aiega eapitch Khisadkihirari8i Khi8aparmir, s8uga8iechimir. Ni-Misens, mi8itch Kasasadkihatch Dieu, Kihisadkihir. That is what came out. That is to say in our language: My Sister even though you are very far away, nonetheless I still love you, more than if I could see you. I firmly embrace you, my sister, and because you love God, that is why I love you.[68]

In this letter, Marie explained that she 'could not resist' greeting her sister in this way 'and saying to her almost exactly [*a peu près*] what we usually say to our dear Neophytes'.[69] Through imagined verbal communication with her sister, Marie envisioned herself closer to her. Conversely, her love of her sisters in France could also be demonstrated through her love of the Indigenous girls she instructed in the seminary. By imagining her sisters in the place of the seminarians (and greeting them as she would the young women), she embraced them textually, reaching out across time and space (given the distance the letter had to travel it would be many weeks before her sister read her words).[70] Marie's statement that an Anishinâbemowin greeting suddenly 'burst out' of her (*'ce qui m'a echapé'*), suggests her familiarity with local culture. She had, she implied, quickly become accustomed to speaking Anishinâbemowin, 'our language', as she called it. The repetition of 'our' (*'our* dear Neophytes', *'our* language') was here used to appropriate Indigenous culture and even individuals (i.e., converts). This verbal image of a nun moved (by her correspondent's letter) to exclaim *'en savage'* (i.e. in a Native tongue), is reminiscent of mystical accounts of vows pronounced during or after mystical visions.

Marie's juxtaposition of Catholic imagery with the Anishinâbemowin language would have been unfamiliar – and jarring – to her correspondent. In the context of the description that follows, of the nun sitting amongst Indigenous women (whose clothes, Marie exclaimed, 'do not smell as good as those of the Ladies of France!'), the reader is invited to laugh at the unexpected scene.[71] Punctuated with a jaunty exclamation mark, the nun's statement appears to have been a joke intended to imply European cultural superiority. The evocation of the unpleasant smell, and thus bodily 'uncleanliness', of the Indigenous women she described also denoted their supposed barbarity.[72] Whilst the nuns were happy to learn – and appropriate – Indigenous languages, the evocation of smell is here used to imply cultural difference.[73] 'Our Reverend Fathers', Marie's letter continued, 'although great doctors' (*'quoique grands docteurs'*) learned with the nuns and did so 'with incredible affection and docility'.[74] This description is reminiscent of some of the nun's descriptions of well-behaved, pious seminarians, and pokes affectionate fun at the learned priests who, through their language learning, were once again pupils (and whose demeanour reflected this change in status).[75] Many early modern Europeans believed that language shaped identity; speaking an Indigenous language could therefore render an individual 'wild'.[76] But Marie pre-empted any such reading by her correspondent, asserting that when she had lived in France she had 'never troubled myself to read a history book'. Now, however, she had to read and meditate on all sorts of things *'en sauvage'*.[77] For Marie, language learning had become a gateway to all kinds of new knowledge.

How then might these Indigenous-language texts have been perceived by readers who did not understand them? Given the communal lifestyle of early modern conventual orders, it is likely that Marie's letter would have been read aloud. Missionaries expected their letters to be shared, particularly when time – and sometimes, lack of paper – prevented them from writing to all those whom they wished to send tidings.[78] The practice of sending 'circulars' (letters which 'circulated' around religious orders to update the community on the latest events) also encouraged a culture of communal reading.[79] Like Sain when he encountered the Wendat words in his letter from the Ursulines, Marie de l'Incarnation's sisters at the Visitandine convent would likely have struggled to pronounce the Anishinâbemowin phrases she had penned for – and to – them (when the letter was published in 1681, a margin note explained how the unfamiliar character '8' should be pronounced).[80] They may have been impressed by her ability to learn a language so different from their own. Perhaps they found the sounds strange or even amusing. Jesuit missionaries, for instance, acknowledged that their own mispronunciation of Indigenous languages often made them the subject of ridicule among those they sought to convert.[81] Any attempt at pronunciation, however, would no doubt have led to a bodily awareness that the language in front of them required the mouth to form words in ways to which they were unaccustomed.[82]

Evidence of the collective enjoyment and affective qualities of letters can be found in abundance in seventeenth-century correspondence. Letters could be shown to the recipient's friends and networks (commercial, intellectual, and so on). The letters of Marie de Rabutin-Chantal, marquise de Sévigné (1626–1696), famous for her prolific, almost fifty-year-long correspondence with her daughter, Françoise-Marguerite de Sévigné, comtesse de Grignon, provide useful insights into the public enjoyment of letters. A close friend of Madame de La Fayette and La Rochefoucauld, Madame de Sévigné often read and composed letters with some of Paris's most renowned literary figures. 'I have never seen anything so funny as what you write about that', Madame de Sévigné praised her daughter's description of the disastrous Lenten sermon of a Minim at Aix, 'I read it to M. de la Rochefoucauld, who laughed heartily'.[83] 'We laughed til we cried', the marquise enthused as she recounted reading another letter, 'about that girl who sang at the top of her voice in church that bawdy song she was confessing to have sung elsewhere'.[84] We can imagine the sisters of the Visitation of Tours taking similar enjoyment from Mother Marie's letter to Mother Marie-Gillette.

Letters from New France could therefore allow their recipients in France to live vicariously through their correspondents. To some, Canada seemed inhospitable; its winter climate 'rude' and unforgiving. In a 1645 letter to her son, Marie de l'Incarnation wrote that before learning that Canada was a country, she had thought that it was a term that had been invented to frighten children.[85] Madame de Sévigné, upon finding out that her daughter's husband had not been offered the governorship of Canada as his wife had hoped, wrote to her daughter to console her. 'Look at Canada as a good thing no longer available', she advised, 'But whatever your philosophy leads you to suppose, it's a dreary business to live in another climate with people you would hate to know in this one'.[86] As a woman of letters, Madame de Sévigné was not opposed to learning about other countries, but she preferred to do so from the comfort of her Parisian *hôtel*. In the same letter to her daughter, she asserted, '"We belong to all countries" – that is from Montaigne, but while saying that he was *very glad to be in his own home*'.[87] Written correspondence could therefore allow a person to learn about Canada without ever leaving French soil. Yet, since there was often no way of verifying a letter's content, recipients had to trust that the information they had been given was accurate and authentic. Natural histories and other books written about the New World provided a source of reference, but like Montaigne's essays, many of these were written without any first-hand experience of the distant lands they described.

In contrast to other forms of communication, such as travel narratives, birch bark letters offered the ultimate 'proof' of their contents' authenticity. They were – quite literally – small pieces of Canada that enabled an individual to experience the mission terrain, whether or not they could read the written text. Simultaneously relations and curiosities, they could provide not only textual information (in the form of body-witness accounts) but novel sensory experiences: the textual evocation of sensation (e.g. bad smells); the sensory investigation of the object; the speaking or hearing of unfamiliar sounds. Since birch bark letters would have been unfamiliar to most early modern French women and men, it is likely they stimulated a certain amount of sensory curiosity (they could be opened, smoothed out, held, smelled, passed around, displayed, regarded, and so on). Early modern curiosities were often examined using a hands-on, investigative approach: holding an object to gauge its weight, for instance, might allow a curious individual to learn more about it than she would if she were to only look at it.[88] But while letters (both birch bark and paper) gave the illusion of experiencing New France, they represented – as sensory synecdoches – only a small part of the whole.

Furthermore, the ability to touch – and the ability to bestow the right to touch – was a privilege that revealed dynamics of power between individuals (particularly private collectors and the guests who they permitted to handle objects from their collections).[89] Possessing a birch bark letter may have held connotations of ownership of the New France mission. In the French language, hands and possession were intimately linked. When a fiefdom 'changed hands', the *Thresor de la langue françoyse* (1606) noted, its lord and owner changed.[90] The subentry for 'to change hands' (*'changer de main'*) continued, 'we say I have it in hand, that is to say, in my power, hold, and possession'.[91] 'Careful', Charles Sain might have warned, as he handed his newly acquired birch bark letter to one of his acquaintances, '*feel* how fragile it is'. Touch has long been associated with proof; in scripture, 'doubting' Thomas was invited to touch Christ in order to prove his resurrection.[92] Although Joseph Poncet's 1647 letter to Claude Martin is almost indecipherable, it is nonetheless possible to glean meaning through its form and paratextual elements (in this case, text added after the letter's receipt). The letter is marked (in the same hand that recorded the letter's entrance into the collection of the library of Saint-Germain-des-Prés in 1653), '*Dominus meus & Deus meus*', the phrase that Thomas uttered in John's Gospel after he was invited to touch Christ's wounds.[93] Read in this context, birch bark letters authenticate the texts they support and embody. Having received tangible proof of the 'successes' (that is, the conversions) of the New France mission, Charles Sain and its other benefactors could rest safe in the knowledge that their money was being put to good use.

V.

In conclusion, since scholars of New France rely heavily on nineteenth-century source collections, attending to the editorial choices of their compilers – and, in particular, to their omissions – is important. Nineteenth-century scholars viewed birch bark letters as objects, rather than texts, and, as a result, these sources have been largely excluded from historiographical accounts. Attending to the materiality of these texts, however, highlights the sensory complexities of communicating across the early modern Atlantic World.

Letter writers were well aware of the significance not only of their words, but also of the writing materials they employed, and of the bearers who carried their missives. Further research, however, is necessary in order to examine the roles of letter bearers, in particular Indigenous letter bearers, in early modern correspondence networks.[94] For those receiving letters from Canada, the materiality of these missives would likely have been even more significant when they were unable to read their textual contents. Very few would have been able to read Indigenous languages, and some may also have been illiterate (a circumstance not uncommon in the early modern world). The study of materiality, therefore, has wide-ranging implications for the history of transatlantic reader reception. While many missionary letters described their own first-hand experiences of the mission, others were subtler, combining text and form to create sensory curiosities for their recipients, and functioning as material recompenses for financial support. Although missionary conveyers of sacred missives retained the power to bestow these little pieces of New France, their recipients were nonetheless permitted to possess small, *sensible* samples of the colonial terrain.

Notes

During the writing of this essay, Robin Macdonald was the recipient of an Australian Research Council Post Doctoral Fellowship (project number CE110001011) at the Australian Research Council Centre of Excellence for the History of Emotions at the University of Western Australia.

1 Henri Omont (1857–1940) graduated from the École des Chartres in 1881 when he was hired by the *Bibliothèque nationale* to work in the department of printed books. The following year, he began working in the manuscripts department, and became curator in 1899. See Bernard Joassart, 'Henri Omont et les Bollandistes: Correspondance', *Analecta Bollandiana* 123 (2005), 378.

2 Henri Omont to [Camille de Rochemonteix], Paris, 27 September 1894, Archives des jésuites au Canada [AJC], Fonds Rochemonteix, 4013, 359. All translations of this letter are my own. The original French reads: 'Vos études sur les missions en Amérique vous feront sans doute trouver quelque intérêt à deux documents tres [*sic*] fragiles que vous me permettrez de vous signaler'.

3 Joseph Poncet to Dom Claude Martin, Sainte-Marie-des-Hurons, 28 June 1647 and 'Lettre de remerciements de jeunes Huronnes "à M. Sain, receveur général des finances à Bourges"', October 1676, Bibliothèque nationale de France [BNF], Nouvelles acquisitions françaises [NAF], 6561. The *Receveur général* collected direct taxes (*taille, capitation,* and *vingtièmes*). See Roland E. Mousnier, *The Institutions of France under the Absolute Monarchy, 1598–1789,* vol. 2, *The Organs of State and Society,* trans. Arthur Goldhammer (Chicago, IL: University of Chicago Press, 1984), 207. The letter to Sain gives no place of authorship, but Natalie Zemon Davis identifies it as a letter written by Indigenous seminarians at the Ursuline convent. See Davis, *Women on the Margins: Three Seventeenth-Century Lives* (Cambridge, MA: Harvard University Press, 1995), 96. This seems likely, since Sain donated generously to the convent. I use 'Wendat' and 'Wendake' (instead of 'Huron' and 'Huronia'), except when quoting. These terms were used by seventeenth-century Wendat people. See Georges E. Sioui, *Huron-Wendat: The Heritage of the Circle,* trans. Jane Brierley (Vancouver: UBC Press, 1999), 3.

4 Despite an extensive search, I have been unable to identify Prempain.

5 A. Prempain to [Camille de Rochemonteix], Tuesday 11 December 1894, AJC, Fonds Rochemonteix, 4013, 361–63. My emphases. 'Voilà tous ce qu'on peut recueillir de suivi qui offre un sens. L'encre de mauvaise qualité s'est effacée,

et on n'aperçoit plus çà et là que quelques mots de loin en loin. Pour pouvoir les lire, il faut un beau soleil et des instruments. M. Omont me dit qu'il n'y a qu'un moyen de tirer parti de ce qui reste de ce monument[.] Relever les mots qu'on peut à moitié lire, à moitié deviner. . . les étaler un à un sur le papier, en laissant entre eux des intervalles, puis à l'aide de ces mots, construire des phrases où ils entreront et qui aient un sens[.]Ce travail très-fatiguant durerait longtemps; puis ou serait l'authenticité d'une lettre fabriqué de cette manière'.

6 The letters had previously been held at the library of the Abbey of Saint-Germain-des-Près, the motherhouse of the Congrégation de Saint-Maur, the Benedictine order to which Claude Martin belonged.

7 Omont to [Rochemonteix], Paris, 27 September 1894, 360: 'chez l'encadreur'.

8 This mirrors the nineteenth-century emphasis on looking at, but not touching, museum collections. This 'hands-off' approach was also geared towards preservation of rare objects, one of museums' principal functions in the period. See Constance Classen and David Howes, 'The Museum as Sensescape: Western Sensibilities and Indigenous Artifacts', in *Sensible Objects: Colonialism, Museums, and Material Culture*, ed. Elizabeth Edwards, Chris Gosden, and Ruth B. Phillips (Oxford: Berg, 2006), 208.

9 The letters are absent from the following major edited source collections: Reuben Gold Thwaites, ed., *Jesuit Relations and Allied Documents: Travels and Explorations of the Jesuit Missionaries in New France, 1610–1791*, 73 vols. (Cleveland: Burrows Brothers, 1896–1901), hereafter, JR; Lucien Campeau, ed., *Monumenta Novæ Franciæ*, 9 vols. (Rome/Montreal: Institutum Historicum Soc. Iesu/Les Éditions Bellarmin, 1989–2003), hereafter, MNF.

10 Although the birch bark letter written from the Ursuline seminary appears as an image in Natalie Zemon Davis's *Women on the Margins*, Davis provides no analysis of this object, which has an illustrative, rather than an analytical, function.

11 Roger Chartier, 'Meaningful Forms', *Times Literary Supplement* (London), 6 October 1989, Issue 4514, *Liber* 1, 8; on the materiality of letters in early modern England, see James Daybell, *The Material Letter in Early Modern England: Manuscript Letters and the Culture and Practices of Letter Writing, 1512–1635* (Basingstoke: Palgrave Macmillan, 2012); James Daybell and Peter Hinds, 'Introduction: Material Matters', *Material Readings of Early Modern Culture: Texts and Social Practices, 1580–1730*, ed. James Daybell and Peter Hinds (Basingstoke: Palgrave Macmillan, 2010), 1.

12 For an examination of reading as a bodily practice, see Helen Smith, '"More swete vnto the eare / than holsome for ye mynde": Embodying Early Modern Women's Reading', *Huntingdon Library Quarterly* 73 (2010): 413–32.

13 Julia Boss, 'Writing a Relic: The Uses of Hagiography in New France', in *Colonial Saints: Discovering the Holy in the Americas*, ed. Allan Greer and Jodi Bilinkoff (London: Routledge, 2003), esp. 222–29 (quotation at 229).

14 Boss, 'Writing a Relic', 213. Karin Vélez makes a similar argument for gift exchange between the Wendat Christians of Lorette and other Catholic communities in Canada and Europe. See Vélez. '"A Sign That We Are Related to You": The Transatlantic Gifts of the Hurons of the Jesuit Mission of Lorette, 1650–1750', *French Colonial History* 12 (2011): 31–44. For a nuanced discussion of these gifts, see Muriel Clair, 'La Chapelle de Notre-Dame-de-Lorette', in *Les arts en Nouvelle-France*, ed. Laurier Lacroix (Quebec: Musée Nationale des Beaux-Arts du Québec/Les Publications du Quebec, 2012), 72–84.

15 See, for example, Claude Du Molinet, *Le Cabinet de la Bibliotheque de Sainte Genevieve: Divisé en deux parties: Contenant les Antiquitez de la*

Réligion des Chrétiens, des Egyptiens, & des Romans; des Tombeaux,
des Poids & des Médailles; des Monnoyes, des Pierres antiques gravées, & des
Mineraux; des Talismans, des Lampes antiques, des Animaux les plus rares &
les plus singuliers, des Coquilles les plus considérables, des Fruits étrangers,
& quelques Plantes exquises (Paris, 1692), 33.

16 On the utility of Jesuit correspondence networks for the communication of scientific knowledge, for example, see Steven J. Harris, 'Confession-Building, Long-Distance Networks, and the Organization of Jesuit Science', *Early Science and Medicine* 1 (1996), esp. 289.

17 Neil Kenny, 'La collection comme mode discursif dans les relations de voyage françaises aux XVIe et XVIIe siècles', *French Studies* 65 (2011), 360, 361, 365.

18 My thanks to Mark Jenner for suggesting the use of the term synecdoche to describe these letters and for his helpful comments on an earlier draft of this essay.

19 To the best of my knowledge, the letters examined in this essay are the only two extant examples of birch bark letters from the seventeenth century. For mentions of birch bark letters in missionary accounts, see Marie de l'Incarnation to Dom Raymond de S. Bernard, Tours, end 1638, in *Marie de l'Incarnation (1599–1672): Correspondance*, ed. Dom Guy Oury (Solesmes: Abbaye Saint-Pierre, 1971), Lettre XXX, 68, hereafter MI, *Corr.*; Louis Nicolas, *The Natural History of the New World*, trans. by Nancy Senior, in *The Codex Canadensis and the Writings of Louis Nicolas: The Natural History of the New World*, ed. with an introduction by François-Marc Gagnon, trans. by Nancy Senior, modernization by Réal Ouellet (Montreal: McGill-Queen's University Press, 2001), 299; *JR*, 32: 165; *JR*, 41: 167; *JR*, 47: 83–85.

20 On the editorial process for the *Relations*, see Allan Greer, 'Introduction', in *The Jesuit Relations: Natives and Missionaries in Seventeenth-Century North America* (Boston: Bedford/St-Martin's, 2000), 14.

21 For an example of a letter written on gunpowder wrapping paper, see *JR*, 47: 85–87.

22 *JR*, 47: 83–93. On the role of bodily 'fragmentation' in the Jesuit 'martyrs'' memorialisation, see Boss, 'Writing a Relic', 225–26.

23 This practice ensured that captives were identifiable and was intended to prevent them from using weapons against their captors. See Daniel K. Richter, *The Ordeal of the Longhouse: The Peoples of the Iroquois League in the Era of European Colonization* (Chapel Hill: University of North Carolina Press, 1992), 66.

24 *JR*, 47: 85.

25 *JR*, 47: 87.

26 *JR*, 39: 55. Italics in original.

27 The first ships from France set sail in March and the last, in May. They might spend a month or more at the port of Quebec before returning to France. The last vessels usually left in October, and sometimes as late as November. See Jane E. Harrison, *Until Next Year: Letter-Writing and the Mails in Canada, 1640–1830* (Waterloo, ON: Wilfred Laurier University Press, 1987), 55. See also Harrison, 'The Intercourse of Letters: Transatlantic Correspondence in Early Canada, 1640–1812' (PhD thesis, University of Toronto, 2000), TSpace. Available at: https://tspace.library.utoronto.ca/bitstream/1807/14534/1/NQ53759.pdf.

28 The messenger who carried the letters that comprised the *Copie de deux lettres*, published in place of the 1655 *Relation* (which had been lost at sea), was robbed by highwaymen on the road from La Rochelle to Paris. See *Copie*

de deux lettres envoieés de la Novvelle France, Au Pere Procureur des Missions de la Compagnie de Iesvs en ces contrées (Paris, 1656), 6.

29 The importance of a letter's bearer stretches back to biblical times. See Alain Boureau, 'The Letter-Writing Norm, a Mediaeval Invention', in Roger Chartier, Alain Boureau, and Cécile Dauphin, *Correspondence: Models of Letter-Writing from the Middle Ages to the Nineteenth Century*, trans. Christopher Woodall (Oxford: Polity Press, 1997), 27.

30 Relatively little work has been done on the roles of Indigenous people in early modern North American correspondence networks. For a notable exception, see Katherine Grandjean, *American Passage: The Communications Frontier in Early New England* (Cambridge, MA: Harvard University Press, 2015), for instance, 45–75.

31 *JR*, 9: 251. Italics in original.

32 *Relation de ce qui s'est passé en la Novvelle France en l'année 1636: Enuoyée au R. Pere Provincial de la Compagnie de Iesvs en la Prouince de France: Par le P. Paul le Ieune de la mesme Compagnie, Superieur de la Residence de Kébec* (Paris, 1637), 233–34.

33 Marie famously 'abandoned' her young son Claude when she joined the Ursulines at Tours in 1631 (she professed in 1633). Claude later followed his mother into a religious vocation and became a Benedictine. For an account of Marie's life, see Davis, *Women on the Margins*, 'New Worlds: Marie de l'Incarnation', 63–139. For a biographical account of Claude's life, see Guy-Marie Oury, *Dom Claude Martin: Le Fils de Marie de l'Incarnation* (Solesmes: Abbaye Saint-Pierre, 1983).

34 Marie de l'Incarnation to her son, Quebec, 30 October 1650, MI, *Corr.*, Lettre CXXXI, 406. My translation and emphasis. All translations from Marie's correspondence are my own. 'Vous verrez un Martyr vivant, des souffrances duquel vous avez cy-devant entendu parler, sur tout de sa captivité au païs des Hiroquois'.

35 *Dictionnaire de l'Académie française* (1694), s.v. "bruit."

36 Marie de l'Incarnation to her son, 30 October 1650, 406. 'Sans faire semblant de rien, regardez ses mains; vous les verrez mutilées, et presque sans aucun doigt qui soit entier'. Cfr. Emma Anderson's discussion of Isaac Jogues's meeting with Anne of Austria in 'Blood, Fire, and "Baptism": Three Perspectives on the Death of Jean de Brébeuf, Seventeenth-Century Jesuit "Martyr"', in *Native Americans, Christianity and the Reshaping of American Religious Landscapes*, ed. Joel W. Martin and Mark A. Nicholas (Chapel Hill: University of North Carolina Press, 2010), 131.

37 For examples, see Cornelius J. Jaenen, *Friend and Foe: Aspects of French-Amerindian Cultural Contact in the Sixteenth and Seventeenth Centuries* (New York: Columbia University Press, 1976), in particular, 12–14.

38 Silvia Spitta, *Misplaced Objects: Migrating Collections and Recollections in the Americas* (Austin: University of Texas Press, 2009), 9. For a discussion of bodies in cultures of collecting from the sixteenth century onwards, see Peter C. Mancall, 'Collecting Americans: The Anglo-American experience from Cabot to NAGPRA', in *Collecting Across Cultures: Material Exchanges in the Early Modern Atlantic World*, ed. Daniela Bleichmar and Peter C. Mancall (Philadelphia: University of Pennsylvania Press, 2011), 192–213.

39 Marie de l'Incarnation to her son, Quebec, 17 September 1650, MI, *Corr.*, Lettre CXXIX, 403. My emphasis. 'Recevez, s'il vous plaist, ces saints Personnages comme autant de Martyrs vivans, qui ont entrepris des travaux, et souffert des croix incroïables à ceux qui n'ont pas l'expérience des Missions Huronnes'.

40 Nuns in New France also performed the *Exercises*. See Mutius Vitelleschi to Marie de l'Incarnation, Rome, 7 January 1640, *MNF*, Vol. 4, *Les grandes épreuves (1638–1640)*, Doc. 110, 444.

41 Ignatius of Loyola, *The Spiritual Exercises*, in *Spiritual Exercises and Selected Works*, ed. by George E. Ganss with the collaboration of Parmananda R. Divarkar, Edward J. Malatesta, and Martin E. Palmer (New York: Paulist Press, 1991), 141.

42 *JR*, 51: 137.

43 *JR*, 51: 137.

44 Cécile de Sainte-Croix to the superior of the Ursulines at Dieppe, Quebec, 2 September 1639, MI, *Corr.*, Appendix II, 951–52. My translation. 'Il m'a, dis je, souvent passé par l'esprit que c'est autre chose d'expérimenter les incommoditez de la mer que d'en ouïr parler seulement'.

45 Marie de l'Incarnation to her son, Quebec, 19 September 1650, MI, *Corr.*, Lettre CXXX, 405. 'C'est par le Révérend Père Bonnin fidèle témoin des souffrances de nos Saints Martyrs que je vous envoie de leurs reliques'.

46 *JR*, 20: 77–79.

47 *JR*, 20: 79–81.

48 *JR*, 20: 81.

49 On the importance of local, lived Catholicism in the creation of holy persons in New France, see Timothy G. Pearson, *Becoming Holy in Early Canada* (Montreal: McGill-Queen's University Press, 2014), 7–10. Julia Boss speculates that the colonists' limited access to relics may have made them more open to the notion that a book could be a holy site. Boss, 'Writing a Relic', 228–29.

50 Poncet had been one of Claude's teachers during the latter's time at the Jesuit college in Orléans (1633–36), and sailed to New France in the same fleet as Marie de l'Incarnation. See Marie de l'Incarnation, *Relation de 1654*, in Dom Albert Jamet, ed. *Écrits spirituels et historiques* (Paris: Desclée de Brouwer, 1930), 2: 299.

51 See Claude Martin, *La Vie de la venerable Mere Marie de l'Incarnation: Premiere superieure des Ursulines de la Nouvelle-France: Tirée de ses lettres et de ses Ecrits* (Paris, 1677). On Claude's role in the production of Marie's life narrative, see Jodi Bilinkoff, *Related Lives: Confessors and the Female Penitents, 1450–1750* (Ithaca, NY: Cornell University Press, 2005), esp. 59–64.

52 Musée du Québec, *Trésors des communautés religieuses de la ville de Québec*, exhibition catalogue (1973), 68 and 79.

53 *Annales du Monastère des Ursulines de Québec, 1639–1822*, Archives du Monastère des Ursulines de Québec [AMUQ], 1/E,1,1,3,2,1 (page 33). Sain's name also appears in the Ursuline's *Registre des dons, 1640–1815*, AMUQ, 1/E,3,4,6,1, f.9r-v. My thanks to Marie-Andrée Fortier, archivist at the AMUQ for locating this reference for me.

54 I am very grateful to John L. Steckley for confirming that this letter is written in Wendat and for kindly providing me with an English translation of the Wendat text. Personal correspondence, 14 November 2016.

55 'Lettre de remerciements de jeunes Huronnes', October 1676. My translation from the French text. 'tres humbles filles servantes les huronnes, Gaspésienne, d'onnontagué d'oiog8en, algonquines, montagesses, et 8taoises'.

56 'Lettre de remerciements de jeunes Huronnes', October 1676. My translation from the French text. 'Prenez courage continuez à avoir compassion de nous mais sur tout priez continuellement Dieu quil nous donne la grâce de bien croire afin que nous vous voyons au ciel apres nostre mort'.

57 Fay Bound, 'Writing the Self? Love and the Letter in England', *Literature and History* 11, (2002), 10.

58 See, for instance, MI, *Corr.*, Lettre XLVIII, 114. On missionary correspondence networks and the development of Jesuit science, see Harris, 'Confession-Building, Long-Distance Networks, and the Organization of Jesuit Science', 287–318.
59 *JR*, 63: 291. The original French (on page 290) reads: 'Des écorces figures avec les dens'. On Villermont see, Augustin Val, *Dictionnaire critique de biographie et d'histoire errata et supplement pour tous les dictionnaires historiques d'après des documents authentiques inédites* (Paris: Henri Plon, 1867), 1271.
60 Few academic works have been devoted to birch bark. For an early example, see Frank G. Speck, *Montagnais Art in Birch-Bark: A Circumpolar Trait* (New York: Museum of the American Indian, Heye Foundation, 1937). On birch bark biting, see 74–80.
61 Classen and Howes, 'The Museum as Sensescape', 203.
62 See, for example, *JR*, 5: 29. Whilst, broadly speaking, the early modern Church tended to condemn curiosity, which could lead to all manner of sins, there was recognition that curiosity could be accommodated and even exploited. See Neil Kenny, *The Uses of Curiosity in Early Modern France and Germany* (Oxford: Oxford University Press, 2004), in particular, chapter 2: 'Institutions: Church'.
63 On experience without danger see Classen and Howes, 'The Museum as Sensescape', 203. Classen and Howes here draw on Nicholas Thomas's *Entangled Objects: Exchange, Material Culture, and Colonialism in the Pacific* (Cambridge, MA: Harvard University Press, 1991).
64 Jesuit missionary Paul Le Jeune identified the three stages through which humanity had apparently passed before reaching its 'civilised' peak: at first, men required only the basic necessities, then, they learned to combine the 'tasteful and the necessary', and finally, they began to contemplate science in order to perfect the human condition. *JR*, 7: 7–9. Cfr. José de Acosta's three categories of barbarism, which ranked cultures according to whether or not they had formed urban societies or established writing systems. For an explanation of this model, see Simon Ditchfield, 'What Did Natural History Have To Do With Salvation? José de Acosta SJ (1540–1600) in the Americas', in *God's Bounty? The Churches of the Natural World*, Studies in Church History 46 (2006), 157–59.
65 *JR*, 8: 131–33. Presumably Brébeuf was referring to the Greek and Roman usage of papyrus, rather than birch bark.
66 Whilst Indigenous North American cultures prior to European colonisation have often been described as 'oral', many scholars now challenge this designation, highlighting the long history of sign-making present in the archaeological record. See Germaine Warkentin, 'In Search of the "Word of the Other": Aboriginal Sign Systems and the History of the Book in Canada', *Book History* 2 (1999), 3–4. Birch bark scrolls are used in sacred ceremonial practices of the Anishinâbe Midewiwin. See, for example, Michael Angel, *Preserving the Sacred: Historical Perspectives on the Ojibwa Midewiwin* (Winnipeg: University of Manitoba Press, 2002); Joan M. Vastokas, 'Interpreting Birch Bark Scrolls', *The Papers of the Algonquian Conference/Actes du Congrès des Algonquinistes* 15 (1984), 425–44.
67 I would like to thank Kevin Brousseau for identifying this language as Anishinâbemowin and for kindly providing me with an analysis of the sentences. Personal correspondence with Kevin Brousseau, 21 September 2015. Marie would have referred to this language as 'Algonquin'. The missions in the seventeenth-century Saint Lawrence Valley were frequented by Anishinâbe ('Algonquin') and Nêhiraw ('Montagnais') people; extant linguistic sources from the region therefore tend to be in Anishinâbemowin ('Algonquin') and

Nêhirawêwin ('Montagnais'). These two communities were closely linked: intermarriage was common and bilingualism was also likely to have been frequent. Personal correspondence with John E. Bishop, 21 September 2015. I am grateful to John for sharing his expertise. The dialects of the Nêhiraw Iriniw are referred to by some linguists as 'Nêhirawêwin' ('Montagnais' was the term employed by seventeenth- and eighteenth-century French people). See John E. Bishop and Kevin Brousseau, 'The End of the Jesuit Lexicographic Tradition in Nêhirawêwin: Jean-Baptiste de la Brosse and his Compilation of the *Radicum Montanarum Silva (1766–1772)*', *Historiographia Linguistica* 38 (2011), 293n1.

68 Marie de l'Incarnation to Mother Marie-Gillette Roland, Quebec, 4 September 1640, MI, *Corr.*, Lettre XLVI, 108. 'J'ay reçu une singulière consolation à la lecture de votre lettre. Ni-Misens, criᵹek ᵹasa ᵹapicha entaien aiega eapitch Khisadkihirariᵹi Khiᵹaparmir, sᵹugaᵹiechimir. Ni-Misens, miᵹitch Kasasadkihatch Dieu, Kihisadkihir. Voilà qui m'est échapé. C'est à dire en notre langue: Ma Sœur encore que vous soiez bien loin, néanmoins je vous aime toujours, plus que si je vous voiois. Je vous embrasse fortement, ma Sœur, et parce que vous aimez Dieu, c'est pour cela que je vous aime'.

69 Marie de l'Incarnation to Mother Marie-Gillette Roland, 4 September 1640, 108. 'lui dire à peu près ce que nous disons ordinairement à nos chères Néophites'.

70 Julia Boss argues that reading the same hagiographic narratives on both sides of the Atlantic could create an 'imagined community'. See Boss, 'Writing a Relic', 305.

71 On incongruity and the humour of the unexpected, see Guy Halsall, 'Funny Foreigners: Laughing with the Barbarians in Late Antiquity', in Guy Halsall, ed. *Humour, History, and Politics in Late Antiquity and the Early Middle Ages* (Cambridge: Cambridge University Press, 2002), 89–90.

72 When new students arrived they were washed (many wore protective grease) and clothed in French garments. See Marie de l'Incarnation to a lady of quality, Quebec, 3 September 1640, MI, *Corr.*, Lettre XLIII, 97.

73 The attribution of a foul odour to a particular social or cultural group is usually a sign of animosity, and rarely a conclusion drawn from actual sense perception. See Constance Classen, 'The Odor of the Other: Olfactory Symbolism and Cultural Categories', *American Anthropological Association* 20 (1992), 134.

74 Marie de l'Incarnation to Mother Marie-Gillette Roland, 4 September 1640, 108. 'ils le font avec une affection et docilité incroiable'.

75 See, for example, Marie's description of a particularly pious young seminarian, who – though she was barely old enough to speak – said her prayers with fervour in both her mother tongue and in French. Marie de l'Incarnation to her son, Quebec, 29 August – 10 September 1646, MI, *Corr.*, Lettre XCVII, 286–87. In a recent book, *Masters and Servants*, Micah True argues that while missionaries, as educators and priests, were 'masters' and 'teachers', they were simultaneously 'students', who learned Indigenous languages and cultural norms from those they sought to convert. See Micah True, *Masters and Students: Jesuit Mission Ethnography in Seventeenth-Century New France* (Montreal: McGill-Queen's University Press, 2015), 6.

76 See Sara E. Melzer, *Colonizer or Colonized? The Hidden Stories of Early Modern French Culture* (Philadelphia: University of Pennsylvania Press, 2012), 116.

77 Marie de l'Incarnation to Marie-Gillette Roland, 4 September 1640, MI, *Corr.*, Lettre XLVI, 108: 'en France je ne me fusse jamais donné la peine de lire une histoire; et maintenant il faut que je lise et médite toute sorte de choses en sauvage'.

78 'I ought to write to many Fathers in your Province;' wrote Jesuit Father Pierre-Joseph-Marie Chaumonot to Philippe Nappi, Superior of the Professed House in Rome, in 1640, 'but the paper and the time fail me'. *JR*, 18: 33.

79 During meals in the refectory, for instance, one of the nuns would be charged with reading devotional texts or sacred histories. See Jérome Lalemant, *Constitutions et Règlements des Premières Ursulines de Québec* (1647), ed. Soeur Gabrielle Lapointe (Québec, 1974), esp. Chapter 20, 'Des choses appartenant au refectoir', 166–73.

80 As this note affirms, the letter represents 'ou', the Greek ligature for the letters 'o' and 'u'. See Claude Martin, *Lettres de la venerable Mere Marie de l'Incarnation, premiere superieure des Ursulines de la Nouvelle-France: Divisées en deux parties* (Paris, 1681), 335.

81 On the mocking of Jesuit missionary Father Paul Le Jeune for his inability to pronounce Montagnais, see Marie-Christine Pioffet, 'Le Rire de Paul Lejeune: Du rire jaune à l'humour noir', *Nouvelles Études Francophones* 22 (2007), 125.

82 Brébeuf wrote of the Wendat language: 'The greater part of their words are composed of vowels. They have no labial letters. This is probably the reason why they all open their lips so awkwardly, and why we can scarce understand them when they whistle or when they speak low'. *JR*, 10: 117.

83 Madame de Sévigné to Madame de Grignon, Paris, Wednesday 1 April 1671. Madame de Sévigné, *Selected Letters*, trans. by Leonard Tancock (London: Penguin Books, 1982), 83.

84 As discerning critics of both theatre and literature, it is no wonder that Madame de Sévigné and her daughter frequently described and critiqued sermons and church-related 'performances'. Madame de Sévigné to Madame de Grignon, Les Rochers, Sunday 12 January 1676. Madame de Sévigné, *Selected Letters*, 177.

85 Marie de l'Incarnation to Claude Martin, Quebec, 3 October 1645, MI, *Corr.*, Lettre XCIV, 270.

86 Madame de Sévigné to Madame de Grignon, Paris, Wednesday 6 April 1672. Madame de Sévigné, *Selected Letters*, 134. It was Louis de Bouade, Comte de Frontenac, who became Governor General in 1672. See W.J. Eccles, *Canada Under Louis XIV, 1663–1701* (Toronto, ON: McLelland and Steward, 1964), 77.

87 Madame de Sévigné to Madame de Grignon, Paris, Wednesday 6 April 1672. Madame de Sévigné, *Selected Letters*, 134. My emphasis.

88 Constance Classen, 'Museum Manners: The Sensory Life of the Early Museum', *Journal of Social History* 40 (2007), 900.

89 Classen, 'Museum Manners', 898.

90 *Thresor de la langue françoyse, tant ancienne que moderne...* (Paris, 1606), s.v. "main."

91 *Thresor de la langue françoyse*, s.v. "changer de main." My translation. 'on dit ie l'ay en main, c'est-à-dire, en ma puissance, tenuë et possession'.

92 Classen, 'Museum Manners', 900. Whether or not Thomas took up the invitation to touch is unclear. See Subha Mukherji's essay in this volume.

93 John 20: 27–28. This inscription appears on the top right had corner of the address leaf (the address is now almost completely faded). In the centre of the same side of this letter, just below the address, the date of the object's entrance into the collection is recorded. This inscription reads: 'Bibliotheca S. Germani à pratis die 21. apriles 1653.-'

94 For a notable exception relating to early New England, see Grandjean, *American Passage*, esp. 45–75.

Part IV
Figuration and feeling

9 "O, she's warm": evidence, assent, and the sensory numinous in Shakespeare and his world

Subha Mukherji

I.

> If you should dip your hand in,
> Your wrist would ache immediately,
> . . .
> If you tasted it, it would first taste bitter,
> then briny, then surely burn your tongue.
> It is like what we imagine knowledge to be:
> dark, salt, clear, moving, utterly free,
> drawn from the cold, hard mouth
> of the world. . .[1]

Elizabeth Bishop, in her secular twentieth-century poem, captures the feel of knowledge in sharply sensory terms, by way of an analogy with the water at the fishhouses. Bishop is, however, channelling a far earlier descriptive tradition: the pre-history of sensuous perception and portrayal of knowing has featured persistently, if slipperily, in religious epistemologies. In early modern England, sceptical mistrust of the senses was a commonplace, as were religious warnings against their limits: as Richard Smith put it, 'the senses. . . oft do deceave'.[2] Yet, literary perceptions of the divine are arrived at, again and again, through the senses. Sensible tokens were, of course, valued in legal practice, despite a theoretical preference for probabilistic reasoning. The sensory spiritual register of imaginative literature, however, manifests a vexed, often antagonistic, relation to evidence, unmooring the senses from their usual demonstrative domains. Their role in such literature suggests a distinct understanding of the relation between knowledge and belief. Moments that have seemed confused or puzzling in their mixing of evidentiary and religious languages illuminate an interdisciplinary transaction of ideas, if we know how to read their apparent strangeness. Early modern culture was juggling Reformation theology, with its stress on *sola fide*, alongside a complex sensory inheritance deriving from late medieval liturgical practices, and Aristotelian and Galenic affective physiology. Added to this was a vocabulary of spiritual perception that went back to the early Church fathers (notably Origen, Gregory of Nyssa, and Augustine), and which was systematised in medieval theology. This pre-modern history of sensing the sacred feeds into the early modern in its literary manifestations, where it joins a classical legacy as well as a secular aesthetic imagination to form something too hybrid to have been recognised as a transformed theological percept. In their pioneering book *The Spiritual Senses*, Paul Gavrilyuk and Sarah Coakley suggest that 'the spiritual senses tradition was to undergo [an] eclipse' in early modernity.[3] While I address a more diffuse spectrum of sensory-spiritual texture in the writing of the time than the 'spiritual sense tradition' technically suggests, the history they chart might look different, and the gaps they spot might look like diversions, if we let in the testimony of literature. To the list of disciplines they invite to extend research on the relation between Western spirituality and the senses – 'cognitive science, comparative religion, systematic theology, spiritual anthropology and philosophy of religion'[4] – I propose that we need to add literary, including theatrical, production.

The first of my main examples will be the climax of Shakespeare's *The Winter's Tale*, where Leontes arrives at his assent to an improbable resurrection through touch, and through an imagining of the moment of recognition as an act of magic 'lawful as eating'.[5] That it is not a play directly about religion is germane to my argument, for I suggest that the more elusive narratives of the sensory sacred in early modern literature are to be looked for in explorations of the numinous, rather than solely of the divine or theological in a straight-forward sense. I use the term 'numinous' to mean textual moments, processes, or components that go beyond reference, to actually evoke the presence of the invisible and the immanent in the visible, material world. I build on Rudolph Otto's originary definition of the term as an experience of '*mysterium tremendum*', to examine equivalent early modern spiritual affects as captured in literature. In Otto's conception, the numinous was a combination of three main components: wonder inspired by an absolute otherness from the ordinary, overwhelming awe, and speech-defying grace.[6] It is the numinous that suffuses the ending of *The Winter's Tale*, as it also does beatific moments in several other Shakespearean plays, sometimes where you least expect it, as in my second example: Bottom's account of his dream in *A Midsummer Night's Dream*.

Mainstream Reformist thought posited a duality between the perceptual clarity of the elect and the fogginess of the reprobate or the base, when it comes to physical sensations. As the hugely influential Cambridge Puritan preacher, William Perkins, explicates in his commentary on the first five chapters of the Epistle to the Galatians, sensible religious signs were only valuable in so far as they were components of a process of logical persuasion and judgement, and that too, only in application to the elect. The language of the spiritual senses – inward sensations corresponding (but superior) to physical ones – was co-opted into this polarity: it was for the elect alone that the Holy Ghost could 'clear the eies of the mind'.[7]

Both the dramatic episodes I focus on are among literary works which collapse or even reverse such hierarchies. Often, these inversions are effected by probing the duality inherent in the language of the spiritual senses. Perkins's phrase, 'eies of the mind', is typical of articulations of spiritual sensation, consisting of the coupling of a physical sense with a spiritual, abstract referent (and sometimes, the mixing of disparate physical senses). Remember Augustine's famous lament that we have lost our *palatum cordis* – the palate of the heart; or his prayer to the Lord at the opening of *Confessions* to 'see the ears of [his] heart [*aures cordis*] . . . [and] open them. . .'.[8] Significantly, the 'heart', while it is a spiritual reference here, suggesting affect, also has a corporeal reality and application, which further confounds the basic dichotomy of physical and abstract. This language represents an attempt to find a register for a sensory experience that is extraordinary, in keeping with its object. The disorientation caused by the coupling of physical organs and mental functions is part of that estrangement.

II.

I want to start with a text that is directly about the sacred, as a point of departure: George Herbert's poem, 'Prayer 1':

> Prayer the Churches banquet, Angels age,
> Gods breath in man returning to his birth,
> The soul in paraphrase, heart in pilgrimage,
> The Christian plummet sounding heav'n and earth;
>
> Engine against th' Almightie, sinners towre,
> Reversed thunder, Christ-side-piercing spear,
> The six-daies world transposing in an houre,
> A kinde of tune, which all things heare and fear;
>
> Softnesse, and peace, and joy, and love, and blisse,
> Exalted Manna, gladnesse of the best,
> Heaven in ordinarie, man well drest,
> The Milkie way, the bird of Paradise,
>
> Church-bels beyond the starres heard, the souls bloud,
> The land of spices; something understood.[9]

While phrases such as 'soul's blood' or 'the soul in paraphrase' resonate faintly with the language of the spiritual senses, the very arrangement or *collocatio* of the poem creates a striking sensory impact – a rush of ascending aural darts forming a missive probing at once God's ear and the reader's. But the content has its own sensory dimension too. The poem is structured around the figure of 'systrophe', a piling up of definitions without getting to the core; a chain of asyndetically juxtaposed, vividly sensuous metaphors that translate a given term of reference – in this case, prayer. As Henry Peacham writes in his popular rhetorical manual, *The Garden of Eloquence* (1577), 'systrophe' or 'conglobatio' of definitions is 'when we bring in diffinityons of one thing, yet not of such defynitions as doe declare the pith of the matter, but others of another kynde all heaped together, which doe amplifye most pleasauntly. . .'.[10] The definitions in Herbert's systrophe are a succession of vividly sensory images and metaphors for prayer, which make way for the adequate register the poem finds at last in the plain, unmetaphorical 'something understood'. In a sense it enacts what Herbert's near contemporary Richard Crashaw calls 'Types [yielding] to Truths' (*Lauda Sion Salvatorem*. The Hymn of the Blessed Sacrament');[11] a shift that registers a transition from physically perceptible sensations (as implicit analogies) to an inner sense, almost an intuition; from created things to the creator himself. This journey is Augustinian: the bodily senses are conceived by Augustine as points of entry – *fores* (doors) and *nuntii* (messengers) – leading to a path back across our sensory exile and dysfunction to the *sensus interiores* we have lost.[12] Crashaw, while denigrating 'poor sense' in 'Adoro Te: The Hymn of St Thomas' (1648), addressed to the undisciplined doubter, allows the senses the function of doorkeeper:

> Nor touch nor tast must look for more
> But each sitt still in his own Dore.[13]

Like his unnamed friend's preface to his *The Steps to the Temple* (1646), Crashaw's poems, offered in the wake of his nightly prayers, are likened to 'Stepps for happy Souls to climbe heaven by'. The metaphor of doors goes back to the classical elegy of desire, *paraklausithyron* or 'lament by a door', as well as to the wandering knight of medieval romance, seeking entrance at his lady's gate. But this language of longing is harnessed by Crashaw to the idea of Christ's wounds as our doors to heaven, most eloquently expressed in St Bernard's homilies on the Song of Songs, intimating a world of reference that was accessible to his readership.[14]

While doors, windows, and porches structure the sequence of Herbert's *Temple*, in 'Prayer 1' these sensory thresholds are mobilised as stages of a process which leads the devotee to the place where, finally, he can achieve cognitive clarity and dispense with the structural code of repeated, serial analogy through which we struggle to inadequately express the inexpressible; to the end of the soul's need to paraphrase. Yet the last, unadorned phrase of 'Prayer 1' is also, in rhetorical terms, the *conclusio* – the logical end of the systrophe. Could it have been reached without the energetically spiralling sensible images that try to divine the meaning, and experience, of prayer? Is it not, in some senses, an apprehension that accommodates all the meanings conveyed by the attempted definitions, and then, from that platform, makes an intuitive leap?

The poem not only attempts a definition of prayer, but enacts it too. In doing so, it performs and invites a reading process that is the necessary route to understanding. The soul that is 'in' paraphrase is not only the object of paraphrase but a subject in the act of paraphrasing, vivid and present as the spear that is in the act of 'piercing' Christ's side, eliciting Eucharistic grace and opening up a sensory portal not unlike the corporeal doors of Augustine's human vessel, or – especially – the salvific wounds of St Bernard's Christ. Likewise, the plummet that is 'sounding' heaven and earth, and even the 'transposing' that happens ceaselessly and repeatedly in an hour of prayer, are functions of an ongoing activity that finds its material, in the world and on the page, in sensory forms. The aural symmetry of 'soul in paraphrase, heart in pilgrimage' reinforces the equivalence between paraphrasis and journey. Herbert's paraphrase is for, and on behalf of, his fallen readers; but in as much as the poem embodies prayer, paraphrase is also what makes the soul audible to God. It is what bridges the gap between human chatter and the silence of God; and like the elegy of desire, it acts as the medium of longing, of the instinct towards communion.

The affective function of paraphrasis is co-joined by a doctrinal idea: the implication that the poem is mimetic of the reading process that God initiates in the world. Herbert's 'The Windows' throws light on this, for there, God himself is the ultimate image-maker: 'thou dost anneal in glass thy story'.[15] The ultimate artist, God figures forth his story in the glass that is his preacher and poet. This is not only a reclaiming of the value of stained glass windows that depicted the story of the Bible (just as, elsewhere, Herbert reclaims the prayer-book and liturgy denounced by Puritans like Richard Baxter and John Bunyan). It is, at the same time, a pointer to yet another reader-relation: just as Herbert tries to read God (or prayer), explicating the sense through signs, we need to interpret Herbert's poetry as it records the process towards discovery, and figures the hermeneutic field that fallen man must plough before arriving at the place of holiness. 'Thy word is all, if we could spell', Herbert writes in 'The Flower'.[16] To 'spell' connotes literacy at two levels: not only writing but also reading. In reformed thought, we are inheritors of a certain illiteracy by virtue of being human. But it is not enough, therefore, to give up. The act of interpretation itself becomes a necessary process, just as signification is a function of the fallen world.

This is where Augustine's theory of signs finds a straight route into Herbert.[17] Augustine said that God indicates his presence through sensible signs, as man needs to travel the path from obscurity to understanding, in proportion to what he has lost through the Fall. The created world is a semiotic of divine metaphors in which the Creator is manifest, but needs to be read right. The implicit analogy makes 'discovery' a more actively engaged process than the apparently passive grace of revelation suggested in the 'Jordan' poems, or in 'Love Unknown', where 'discovery' is defined pointedly as uncovering, as opposed to invention: 'Lord, in thee,/The beauty lies in discovery'.[18] It also complicates the seeming redundance of sensory apprehension suggested by the suddenly achieved post-figurative simplicity of 'something understood' after the aural climax of 'church-bells beyond the stars heard'. This ineradicability of the material sign blends easily into Christian theology which is based on a figuring forth – the poetics of the incarnation. So, Herbert's own figurations are as legitimate as our hermeneutic effort is necessary, if only to realise that the truth both is, and is not, the fruit of these labours. There is pleasure in the reading of sensible signs accretively; but it is also a required discipline. The material, audible, metaphorical, and visualisable content provided by paraphrase, then, is the substance and medium of 'Prayer 1'. Roger Ascham's section on *paraphrasis* in *The Scholemaster* is tellingly para-doxical: it addresses the potential for this mode of translation or imitation to become a form of 'chopping and changing the best to worse', but goes on to admit of the possibility of 'an other kinde of Paraphrasis, to turne rude and barbarous into proper and eloquent', and concludes that it is an exercise best left to the absolute masters.[19] It is at once a potential mark of expressive excellence and of inadequate groping prior to complete grasp, trying to capture the supreme in terms that are necessarily inferior.[20] 'Something understood' is, and is not, the sum of all the rest; both an epiphany and an anti-climax.

Even when Herbert abjures the senses in *Jordan II* – a poem that explicitly rejects secular poetics – the textile energy of his poem takes life from his weaving himself into the sense, just the activity he ostensibly critiques in his earlier, erroneous poetic practice:

> As flames do work and winde, when they ascend,
> So did I weave my self into the sense.[21]

When Herbert follows Augustine in *Denial* to chart his spiritual (and hence poetic) recovery through grace, the healing harmony, correcting and redirecting his sensory dysfunction, is nevertheless heard – and '[relished]' by the '[verser]'– in a final rhyme that rings in the corporeal ear:

> That so thy favours granting my request,
> They and my mind may chime
> And mend my rhyme.[22]

Even in sacred poetry that has a *telos*, there is a pull against the de-prioritisation – or mere instrumentalisation – of the physical senses.

III.

An even less linear trajectory is worked out in drama. Take the recognition scene of *The Winter's Tale*.[23] Literary recognition scenes in the Renaissance have been seen as going back to their roots in Greek romance, drama, and Aristotle; but they are also mediated by the foundational moments of recognition and uncertainty in the Christian narrative. These moments bring together knowledge – *gnosis* being the Greek root for the generic term 'anagnorisis' – and incredulity about seemingly impossible truths. The originary Christian empiricist, doubting Thomas, was cured of his mistrust of the Resurrection when he was invited to put his finger into Christ's wound. But Jesus said to him, 'Have you believed because you have seen me? Blessed are those who have not seen and yet believe' (John 20:29). This ability to believe *against* the evidence, or in excess of the proof, is a distinct definition of faith in religious discourse. For Aquinas, for instance, faith was defined by absolute assent in the face of inadequate proof.[24]

The Reformation sharpened these long-standing theological debates on proof and certainty. In his sermon on certainty, Richard Hooker, Anglican priest and theologian, negotiates the central paradox of Protestantism – that justifying faith has to be assured, yet is inevitably mingled with doubt – by distinguishing between 'certainty of evidence', based on sensible things, and the superior 'certainty of adherence'.[25] The latter is activated 'when the hart doth cleaue and sticke vnto that which it doth beleeue. . . *against all reason of believing*'.[26] In this theological tradition, faith is predicated precisely on a gap between evidence (literally, what is visible) and the belief that it engenders.

This gap offers a productive space for the poetics of improbability. *The Winter's Tale* – going live more or less contemporaneously with the printing of Hooker's sermon – builds up its trial scene towards a piece of supernatural evidence that will resolve all uncertainties: the verdict of Apollo's oracle.[27] But when it vindicates his wife, Leontes declares, 'There is no truth at all i'th'oracle. The sessions shall proceed' (3.2.140–41). Suspicion hardens into conviction and overtakes the original purpose of truth-finding. And yet, in the reason-robbed Leontes, it comes paradoxically, perilously close to the rationalist legal impulse that, from 1215 onwards, steadily outmoded the older form of trial by divine proof.[28] The presumption of the rationality of suspicion – the new orthodoxy by the Jacobean period – is what Hermione's trial puts on the dock.

Against Leontes's perverse dismissal of absolute evidence, Shakespeare counterpoints another pivotal moment of dramatic reversal where belief, instead of disbelief, is induced: but it is equally at odds with probability and proof. Paulina exhorts, before presenting and animating Hermione's supposed statue after sixteen years: 'It is requir'd / You do awake your faith' (5.3.94–95). To be the beneficiary of that unlikely, impending miracle, Leontes needs an absolute leap of faith, having failed in (what natural theologians would call) moral certainty. His apparent irrationality is to be corrected not by rationalist certainty, but by a training in believing *against* proof, a surrender to the possibility of grace that accommodates uncertainty and inexplicability. The replacement of legal epistemology here tunes into a contemporary understanding of the psychology of belief – anticipating the distinction between persuasion and faith that Thomas Browne was to formulate, later, in discussing Christ's resurrection:

> I desire to exercise my faith in the difficultest point; for to credit ordinary and visible objects is not faith, but persuasion. . . . 'Tis an easy and necessary belief, to credit what our eye and sense hath examined.[29]

What the final scene of *The Winter's Tale* demands is nothing short of the acceptance of an incredible resurrection, both from Leontes and his court, and from the audience. The disproportion that is the ingredient of faith is the counterpart of what Terence Cave calls the 'scandal' of recognition in dramatic plots, where momentous knowledge often turns on inadequate sensory proofs, and 'a deal of wonder' breaks out from perfunctory antecedents.[30]

Yet the play itself uses Hermione's statue – potentially unlawful also because it is false – as a kind of *entechnic* evidence to manage belief, at the same time as it challenges and elicits a submission premised on a lack of proof. This paradox evokes the central legend of doubt and belief in the Western tradition. In his gripping exploration of the story of St Thomas, Glenn Most demonstrates that John's gospel – by far the fullest and the most narratologically sophisticated – makes it clear that though Thomas asked for material proof, there is no basis for thinking that he was given any.[31] When he was told by the other disciples that they had 'seen the Lord' (20:25), he replied, unforgettably, 'Unless I see in his hands the print of the nails, and place my finger in the mark of the nails, and place my hand in his side, I will not believe' (20:25). Implicit in this story is a hierarchy of proofs. While we have seen Browne denigrating the belief that is based on the sight of Christ or his miracles, Thomas not only demanded to see the nail-marks but went on to demand to touch, indeed, to invade Christ's wounds with his fingers. This second stage Glenn Most calls the stage of 'hyperbolic doubt', as distinct from conventional doubt which requires the evidence of the eyes.[32] The violent and sceptical passion of Thomas's stance has so mesmerised the cultural and aesthetic imagination of ages to follow that we have almost forgotten that when Jesus said to Thomas, 'Put your finger here, and see my hands; and put out your hand, and place it in my side' (20:27), that offer, and promise, of touch, seems to have been enough to elicit Thomas's answer, 'My Lord and my God!' (20:28).[33] It is a narrative that evokes the temptation to crave tactile proof as further confirmation of visual proof, at the same time as it shows that complete submission transcends that temptation. It is a parable at once of scepticism and faith. That touch is inaudible and implicit at this crucial moment – deliberately leaving

Christ's materiality open – is suggestive of the link between the unspoken and the unspeakable.

The optical illusion of the statue offered by *The Winter's Tale* as a healing instrument signifies the play's accommodation of the Biblical narrative to the limits of human faith and trust. But from Leontes's assent to Paulina's call for her audience to awake their faith before her act of revival – 'Proceed; / No foot shall stir' (5.3.97–98) – there is a gentle transition to his grateful acceptance of the gift of touch as Hermione descends from her pedestal: 'O, she's warm' (109). This passage enacts the promised sequence that is left tantalisingly incomplete in the Gospel story, for this is not the world of the Gospels but a world where God's word has less power than Paulina's trick. Warnings preface the gift: 'Do not shun her / Until you see her die again; for then you kill her double. Nay, present your hand' (105–7). Unlike Christ with Mary Magdalene and perhaps Thomas, Hermione does touch, and embrace, Leontes.

Despite the demotion of the senses in traditional religion and Aristotelian rhetoric and poetics, the epistemology of the law-court in this period was based on the assumption that first-hand sensory experiences would provide the best proofs. But given how difficult these might be to obtain, substitutes were designated, including material, sensuously apprehensible tokens that had remarkable impact in court, even though, theoretically, they did not count as full proof.[34] Theology was not untouched by this strain of pragmatism, but it showed a simultaneous anxiety that often resulted in a dissolution of the physical into the figurative. Lancelot Andrewes's Sermon on a Seraphim touching the Prophet's mouth with a coal vividly suggests this duality.[35] First, Andrewes cites the Seraphim's comments on the '[effects] of this touching': 'Secondly, the certainty; that as sure as this coale hath touched thy lips; so surely are thy sinnes taken away',[36] evoking touch as a surety against doubt, for this 'outward element [was] appointed by God to confirme his faith';[37] 'As Christ himself is spirituall and bodily; so he taketh away our sinnes, by means not only spiritual but bodily; as in the Sacrament'. Yet at the same time, Andrewes stresses that the 'Seraphim did not take the coale in his mouth, but with tongs'. Then again, he 'applied it not to the Prophets eare, but to his tongue. . .it is not the hearing of a sermon that can cleanse us from sinne; but we must taste of the bodily element, appointed to represent the invisible grace of God'.[38] The sermon swings back and forth between a sense of corporeal contact and a figurative idea of touch, till it settles on an exposition of the symbolism of the Eucharist.

The instinct towards the bodily is never erased, however, and although the late Protestants talk about 'feeling' in entirely immaterial terms, the early reformers were tactile in their imagination. Hooker's 'perseverance' is an inheritor of what Tyndale earlier called 'feeling faith': the kind of subjective conviction against which the persuasions of 'all the preachers of the world' 'would not prewayle, no more then though they would make me beleue the fire were cold, after that I had put my finger therein'.[39] Curiously, the terms in which this supra-evidential feeling is configured evokes the precise sensory voucher that jolted St Thomas out of doubt into faith. The kind of touch that makes Leontes exclaim, 'O, she's warm / If this be magic, let it be an art / Lawful as eating' (109–11), collapses the mechanics of doubt into the workings of faith in the human condition. It is no accident that in Luke's Gospel, when some of the disciples 'still disbelieved for joy, and wondered' at the risen Christ, there were two responses from Christ. First, he said, 'handle me' (24:39), an offer (once again) not taken up or commented on by them; next, he sat down in front of them and ate fish (24:42–43) – a banal activity, and an emphatically everyday foodstuff in the context of contemporary Palestine.[40] Any residual doubt in their minds about his materiality dissolved at this point. In Luke, the disciples at Emmaus have their eyes opened when 'he was known of them in the breaking of bread' (24:35; cp. 30–31). Significantly, post-Resurrection recognition scenes are more explicitly suggestive of the self's reliance on physical senses than the pre-resurrection Biblical moments which provide inspiration for the spiritual senses tradition.[41]

IV.

The history of doubt and belief is inextricably bound up with sensory history: no wonder, then, that the theatre provides Shakespeare with the perfect medium for exploring the phenomenology of faith. Biblical tradition and commentaries, as the Gospels and the Andrewes sermon indicate, strain to pull back from their engagement with the senses and take refuge in the figurative; consider Cranmer's defence of his description of Christ's manifestation to us in the sacraments 'as it were face to face' and our '"smelling of him with our noses, and a feeling and groping of him with our hands"', to make the point that that does not therefore mean that we 'see or feel him in deed . . . If it were so indeed, I would not add these words to say, "as it were"'.[42] As St Paul said, 'For now we see in a mirror, dimly, but then face to face' (1 Corinthians 13:12). By contrast, 'face to face' art forms[43] – such as drama and sculpture – actively embrace the tactile, as part of their understanding both of the limits of human perception, and of the productive fraudulence of artifice. Leontes's 'let it be. . .' suggests that the identity between magic and eating, the lost and the restored, is at once a felt longing and a fantasy. 'To understand a metaphor', as Jan Zwicky puts it, 'is always to experience loss at the same time as connexion'.[44] Analogy with the bodily offers Leontes, and the audience, familiar cognitive parameters to make sense of the unintelligible but retains the mystery, and the cognitive dissonance, of Hermione as a 'statue', as it were, resurrected, 'as it were'. As the disoriented Hermia puts it in *A Midsummer Night's Dream*, 'methinks I see these things with parted eye, / When everything seems double' (4.1.189–90); or in the words of Helena, who has found Demetrius 'like a jewel, / Mine own, and not mine own' (191–92).

The sensory dimension of this disjunctive vision is specifically connected by Shakespeare to the way in which the theatre plays havoc with our senses, making us take live flesh for corpse or marble, flat ground for Dover Cliff, or see sounds and hear sights. It is no accident that Helena uses a characteristic Bottom word – 'methinks' – here. For it is in Bottom's account of his dream that we find the most extreme example of how the moving around of a stage-prop – an ass's head – can not only signal but *effect* a transfiguration of sensibility that allows the unromantic, literal-minded weaver to acquire an intuitive understanding of the significance of his 'most rare vision', and to simultaneously fail and refuse to describe it. In the process, he succeeds in forging a language that perfectly captures the cognitive indeterminacy of such visions:

> I have had a most rare vision. I have had a dream, past the wit of man to say what dream it was. Man is but an ass if he go about to expound this dream. Methought I was – there is no man can tell what methought I was – and methought I had – but man is a patched fool if he will offer to say what methought I had. The eye of man hath not heard, the ear of man hath not seen, man's hand is not able to taste, his tongue not able to conceive, nor his heart to report what my dream was! . . . it shall be called 'Bottom's Dream', because it hath no bottom. . .
>
> (4.1.204–16)

Here is a collapse of both theological and epistemological elitism as the idiot boy of the play goes through the strangest imaginative experience. He comes to terms with, and responds to his dream with all the folly and susceptibility that gives him the cognitive equipment for this vision, and all the incomprehension that indicates his acknowledgement of its nature. This is a comedic version of the 'faith' that Paulina calls for, before her act of animation; and indeed of the capacities that Origen called 'the faculties of the heart';[45] a certain attunement. Imperfect knowledge was itself potentially a criterion of the highest truths, not only in medieval negative theology, but also in Aristotle's discussion of knowing 'celestial things', like 'a half-glimpse of persons that we love'.[46] The inverse relation between the excellence of the subject and its knowability, the 'ancient dilemma' Wesley Trimpi identifies, finds its way into early modern episte-mology.[47] But unlike Aristotle's knower, Shakespeare's Bottom would not have been so transfigured, had he not been disfigured first by a physical change – wearing an animal head. In Bottom, such unknowing is dissolved into sense, and translated through his confused apprehension of his dream, and indeed into the contrast between *apprehension* as a mode of cognition and Theseus's rationalist 'comprehension':

> Such tricks hath strong imagination
> That if it would but apprehend some joy,
> It comprehends some bringer of that joy;
> Or in the night, imagining some fear,
> How easy is a bush supposed a bear?
> *MSND*, V.i.18-22

For Theseus, a bush is a bush and a bear is a bear; but the play shows us that a man can become a donkey. The lovers are both tricked and healed by a potion in their 'charmèd eye' (III.ii.376), and the audience are given the gift of transformation through the theatrical manipulation of the senses. As Hippolyta says:

> And all their minds transfigured so together,
> More witnesseth than fancy's images.
> And grows to *something* of great constancy. . .
> Howsoever, strange and admirable.
> *MSND*, V.i.24-7 [italics mine]

Here we recall Herbert's 'something' – that hint of approximation, of intuitive grasp – the traces of something understood, and retained, that they carry back with them to Athens, beyond the stripping of the magic and sensory mayhem of the woods and the play.

The sense of the numinous underpinning Theseus's distinction, but brought to light in Hippolita's response, is ingrained in the devotional writing of the period. A single eloquent example will suffice here – Donne's Christmas 1621 sermon, where divine light is described as 'the hardest to be looked on': 'It is apprehensible by *sense*, and not comprehensible by *reason*. If wee winke, we cannot chuse but see it, if we stare, wee know it never the better'.[48] Bottom winks when he puts on the donkey head and opens himself up to the mystery of what appears to happen to him. While Hippolyta's speech has the gravity and rhythm of a philosophically sophisticated *response*, a post-factum reflection on the truth-value of the unverifiable, Bottom's insouciance is a simultaneous register of threshold *experience*: the blurry boundary between dreaming and awakening. Like Keats's Adam (and indeed Milton's Eve, echoed by Adam), he 'awoke and found it truth'.[49] In *Dream*, however, the ineffable is specifically linked with the theatrical: when the ass's head is removed, Bottom awakes not into noetic illumination but into folly: 'with thine own fool's eyes peep' (IV.i.81). The disjointed, anti-discursive syntax of Bottom's attempted paraphrase – a prose equivalent of Herbert's asyndetical arrangement of approximation in grasping 'prayer' – intimates an attempt to find a grammar for the numinous.

This is a grammar of apprehension, necessarily glimpsed rather than mastered in human experience: for 'now I know in part', as Paul said

(1 Corinthians 12).[50] There are also more obvious echoes of Corinthians. On the one hand, Bottom's language verbally recalls Paul on the senses, and resonates with the idea of 'the deep things of God' revealed to the spirit:

> The eye of man hath not seene, and the eare hath not heard, neither have entred into the heart of man, the things which God hath prepared for them that love him. But God hath revealed them unto the spirit, for the spirit searcheth all things, yea the deep things of God. . . [1 Corinthians 2: 9–10][51]

The context of the Biblical speech is the mysterious manifestation of the wisdom of God in the apparently foolish and base: 'God hath chosen the foolish things of the world to confound the wise; . . . and base things of the world, and things which are despised hath God chosen, yea, and things which are not, to bring to nought things that are' (1 Corinthians 1: 27–28). On the other hand, the Bottom register introduces resonances of the diction of spiritual senses with a twist, retaining its dislocations, but reconnecting it with physical sensations. Bottom's conflation and confusion of senses has a ring of Augustine's unity or confusion of the senses in describing God as a richly polymorphous sense-object:

> Neither is God bread nor is God water, nor is God this light, nor is God clothing, nor is God a house. For all these are visible things and are individual . . . God is everything for you. If you are hungry, he is bread for you; if you are thirsty, he is water for you. . .[52]

Bottom's dream is also a translation of a miraculous translation *into* sense, even while the inadequacy of sensory language is acknowledged. This evokes a strand in Reformist thinking about intellectual intuition, as exemplified in the Cambridge Platonist John Smith's statement that 'when reason once is raised by the mighty force of the Divine Spirit into a converse with God, it is turned into sense', though the context is that of '[shutting] the eye of the sense'.[53] This is turn is a development of Origen's increasingly sympathetic understanding in his later works of the role of the physical senses, and their capacity for transformation in close converse with the divine. Simultaneously, it is a departure from Reformist thought, in that the senses are not just a sign of election but the means of the perceptual transformation that allows the reception of grace. Bottom being Bottom, however, his *conclusio* and digest will be the ballad, 'Bottom's Dream', to be written by Peter Quince. This, along with the repeated 'methoughts', moor this 'rare vision' in the hyper-quotidian. Meanwhile the rough-hewn, unfinished texture of his prose captures the immediacy and the ongoing feel of *process*, and the anti-syntactical drive in the experience of the numinous.

The Winter's Tale's climax, like Bottom's, brings the bodily and the wondrous together, by an 'art' that is 'lawful as eating' – a phrase that is itself homely, yet 'strange and admirable', and recalls the eldritch lawful-ness of that other act of eating in the play, which is all Nature: the bear eating Antigonus. The play's own brand of uncanny, yoking the wrinkles of age with the 'grace' of resurrection, transforms an inherited lexicon that conjoins the abstract and the physical. Its medium, meanwhile, shifts the balance of emphasis and translates the abstraction of doctrine into the particulars of affect through embodied mediation. But the sensible also makes it impossible not to notice the joins. The gap between evidence and assent produces a peculiar realism which is inseparable from the doubleness of human perceptual mechanisms. Like Hermia's shaky double-seeing, or Helena's uncertain re-possession of Demetrius who loves her because his eyes are still laced with love-juice, Leontes's ifs and lets – 'If this be magic', 'let it be' – inhabit the space between desire and actuality, even as Hermione's wrinkles at once point up the gap and the potential (if costly) bridge between improbability and possibility.

V.

The first variation on the discourse of spiritual senses on the early modern stage, then, is that it breaks down the hierarchy inherent in the pre-modern register between inner and outer senses. The implicit analogy is retained, but adapted to the disorientations of the numinous, within the play and in the audience, and theatrically deployed to tap into the zone of double-seeing and double-being that the post-lapsarian world, at its improbably best moments, is. The further twist is that the senses – both erroneous and corrective – are prized apart from supernatural evidence, and thus demarcated from the spiritual senses which were traditionally understood to be the evidence of things unseen.[54] The mediation is effected not through the inner senses, but through art playing on – and with – our physical senses, creating semblances and analogies which both are, and are not. Finally, the sensory grounding allows transformation, both affective and spiritual. If a live Hermione had been sprung, unmediated, on Leontes the moment he seemed to come to his senses, at the end of that frenetic trial scene driven by '*tremor cordis*', we might have had a lurch into certitude more generic than psychological, the event rather than the process of conversion. Even in the final scene, when Leontes attempts to kiss the 'statue', Paulina intervenes and stalls: 'Good my lord, forbear. / The ruddiness upon her lip is wet; / You'll mar it if you kiss it; stain your own / With oily painting' (80–83). A premature kiss would indeed fail to translate the moment from an encounter with artifice to a leap of faith. But the gradual accretion of sensory experiences makes space, in the final scene, for an enactment of process, as flesh and faith conjoin. No cryptic oracle could have brought the gradual epiphany that the compound of deictic art, vision, hearing, music, touch, and (even the idea of) taste make possible.

Touch, in particular, has a special role in mediating between the visionary and the real, the incredible and the believed. Indeed, *Dream*'s evocation of *Corinthians* – 'the spirit searcheth all things, yea the deep things of God' – has implications for *Winter's Tale*'s evocation of Thomas's reliance on touch, for 'searcheth' carries an overtone of *OED* sense 8, 'to probe a wound': we might remember Saturnius' words, 'Now to the bottom dost though search my wound' (*Titus Andronicus*, 2.3.262). It is as though even if our eyes and ears are not up to the task of the spirit, touch might be. This in turn creates a further allure which is the other side of an aesthetic illusion: for we can see and hear a play but not touch it, and so Hermione being 'warm' is a particularly vivid claim because it is testimony to a sensual certainty that an audience cannot share. Touch is thus brought to the heart of the theatrical experience. So, as it turns Aristotle on his head by giving us the improbable possible, the play also turns the traditional hierarchy of senses upside down. It is significant that the theological strands in which this hierarchy was complicated include the spiritual senses tradition in which the contact senses of touch, taste, and smell subsumed and surpassed the abstract senses of sight and hearing; mystical theology where touch was thought to allow the closest access to the subject; and Eucharistic theology which often aligned *sapor* with *sapientia*: all ways of articulating affective cognition. This essay, then, is a first step towards re-examining the gap in Gavrilyuk and Coakley's chronology which traces the parallel Patristic and medieval traditions of *inner* and *spiritual* senses to Cusa's fusion of the two 'on the cusp of early modernity', and picks up the thread again in the Enlightenment, when epistemology and spirituality were being separated (notwithstanding residually entwined strands).[55] The continuing but particular role of the senses as transformative agents in the wider life of 'faith' understood imaginatively in the sixteenth and seventeenth centuries comes into focus if we treat literary representations of numinous experience as historical evidence; if we resist the binary of the religious and the secular Renaissance(s), and open up to the affects generated at their interface. Imaginative literature is a playground for such hybrid histories and elusive overlaps, free as it is of doctrinal responsibility, and ready to embrace the tentative, the indeterminate, and the pre-conceptual.

Notes

The research for this essay has received funding from the European Research Council under the European Union's Seventh Framework Programme (FP7/2007–2013)/ERC."

1 Elizabeth Bishop, 'At the Fishhouses', in Elizabeth Bishop, *Poems*, ed. By Saskia Hamilton (New York: Farrar, Straus and Giroux, 2011), 62–4 (64). Excerpt at the beginning of the chapter from *Poems* by Elizabeth Bishop,

Published by Chatto & Windus Ltd., Reprinted by permission of The Random House Group Limited. © 2011 (UK & Commonwealth Rights, Excluding Canada), and Elizabeth Bishop, 'At the Fishhouses', in Elizabeth Bishop, *Poems*, ed. By Saskia Hamilton (New York: Farrar, Straus and Giroux, 2011), 62–4 (64). Copyright © 2011 by The Alice H. Methfessel Trust. Publisher's Note and compilation copyright © 2011 by Farrar, Straus and Giroux. Reprinted by permission of Farrar, Straus and Giroux. (United States, Canada, and Rest of World).

2 Richard Smith, *The Assertion and Defence of the Sacrament of the Aulter* (London, 1546), f. 77v.

3 Paul L. Gavrilyuk and Sarah Coakley, 'Introduction', in *The Spiritual Senses: Perceiving God in Western Christianity*, ed. Gavrilyuk and Coakley (Cambridge: Cambridge University Press, 2012), 16.

4 Gavrilyuk and Coakley, 'Introduction', 19.

5 William Shakespeare, *The Winter's Tale*, in *The Riverside Shakespeare*, ed. G. Blakemore Evans, 2nd edn (Boston: Houghton Mifflin, 1997), 5.3.111. All references to Shakespeare's plays are to this edition unless otherwise stated.

6 Rudolph Otto, *The Idea of the Holy*, trans. John W. Harvey (Oxford: Oxford University Press, 1950, first pub. 1923), esp. 1–30. On the mixture of the daunting and the fascinating, the dreadful and the ravishing, in the numinous, see 31–40.

7 William Perkins, *A treatise tending vnto a declaration whether a man be in the estate of damnation or in the estate of grace* (London, 1590), 34. See also Cranmer's explication of how the spiritual signification of the Eucharist was only accessible to the elect who were blessed with the spiritual senses and, unlike the reprobate or the Papist, able to read the thing that was signified by the outward signs: Thomas Cranmer, *A Defence of the True and Catholic Doctrine of the Sacrament of the Body and Blood of Christ* (1550), in John E. Cox, ed., *The Works of Thomas Cranmer* (Cambridge: Cambridge University Press, 1846), 41, 207. On the perceptual privilege of election, often discussed in the context of the Reformed understanding of Eucharistic sensing, see Matthew Milner's magisterial book, *The Senses and the English Reformation* (Farnham: Ashgate, 2011), passim, but especially 255–65.

8 Augustine of Hippo, *Enarrationes in Psalmos*, XXX. S3. 6; Augustine of Hippo, *Confessions*, I.5.5.

9 *The Works of George Herbert*, ed. F.E. Hutchinson (Oxford: Clarendon Press, 1941) (hereafter, 'Herbert'), 51. All references to Herbert's poems are to this edition.

10 Henry Peacham, *The Garden of Eloquence* (Menston: Scholars Press, 1971), Tir.

11 George Walton Williams, ed., *The Complete Poems of Richard Crashaw* (hereafter, 'Crashaw'), 178–85 (at 181). All references are to this edition.

12 Augustine of Hippo, *De Genesi ad Litteram*, XII.20.42, and XII.24.51. On the threshold function of the senses in Augustine, see Gerard J. P. O'Daly, *Augustine's Philosophy of Mind* (London: Duckworth, 1987), 80 ff. Another key text is *Sermo de Providentia Dei*, also known as '*Sermo Dolbeau 29*': see *Sermo inédit de saint Augustin sur la providence divine*, RÉAug 41, no.2 (1995), 267–289. For the provenance of the idea in Augustine studies, see, e.g., Karl Barth, *Church Dogmatics III.I: The Doctrine of Creation* (New York: T & T Clark International, 2004; first pub. 1958), 10.

13 Crashaw, 173–77 (173). This is, of course, a translation (with differences) of St Thomas Aquinas's Eucharistic Hymn, '*Adóro te devóte, latens Déitas*': see Charles Herbermann, ed., 'Adoro Te Devote', in *Catholic Encyclopedia* (New York: Robert Appleton, 1913). But on the controversies around the Thomistic authorship of this hymn, and by extension of this statement on the error of

the senses, see Jean-Pierre Torrell, O.P.'s suggestive discussion in *St. Thomas Aquinas, Vol. I*, rev. ed., trans. Robert Royal (Washington: The Catholic University of America Press, 2005), 132–36.

14 St Bernard of Clairvaux, *Sermon 61, 3–5, Opera Omnia*, 2 (Paris: Frederic Leonard, 1666), 102–103 (at 102); and J. Leclercq, C.H. Talbot and H.M. Rochais, eds., *Sancti Bernardi Opera*, 8 vols. (Rome: Editiones Cistersienses, 1957–77), vol. 2: Sermon 61, 149.

15 Herbert, 67–68.

16 Herbert, 165.

17 On Augustine's hermeneutics, see Richard Todd, *The Opacity of Signs: Acts of Interpretation in George Herbert's "The Temple"* (Columbia: University of Missouri Press, 1986), esp. chapter 2 ('Augustinian Theory: Divine Signs as "Visible Words"'), 21–41.

18 Herbert, 129–30.

19 Roger Ascham, *The Scholemaster* (first pub. 1570), ed. J.E.B. Mayor (London: Bell and Daldy, 1863), Book II, 106–118 (106–107).

20 Herbert cannot have been unaware, either, of the period's practices and understanding of paraphrasing as a way of translating and opening up the Bible – potentially both a making sense of things known, and an opening of secrets unnoticed. On the connection of Biblical paraphrase in this period with translation as 'opening', see Matthew Reynolds, *The Poetry of Translation: From Chaucer & Petrarch to Homer & Logue* (Oxford: Oxford University Press, 2011), 73–81.

21 Herbert, 102–103.

22 Herbert, 79–80. Compare 'The Flower' (165) which registers the healing of the devotee's withered soul in a breathlessly awaited, perfect, clinching rhyme.

23 An earlier version of my argument about the poetics of doubt (and by extension, faith) in *The Winter's Tale*, among other plays, is in Subha Mukherji, 'Trying, knowing, believing: the epistemic plot and the poetics of doubt in early modern literature', in Yota Batsaki, Subha Mukherji, and Jan-Melissa Schramm, ed., *Fictions of Knowledge; Fact, Evidence, Doubt* (New York: Palgrave Macmillan, 2011), 84–109.

24 This idea pervades the *Summa Theologica*. On Aquinas' epistemology of faith, and its apartness from proof, see Creighton Rosental, *Lessons from Aquinas: A Resolution of the Problem of Faith and Reason* (Macon: Mercer University Press, 2011).

25 Richard Hooker, 'Of the Certainty and Perpetuity of Faith', in *The Works of Richard Hooker* (London, 1682), 527–32 (at 527–28).

26 Hooker, 'Of the Certainty and Perpetuity of Faith', 528. Italics mine.

27 Hooker's sermon was printed in 1612, though it was composed around 1586/87. The earliest performance of *The Winter's Tale* appears to have been in 1611, and its popularity on stage and in court between 1611 and 1613 is recorded.

28 The Lateran Council of 1215 marked the beginning of the secularisation of judicial tests and ordeals (Canon 18), by taking away clerical control over these. Trial by divine proof was henceforth gradually outmoded, and in England, it was replaced by procedures of pre-trial arrest and questioning based on suspicion, and, at the next stage, witness testimony and jury trial where adjudication depended on a rational assessment of the probability of evidence. Lorna Hutson builds on Barbara J. Shapiro's finding, in *A Culture of Fact: England 1550–1720* (Ithaca, NY: Cornell University Press), 8–33, to write on *The Invention of Suspicion: Law and Mimesis in Shakespeare and Renaissance Drama* (Oxford: Oxford University Press, 2007) as a dramatic phenomenon deploying common notions of the bases of legal adjudication,

transmitted through the new model of jury trial. A caveat is necessary, however, against over-estimating the prevalence of the jury trial and its indicative nature for participatory justice. Felony trials were only a small part of the total legal business of the period, not all civil or criminal action used the jury format, treason trials began using it at the very end of the seventeenth century, the intensification of interest in contract law indicated an increasing emphasis on resolving matters through negotiation rather than jury trial, and members of the jury were often limited to the middling status who were deemed to be 'epistemologically competent' (Shapiro, 24). But that the new procedures were seen as rational replacements of the older forms of supernatural or divine proofs is clear.

29 Browne, *Religio Medici*, Part I, section 9, in *Works*, 13–14.
30 Cave, *Recognitions*, passim, but esp. 1–9 (Introduction).
31 Glenn W. Most, *Doubting Thomas* (Cambridge, MA: Harvard University Press, 2005), passim.
32 Most, *Doubting Thomas*, 50–55.
33 What gives credence to Most's reading is that Jesus, in immediate response to Thomas's 'hyperbolic submission' (52) (which in turn is an immediate response to Christ's offer of tactile proof) in this Biblical recognition scene, says, 'Have you believed because you have seen me? Blessed are those who have not seen and yet believe'. No reference is made to touching. As Most argues, those who want to see a narrative lacuna here would have to assume verbal omission at the expense not only of textual arrangement but of a crucial textual fact – that John does not say that Thomas 'said' or 'uttered' the words 'My Lord and my God', but that he 'answered him' (John 20:27–28), and that verb consistently indicates immediacy of response throughout the Bible (57–58).
34 See Subha Mukherji, *Law and Representation in Early Modern England* (Cambridge: Cambridge University Press, 2006), esp. chapter 1.
35 Lancelot Andrewes, 'A Sermon on Isaiah 6:6–7, Preached at St Giles Cripplegate, 1 October 1598', in *Lancelot Andrewes: Selected Sermons and Lectures*, ed. Peter McCullough (Oxford: Oxford University Press, 2005), 138–45 (138).
36 Andrewes, 'A Sermon on Isaiah 6: 6–7', 144.
37 Andrewes, 'A Sermon on Isaiah 6: 6–7', 140.
38 Andrewes, 'A Sermon on Isaiah 6: 6–7', 143.
39 *The Whole Workes of W. Tyndall* (London, 1573), 266b.
40 Most, *Doubting Thomas*, 21.
41 This is noted in passing in Gavrilyuk and Coakley, 'Introduction', 11.
42 Thomas Cranmer, *An Answer to a Crafty and Sophistical Cavillation devised by Stephen Gardiner* (London, 1580; first published 1551), 160. For a fuller discussion of how this dramatic moment relates to sermon literature on touch, see Mukherji, 'Trying, knowing, believing' (2011), 84–109. On Cranmer's 'as it were', and how it negotiates a fine line between sensation and figuration, see my discussion in op cit, 101, and Joe Moshenska's extensive and acute discussion of it in his subsequent book, *Feeling Pleasures: The Sense of Touch in Renaissance England* (Oxford: Oxford University Press, 2014), 37–39.
43 Susan Stewart's term, in *Poetry and the Fate of the Senses* (Chicago: University of Chicago Press, 2002), 146.
44 Jan Zwicky, *Wisdom and Metaphor* (Kentville, NS: Gaspereau Press, 2008), 56.
45 Origen, *De Principiis*, 1, II.
46 Aristotle, *Parts of Animals*, 1.5.644b.
47 Wesley Trimpi, *Muses of One Mind: The Literary Analysis of Experience and its Continuity* (Princeton, NJ: Princeton University Press, 1983), 87–195.

48 John Donne, Sermon Preached at St Paul's upon Christmas day, 1621, in *The Sermons of John Donne*, ed. George Potter and Evelyn Simpson, 10 vols. (Berkeley, CA: University of California Press, 1962), vol. III, no. 17, 348–75 (at 356).

49 John Keats, Letter to Benjamin Bailey, 22 November 1817: Maurice Buxton Forman, *The Letters of John Keats* (New York: Oxford University Press, 1947), 66–70 (68). His mode of understanding – encapsulated by 'methinks' – is also echoed by the most unlikely literary inheritors: Milton's Eve recounts her terrifying dream to Adam in a narrative that begins and ends with 'methought', and repeats it twice in between (*Paradise Lost* Bk V, 35, 50, 85, 91); Adam, in response, trying to make sense of her report, muses, 'Some such resemblances methinks I find/Of our last Ev'ning's talk, in this thy Dream,/But with addition strange' (114–16). Vivid dreams, strangeness, and tentative grasp characterises all these speakers.

50 A fuller discussion of 'apprehensive knowledge' in the period's literary writing appears as a chapter in my book in progress, *Knowing Encounters: Questioning Knowledge in Early Modern Literature*.

51 See also 1 Corinthians 1: 27–28.

52 St Augustine, *In Iohannis evangelium tractatus* (CCL 36), trans. J.W. Rettig, FC 79 (Washington, DC: The Catholic University of America Press, 1988), 49.

53 John Smith, *Select Discourses* (New York: Garland, 1978), 15–16.

54 As Mark T. Mealey demonstrates, the theologian John Wesley, as late as the eighteenth century, writes about spiritual senses as a type of *elenchus* – supernatural proof – suggesting at least a continuing strand against the grain of Enlightenment thought; and as Mark J. McInroy indicates, they acted as a buffer-zone in theological aesthetic from Bonaventura onwards, mediating revelation to human apprehension. See Mealey, 'John Wesley', in *The Spiritual Senses*, ed. Gavrilyuk and Coakley, chapter. 14 (241–56), and McInroy, 'Karl Rahner and Hans Urs von Balthasar', in Ibid., chapter 15 (257–74).

55 Gavrilyuk and Coakley, 'Introduction', 16.

10 Robert Southwell's intimate exegesis

Bronwyn V. Wallace

According to the gospel of John, following Christ's resurrection, Mary Magdalen arrives at his empty tomb with John and Peter, who promptly flee. 'But Mary stood at the sepulchre without, weeping' (20:11).[1] Unlike the synoptic gospels, John leaves Mary alone there by the empty tomb, and leaves her there for some time, fixed in place by her loss and her confusion. When the angels who attend the tomb ask the potentially consoling question, 'Woman, why weepest thou?', she takes it literally, and expresses in reply her basic misconception: 'Because they have taken away my Lord, and I know not where they have laid him' (20:13). She has failed to recognise the resurrection. When Christ does arrive, she still does not recognise him – he, too, asks her (woman) why she weeps. Taking him for the gardener, in a moment of desperate irony she asks if he knows where his own body might be (20:15). It is not until he says her name that realisation dawns: 'Jesus saith to her: Mary. She turning, saith to him: Rabboni (which is to say, Master)' (20:16). In this scene of divine interpellation, Mary turns from bereft longing toward the plenitude of perfect presence. As Robert Southwell describes it in his 1591 treatise *Mary Magdalen's Funeral Tears*, the reconstitution of her mourning as intimacy with the risen Christ provokes 'so strange an alteration in her, as if she had beene wholie new made when she was onlie named'.[2] But in the next verse, the prohibition of touch comes so abruptly and so starkly that it has disoriented centuries of commentators: 'Jesus saith to her: Do not touch me, for I am not yet ascended to my Father' (20:17). There is another turn to come: he dispatches her to tell the other disciples of the resurrection, and she goes. The interpellative scene of the turn moves into her commission as *apostola apostolorum* – it sets her on a new path, directs her into a new orientation toward the community, a new relationship to the apparent absence of Christ from the world.

But Mary stood at the sepulchre without, weeping. Before that transformative turn can occur, she must *stand there*, arrested by her extremity of feeling. *But:* her divergence from the path laid out by John's and Peter's flight is her refusal to move or be moved, a standing still that is also an extension into her desire for the absent body of Christ. The

others move on, *but Mary stood*. Lancelot Andrewes identifies this as one
of the 'arguments of her great love' in the text of John 20:

> But Mary stood (that is as much to say, as) others did not, *But*, shee
> did. [. . .] *But Mary* went not, shee *stood still.* Their *going
> away* commends her *staying behinde*. [. . .] *Fortior eam figebat
> affectus*, saith *Augustine*, a stronger affection fixed her, so fixed her,
> that shee had not the power to remove thence. Goe who would, shee
> would not, but *stay still. To stay*, while others doe soe, while company
> stayes, that is the worlds love: But *Peter* is gone, and *Iohn* too : all
> are gone, and we left alone; then to *stay*, is love.[3]

But has at least two functions here according to Andrewes: to signal the
distinction between Mary and the others, and to signal the difference
between going and staying. Her fixity becomes her exceptionality, and in
turn her exemplarity. In Andrewes's citation of Augustine, we discover
that it happens *to* her: *affectus* is the subject of this fixity and she its
object; she has no power against it. But to be thus overcome is her virtue:
to stay still, to be unmoving and unmoveable, is the necessary condition
of her being in the way of Christ when he arrives. It is this period of
prolonged stasis in extreme feeling, in the space opened by the deferral
of Christ's arrival, that Southwell takes as the occasion for his meditation:
his dilation of the text of John resists movement, exerting on the time of
the gospel text the same kind of refusal to move on that Mary's standing
and weeping embodies.

Dilation

The dilation of Mary's mournful desire is the condition of her disposition
toward Christ upon his arrival. Southwell expands the time of that delay
to include the reader in Mary's longing, deferring the end that we know
(though she doesn't) must arrive in order that we might dwell in that
suspension of desire. In one of Southwell's source texts, a sixth-century
homily on John 20, Gregory IV likewise invests in delay, configured as
dilation in both senses of expansion and of deferral, as he reads Mary's
'dilated desires' as the very mechanism of her seeking and eventual finding
of Christ. 'She sought for him', Gregory writes, and 'burned with desire
for him', and 'so it happened that she who stayed behind to seek him was
the only one who saw him [Unde contigit ut eum sola tunc videret, quae
remansit ut quaereret]'.[4] What appears to be a tautology – Mary is the
only one who found him because the only one who sought him – creates
in syntactic parallel (*videret*; *quaereret*) a strong relation between seeking
and seeing. By remaining, by refusing to move on, in the paradoxical
simultaneity of seeking and stasis, Mary gains access to the object of her
desire. The condition of that remaining is indeed her burning desire itself:

'It came about that her unfulfilled desires increased, and as they increased they took possession of what they had found [desideria dilata crescerent, et crescentia caperent quod invenissent]'.[5] If 'holy desires [. . .] increase by delay [dilatione crescunt]', that increase only enables the eventual seizure of the desired object.[6] *Crescentia caperent:* the expansion of desire – its crescence; its dilation – is itself the mechanism of possession. In that homely little conventional *contigit* – 'contigit ut eum sola tunc videret'; 'contigit ut inveniret' – is revealed the contingency of Mary's seeing or finding of Christ. Contingent, of course, on her desire: first, 'ardebat desiderio', she burns with desire, *unde* contigit: her sole seeing of Christ is predicated on her ardour. Gregory then repredicates her finding of Christ on the perseverent seeking that arises from that desire: '*unde* contigit ut inveniret'. From contingency to contingency, Mary eventually arrives at the moment of finding and of taking hold – in the subjunctive; the verb itself registering its own syntactic contingency. As Carolyn Dinshaw has observed, 'contingency' as *com+tangere*, touching-with, has a special value for queer literary history in its emphasis on the 'sensible' and the 'tactile'.[7] Gregory's emphasis on contingency thus accrues a crucial kind of irony, as it describes the uncertain route to a touch that is at first deferred and ultimately prohibited.

It matters, too, that Gregory describes what happens as *finding*: contigit ut *inveniret*. As a term of rhetoric and hermeneutics, *inventio* here invites us to understand Mary's desire as an interpretive disposition. In the very first sentence of *De Doctrina Christiana*, Augustine turns rhetorical *inventio* – the discovery of topics for argument – toward scriptural hermeneutics: 'There are two things on which all interpretation of scripture depends: the process of discovering [modus inveniendi] what we need to learn, and the process of presenting [modus proferendi] what we have learnt'.[8] For Augustine, the 'most hidden meanings' of scripture are 'discovered [inventa sunt]' by the interpretation of figures and tropes.[9] The term is everywhere in *De Doctrina*, as in this passage on the pleasure of figurative difficulty: 'no one disputes that it is much more pleasant to learn lessons presented through imagery, and much more rewarding to discover meanings that are won only with difficulty [Nunc tamen nemo ambigit et per similitudines libentius quaeque cognosci et cum aliqua difficultate quaesita multo gratius *inveniri*]'.[10] The obscurity of the difficult text that yields pleasure in *inventionem* is analogous to the impassable difficulty Mary encounters at the empty tomb: the yawning absence of Christ is a figure she does not (yet) know how to interpret. The challenge of comprehending the resurrection, the peculiar mixed presence and absence of Christ, aligns with the challenge of interpreting the gospel text, and Mary's dilated desire provides the opportunity to dwell in the difficulty, to experience it with her as an emotional as well as interpretive challenge.

It is error, a mistake of doctrine, that motivates the scene in John 20, and Southwell's whole project in *Mary Magdalen's Funeral Tears*: Mary's misrecognition of the resurrection. Yet that failure creates space for her mourning desire and motivates the extensive discourse between her and the narrator. For Southwell, that is, error is an opportunity in itself: his aim is not to contain but to inhabit Mary's debilitatingly desiring femininity – and to invite his reader to inhabit it too. Mary's weeping is excessive, her faith imperfect, but precisely in her somatic affective disorder, she offers an alternative to the patriarchal rhetoric in which feminised textual dilation is always already the object of a disciplinary apparatus that seeks to neutralise it.[11] The most striking feature of Southwell's text might be that its motive is not containment but empathy.

Intimacy

Seeking to capture the interpretive register of empathy, the 'intimacy' of my title indexes several circuits of attachment and feeling in the rhetoric and hermeneutics of devotion: the relation in devotional reading and writing between the scriptural text and its expansion in interpretation; the relation these texts sought to provoke with their contemporary readers; the relation between these texts and the modern reader. My interest is thus engaged in its own intimate way with studies in queer literary history that articulate a 'queer temporality' in the relation between modernity and premodernity: the encounters across the gulf of history that do not proceed according to the ordinary unfolding of linear time or according to the progressive logic of literary-historical reproductivity and inheritance. Studies in queer temporality are dense with the metaphorics of the senses, especially touch. For Elizabeth Freeman, the 'close' in the 'close-reading' that sutures gaps in historical time is characterised by 'a grasp, a clutch, a refusal to let go'.[12] For Carolyn Dinshaw, the affective and often erotic charge of intimacy with the past is a 'touch across time'.[13] Meanwhile, scriptural hermeneutics routes interpretation through the dialectical system of spirit and body: for example, in his figure of scripture as 'treasure in earthen vessels' (2 Corinthians. 4:7), Saint Paul conflates the capacity of the gospel as text to express divinity in human terms and the capacity of the base material of humanity to exceed itself in preaching that gospel – that is, for Saint Paul here as elsewhere, the body and spirit of scripture and of human being are so nearly analogous as to be almost identical. The shared set of concerns between these two apparently disparate bodies of work thus seems to offer a ready explanatory apparatus for how reading generates a presence that can be intimately felt – can be touched.[14]

How, then, to address a text in which the senses are compromised, and such a touch or grasp remains out of reach? *Mary Magdalen's Funeral Tears* centers on an absence, dilating the few verses in which Mary Magdalen stands disconsolate before the empty tomb of Christ – the first confrontation in Christian history with the absence of Christ from the world. In Mary, Southwell makes a study of the defeat of the senses in

John 20, a text whose climactic *noli me tangere* expressly renders touch problematic. As Shelly Rambo has argued, the gospel text 'dismantles sight, sound, and even touch as vehicles constituting Mary's witness':

> [Mary] points to a different kind of presence, whose form cannot be readily identified or can only be received through multiple experiences of misrecognitions. She encounters not simply the absence of Jesus, but a mixed terrain of his absence and presence. He is there but not there; he is present in a way that she has not known before.[15]

Something must take the place of, or at least supplement, the bodily senses in the scene of Mary's longing for and eventual apprehension of Christ. As Joe Moshenska has observed in his recent study of touch in the Renaissance, 'feeling', like 'touch', has a peculiar relationship to language, 'shifting restlessly between literal and metaphorical', productively capacious and gesturing simultaneously to the materiality of the body and to a spiritual or emotional dwelling in that body.[16] Feeling as affect, I further argue, captures the circuit that runs between text and reader, as between soul and body, in the procedure of interpretation, providing a response to the dilemma of overinvestment in touch as the primary category of phenomenal experience, be it of divinity or of literary history. In devotional reading, feeling mediates between the letter of the text and its figurative resources, as it does between the material body and the perceiving mind or soul. For Southwell, it is such feeling that mediates the problem of partial and difficult knowledge in the gospel scene he dilates. And it is feeling, too, that structures his text's disposition toward its reader. In order to access the devotional amenities of affect, Southwell invests his reading of Mary Magdalen with an empathy that solicits her feeling in order to make it available to the reader as her own empathetic investment, as a way of feeling *with* Mary as she mourns for and desires the body of Christ, as she copes with the peculiar problem of his simultaneous presence in and absence from the world following the resurrection. Tracing Southwell's method in this essay, I hope that it will offer, if only implicitly, something to our own critical practices: what might it mean, I ask, to *feel with* the texts we read, as Southwell does with his gospel-reading?

Tears

As his epistle dedicatory to Dorothy Arundell indicates, Southwell's project is in part a manifesto of devotional eroticism in poetry: he makes a strong claim for the orientation of erotic poetics toward divinity (a claim about writing) that also entails a claim for the capacity of feeling to generate meaning (a claim about reading).[17] Drawn into the 'right chanel', desiring inclination – 'passions and loves' – takes the path it was always already supposed to take: toward God (A3ᵛ). A 'floud of affections' that might otherwise register as excess is perfected by its object: Mary's 'passions', Southwell writes, were 'commaunded by such a love as could never exceede, because the thing loved was of infinite perfection' (A5ᵛ). Southwell's habit of positioning Mary and her thought as the objects of verbs whose subjects are terms of feeling – love, desire, passion – emphasises how, like Augustine's *affectus*, 'passion' is something that happens *to* her.

In order to pursue his reading of John 20, Southwell locates in Mary's wet, desiring femininity – in her tears – the ground of his exegetical method, mobilizing embodied affect for meditative and interpretive purpose. Mary's weeping, as the index of her error of doctrine, her ostensible 'weakenes' (A5ᵛ), becomes an occasion to inhabit her extreme longing for the presence of Christ, the scriptural ground on which Southwell builds his investment in the affective phenomena of devotional reading. In the letter to Arundell, Southwell further declares that 'among other glorious examples of this Saints life, I have made choise of her Funeral Tears, in which as shee most uttered the great vehemencie of her fervent love to Christ, so hath she given therein largest scope to dilate upon the same' (A3ʳ⁻ᵛ). As utterance, as the embodied sign of mourning and desire, Mary's tears constitute the kind of exegetical ground usually associated with the text of scripture. Their capacity – their *scope* – demands interpretation and commentary, demands *dilation*. In his more sober preface 'To the Reader', Southwell situates his work in the context of a long exegetical tradition, 'the ground therof being in scripture, and the form of enlarging it, an imitation of the ancient doctors' (A8ᵛ). Taken together, the two prefaces sketch an analogy between Mary's capacious tears and the capacious text of scripture, between dilating on her love and enlarging the gospel text, between emotion and interpretation. Feeling – love, desire, mourning – itself emerges as the ground of interpretation, and also as a method of reading.

Southwell's method turns the text of John back on itself, taking up each of its verses in turn in order to dwell in them, perhaps most importantly in its abiding question of affect: *Woman, why weepest thou?*, Southwell's major refrain in his meditation's opening movements. The question is the occasion for Southwell to dwell at length on the question of the propriety of Mary's weeping (did not Christ forbid the daughters of Jerusalem to weep for him?), on her preference for weeping over reasoned thought, and on the excessive somatic femininity of her weeping. With its emphasis on *woman* (and 'too much a woman' [E6ᵛ]), the repeated citation challenges at once her mourning itself (apparently causeless) and the peculiarly feminine mode of her mourning (too wet, too porous, too undisciplined).[18] As a result of her 'incredulous humor' (E6ᵛ), her unbelief coded as a somatic disorder, Mary's 'wittes are smoothered with too thicke a mist, to admit these unknown beames' of right belief (F1ʳ). Yet the question also gestures to the most generative problem posed by this passage from John: in Southwell's appropriation of it, we might also paraphrase 'Why weepest thou?' as 'What is the significance of this figure of weeping in the gospel text?' Southwell recreates a problem of the gendered embodiment of feeling as a problem of interpretation: his questions excavate the surface of John's text, bringing Mary's consciousness into the frame. When Mary's reply comes at last, she objects that 'if this [weeping] be a fault, I will never amend it [. . .], for my part, sith I have lost my myrth, I will make much of my sorrow' (C8^v). As she later protests, 'What needeth my answere, where the miserie itselfe speaketh?' (F3^v). Voicing Mary's own defense of her weeping and her static standing by the tomb creates the dilated space in which the importance of 'making much of sorrow', of dwelling in feeling, can be elaborated and understood.

Dwelling

Mary Magdalen's Funeral Tears faces a dilemma in the historical gulf between its reader and Mary's scene of feeling. Her misery speaks, but how are we to hear it? How, more importantly, are we to inhabit it, from our so distant vantage? Southwell confronts this challenge by stalling his reader alongside Mary, making the time of reading coextensive with the long period of Mary's astonishment and confusion. Convinced of Christ's death, in the worldly sense, Mary can only conclude that his body has been stolen: 'They have taken away my lord, and I know not where they have laid him', reads John (20:13). For Southwell's Magdalen, this proves to be an epistemological problem so profound that it dislocates her very self: 'She was not there where shee was, for shee was wholly where hir master was, more where she loved then where she lived, and lesse in her selfe then in his bodie, which notwithstanding, where it was shee could not imagine' (B6^v). Like the misty cognitive challenge posed by her weeping, this disarticulation or distension registers first as an impairment. Reduced to her tears, she is deprived of even the basic cognitive capacity that would enable her to recognise the resurrection, or to react to the pastoral empathy of Southwell's narrator, or to answer the angels who seek to comfort her with anything but irrational refusal of clarity, or indeed to make any decision at all that would enable her to pursue the knowledge she seeks: 'Her wittes were astonied, and all her senses so amased, that in the end finding she did not know, seeing she could not discern, hearing she perceived not' (B6^v). Yet Mary's astonishment is also distension, not there where she was, more where she loved than where she lived: it is a signal characteristic of devotional desire. As Pseudo-Dionysius writes, arguing for the recuperation of *eros* as a vital theological category, 'divine yearning [*eros*] brings ecstasy so that the lover belongs not to self but to the beloved'.[19] Mary's astonished weeping, ostensibly an impairment, replaces the orderly mechanics of the senses with a counterintuitively generative ecstasy. What began as a cruel dramatic irony (Mary in her mistakenness looking ridiculous to the knowing reader) becomes an empathetic investment in the impasse Mary faces.

As Southwell argues in the epistle dedicatory, Mary's 'perfect love' repairs her 'want of beliefe, with the strange effectes of an excellent charitie' (A5ᵛ-A6ʳ). Mary echoes this sentiment: 'as in him alone is the uttermost of my desires, so he alone is the summe of all my substance' (G7ʳ⁻ᵛ), and from such desires, such substance, 'such effectes must follow as are without example' (H1ʳ). The strangeness, the unexampledness of the 'effectes' of Mary's love register the central paradox of Southwell's text: that feeling both debilitates and enables devotional disposition toward divinity, that desire and delay, indices of radical absence, are at the same time the very mechanisms of presence and possession. Yet Mary's disarticulated self remains the site of a fundamental impairment: she remains stubbornly stuck in the problem of the absence of Christ's fleshly body. Southwell in turn commits to remaining with her in that stuckness, engaging his narrator in a debate with Mary on her own terms: unable to persuade her out of her stasis, he must accept her faulty premise in order to contend with her at all. Or rather, instead of persuading her, he provides an opportunity to her voice.

In the text's most stunning account of its own method, Southwell breaks off mid-argument to make an extradiegetic observation on his practice: 'But to feel more of their sweetnesse, I wil pound these spices, and dwell a while in the peruse of thy resolute fervour' (G5ᵛ). The material, sensory quality of meditative prose emerges vividly here in the relentlessness of a stylistic pestle releasing the sweet essential property of spiritual spice. In the ambiguity of Southwell's sensory lexicon, the sweetness of spice is not to be smelled or tasted specifically but more generally, and perhaps more capaciously, *felt*. Mary Carruthers, in her study of *sweetness* as a medieval term of aesthetics, suggests that a sensibility of sweetness as a 'definable sensory phenomenon' coordinates feeling with perception, with affect, bodily sense, and knowledge, bringing to a kind of aesthetic fruition the ambiguity that always resided in Latin *sentire*.[20] In a sixteenth-century variation on this perceptual figure, Southwell's conspicuous attention to the sensory as a figurative vehicle for a method of reading (and of writing, even of the movement from reading to writing) recalls Ignatius of Loyola's insistence in the *Spiritual Exercises* on the sensory involvement of the '*the whole composite self*, I mean body and soul together', in the process of meditation.[21] Southwell's complex figure may after all be more literal than it appears, extending the moment of 'dwelling' by insisting on its activation of embodied perception. The metaleptic movement from the figure of spice-pounding to the figure of dwelling, itself a 'strange effecte', registers the challenge of spending time with a text, of an act of meditation that is also necessarily an act of interpretation and an act of writing. The figure renders the dilation of the text as a felt phenomenon, an embodied experience simultaneously receptive and appropriative, passive and active, dwelling and pounding – and, as the figure's contortion suggests, difficult or even impossible to describe. What is clear is that the pounding of spices means internalising the text, consuming it bodily, in order to have an experience of Mary Magdalen's 'fervour' – in order, through a meditative interpretation, to approach her affectively. Southwell's figure makes clear the significance of the body to interpretation, to this process of turning and returning to the text that shapes the reader in the most material ways: to feel and to know are not so dissimilar; to desire is not merely to lack but to move toward the sweetness of knowledge. Yet the figure also risks catachresis at the site where the sensory meets the affective, in the difference between the sensory 'feeling' of spice and the affective 'feeling' of fervour. Southwell, in other words, materialises the figure of dilation to explicitly include the circuitry that runs between affect, embodiment, and interpretation. The aim is to distort the time of reading, to produce in the devotional sensorium a means of extending that time. The figure's own contortion registers its resistance to the normal order of time in reading, the bind of dwelling like a gloss on John 20:11, '*But* Mary stood without at the sepulchre, weeping'.

Mary echoes this language of dwelling, too, as she begins to recognise the impossibility of moving out of her grief-stricken stasis into action: 'stil I am forced to dwel in this answere. *They have taken away my Lord, and I knowe not where they have put him*' (H3ᵛ). She *dwells* in a citation of her own words in John (20:13), as Southwell dwells in his perusal. As Mary begins to speak in the terms of Southwell's method, the full richness of the text's master tropes of speech and address begins to emerge. 'Still I am forced to dwell in this answer': Southwell's meditative method enacted in Mary's impassioned stasis. Just as earlier she queries the angels' response to her weeping, here she performs Southwell's method of putting interpretive pressure on the text of John. At the first citation of this 'answer' in which she dwells, the text draws the reader's attention to the textuality of her words: '*They have taken away*, O unfortunate word. *They have taken away my Lord*' (F3ᵛ). Mary's interjection reads like a reader's response to the gospel text, a kind of affective gloss. The typographic distinction between the conventional italics of citation and the roman type of Mary's lamenting interjection creates a strange effect of its own: Mary's speech comes to us as always-already citational, as though she is quoting the text of John and issuing a commentary on it. It is as though she reads the same gospel text that we do: a dizzying historical impossibility. When she later reiterates the verse, slightly paraphrased, it is no longer italicised and thus easier to understand as proleptic, as historical speech awaiting its record: 'And nowe (O griefe) because I know not where he is, I cannot imagin how to help, for they have taken him away, and I know not where they have put him' (F8ʳ). But when at last she observes her enforced static dwelling in her answer, the verse is once more citational, in italics emphasised by her deixis, *this* answer. She dwells as we do, caught in the time of this one half-verse by Southwell's spice-pounding. Southwell's implicit argument is that understanding the gospel text requires the reader's empathetic investment: in order to read John adequately, we must be able to think and feel as Mary Magdalen does. We must, in other words, be able to speak in her voice. And when we do, historical time seems to collapse.

Time binds: prosopopoeia

The strange effect of Mary's anachronic citation registers as what Elizabeth Freeman calls a 'time bind': the moment when 'an established temporal order gets interrupted and new encounters consequently take place', interruptions that constitute 'points of resistance to [the] temporal order that, in turn, propose other possibilities for living in relation to indeterminately past, present, and future others: that is, of living historically'.[22] For Freeman, the 'bind' of queer temporality is multiple: it signifies asynchronous attachment (willing or otherwise) to moments in history, the possibility or the danger that such anachronic investment might bind the subject in time, and also that the subject might create in her temporal resistance an effect of 'drag'. Drag both in the sense of dressing-up out of time and in the sense of kinetic resistance – the capacity, as a young Shulamith Firestone put it, to 'catch time short, and not just drift along in it'.[23] 'Temporal drag', for Freeman, registers the importance of 'retrogression, delay, and the pull of the past' to the unfinished business of queer feminism: how a return, in the present, to the stylised intellectual modes of an earlier moment of feminist history can constitute 'a *productive* obstacle to progress, a usefully distorting pull backward, and a necessary pressure on the present tense'.[24]

The invitation to identification in feeling that occurs through the pressure Southwell's method puts on the 'present tense' of the time of reading the gospel is a signal feature of prosopopoeia, in both classical and early modern understandings of its rhetorical capacities.[25] As a figure of speech that is also a figure of speaking, prosopopoeia necessarily demands identification. The long history of rhetorical personification in the Christian tradition is richly suggested by Paul de Man in an otherwise archly secular essay on prosopopoeia, where the ensouled body serves as his aptest analogy for figurative language in general: 'The language of tropes [. . .] is indeed like the body, which is like its garments, the veil of the soul as the garment is the sheltering veil of the body'.[26] But where de Man understands prosopopoeia to be therefore (only) 'privative' – because the very purpose of the figure is to revive the voice it stages only to replace it – the tradition on which he calls for his analogy of embodiment has a more complex understanding of the relationship of language to absence. The Pauline lexicon at work in de Man's analogy is the source of Origen's foundational hermeneutics of the inner and outer senses of body and of text, the spiritual sense finding expression in the material of body and letter, just as prosopopoeia gives voice to what is missing, what is inapprehensible. In this tradition, figure can *never* be privative: on the contrary it is the vehicle of the ongoing process of interpretation, of what Origen called the transformation of 'the sensible gospel into the spiritual'.[27]

As the reader takes on the voice (puts on the persona) of the speaking figure, she also internalises the text – transforms its sensible letter into spiritual apprehension of figurative meaning. That interpretive performance is what is happening in Southwell's personation of Mary Magdalen quoting from the gospeller's account of Mary Magdalen's speech: amplified by its italics, it stops us short. Like Mary, *still* – stalled in long duration, unmoving in extended time – we are *forced to dwell*, literally arrested by the site where prosopopoeia meets citation, figure meets interpretation, rhetoric meets hermeneutics. If, as John Parker wryly suggests, the mimetic personifications of poetry are themselves in some way 'even more hollow' than the casual deceptions of theatricality,[28] do they not then also, as Parker writes elsewhere of typological figures, 'yawn for fulfillment'?[29] And what might fulfill them but the investment of a reader's attention – her identification with the voice that speaks, her inhabiting of the text she reads, filling it out?

As the problem of Mary's gospel-citation makes clear, voice puts pressure on the present tense. For Freeman, rhetorical figures of time and its order or disorder signal those sites where queer ways of being in time surface in literary language: hysteron proteron, prolepsis, anastrophe, asynchrony, anachronism, delay, repetition, all resist the ostensible linearity of historical life and register in reading the felt experience of time out of order.[30] I'll add to her list Southwell's dilatory metalepsis in the figure of spice-pounding, as well as prosopopoeia. Not conventionally understood as a figure of time, prosopopoeia nevertheless demonstrates its anachronic potential as it asks us to cross a historical divide in order to inhabit Mary Magdalen's voice, and as it forces us to dwell in Mary's stalled time of loss and longing. As Margreta de Grazia has suggested, prosopopoeia 'encourages anachronism'.[31] In voicing the past, and in asking a reader to dwell with that voicing, the figure necessarily stands outside of ordinary time. Southwell understands this problem of time also as a problem of feeling. Mary's grief has removed her from herself in more ways than one: she's not only 'not there where she was', but not, in a sense, *when* she was, either. This challenging temporality is vital to those aspects of Southwell's project that require the reader's investment in and identification with the text of *Mary Magdalen's Funeral Tears* in order to have the affective purchase that motivates them. Southwell's dilation of the text of John, configured as delay, exerts the 'distorting pull' of kinetic and interpretive drag: in order to 'dwell a while', to persist in perusal, his text resists the ordinary progress of reading in time. In the language of 'dwelling', Southwell conjoins his own meditative method with the anachronic quality of Mary's voice and with her suspension in time, her recalcitrance and refusal as well as her cognitive impairment. Mary's citation of her own words in John exhibits the dangerous side of this: to be *forced to dwell* in one fixed moment, to be unable to move into a more promising future, is to live the discomfort of being caught in time, trapped in the undertow.[32]

Collation, or repair

At the climax of Southwell's work, just before Christ appears at last, the narrator apostrophises him in a desperate defense of Mary's desire: 'To what end, O sweet Lord, doest thou thus suspend hir longinges, prolong hir desires, and martyr hir with these tedious delaies?' (H5ᵛ) By now this is the reader's own question – but Southwell has already answered it. Not only do holy desires increase by delay, but delay itself gives to desire an interpretive force, by making time and space for the process of reading. An analogy emerges between Southwell's method – his own suspension and delay – and the apparent belatedness of Christ's appearance to Mary, between the sweetness of extended dwelling in the text of scripture and the sweetness of Christ himself. When Christ finally does appear, Mary makes, of course, one last mistake: taking him for a gardener, she asks him, too, whether he might know where her lord's body has been laid. The outrageous irony of her misprision is initially an opportunity for the narrator to excoriate her: how could she not recognise him for whom she has so longed? 'But', Southwell writes, 'thy mistaking hath in it a farther mysterie' (H7ᵛ). The consonance of *mistake* and *mysterie* in sound contravenes their dissonance in sense as once more, Mary's error provides an opportunity. Southwell takes Mary's mistake as an occasion to enlarge on the conventional typological association between Christ and the first gardener, Adam, according to which Christ sows salvation to cancel Adam's condemnation, and labours in death to provide the fruits of the heavenly banquet to come. 'For this', Southwell writes, meaning this reading in 'mysterie', this interpretive gesture, 'for this also was *Mary* permitted to mystake, that we might be infourmed of the mysterie, and see how aptlie the course of our redemption did answere the process of our condemnation' (H8ᵛ-I1ʳ).

'O woonderfull effectes of *Maries* love!' (H6ᵛ): Southwell cannot stop commenting on the strangeness, the wonder, the unexampledness, of the 'effectes' of Mary's passion for Christ. There is one more wonderful effect to come, of course, in the moment of recognition, the anagnorisis that transforms Mary's tragedy into a comedy of devotional ecstasy. The dilated desire that has yawned for fulfillment all this time at last reaches its climax when Christ at last says Mary's name, and at last she turns and *sees* him, in the scene of salvific interpellation that creates in her 'so strange an alteration [. . .] as if she had been wholie new made when she was onlie named' (K7^r). Her strange alteration repeats the trope that characterises the 'strange effectes' of her love: in some sense, the affective movement of Southwell's text lies just beyond language, registered in his repeated insistence on the ineffable. In only the single word of Mary's name – the little word spoken by the Word, as Southwell wonderingly observes (K7^v) – can the full erotic potential of the prolonged period of Mary's longing at last achieve some release: 'And as all this while she hath sought without finding, wepte withoute comforte, and called without answer: so now thou satisfiest her seeking with thy coming, her teares with thy triumph, and all hir cries with this one word, *Mary*' (K7^r). In the voice of god, interpellation becomes consummation, becomes erotic and literary climax.

Or, as it turns out, not quite a climax, or at least not the final one: after this exuberant erotic communion, the *noli me tangere* that inevitably arrives registers as tragedy, as a scene of devastation. Ventriloquizing the bafflement of commentators on this verse, and perhaps anticipating the reader's own shock, hurt, and disappointment at the evident violence of Christ's prohibition, Southwell's narrator launches an indignant protest:

> O Iesu what mysterie is in this? [. . .] If the multitude of hir tears have won that favor for hir eies, and hir longing to heare thee so great a recompence to hir eares, why doost thou not admitte her hands to touch, & hir mouth to kisse thy holy feete, sithe the one with many plaints and the other with their readinesse to all services, seem to have earned no lesse reward.
>
> (L3^r-L4^r)

In querying the *mysterie* of Christ's words, Southwell continues to make explicit the interpretive posture of the work: as in the mystery of Mary's mistaking, the interpretive and affective crux must be dwelled in. The answer to the question will be the conventional one of the commentary tradition: that Mary has failed to proceed from devotion to Christ in his humanity to devotion to Christ in his divinity, so that 'eyes' and 'ears' stand in for spiritual perception whereas in 'mouth' and 'hands' is located the fleshly grasp that is prohibited. To resolve the pain of the apparent rebuff, then, Southwell first ventriloquises Christ, expanding on his words in a mild chastisement of Mary's ongoing misprision: 'O *Mary* know the difference betweene a glorious and a mortall body, betweene the condition of a momentarie and of an eternall life' (L4^r). This lesson in trinitarian spirituality may be the standard line on the *noli me tangere*, but for Southwell and others this alone cannot suffice.

Southwell looks to collation as a method of repair, as though the prohibition of touch is too unbearable to sustain. He makes recourse to the text of Matthew in the work's sole moment of deviation from the Johannine account, an act of collation not unusual in itself but exceptional in *Mary Magdalen's Funeral Tears*.

But as she was in this perplexed manner, now falling, now rising in her own uncertainties, shee findeth on the waie, the other holy women that first came with hir to the grave, whom the angels had now assured of Christes resurrection. And as they passed all forwardes towardes the Disciples: *Behold Jesus met them, saieng: All hail. But they came neere, and tooke hold of his feete, and adored him. Then Jesus said to them, feare not. Go tell my brethren, that they goe into Galilee, there they shall see me.*

(M1ᵛ, quoting Matthew 28:9–10)

In this quotation, unmarked by the text's usual habit of marginal citation, Southwell sutures the events of John to those of Matthew with this brief narrative in which Mary *finds* the other two Marys *on the way*. Her finding returns us to Gregory's *inventio*: Southwell's act of interpretive collation encoded as Mary's discovery repairs her solitude and prepares for the moment of touch that John alone prohibits. Southwell characterises his act of collation – of finding on the way through scripture – as a curative gesture inherent to the scene itself: 'But O most milde phisition', he apostrophises Christ, 'wel knowest thou that thy sharp corrosie, with bitter smart angred hir tender wound, which beeing rather caused, by unwitting ignorance then wilfull error, was assoone cured as knowne' (M2ʳ). This touch is the source of Mary's ultimate 'satisfaction': it precipitates the ecstatic, even orgasmic, climax of the whole work. This careful affective physics, in which the pain of the *noli me tangere*'s rebuff is recompensed with perfect pleasure, the injury of alienation cured by the miracle of communion, is for Southwell the purpose of interpretation. The exegetical gesture of collation, in which Matthew supplies an absent encounter, could likewise be described as a 'cure' to the 'corrosie' of John, the 'requital' of John's 'refusall'. It is an act of intimate mercy on Southwell's part.

What has happened between *corrosie* and *cure* is, in some sense, a reorientation of the logic of embodiment itself: a transformation of the devastated space of mourning conditioned by Mary's fixation on Christ's fleshly body and by the reduction of embodiment to flesh alone, into a new mode of ensouled embodiment, the restoration of Ignatius' 'whole composite self' and the recuperation of *all* the senses into the interpretive frame of the dialectic between inner and outer, spiritual and material, figurative and literal. For Augustine, too, collation provides relief from the exegetical and affective difficulty of the text of John: 'Who could be so absurd', he writes in his homily on the passage, 'as to affirm that He was willing indeed to be touched by the disciples before He ascended to the Father, but refused it in the case of women till after his ascension?'[33] But it is impossible to 'run into such folly' because of the account in Matthew:

This was passed over by John, but declared as the truth by Matthew. It remains, therefore, that some sacred mystery must lie concealed in these words, and whether we discover it [quod sive inveniamus] or utterly fail to do so [invenire], yet we ought to be in no doubt as to its actual existence.[34]

Inventio is once again at stake in the process of interpretation. For Augustine, the mystery lies in determining the moment at which Mary Magdalene developed an adequate understanding of the Trinity:

[T]he words, 'Touch me not, for I am not yet ascended to my father', had this meaning, [. . .] that in this way Christ wished Himself to be believed on; in other words, to be touched spiritually, that He and the Father are one. For He has ascended to the Father, to the inward perception [intimis sensibus] of him who has made such progress in the knowledge of Christ that he acknowledges Him as equal with the Father: in any other way He is not rightly touched, that is to say, in any other way He is not rightly believed on. But Mary might have still so believed as to account Him unequal with the Father, and this certainly is forbidden her by the words, 'Touch me not;' that is, Believe not thus on me according to thy present notions; let not your thoughts stretch outwards to what I have been made in thy behalf, without passing beyond to that whereby thou hast thyself been made.[35]

The *intimus sensus* on which Augustine calls here invokes the 'inner senses' of both the body and the text of scripture as developed by Origen, the spiritual reading of Christ's presence that both depends on and supersedes Mary's more material desire for his bodily presence. What is rebuked by the *noli me tangere*, according to Augustine, is Mary's mistaking of Christ in his divinity for Christ in his humanity – a failure, in other words, of Trinitarian doctrine. Augustine interprets the prohibition further as an injunction to transcendence – and a transcendence, moreover, with a futural orientation: 'believe not [. . .] according to thy *present* notions'; 'pass *beyond*'. Allowing her thought to 'stretch outwards', gesturally like an embodied reach, toward the incarnational Christ is only the first movement in a becoming, toward the almost apophatic 'that whereby' ('per quod'), the demonstrative pronoun standing in for the threefold divinity that stands behind and before all created things. In going on to collate John with Matthew, Augustine suggests that Mary and the other women must by the time of embracing Christ's feet have likewise embraced this Trinitarian extension of thought and passed beyond the incarnational moment to, paradoxically, the time of belief in which embodied touch is not only not forbidden, but commended. To believe and to touch 'rightly', then, is not to depart from the body but to return to it. In Augustine's pun, the 'intimus sensus', the innermost sense that makes this movement possible, is then also 'the most intimate sense'.

Mary's *inventio* provides a model for interpretation, for intimate reading. As Debora Shuger expresses it, in early modern Magdalen narratives, 'the movement from desire to enjoyment, from deferred longing to loving union, configures knowledge as an erotic praxis'.[36] This is true not only diegetically, of the longing Magdalen, but also of the reader, whose procedure through interpretation, motivated by her own devotional desire, brings her into a queer kind of loving union with the text she reads. Reading, too, is an erotic praxis. If dilation implies an opening, the generation of space, of capacity, the rhetorical maneuvers of prosopopoeia fill and amplify that space and give it meaning, make it legible. Yet Southwell's investment in Mary's spatial and cognitive stasis – '*But Mary stood* alone at the sepulchre weeping' – stalls the time of Augustine's futurity, Shuger's 'movement'. Mary's intensity of affect is her way of *refusing* to move, or to move on. This is in some way the answer to Southwell's earlier question: the end to which Christ suspends Mary's longings, prolongs her desires, martyrs her with delay. In the dilation of desire resides the time and space of exegesis. In the dilation of a gospel scene in meditative prose, in the pounding of the spices of scripture, Southwell undertakes a mode of reading and of writing that assumes the dilated time of afflicted feeling – of passion – as the very ground of both reading and writing. In the exegetical analogy between the senses of the ensouled body and the senses of scripture, reading is necessarily an embodied, phenomenal event: to read is to *feel* the thing read; feeling is in turn an act of interpretation. What, then, is Mary Magdalen's desire for Christ but the reader's desire for the text she reads?

Notes

1 All citations from the Douai-Rheims Version.
2 *Marie Magdalens Funerall Teares*, 2nd ed. (London, 1592), K7ʳ. Further citations noted parenthetically. I have silently expanded contractions and regularised u/v, i/j, and the long s, but otherwise preserved original spelling and punctuation.
3 *XCVI Sermons* (London, 1631), Bbb5ʳ. Italics original.
4 English taken from 'Homily 25', in *Forty Gospel Homilies*, trans. David Hurst (Kalamazoo, MI: Cistercian Publications, 1990), 188; Latin from the digital *Patrologia Latina*, http://pld.chadwyck.com, vol. 76, *XL Homiliarum in Evangelia*, XXV.1.
5 Homilies, 188; Homiliarum, XXV.2.
6 Homilies, 189; Homiliarum, XXV.2.
7 Carolyn Dinshaw, *Getting Medieval: Sexualities and Communities, Pre- and Postmodern* (Durham, NC: Duke University Press, 1999), 39.
8 Augustine, *On Christian Teaching*, trans. R.P.H. Green (Oxford: Oxford University Press, 1997), 8; *Patrologia Latina* vol. 34, I.i.1.
9 Augustine, *On Christian Teaching*, 88; III.xxix.41.
10 Augustine, *On Christian Teaching*, 33; II.vi.8; my emphasis.

11 See Patricia Parker, *Inescapable Romance: Studies in the Poetics of a Mode* (Princeton, NJ: Princeton University Press, 1979); 'Dilation and Delay: Renaissance Matrices', *Poetics Today* 5 (1984): 519–35; *Literary Fat Ladies: Rhetoric, Gender, Property* (London: Routledge, 1988); 'Othello and Hamlet: Dilation, Spying, and the "Secret Place" of Women', *Representations* 44 (1993): 60–95. Parker's expansive body of work on Renaissance *dilation* demonstrates its centrality as a 'semantic crossroads' that becomes 'a synonym for temporality itself' ('Matrices', 520). Her important argument that Renaissance rhetoric produces 'the dilation and control of a copiousness figured as female [. . .] in order finally to dramatise the very process of its containment, the limiting structures of authority and control' (*Fat Ladies*, 31) helps to demonstrate the particularity of Southwell's dilatory method in *Mary Magdalen's Funeral Tears*, where his purpose is not to contain but to dwell in Mary's dilated affective and rhetorical femininity.

12 Elizabeth Freeman, *Time Binds: Queer Temporalities, Queer Histories* (Durham, NC: Duke University Press, 2010), xx.

13 Dinshaw, *Getting Medieval*, 21.

14 Such an understanding would be in line with the recent a vogue for 'sacramental poetics', in which scholars have read devotional poetry as performing the presence-making work of the sacraments, or as a replacement for that work, with a particular focus on the sacrament of the eucharist as the semiotic *sine qua non* of post-reformation Christianity. See e.g. Regina Schwarz, *Sacramental Poetics at the Dawn of Secularism* (Stanford, CA: Stanford University Press, 2008); Ryan Netzley, *Reading, Desire, and the Eucharist in Early Modern Religious Poetry* (Toronto, ON: University of Toronto Press, 2011); Sarah Beckwith, *Shakespeare and the Grammar of Forgiveness* (Ithaca, NY: Cornell University Press, 2011); Sophie Read, *Eucharist and the Poetic Imagination in Early Modern England* (Cambridge: Cambridge University Press, 2013); Kimberly Johnson, *Made Flesh: Sacrament and Poetics in Post-Reformation England* (Philadelphia: University of Pennsylvania Press, 2014).

15 Shelly Rambo, *Spirit and Trauma: A Theology of Remaining* (Louisville, KY: Westminster John Knox Press, 2010), 89–90.

16 Joe Moshenska, *Feeling Pleasures: The Sense of Touch in Renaissance England* (Oxford: Oxford University Press, 2014), 12, 7–8. For Moshenska, crucially, the historical specificity of this semiotic and phenomenal challenge disappears in casual appropriations of touch as a model for engagement with the past such as those that characterise Carolyn Dinshaw's work (11–12).

17 Dorothy Arundell, daughter of a prominent recusant family and later co-foundress of the English Benedictine convent in Brussels, is identified as the patroness of *Mary Magdalen's Funeral Tears* by Pierre Janelle in his literary biography of Southwell, *Robert Southwell the Writer: A Study in Religious Inspiration* [1935] (Mamaroneck, NY: Paul Appel, 1971), 59. Christopher Devlin speculates in his biography on the encounter that brought Arundell and Southwell together, citing a spy's report to Walsingham on a sermon at Marshalsea Prison: 'Among other guests were three gentlewomen very brave in their attire, two of them daughters to Sir John Arundell. . . It was Magdalen's day, and the priest catechized the company with the doctrine of popish reprentance, taking for his theme the story of the Magdalen'. Devlin suggests Southwell as the anonymous catechist, and that his sermon prompted from Arundell a request for a lengthier meditation. See *The Life of Robert Southwell, Poet and Martyr* (London: Sidgwick and Jackson, 1967), 117–18.

18 On the excessive humoral wetness of femininity, see Gail Kern Paster, 'Leaky Vessels: the Incontinent Women of City Comedy', in *The Body Embarrassed:*

Drama and the Disciplines of Shame in Early Modern England (Ithaca, NY: Cornell University Press, 1993), 23–63.

19 Pseudo-Dionysius, 'The Divine Names', in *The Complete Works*, ed. and trans. Colm Lubhéid and Paul Rorem (New York: Paulist Press, 1987), 82.

20 Mary Curruthers, 'Sweetness', *Speculum* 81 (2006): 999–1013 (at 999).

21 Ignatius of Loyola, 'Spiritual Exercises', in *Personal Writings*, ed. and trans. Joseph A. Munitiz and Philip Endean (London: Penguin, 1996), 295. Emphasis mine.

22 Freeman, *Time Binds*, xxii.

23 Cited in Freeman, *Time Binds*, 77.

24 Freeman, *Time Binds*, 62 and 64, italics original.

25 On Renaissance prosopopoeia, see Gavin Alexander, 'Prosopopoeia', in *Renaissance Figures of Speech*, ed. Sylvia Adamson, Gavin Alexander, and Katrin Ettenhuber (Cambridge: Cambridge University Press, 2008), 97–114; John Parker, 'Persona', in *Cultural Reformations: Medieval and Renaissance in Literary History*, ed. Brian Cummings and James Simpson (Oxford: Oxford University Press, 2010), 591–608; Lynn Enterline, *Shakespeare's Schoolroom: Rhetoric, Discipline, Emotion* (Philadelphia: University of Pennsylvania Press, 2012).

26 Paul de Man, 'Autobiography as De-facement', *MLN* 94:5 (1979): 929–30.

27 Origen, *Commentary on John, Book I* in *Origen*, ed. and trans. Joseph W. Trigg (London: Routledge, 1998), 109.

28 'Persona', 605.

29 John Parker, *The Aesthetics of Antichrist: From Christian Drama to Christopher Marlowe* (Ithaca, NY: Cornell University Press, 2007), 50.

30 *Time Binds*, xxii.

31 Margreta de Grazia, 'Anachronism', in *Cultural Reformations* ed. Cummings and Simpson, 22.

32 Freeman's epigraph to her temporal drag chapter is a quotation from Meryl Altman on 'Teaching 70's feminism': 'Every wave has its undertow'. *Time Binds*, 59.

33 Augustine, *Homilies on the Gospel of John*, ed. Philip Schaff, trans. John Gibb and James Innes, *Nicene and Post-Nicene Fathers*, vol. 7 (Peabody, MA: Hendrickson, 1994), 437.

34 Ibid., 437–8. Latin from the *Patrologia Latina* online, vol. 35, Tractatus CXXI.3.

35 Ibid., 438.

36 Debora Shuger, *The Renaissance Bible: Scholarship, Sacrifice, and Subjectivity* (Berkeley: University of California Press, 1994), 187.

11 God's nostrils: the divine senses in early modern England

Elizabeth L. Swann

I.

In a sermon on the topic of prayer published in 1611, Lancelot Andrewes expounds on Psalm 141, verse 2, translated in the King James Version as 'Let my prayer be set forth before thee as incense'.[1] The analogy, Andrewes explains, is explicable by reference to Hebrew ritual practice:

> In the time of the law a speciall part of the service, which the people performed to God, was the offering up of incense, and therefore the Prophet *compareth prayer to incense*. . . And it is most fitly resembled to incense, for the use of incense was to sweeten those places which are unsavory: Even so the wicked imaginations, and unchast thoughts of our heartes, which yeeld a stinking smell in the nostrils of God, are sweetned by no other meanes then by prayer.[2]

For Andrewes, the Psalmist's analogy is apt because prayer functions as incense did under the old law, sweetening and purifying the heart of the worshipper. As such, this passage seems to lend support to Holly Dugan's argument that whereas early modern Catholics preserved a medieval tendency to view the senses as a direct route to the divine, Protestant reformers expunged sensation from liturgical experience whilst continuing to exploit its symbolic and figural possibilities in their written works. Focusing on smell, Dugan shows that whilst reformers limited the use of incense in ritual, denouncing it as sinfully luxurious, they frequently employed incense 'as a metaphorical abstraction', associating sacrifice and prayer with sweet and aromatic scents.[3] In this way, Dugan contends, reformers prioritised the symbolic meanings of incense over direct, sensory engagement with it.

Dugan's argument is rich and persuasive in a number of respects, but it should also give us pause, for it replicates the older historiographical narrative – challenged at a number of points in this volume – that takes the Reformation as precipitating a progressive disembodiment of religious belief.[4] Protestant metaphoricity is supposed to evacuate sensory language of its physical referents: invocations of the sweet smell of incense are to be taken as abstractions, not as experiential realities. As we have seen, however, this is not always the case, both because Protestant uses of metaphor and other forms of figurative language do not always entail the disembodiment of such language, and because Catholic writers, too, made extensive use of sensory imagery.[5] Indeed, whilst Andrewes clearly intends the reek of sin and the fragrance of prayer to be taken as metaphorical, they are not unproblematically disembodied: his reference to 'the nostrils of God' is strikingly corporeal, associating God's apprehension of the smells of sin and prayer with a specific physical organ. As Joe Moshenska has argued, the ways in which reformers employed sensory language was neither purely abstract and metaphorical, nor exclusively corporeal and literal. Rather, it was carefully calculated to 'hover' between the two, exploiting the affective force of physical experience whilst circumventing the potentially heretical implications of over-emphasising the literal nature of humankind's sensory apprehension of the divine.[6] Sensory language does not have to be associated either with objective physical realities, or with abstract, disembodied metaphor, for it can have – so to speak – a foot in both camps.

With this established, what is striking in Andrewes's assertion that prayer and incense are alike is not the precise extent to which we should take the analogy as describing an embodied reality as opposed to a purely figurative, conventional formulation. Instead, I am interested in *where* Andrewes locates sensation in the analogy: not with the worshippers, but with God himself. The sweet incense of prayer, and the stench of wickedness that it displaces, are experienced not by those who pray, but by the deity they venerate. Put another way, what is at stake here is not (as Dugan and others tend to presume in discussions of sensory metaphor) humankind's sensory perception of God; rather, it is God's sensory perception of humankind.

Andrewes's discussion of prayer, then, highlights a gap in the scholarship on early modern religion and the senses. The essays in this volume – and research on religion and the senses in medieval and early modern culture more generally – differ in method, topic, and scope, but they are united in a focus on what premodern men and women thought about, or how they experienced, the role of their senses in apprehending the divine. The question of how humankind perceives God, however, invites the chiastic reversal of its own terms: how does God perceive humankind? Does God sense us in any recognisable, human way? Is his apprehension of humanity a source of pleasure (as he delights in his creation) or suffering (as he shares in our sorrow and deplores our sin)? Is divine attentiveness a form of intimacy and vehicle of grace, or an expression of power, a form of surveillance? And what of the lower senses? If God can see and hear humankind, might he also be able to smell, touch, and taste us? If so, how should we understand this kind of anthropomorphism: as accommodation, as error, or as literary flourish?

If these questions seem absurd, then perhaps our discomfort might alert us to the pull that conventional sensory hierarchies – which present vision and hearing as the most dignified and reliable senses, and which associate smell, taste, and touch with vulgar, immoral desires – continue to exert on us.[7] We are used to thinking of God's omnipotence and omniscience in terms of the comprehensive scope and penetrating acuity of the divine senses, but usually the focus is on God's aural and visual supremacy: God is all-seeing and all-hearing. A God who looks and sees us, who listens to and hears us, is clearly easier to stomach than a God who tastes, smells, and touches us, for a God with the full set of senses is a fleshy, corporeal God, unsettlingly subject to physical appetites.

Despite the potential for blasphemy, however, early modern reformed thinkers from a variety of backgrounds were deeply interested in the question of divine sensation. As the Church of England clergyman and theologian Richard Sibbes writes in a sermon published in his *The returning backslider* (1639):

> Scripture. . . attribute[s] senses unto God, of feeling, smelling and touching, *&c.* So God is said to looke upon his children with delight, and to heare their prayers. . . And he tastes the fruit that comes from them. So on the contrary, all his senses are annoyed with wicked men and vile persons. . . As a man that goes by a stinking dung-hill stops his nose and cannot endure the sent. So the blasphemous breath of gracelesse persons, it is abhominable to God. . . and for his *eyes* he cannot endure iniquity, to looke upon the wicked, and for his *eares,* their prayers are abhominable. . . And so for *feeling*. . . the Prophet complaineth that God was burthened and loaded under their sinnes, as a cart pressed till it be readie to breake under the sheaves. All his senses are offended with wicked men.[8]

For Sibbes, human virtue and vice are expressed physically, and all of God's senses are deployed in apprehending 'his children'.[9] In this essay, focusing on the 'lower' senses of smell, touch, and taste, I explore moments where Protestant theologians and authors of different stripes variously hint at, confront, seek, or deny the potentially sacrilegious notion of God's embodied humanity. For sixteenth- and seventeenth-century men and women, God's knowledge of humankind (embodied or otherwise) is both a precondition of and the model for humankind's knowledge of God. Knowing God, these men and women thought, was not just a matter of intellectual apprehension, but neither was it exclusively a matter of feeling, hearing, smelling, tasting, and desiring him, for such affectively-charged apprehension was only perfected when it incorporated a sense of being reciprocally *recognised* by God – that is, of being desired, felt, and touched by Him in return. Taking George Herbert and Guillaume Du Bartas as examples, I propose that poetry offered one way to facilitate such recognition, serving as a means of inviting and directing God's sensory attention. Like Paul in his letters to the Corinthians, early modern men and women longed for a time when the darkness of human vision would clear, and it would be possible to 'see' God 'face to face', and to 'know even as also I am known'.[10] In striving to achieve, or at least emulate, such a state of sensory and epistemic felicity on earth, the question of divine sensation was paramount – and the resources of poetry were indispensable.

II.

In one instantiation at least, of course, the Christian God does possess the full quota of human senses. Taking on form and flesh in the figure of his own son, the impassable deity lives, loves, and suffers (and eats, sleeps, spits, and weeps) in Christ.[11] The book of Isaiah, which is usually taken to prophesy the advent of Christ, is a crux for the problem – or possibility – of divine sensation:

> And there shall come forth a rod out of the stem of Jesse, and a Branch shall grow out of his roots: And the spirit of the LORD shall rest upon him, the spirit of wisdom and understanding, the spirit of counsel and might, the spirit of knowledge and of the fear of the LORD; And shall make him of quick understanding in the fear of the LORD: and he shall not judge after the sight of his eyes, neither reprove after the hearing of his ears: But with righteousness shall he judge the poor, and reprove with equity for the meek of the earth. . .[12]

Here, Christ's divine wisdom is attributed to his repudiation of his human senses: his preternatural ability to know and judge is explicitly *not* dependent on 'the sight of his eyes' or 'the hearing of his ears'. This prophesied rejection of sensory evidence, however, is somewhat complicated by the beginning of verse 3, which in the King James Version reads '[the spirit of the Lord. . .] shall make him of quick understanding in the fear of the LORD', but which can be more literally translated from the Hebrew as 'and his smelling is with the fear of Yahweh'.[13]

Early modern commentators recognised that the King James Version's use of 'quick understanding' represented a departure from this literal meaning. Thus, in his 1682 *Annotations upon. . . Isaiah*, the Presbyterian clergyman Arthur Jackson writes that:

> It is in the original, *And he shall make him sent or smell in the fear of the Lord;* which therefore some expound thus: That by reason of this his being so abundantly anointed with the holy Spirit of God, he should breathe forth nothing but what was sweetly pious and religious; or that in all his courses he should send forth a sweet sent

suitable to the precious savour of his spiritual unction. But rather by this figurative expression is only meant that which we have in our Translation, *And shall make him of quick understanding in the fear of the Lord.* By the smell we discover things more secret, than those things are which appear to the eye or ear; and likewise by the smell we discover things more easily and quickly than any other way; so that when it is said, That the Spirit should make Christ *sent or smell in the fear of the Lord;* This seems to intend, that he should be of a sharp and quick understanding.[14]

Jackson acknowledges – only to deny – a tradition according to which Christ is positioned as the object, rather than the subject of smell. According to this interpretation, Christ emits something like the odour of sanctity attributed to saints in the Catholic tradition, and both his words and deeds are perfumed with virtue.[15] Against such readings, Jackson defends the authority of the King James Version: the reference to Christ's sense of smell in the original Hebrew, he argues, serves as a metaphor or 'figurative expression' for his '*quick understanding*'. The association, he explains, is appropriate, for smell itself is a valuable source of knowledge: 'by the smell we discover things more secret, than those things are which appear to the eye or ear'.[16] Jackson thus preserves Christ's autonomy as a sensing and knowing subject by highlighting the figurative associations of smell, which indicate Christ's exceptional ability to perceive truth.

Other early modern authors – both Catholic and Protestant – evince a deep interest in Christ's use of his physical senses, as well as his spiritual senses, taking him as an exemplary model in this regard. Robert Southwell, for instance, describes him as 'the most experienced and perfitt taster', citing his acceptance of the sour vinegar which he was offered to drink during the crucifixion, as well as his choice of the metaphorical 'gall' of death over the 'honye' of sensuous pleasure, as evidence of his irreproachable disregard for worldly pleasures.[17] A number of writers and thinkers also suggest, however, that a keen sense of smell and taste also belong to God in his transcendent, paternal manifestation – that is, to God the lawgiver and judge – and it is this phenomenon that I will focus on here.

In suggesting that God possesses the lower senses, early modern authors follow scripture, which itself attributes distinctly human features, sensations, and affects to the father, as well as to the son: the Bible refers to God's hands, face, mouth and breath, eyes, and ears.[18] He is also described as experiencing passions, along with the corresponding physiological responses: at various points, God is said to love us, to feel jealousy, to become angry, to rejoice, to be cheered by wine, to laugh and scoff, and to 'cry like a travailing woman'.[19] God's nostrils – singled out in the earlier quotation from Andrewes – are also explicitly invoked elsewhere in scripture, as Moses and the Israelites celebrate the parting of the red sea as an effect of God's powerful breath: 'And with the blast of thy nostrils the waters were gathered together'.[20] God is said to apprehend sacrifice in terms of smell, and to experience both olfactory pleasure and irritation as a result of human actions. In Genesis, God smells and is pleased by the 'sweet savour' of Noah's burnt offerings; in Isaiah, however, He excoriates the proud Babylonians: 'These are a smoke in my nose', he fulminates, 'a fire that burneth all the day'.[21]

The coming of Christ entailed a wholesale transformation of the notion of sacrifice, and a corresponding shift in divine olfaction. As St Paul's Epistle to the Ephesians states, 'Christ. . . hath loved us, and hath given himself for us an offering and a sacrifice to God for a sweetsmelling savour'.[22] In offering himself in this way as a substitute for the burnt sacrifices of the old law, Christ internalised sacrifice, which was no longer to be a matter of material burnt offerings, but of continual self-abnegation. Subsequently, God's olfactory pleasure in the sacrifices presented to him must be understood not as physical, but as spiritual or metaphorical. The incarnation, then, was doubly significant for humankind's sensory relationship with the divine: in assuming a body, Christ took on the pleasures and pitfalls of the human senses, but he also reconfigured the sensory relationship between God the father and earthly believers, spiritualising the sacrificial exchange. In the incarnation, the connection between humankind and the divine was *simultaneously* embodied, and spiritualised.

During the Reformation, the sensory dimension of sacrifice – that it is 'sweetsmelling' – became particularly freighted in the context of debates around Socinianism, an unorthodox movement originating in the reformed Polish church in the sixteenth and seventeenth centuries. Amongst other things, Socinians argued that the crucifixion did not serve a propitiatory function; that is, it did not expiate our sins in the eyes of God. Paul's use in Ephesians of the phrase 'sweetsmelling' to describe Christ's sacrifice was supposed to support this position. As the theologian and bishop of Worcester Edward Stillingfleet notes in his 1673 *A Discourse Concerning the True Reason of the Suffering of Christ*, the Socinian theologian Johann Crell argued that in the Old Testament 'that phrase of a sweet-smelling savour is generally and almost always used of sacrifices which are not expiatory'. Furthermore, Crell contended, if the words *were* ever applied to an expiatory sacrifice, 'they are not applied to that which was properly expiatory in it, *viz.* [namely] the offering up of the blood'. The expiatory part of the burnt offering is the blood, and burning blood, according to the literal-minded Crell, does not produce a smell. 'Sweetsmelling', therefore, must refer to 'the burning of the fat, and the kidneys, which although required to perfect the expiation' were not instrumental to it, and therefore 'hath nothing correspondent to the expiatory Sacrifice of Christ'.[23]

Stillingfleet answers Crell's argument, which he calls 'gross' and 'corporeal', by considering Genesis' description of Noah's sacrifice as 'sweetsmelling'. In the Syriac Version of Genesis, Stillingfleet notes, the smell of

Noah's sacrifice is described as '*the savour of rest* . . . and so it imports a *rest* after some *commotion*, and in that sense is very proper to *Atonement*, or that whereby God makes *his anger to rest*'. [24] In Syriac – a dialect of the Aramaic spoken by Christ, and therefore a language with some authority in such matters – the expiatory dimensions of the phrase 'sweet-smelling savour' are evident. Stillingfleet goes on: 'from whence it follows, that the phrase of a *sweetsmelling savour,* being applied under the Law to *Expiatory Sacrifices,* is very properly used by St *Paul,* concerning Christs giving up himself for us'. [25] Both Crell and Stillingfleet accept that the answer to a key theological question – that is, whether or not Christ's sacrifice should be taken as expiatory – is to be found in scriptural depictions of divine sensation. Both Crell and Stillingfleet, moreover, presume that the exact nature of divine sensation can be accessed via philological analysis. The complexities of theology and the intimate sensuality of smell converge in the technicalities of scriptural translation.

The sweet smell of sacrifice is also invoked when the subject is a contemporary believer acting after the model of Christ himself. Hagiographers often describe the sweet scent supposedly produced by the deaths of martyrs: in his *An exposition of the seven epistles to the seven churches* (1669), for example, the Cambridge Platonist Henry More asserts that 'the Faith, Constancy and devout Sincerity of our blessed Protestant Martyrs went up with the flames and globes of Smoak, sweeter then any Odours or Incense, from the Altar, into the presence of Heaven'. [26] Less drastic forms of self-sacrifice are also figured as a means of providing God with olfactory pleasure: 'I will burn with devotion, that He may smell a sweet savour', proclaims Bishop of Coventry and Lichfield John Hacket, in a 1675 sermon on Genesis which offers an extended account of the divine senses, and smell in particular. [27]

For Hacket, divine sensation is analogous to, but also importantly distinguished from, human sensation. For a start, God's senses are less prone to becoming jaded: 'All sensible smells', Hacket notes, 'be it the *Rose* among the Flowers, or *Cassia* among the Spices, must be often put to the sense, and often taken away to please it; hold them long to the Nostril, and they will prove faint and tedious'. God, however, is 'very tenacious of his mercy, our Sacrifice, our Prayers, our Alms. . . their smell stays long with *God*'. [28] In stressing God's imperviousness to sensory fatigue, Hacket places his senses firmly in the spiritual realm, for – following Augustine – early modern authors often contrasted the enduring nature of spiritual sensation with the ephemerality of physical, worldly sensation. [29]

Another defining characteristic of divine perception for Hacket and his contemporaries is that it must be not merely receptive, but also dynamic: God's senses work on what they perceive in ways that are variously creative and destructive. In Hacket's formulation, God is the ultimate spectator of the human drama:

the spirit of a Christian would be obtuse, and nothing so well excited
to be dutiful, but that we know all the thoughts, words, and works
of piety are within the look of *God*. . . [God's] aspect doth fortify and
animate our strength, like Plants that open themselves to the *Sun,*
and revive when his light is cast upon them.[30]

Hacket suggests that divine surveillance is what gives meaning and pleasure
to our lives: God's sensory awareness of us is not passive but active, rousing
and revitalising us just as the sun's light stimulates and sustains vegetable
matter.[31] Hacket continues, 'the love and complacency of *God* is not a bare
affection like mans. . . Where *God* is said to love, or to smell some sweetness in a thing, this is not to affect it theorically, but to effect some good
for it'.[32] God's affects entail effects, acting on and sustaining the objects
they apprehend.

There is a similar sense of the generative pleasure of being perceived by
God in George Herbert's 'The Glance', although the focus here is on sight,
rather than smell.[33] In Herbert's poem, the narrator recalls how God's
'sweet and gracious eye' turned briefly on him 'in the midst of youth and
night', making him feel 'a sugred strange delight' and precipitating a
conversion experience.[34] Here, the experience of grace is not an experience
of *seeing* God, but rather of being *seen* by him; it is an awareness that one
is being perceived by God. Donne's *Devotions upon Emergent Occasions,*
written around December 1623 and published the following year, is
similarly invested in the sustaining force of divine perception. Donne
addresses God directly, describing him as one 'who art of so pure *eyes*, as
that thou canst not look upon *sinn*, and we of so unpure constitutions,
as that wee can present no object but *sin*, and therfore might justly feare,
that thou wouldst turn thine *eyes* for ever from us'.[35] This fear, however,
is appeased, for the incarnation enables a kind of mediated perception
whereby God is able to 'look upon' human sin: 'thogh thou canst not
indure *sinne* in us, yet in thy *Sonn* thou canst, and he hath taken upon
him selfe, and presented to thee, al those *sins*, which might displease thee
in us'.[36] In enabling God to see our sins, Christ also enables him to
strengthen us against them, for God's eye, as Donne writes, '*nourishes* us
by looking upon us'.[37] Christ is both sensing *subject*, God looking through
human eyes, and *object* of sense, presenting human sin and folly to God's
reparative sight in a way that is tolerable to him.

III.

Divine olfaction and vision, then – distinct as they may be from the human
experience of these senses – are vital to the relationship between God and
his creation. The other lower senses, however, also have a part to play. In
his 1616 collection of sermons *A divine herball*, the clergyman Thomas
Adams indicates the importance of taste, as well as smell. Adams attests

to God's olfactory response to sin, noting that whilst 'man is naturally delighted with pleasant savours, and abhorres noisome and stinking smels', God is even more susceptible to odours: 'our God hath purer nosthrils, and cannot abide the polluted heapes of iniquities'.[38] Smell can also mislead, however. In the third sermon in *A divine herball*, Adams recounts the parable of the Pharisee and the Publican related in Luke, in which the apparently pious Pharisee is revealed to be corrupted by pride, whilst the humble Publican is vindicated as a true believer.[39] 'Many a flower', writes Adams

> hath a sweet smell, but not so wholsome a taste. Your Pharisaicall prayers and almes smelt sweetly in the vulgar nosthrils: *taste* them, and they were but rue, or rather worme-wood. When the Pharise sawe the Publican in the lower part of the Temple. . . he could cry, Foh this Publican: but when they were both *tasted,* by his palate that could judge, the Publican hath an *herbe* in his bosome, and the Pharise but a gay, gorgeous, stinking weede.[40]

In a peculiar departure from scripture, Adams describes God's arbitration between the Pharisee and the publican as an act of tasting. Taste, traditionally understood as one of the lowest senses, is here apotheosised as divine judgement: whilst the 'vulgar nosthrils' of the laity may deceive, the divine palate has the capacity to discriminate between adherence to ritual forms, and genuine faith. For Adams, human virtue and vice emerge as sensible to a deity with 'nosthrils', and palate.

In this, Adams is by no means unusual: the notion that God smells and tastes human virtue and vice is ubiquitous in the sixteenth and seventeenth centuries. For the religious writer and bishop of Norwich Joseph Hall, for instance, the sins of men who give themselves over to the inclinations of their own will are like 'wilde grapes for the harshnesse and sowrnesse of the tast. . . to the palate of the Almighty'. The pious people of Israel, however, are described by Hall as 'tastfull. . . [and] delightfull unto God'.[41] Often, humankind's unpleasant taste to God was understood as a manifestation of original sin, traceable to Adam and Eve's tasting of the forbidden fruit. As the poet Edward Benlowes writes in his 1652 devotional epic *Theophilia*, '*both* taste, by tasting, tastlesse *Both* became'.[42] Benlowes's use of polyptoton – the repetition of a word in different cases, as 'taste. . . tasting. . . tasteless' – extends Adam and Eve's action through history, as the simple present tense of 'both taste' is repeated as the present continuous 'tasting'. In tasting, furthermore, Adam and Eve become 'tasteless': a word that indicates both that they become devoid of the capacity to taste, and that they themselves become insipid or flavourless.

Humankind's inherited tastelessness, however, can be exacerbated or palliated by an individual's actions in life. Thus, in his exposition on Matthew, included in the 1573 edition of his *Works*, William Tyndale informs those who fast for self-serving reasons such as pride in their own piety that 'thy sacrifice were cleane without salt, & all together unsavery in the tast of God'.[43] Invoking the Sermon on the Mount, in which Christ calls his disciples the salt of the earth, Tyndale suggests that the individual's vainglorious rejection of the legitimate pleasures of taste deprives him or her of the seasoning of genuine faith.[44]

Nonetheless, it is possible for the individual believer to palliate his or her unpleasantness to God's palate, either by partaking in the Eucharistic sacrament, or through immersion in Gospel.[45] For the radical Essex minister John Smith, participating in the Lord's Supper effects change for the better in the sensory qualities both of the communicant's body and of his or her soul. As the physical wine sweetens the communicant's breath ('a man having tasted of it', Smith claims, 'it will make his very breath smell the sweeter'), so too will the spiritual blood of Christ sweeten his mind and actions: 'a man having tasted of it by faith, all his actions and all his thoughts will be full of the good taste, and good relish of the same'.[46] For the Sussex minister George Petter, writing in his 1661 commentary on the gospel according to Mark, reading scripture and listening to 'the Word Preached' serves a similar function. Again, making reference to the Sermon on the Mount, Petter advises that 'as salt being put upon the Sacrifices, did. . . give unto them a good savour and rellish; so the Word Preached is a means. . . to make them savoury and pleasant (as it were) unto Gods own taste'.[47] As the believer consumes – whether the Eucharistic elements or the word of God – he or she takes on the nature of the objects of his taste, becoming more palatable to God in the process. For Benlowes, Tyndale, Smith, and Petter alike, human and heavenly sensation exist in a reciprocal relation. In sinfully tasting the forbidden fruit, Adam and Eve became tasteless to God, and in engaging in pointless and prideful acts of gustatory self-denial, fasters exacerbate this state of insipidness; but in tasting of the licit and redemptive feast of the Eucharist or the Word of God, the believer can regain some of his or her pleasantness to God. In engaging in active, and religiously significant, acts of tasting, then, believers are also constituted as *subjects* of taste, acquiring the flavour (or insipidness) of the things that they consume. Humankind's perception of God is both predicated on and entails God's perception of humankind.

God, then, was understood to possess acute and frequently exercised (albeit perfectly regulated and benevolent) senses of smell and taste. But what of what was often considered the very lowest of the senses – the sense most intimately entangled with sensuality – namely touch? Here, too, we find a strong emphasis on God's sensitivity. In the first half of the seventeenth century, divine touch took on political significance. In a 1610 sermon preached before the king, Lancelot Andrewes interprets the injunction of Chronicles, 'touch not mine anointed', as referring to the monarch himself.[48] To be anointed and claimed by God as 'mine', asserts Andrewes, is to be touched by God, a state which prohibits the vicious contact of worldly men: 'His hand hath *touched* them with his *anointing*, that no other hand might *touch* them. . . the whole race Royall is folded up in this word. . . that not one of them is to be *touched*'.[49] Speaking only five years after the Gunpowder Plot, Andrewes is vigilant to aver that indirect contact is still a form of touch, and thus falls under the divine injunction against the touching of kings: 'There is none so simple as to imagine there is no touch', Andrewes declares, 'but that with the finger's end, immediate. The *mediate*, with a *knife* or with a *Pistoll*, that is a *touch*: if wee *touch* that whereby they are *touched*, it is all one'.[50] Mediated touch, says Andrewes, is still contact: to touch a monarch with a weapon is no less a violation of God's protective, anointing touch than to strangle him or her with one's bare hands.

In contrast to the monarchist Andrewes, later and more radical theologians interpret the Chronicles verse as referring to the elect, thereby effecting a reversal of its political meaning. 'You see how tender he is of them', writes the nonconformist minister and eventual engineer of the Cromwellian settlement Thomas Goodwin in his sermon *The great interest of states & kingdoms*, preached before the House of Commons in 1645:

> TOUCH *them not*. If you would understand the tendernesse of Gods heart expressed in that word, parallel it with that, *He that* TOUCHETH *them, toucheth the* APPLE OF MINE EYE. . . there is nothing more deare then the eye. . . and of the eye, the *pupa*, the *black* of the eye most.[51]

God's tenderness is both an affective solicitude (a tenderness of the heart), and an intensely intimate physical connection, whereby – as Goodwin warns – to touch the elect violently is to touch the very apple or pupil of God's own eye: the most sensitive part of God. As such, Goodwin's insistence on God's sensory connection with his flock contains a pointed political warning, prohibiting violent action against the self-appointed godly.

Turning again to George Herbert, I now want to argue that for some authors the resources of poetry played a vital role in maintaining a rich and authentic sensory relationship with the divine. As Katherine Craik has shown, for early moderns, language was conceived 'as a material system which could literally touch readers – and be touched by them in return'.[52] For Herbert, I suggest, the sensory exchanges involved in writing, reciting, or reading poetry functioned as a means of inviting divine attention. In Herbert's 'Church-Lock and Key', God's ears are described in terms which reflect the common Augustinian understanding of the human sense organs as doors or windows which may be open or closed. The narrator's transgressions are figured as a kind of key: 'I know it is my sinne', Herbert writes, 'which locks thine eares, / And bindes thy hands'.[53]

If sin is a key, however, it turns both ways: it has the potential to unlock as well as lock up the divine senses. In the final stanza of the poem, the narrator apostrophises God: 'Yet heare, O God, onely for his blouds sake. . . For though sinnes plead too, yet like stones they make / His blouds sweet current much more loud to be'.[54] Sin – which at the beginning of the poem is an obstacle to divine perception – is at the end of the poem understood to contribute to an auditory appeal to the divine senses, functioning as a stony obstruction which amplifies the voluble currents of Christ's expiatory blood.

It is worth noting, however, that the final lines of 'Church-Lock and Key' constitute an appeal to the divine ears that is not, within the scope of the poem itself, answered. This highlights a central feature of human-kind's sensory relation with God, namely the difficulty of perceiving God's perception of (or conversely, obliviousness to) humankind. In other words, we can never be absolutely sure of divine attention: we cannot see God watching us, or hear him listening to us, or smell him smelling us. The best assurance that we have of divine *attentiveness* is divine *responsiveness*, in whatever form this might take. Herbert explores this difficulty in his poem 'Deniall':

> When my devotions could not pierce
> Thy silent eares;
> Then was my heart broken, as was my verse. . .[55]

The metalepsis of 'silent ears' condenses a relatively complex process of reasoning: God's deafness is inferred from his silence, his lack of response to the narrator's 'devotions'. Herbert's narrator, then, presumes an intimate and immediate relationship between divine audition and divine responsiveness: if God hears us, he will immediately reply; if he does not immediately reply, then he has not heard us. Despite this presumed rift between the narrator and God, however, Herbert retains a sense of the shared quality of human-divine perception. This shared quality is attested by the *failure* of his verse, which becomes 'broken', interspersed with silence. God's presumed deafness is reflected in the collapse of the poet's own ability to speak out, and the accord of human and divine senses is evident precisely in their simultaneous breakdown.

This sensory and communicative dysfunction is explored further in the third and fourth stanzas of the poem, as the narrator's 'knees and heart' are 'benumm[ed]' by supplication:

> O that thou shouldst give dust a tongue
> To crie to thee,
> And then not heare it crying! all day long
> My heart was in my knee,
> But no hearing.[56]

Again, we get a catachrestic disorder of body parts ('my heart was in my knee') resulting in sensory deprivation, but despite the narrator's accusations of divine inattention – or arguably, *because* of them – the implication here is that it is the narrator himself who is not listening to God, rather than vice versa. This is suggested initially by the assertion that the narrator's knee, and by extension his heart, are numb from genuflecting; his over-zealous, relentless attempts to make contact with God have resulted in a state of anaesthesia, a lack of responsiveness in his own body. This notion is reinforced by the elliptical, subject-less last line of this verse, which is presumably intended to bemoan God's lack of hearing, but which is ambiguous enough to refer to the narrator himself. The narrator's voluble pleas to be *heard* forestall the possibility that he might himself *hear* God's own voice: his 'crying' drowns it out. Again, the poem ends on a note of supplication. This time, however, the outlook is brighter. 'O cheer and tune my heartlesse breast', the narrator pleads:

> Deferre no time
> That so thy favours granting my request,
> They and my minde may chime,
> And mend my ryme.[57]

The request to God to 'defer no time' draws the reader's attention to a shift of tense, for whilst the poem describes the breakdown of sensory communion between man and God in the past tense (*'could not* pierce. . . *Then* was my heart broken. . .' and so on), the final verse shifts into a present tense imperative ('Deferre no time') and then into the future conditional ('They and my minde might chime'). The possibility of an incipient restoration of the channels of communication is confirmed by the final rhyming couplet – unique in the poem – which fulfils the narrator's appeal to God to 'mend my ryme' in the very act of making that appeal: the request is granted even as it is made, instantaneously. The poem itself, that is, becomes a vehicle of atonement, restoring the sensory communion between the narrator and his God.

IV.

Early modern authors, then, placed a high premium on God's senses: to offer sensory pleasure to God, and to know that one was nourished and sustained by his perceptual attention, was a form of grace, the highest spiritual honour. The notion of a deity who sees, hears, smells, tastes, and touches, and who feels affects of love, jealousy, compassion, anger, and so on, is, however, also problematic, conflicting with a broader insistence on God's transcendence.[58] The first of the Church of England's thirty-nine articles of 1563 specifies that 'there is but one living & true God, and he is everlasting, without bodye, partes, or passions'.[59] And whilst, as I commented earlier, scripture frequently anthropomorphises God, it also contains numerous warnings *against* anthropomorphising God. Sometimes, indeed, God is described in scripture in precisely the terms that scripture elsewhere prohibits: Exodus, for example, describes how 'the LORD repented of the evil which he thought to do unto his people', whilst Numbers states that 'God is not a man. . . that he should repent'.[60]

What are believers supposed to make of this conflict? The question comes to the fore in debates about the value or dangers of religious imagery. In answer to the prominence which reformers gave to the second commandment ('thou shalt not make to thyself a graven thing, nor the likeness of any thing that is in heaven above') Catholic apologists often pointed out that scripture attributes recognisable – and therefore representable – human features to God, arguing that there cannot therefore be any harm in picturing the divine in human form.[61] Frequently mentioned, for example, was the prophet Daniel's description of 'the ancient of days. . . [whose] garment was white as snow, and the hair of his head like clean wool'.[62] As the convert John Nicholls – who embraced Catholicism whilst on the continent then subsequently returned to England and re-converted to Protestantism – puts it in his 1581 *Recantation*, parroting the Roman Catholic church he has just left, 'seeing these things nowe uttered were seene of the Prophets, why then is it unlawfull for us to paint God with colours and karving?'[63] Additionally, many Catholic defences of devotional images cited Genesis's avowal that 'God said, Let us make man in our image' in order to argue that, in making man 'after our likeness', God implicitly sanctioned reciprocal acts of image-making *by* man: because human beings were made in the likeness of God, to represent God as something 'like' us, in physical form, is not irreverent.[64] Reformed writers are scathing about these arguments, which they take to indicate an arrogant presumption of equality between man and God: 'because God made man according to his Image', as Thomas Adams writes, 'therfore they, by way of recompence, will make God according to mans Image'.[65] Adams' sarcasm is pointed: in making God subject to human representation – in attempting in some sense to 'make God' as he was supposed to have 'made' us – Catholics sacrilegiously claim equality with God, an ability to requite the unpayable debt of gratitude owed for our creation.

Nonetheless, in citing this verse of Genesis, defenders of religious images reminded Protestant thinkers that if we are something like God, then – conversely and troublingly – God must logically be something like us.[66] How can this be, when we are mortal and finite, but God is immortal and infinite; when we wander in the mazes of our own error, but God is omniscient; when we are entrenched in sin, but God is immaculately good; when we are feeble, but God is omnipotent? In other words, by foregrounding both the abundance of anthropomorphic depictions of God in scripture, and Genesis' assertion that man was made in God's image, Catholic defences of devotional images forced reformers to confront a central enigma of Christian faith: how can it be that we are like God, and yet God is not like us?

John Calvin offers a two-pronged response to this question. Firstly, in his commentary on Genesis, he makes it clear that humankind's likeness to God is not physical: 'the Anthropomorphites were too gross in seeking this resemblance in the human body'. God, Calvin insists, is totally incorporeal, and humankind's resemblance to God – insofar as this image has escaped the defacement of the Fall – is purely 'spiritual'.[67] Secondly, Calvin posits the doctrine of accommodation as a resolution to the embarrassment of scriptural anthropomorphism.[68] As he writes in Volume 1 of *The institution of Christian religion*, translated by Thomas Norton in 1561:

> the Anthropomorphites are. . . easily confuted which have imagined God to consist of a bodye, because oftentimes the scripture ascribeth unto him a mouthe, eares, eyes, handes, and feete. For what man yea though he be sclenderly witted dooth not understande that God dooth so with us speake as it were childishly, as nurses doo with their babes? Therefore suche maners of speeche doo not so plainely expresse what God is, as they do apply the understanding of him to our sclender capacitie.[69]

From this perspective, the scriptural attribution of human senses and affects to God is simply an accommodation to our weakness, a concession to the human inability to comprehend the spiritual purity of the divine nature. Scriptural descriptions of God in terms which imply his embodiment, therefore, cannot be used to neutralise the second commandment's injunction against devotional images, because these scriptural descriptions are not representative of God's nature, but rather are indicative of human limitations.

There is, then, a tension here. On the one hand, as we have seen, Protestant writers such as Andrewes and Herbert place heavy emphasis on divine sensation, figuring God's perceptual attentiveness to us as central to the experience of grace. On the other hand, Protestant authorities insist strenuously on God's immateriality: God is a spiritual being, and scriptural invocations of his members, senses, and affects are mere accommodation to our human weakness. This tension is also inherent in Protestant discussions of devotional imagery. In such works, reformers accentuate God's physical and affective responsiveness in order to define the divine against the dead, corporeal images of Catholic iconography: paradoxically, Protestant polemic against idolatry insists on God's disembodiment by insisting on his sensitivity.

Reformist iconoclasm is often considered as a response to the (supposedly) hazardous sensuousness of devotional art. As Matthew Milner puts it, 'one of the most enduring stereotypes of the Reformation is the casting of idolatry as the epitome of sensory transgression, sensuality, and sensual excess. Reformers attacked the sensuality of late-medieval religious life'.[70] I do not intend to challenge this pervasive notion: reformers did clearly consider idolatry a sin of the senses, an over-investment in the corporeal. But by focusing so much on worshippers' uses (or rejection) of their senses, I want to suggest, scholars have ignored an equally pervasive conviction that the devotional use of images skews the sensory relation between humankind and God in the other direction, too: even as religious images compel a dangerous, intensely sensuous response from worshippers, they also erect as a deity an insensitive image, anaesthetised to the appeals of believers. Reformers' dread and loathing of the human tendency to sensuality, in other words, has a counterpart in an answering antipathy to – even a terror of – divine *in*sensitivity. Reformist iconoclasts fought against the human propensity to sensory self-indulgence, but they also battled the idea of an impassable, oblivious God.

The convert John Nicholls, for example, asserts that 'God is altogether wisedome and knowledge: whereas your images feele nothing, and understande as much'.[71] The idol is feared and reviled as a *dead* image, a divinity which is incapable of responding – sensorially, affectively, or intellectually – to the embodied devotion it elicits. Psalm 115, which Nicholls cites, is an important source here:

> Their idols are silver and gold, the work of men's hands. They have mouths, but they speak not: eyes have they, but they see not: They have ears, but they hear not: noses have they, but they smell not: They have hands, but they handle not.[72]

Idols are to be doubly despised, as the products of embodied human labour (they are 'the work of men's hands'), and as insensible matter. In his commentary on this psalm, Calvin describes how:

> Therefore as they list not too seeke God spiritually, they [idolaters] pluck him down out of his throne, and thrust him under dead elementes. Wereupon it commeth to passe that they direct their prayers to images, bicause they think that in them gods eares, ye & his eyes and hands are neere unto them.[73]

The desire to perceive the divine materially – to lodge him in or under 'dead elements' – segues into a desire to be perceived *by* the divine. The longing to be physically close to God is, specifically, a longing to be close to his ears, eyes, and hands: that is, his organs of sense. The idolatrous error, then, lies not only in believing that images facilitate human apprehension of God, but also in believing that they facilitate God's apprehension of humankind.

Following Calvin, Protestant thinkers and writers also foreground another threat: namely that in making and worshipping idols, men and women will become like idols, numb to grace. In the words of the clergyman William Bates, in his *The sovereign and final happiness of man* (1680):

> The End has always a powerful virtue to transform a Man into its likeness. . . . Thus carnal Objects when propounded as the End of a Man, secretly imprint on him their likeness, [so that] his Thoughts, Affections, and whole Conversation is carnal. As the Psalmist speaks of the Worshippers of Idols, *they that make them are like unto them, so is every one that trusteth in them:* whatever we adore and esteem, we are changed into its Image. Idolaters are as stupid and senceless, as the Idols to which they pay Homage.[74]

The process of worshipping idols results in a kind of anaesthesia, a loss of sensitivity and subsequently of intelligence. 'For they that crave life at dead things', as Calvin writes in in his commentary on the Psalms, 'do they not (as much as in them is) quenche all light of reason[?]'[75] Calvin's phrasing implies process: it is not (or not only) the case that senseless men make idols, but that the act of making idols makes men senseless. Human creation, here, is a process of self-defacement: in attempting to infuse inanimate images with life, men and women end up destroying the spark of sense and reason in themselves. According to reformers, then, in their sensual over-investment in senseless idols, Catholics transformed themselves into the dead images they worshipped, progressively and paradoxically anaesthetising themselves through an abundance of sensuality.

V.

Earlier in this essay I suggested that, for George Herbert, the resources of verse can serve to renew the sensory relationship between man and God. Just as the Protestant fascination with divine sensitivity is compromised by a conflicting insistence on divine transcendence, however, so too do the sensory resources of poetry have a troubling aspect: they can also corrupt the sensory relation between man and deity. Herbert explores this aspect in his 'Jordan' poems, which describe how even pious verse tends to vain over-elaboration, accruing a troublesome materiality in the process: 'curling with metaphors a plain intention', as Herbert writes, 'decking the sense, as if it were to sell'.[76] Poetry, that is, is inclined to make an idol of itself when it strives to communicate with the divine, substituting an abundance of ornament for plain 'sense'.

For the final section of this essay, however, I turn not to Herbert, but to the Huguenot poet Guillaume de Salluste Du Bartas's creation poem *The Divine weekes and works,* published in instalments between 1578 and 1603, and translated into English by Joshua Sylvester in 1611. Here,

I take Du Bartas as a transnational poet – familiar to English audiences primarily in Sylvester's translation – who offers a sustained and immensely subtle, if strikingly idiosyncratic, exploration of the broader reformist interest in the intimate relations between poetry, idolatry, and sensation. Du Bartas is often described as a poet who avoids, or at least negotiates with consummate care, tricky doctrinal bones of contention.[77] Whatever poise or tranquillity Du Bartas's verse achieves, however, is a result not of delicate conciliation, or an avoidance of the dangerous peaks and troughs of polemic, but rather of a bold holding in balance of radically opposed streams of thought and feeling. In Sylvester's translation at least, the impression of equilibrium that Du Bartas's poetry can give is a result of his careful counterbalancing of a series of extreme contraries, rather than a cautious avoidance of such extremes.

This is certainly the case with his investigation of the relation between divine and human creativity, and of the potentially idolatrous inclinations of the latter, which comes to the fore in his account of God's creation of Adam in the 'sixth day' of first week. Describing Adam's body – and by extension, the human body more generally – as 'the divinest Master-Piece of Art' and as 'a second God, of Earth', Du Bartas describes the human impulse to engage in image-making as a consequence or outgrowth of the fact that mankind itself is a product of divine artistry:

> This curious Lust to imitate the best
> And fairest Works of the Almightiest,
> By rare effects bears record of thy Linage
> And high descent; and that his sacred Image
> Was in thy [i.e. man's] Soule ingrav'n. . .[78]

As we have seen, this notion that humankind's innate inclination to make artistic images attests to our own status as images of God is a key component of Catholic polemic in this period, levied in response to Protestant condemnations of idolatry. For Du Bartas, unlike Calvin, the human impulse to imitate divine creation is not a pernicious by-product of the Fall, but is innate in mankind from the very beginning. In Sylvester's translation, however, the verse veers back from articulating the full implications of this. Whilst Du Bartas's Calvinist credentials were firmly established in English minds, a residual anxiety about the influence of his Catholic compatriots on his verse is evident in Sylvester's efforts throughout his translation to highlight or enhance Du Bartas's reformist sentiments.[79] Here, even as Du Bartas deploys an argument associated with the defence of devotional images, Sylvester's use of the pejorative phrase 'curious Lust' to translate Du Bartas's more neutral term for the artistic impulse – 'chatouilleus desir', literally 'ticklish desire' or 'wish' – resonates with Protestant condemnations of such images.[80] In Sylvester's translation, the Catholic exaltation of human creativity and Calvinist suspicion of the same coexist: humankind's desire to 'imitate' the world around us is part of our divine inheritance, but it is also troublesome and potentially idolatrous.

Of course, Du Bartas's own poem not only describes but is itself profoundly implicated in this dynamic, for *The divine weeks* constitutes nothing less than a poetic recreation of creation itself. Du Bartas's own poem, that is, is itself an image or a series of images which imitate 'the best / And fairest Works of the Almightiest', thereby potentially placing Du Bartas in competition with the God he professes only to glorify.[81] Rather than attempting to circumvent the spiritual pitfalls of his own poetic ambition, however, Du Bartas appears to revel in them, drawing numerous parallels between his own poetic image-making and the originary acts of divine creation that he so powerfully depicts. We can see this in his extensive use of ekphrasis in his description of the creation of Adam. Ekphrasis is a rhetorical figure according to which an author describes a visual image (for example, a painting or sculpture) in a vivid, evocative way that is intended to recreate that image in the reader's mind.[82] As such, in Protestant discourse ekphrasis could be subject to the same charges of idolatry as other forms of visual art with some claim to represent the divine.[83] In describing Adam's body as a 'masterpiece of Art', and then in depicting that body in highly visual terms supposed to invoke the experience of viewing a picture, Du Bartas is doubly vulnerable to such charges.

Du Bartas's poem, however, evades idolatry precisely where it flirts most outrageously with it, and that this evasion is effected in part by the importance that Du Bartas gives to the sensory dimensions of artistic creation: his poetic recreation of the creation of Adam is not idolatrous because the images that he creates are not dead, but alive. Du Bartas's Adam, like God's, is a breathing, sensing, responsive being, vivified by the poet's skill. This animate quality is evident both Du Bartas's account of God's infusion of breath into Adam, and in his ekphrastic descriptions of Adam's sense organs. For Philip Sidney, whose *An apologie for poetrie* (1595) bears witness to his admiration for Du Bartas, humankind's divine origins are expressed in verse 'when with the force of a divine breath [the poet] bringeth things forth far surpassing [nature's] dooings'.[84] The link between divine exhalation and poetic inspiration is brought to the fore by Du Bartas:

> . . . this most peer-les learned Imager,
> Life to his lovely Picture to confer. . .
> . . .breathing, sent as from the lively Spring
> Of his Divineness some small Riverling.[85]

God's infusion of breath into Adam confers life upon him, and subsequently upon the human race. Significantly, however, the economy of breath here is not linear but cyclical, with Du Bartas himself returning it to God in the form of his own poetry: 'Inspired by that Breath', Du Bartas goes on, 'this Breath desire / I to describe'.[86] In this elegant chiastic formulation, Du Bartas's poem both describes the moment that facilitated its own existence, and circumscribes it, re-creating the vivifying 'Breath' of God as a *product* of its own 'inspired' lines. Syntactically, Du Bartas's inspiration precedes the breath that God gave to Adam. Neither breath – 'that' or 'this' – takes ultimate priority. Du Bartas's poem re-creates the moment that enabled it: inspiration is reciprocal. This suggestion that Du Bartas's own poetic virtuosity confers life on the images that it describes is reinforced by his prosody, as the use of the caesura in the middle of the line 'inspired by that Breath, this Breath desire', also present in the original French, inserts the rhythms of breath into the verse itself.[87]

We can see a similar strategy deployed in Du Bartas's vividly visual account of the parts of the human body, exemplified by Adam. Whilst Du Bartas's blazon of Adam's body as a whole is detailed and evocative, the elaboration of ekphrasis peaks in his descriptions of the sense organs. Adam's eyes, for example, are:

> These lovely Lamps, whose sweet sparks lively turning,
> With sodain glaunce set coldest hearts a-burning,
> These windows of the Soule, these starry Twinns,
> These *Cupids* quivers have so tender skins
> Through which (as through a pair of shining glasses)
> Their radiant point of pearcing splendor passes. . .
> The twinkling Lids with their quick-trembling hairs
> Defend the Eyes from thousand dang'rous fears.[88]

In focusing his use of ekphrasis on the sense organs in this way, Du Bartas animates the images he creates, sidestepping the potential accusation that his poem deals in the construction of dead idols. Adam's eye is not a static, lifeless image, but an entity which both feels (it is 'tender'), and which looks back at us, 'turning' its 'sparks' to glance upon us, setting hearts burning, 'twinkling' and blinking. From the very beginning, Du Bartas suggests, human perception was reciprocal: and in recreating the creation of Adam's eyes, he involves the reader in the very first exchange of glances between God and man.

VI.

For early modern men and women, then, the question of the scope, quality, and significance of God's perception of humankind was at least as pressing as the question of the scope, quality, and significance of humankind's perception of God. Protestant writers and thinkers across a broad spectrum (from radical reformers including Calvin himself, to later establishment figures such Hall, Hacket, and Stillingfleet) may have expressed anxiety about the dangerous allure of sensory worship, but they were equally concerned about the prospect of an anaesthetised, imperturbable deity. In the works of such writers, God employs his lower senses of smell, taste, and touch, as well as sight and hearing, in order to apprehend his creatures. God's senses have some distinctive features – they are spiritual and incorporeal, constant and consistent, and active and sustaining – but they also exist in a dynamic, reciprocal relation with the human sensorium. Human virtue and vice emerge as sensible entities; by pursuing the former and rejecting the latter, men and women might make themselves pleasant to God's perception, thereby cultivating a form of attention coterminous with the experience of grace.

The notion of a sensing – and by extension, an embodied – God was also profoundly troubling, however, particularly in the context of debates surrounding devotional imagery. For some Protestants, idolatry was doubly problematic: on the one hand, it represented an excess of sensuality, a heretical effort to give God physical form; on the other hand, idolaters posited an unfeeling, unresponsive deity, thereby revealing their own lack of 'sense'. The resources of poetry, I have suggested, offer a way to negotiate – if not quite a way out of – this double bind. For George Herbert, the aural harmony of verse effects and represents the renewal of sensory harmony between man and God. For Du Bartas, the resources of ekphrasis – vivid visualisation – enable the poet to replicate God's original act of creation, a form of poetic image-making which veers dangerously close to idolatry, but which is redeemed when it is employed in order to animate sensorially the images that it creates. For both Herbert and Du Bartas, the images produced by poetry involve the reader in a perceptual exchange with the divine. And that is not to be sniffed at.

Notes

Research leading to this essay received funding from the European Research Council under the European Union's Seventh Framework Programme (FP7/2007–2013)/ERC grant agreement no 617849. Thanks to Tim Stuart-Buttle for helpful comments on a draft of this essay. Thanks, too, to audiences at Durham University and the University of Cambridge for their generous comments, questions, and suggestions.

1 Psalm 141:2 (KJV).
2 Launcelot Andrewes, *Scala coeli. Nineteen sermons concerning prayer* (London, 1611), E8v. Throughout this essay, I modernise typography in quotations from early modern sources.
3 Holly Dugan, *The Ephemeral History of Perfume: Scent and Sense in Early Modern England* (Baltimore: John Hopkins University Press, 2011), 29. On the ambiguous status of incense, see also Holly Crawford Pickett, 'The Idolatrous Nose: Incense on the Early Modern Stage', in *Religion and Drama in Early Modern England*, ed. Jane Hwang Degenhardt and Elizabeth Williamson (Farnham: Ashgate, 2011), 21–22.

4 In recent decades, some historians have preferred the lowercase plural 'reformations' to the more traditional 'the Reformation'. In preferring the latter, I follow Peter Marshall in his '(Re)defining the English Reformation', *Journal of British Studies* 48 (2009): 564–86. Notably, Marshall demonstrates that '"the Reformation" is. . . not just an artificial construct of later historians but a central perception and organizing category of contemporaries themselves'. Marshall, '(Re)defining the English Reformation', 569.

5 See Abigail Shinn, 'The Senses and the Seventeenth-Century Conversion Narrative', in this volume.

6 Joe Moshenska, *Feeling Pleasures: The Sense of Touch in Renaissance England* (Oxford: Oxford University Press, 2014), 30–45.

7 There are numerous accounts of this traditional sensory hierarchy in scholarly literature. See, *inter alia*, Robert Jütte, *A History of the Senses: From Antiquity to Cyberspace* (Cambridge: Polity, 2005), 55–71.

8 Richard Sibbes, *The returning backslider* (London, 1639), S2v-S3r.

9 Susan Ashbrook Harvey discusses the olfactory coding of religious virtue and vice in the context of late antique Christianity in chapter 5 of her *Scenting Salvation: Ancient Christianity and the Olfactory Imagination* (Berkley: University of California Press, 2006), but the focus is on humankind's apprehension of the divine, rather than vice versa.

10 1 Corinthians 13:12 (KJV).

11 See, for example, Matthew 9:10 (Christ eating); Mark 4: 38 (Christ sleeping); John 9:6 (Christ spitting); and John 11:35 (Christ weeping); all KJV.

12 Isaiah 11:1–4 (KJV).

13 On the complex textual and translation issues arising from this passage, see Jeremiah Unterman, 'The (Non)sense of Smell in Isaiah 11:3', *Hebrew Studies* 33 (1992): 17–23; Ian Ritchie, 'The Nose Knows: Bodily Knowing in Isaiah 11:3', *Journal for the Study of the Old Testament* 25 (2000): 59–73; and Yael Avrahami, *The Senses of Scripture: Sensory Perception in the Hebrew Bible* (New York and London: Continuum, 2012), 105.

14 Arthur Jackson, *Annotations upon the whole book of Isaiah* (London, 1682), S3v.

15 On the odour of sanctity, see Constance Classen, *Aroma: The Cultural History of Smell* (London: Routledge, 1994), 52–54; Harvey, *Scenting Salvation:*, chapter 5; and Jonathan Reinarz, *Past Scents: Historical Perspectives on Smell* (Urbana: University of Illinois Press, 2014), 38–43.

16 Jackson, *Annotations upon. . . Isaiah*, S3v. On the relation between smell and sagacity, see Dugan, *The Ephemeral History*, 183–84.

17 Robert Southwell, *An epistle of comfort to the reverend priestes* (Paris [London], 1587), M8r.

18 See, for example, Exodus 7:5 (God's hands); Numbers 6:25 (God's face); Psalm 33:6 (God's mouth and breath); Deuteronomy 11:12 (God's eyes), Psalm 34: 15 (God's eyes and ears); all KJV.

19 See, for example, Exodus 20:5 (God's jealousy); 1 Kings 11:9 (God's anger); Deuteronomy 28:63 (God rejoicing); Judges 9:13 (God cheered by wine); Psalm 37:12–13 and Psalm 2:2–4 (God's laugher); Isaiah 42:14 (God crying); all KJV.

20 Exodus 15:8 (KJV). See also Psalm 18:15. God's nostrils are also invoked (and said to smoke) in order to express divine fury: see 2 Samuel 22:9; 2 Samuel 22:16; Job 4:9; Job 41:20; and Psalm 18:8 (all KJV). In Hebrew, the word for 'nose' can also mean 'anger'; see G. Johannes Botterweck and Helmer Ringgren, *Theological Dictionary of the Old Testament* (William B Eerdmans Publishing Co., 1978 [revised edition]), 1:351–52.

21 Isaiah 65:5 (KJV). On the close relation between sacrifice, smell, and incense, see Jonathan Reinarz, *Past Scents: Historical Perspectives on Smell* (Champaign, IL: University of Illinois Press, 2014), 27–35.

22 Ephesians 5:2 (KJV).

23 Edward Stillingfleet, *Sermons preached on several occasions to which a discourse is annexed concerning the true reason of the sufferings of Christ* (London, 1673), Yy2v-Yy3r.

24 Ibid., Yy3r.

25 Ibid., *Concerning the true reason*, Zz1r.

26 Henry More, *An exposition of the seven epistles to the seven churches* (London, 1669), G4r.

27 John Hacket, *A century of sermons upon several remarkable subjects* (London, 1675), Iiiii3v.

28 Ibid., Iiiii2v.

29 See Augustine, *Saint Augustines confessions*, trans. William Watts (London, 1631), Cc3v-Cc4r.

30 Hacket, *A century of sermons*, Iiiii4v.

31 There is precedent for this analogy between God's senses and sunlight: as Augustine notes in his *City of God*, the ancient Roman philosopher and natural theologian Marcus Varro had speculated that 'the stones and the earth which we see in the world. . . are as the bones and nails of God, while the sun, moon, and the stars which we perceive by our senses and which are his means of sensibility, these represent God's senses; the ether is his mind'. Augustine, *City of God*, trans. Henry Bettenson (London: Penguin, 2003), 281.

32 Hacket, *A century of sermons*, Iiiii4v.

33 For a brilliant account of the role of the senses, especially taste, in Herbert's poetry, see *Michael Schoenfeldt, Bodies and Selves in Early Modern England: : Physiology and Inwardness in Spenser, Shakespeare, Herbert, and Milton* (Cambridge: Cambridge University Press, 1999), chapter four.

34 George Herbert, 'The Glance', *The Temple* (Cambridge, 1633), G11v.

35 John Donne, *Devotions upon emergent occasions* (London, 1624), L3r-v.

36 Donne, *Devotions*, L3v-L4r.

37 Donne, *Devotions*, L4r.

38 Thomas Adams, *A divine herball* (London, 1616), I4r.

39 Luke 18:9–14.

40 Adams, *A divine herball*, K1r-v.

41 Joseph Hall, *The contemplations upon the history of the New Testament* (London, 1661), Aa1v. Similarly, excoriating the Israelites for apostasy, the independent minister Jeremiah Burroughs explains that 'God will take no delight in them, they will be but sowre things unto the palate of God. . . Gods palate is more delicate than to tast such sowre and sapless things, than those are that comes from them'. Burroughs, *An exposition. . . upon the eighth, ninth, & tenth chapters of the prophesy of Hosea* (London, 1650), Aa2v.

42 Edward Benlowes, *Theophila* (London, 1652), E1r.

43 William Tyndale, Robert Barnes, and John Frith, *The whole workes of W. Tyndall, John Frith, and Doct. Barnes* (London, 1573), Ff5r. Tyndale's emphasis on salt is symbolically significant, for – as a preservative – salt was associated with the safeguarding of purity. 'The Apostles were not without cause called salte of the earth', explains Robert Southwell in his *Epistle of Comfort*, 'for as the salt preserveth flesh from the vermin, stenche, and corruption. . . So doth the true faithe geve remedies, against all stench and corruption of vice'. Southwell, *Epistle of Comfort*, M6r.

44 For the Sermon on the Mount, see Matthew 5–7.

45 As Michael Schoenfeldt writes, 'the intimacy between God and human that was lost because of a dietary transgression – consuming the forbidden fruit – is restored by an act of eating'. Schoenfeldt, *Bodies and Souls*, 100. Matthew Milner comments on a pervasive belief that the believer must be 'seasoned by the salt of faith. [The Eucharist] was a meal where both God and communicant were both feast and feaster'. Milner, *The Senses and the English Reformation* (Farnham: Ashgate, 2011), 152.
46 John Smith, *Essex dove* (London, 1629), K5r.
47 George Petter, *A learned, pious, and practical commentary, upon the Gospel according to St. Mark* (London, 1661), Vvvv2v.
48 Chronicles 12:22 (KJV).
49 Lancelot Andrewes, *A sermon preached before His Majestie* (London, 1610) D3v.
50 Andrewes, *A sermon*, F1v.
51 Thomas Goodwin, *The great interest of states & kingdoms* (London, 1646), F4v. Similarly, see also Thomas Gataker, *Gods eye on His Israel* (London, 1645), F3r; and Richard Baxter, *Directions for weak distempered Christians* (London, 1669), F6v.
52 Katherine Craik, *Reading Sensations in Early Modern England* (Basingstoke: Palgrave Macmillan, 2007), 8.
53 Herbert, 'Church-lock and Key', *The Temple*, C5r.
54 Herbert, 'Church-lock and Key', C5v.
55 Herbert, 'Deniall', *The Temple*, C12r.
56 Herbert, 'Deniall', C12v.
57 Ibid.
58 Paul Gavrilyuk explores how the Church Fathers negotiated the paradox of an impassable God who nonetheless suffers in *The Suffering of the Impassible God: The Dialectics of Patristic Thought* (Oxford: Oxford University Press, 2006).
59 Church of England, *Articles* (London, 1563), A2r.
60 Exodus 32:14 and Numbers 23:19; see also 1 Samuel 15:29: 'the Strength of Israel will not lie nor repent: for he is not a man, that he should repent' (all KJV).
61 Exodus 20:4 (DV).
62 Daniel 7:9 (DV).
63 John Nicholls, *A declaration of the recantation of John Nichols* (London, 1581), G2v.
64 Genesis 1:26 (KJV).
65 Thomas Adams, *Five sermons* (London, 1626), D2v.
66 Philip C. Almond comments on the potential for anthropomorphism inherent in Genesis 1:26 in his *Adam and Eve in Seventeenth-Century Thought* (Cambridge: Cambridge University Press, 1999), 9.
67 John Calvin, *A commentarie of John Calvine, upon the first booke of Moses called Genesis* (London, 1578), C6r-v.
68 On Calvin's doctrine of accommodation, see Jon Balserak, *Divinity Compromised: A Study of Divine Accommodation in the Thought of John Calvin* (Dordrecht: Springer, 2006).
69 John Calvin, *The institution of Christian religion*, trans. Thomas Norton (London, 1561), D6r.
70 Matthew Milner, 'To Captivate the Senses: Sensory Governance, Heresy, and Idolatry in Mid-Tudor England', in *Religion and the Senses in Early Modern Europe*, ed. Wietse de Boer and Christine Göttler (Leiden: Brill, 2012), 307.
71 Nicholls, *A declaration*, G1v.
72 Psalm 115:4–7 (KJV). The Geneva translation is not substantively different.

73 John Calvin, *The Psalmes of David and others. With M. John Calvins commentaries* (London, 1571), Sss9r.
74 William Bates, *The sovereign and final happiness of man* (London, 1680), H7r-v.
75 Calvin, *The Psalmes of David*, Ssss8v.
76 Herbert, 'Jordan [II]', *The Temple*, D12r.
77 Kathryn Banks, for example, writes that 'Du Bartas rarely engages with theological problems in the *Sepmaine*', and refers to 'his general practice in the *Sepmaine* of avoiding complicated and potentially controversial theological issues'. Banks, *Cosmos and Image in the Renaissance: French Love Lyric and Natural Philosophical Poetry* (London: Legenda, 2008), 36 and 39.
78 Guillaume de Salluste Du Bartas, *Du Bartas his devine weekes and workes*, trans. Joshua Sylvester (London, 1611), N5v.
79 As Susan Snyder notes in the introduction to her edition of Sylvester's translation, 'however admirable as poet and Protestant, Du Bartas was after all a foreigner. Sylvester had not only to translate his poem but to naturalize it. . . Sylvester creates in the *Weeks* a distinctively, even violently Protestant point of view which is absent in his original'. Snyder, introduction to Du Bartas, *The Divine Weeks and Works of Guillaume de Saluste, Sieur du Bartas*, trans. Joshua Sylvester, ed. Snyder (Oxford: Oxford University Press, 1979), 1:50–51.
80 Du Bartas's original French phrase, 'ce chatouilleus desir', does not have the same pejorative implications: it can be translated more literally as 'this ticklish desire' or 'ticklish wish'. Guillaume de Saluste Du Bartas, *La sepmaine, ou Création du monde* (Paris, 1578), Aa4r. Thanks to Raphaële Garrod for discussing the connotations of 'chatouilleus' with me.
81 Banks discusses the close relation between divine and human artistry, particularly image-making, in *Cosmos and Image*; see especially chapter 1.
82 In Claire Preston's words, ekphrasis is 'verbal pictorialism'. Preston, 'Ekphrasis', in *Renaissance Figures of Speech*, ed. Sylvia Adamson, Gavin Alexander, and Katrin Ettenhuber (Cambridge: Cambridge University Press, 2007), 117.
83 This suspicion has deep roots: for a penetrating discussion of the relation between ekphrasis and idolatry in Lollard culture, see Bruce Holsinger, 'Lollard *Ekphrasis*: Situated. Aesthetics and Literary History', *Journal of Medieval and Early Modern Studies* 35 (2005): 67–90.
84 Philip Sidney, *An apologie for poetrie* (London, 1595), C2r. On the relationship between Sidney and Du Bartas, see Alan Sinfield, 'Sidney and Du Bartas', *Comparative Literature* 27 (1975): 8–20.
85 Du Bartas, *Devine weekes and workes*, N2v.
86 Ibid.
87 The line reads, 'Inspiré de ce Vent, ce Ventie veus décrire'. Du Bartas, *La sepmaine*, Aa1r.
88 Du Bartas, *Devine weekes and workes*, M7v-M8r.

Afterword: making sense of religion

Michael Schoenfeldt

It is tempting, particularly for those of us who engage in academic study of the products of the religious imagination in earlier cultures, to underestimate or ignore the role of the senses in religion. The cerebral nuances of theology seem so more congenial to our analytical machinery, and our disciplinary expertise, than the wispy, ephemeral stuff of sensation. This volume shows the great virtue of resisting that temptation. The scholars gathered here demonstrate the myriad ways that religious experience involves not just the brain, but the hands and heart and nostrils and eyes and ears and mouth of the worshipper. Indeed, once one starts paying attention to sensuous phenomena, images and experiences of touch and smell and sight and taste leap from the pages devoted to religious discourse. Religion, these scholars demonstrate, is not an escape from the material world, but a deliberate intensification of lived experience, particularly experience achieved through the senses. Some of our suspicion about the role of the senses in Christianity may derive from St Paul; not only did he define faith as 'the substance of things hoped for, the evidence of things not seen' (Hebrews 11:1 AV), but he asserts that 'eye hath not seen nor ear heard... the things which God prepared for them that love him. But God hath revealed *them* unto us by his Spirit' (1 Corinthians 2.9-10 AV). As the essays in this collection make clear, however, religion requires the senses, even to begin to conceive the unseen. And it is through the senses that the mysteries of Christianity begin to enter into the heart of the believer. In its most vital and compelling incarnations, religion engages the raw, wild, primal matter of our entire beings; it addresses body, mind, and soul at once. When religion ignores the sumptuous, unruly stuff of the senses, furthermore, devotion can desiccate. A religion whose practices neglect or demean the senses can succumb to arid intellectualizing or vapid moralizing, and in the process, render itself largely dormant to the common worshiper.

Historically, however, the senses have been perceived as spiritually hazardous, since even devout sensuous experience can drift easily into distracting sensuality. Perversely, Christianity has been much more at ease with sensations related to pain and suffering than with those associated with joy and pleasure. At the core of Christian worship is the crucifix, a conspicuous instrument of torture and death. In much traditional Christian thinking about the senses, only pain and its related sensations carry any ethical legitimacy, probably because they link humans to the unearthly suffering of their savior; pleasure, by contrast, is seen as an engine of the devil, continually tempting humans to ungodly sensual indulgence.[1] One of the many pleasant surprises in this collection that there is remarkably little attention paid to suffering, but perhaps that is because suffering is such a conventional and unsurprising subject for Christianity.

The rampant suspicion about the senses that suffuses so much Christian commentary, moreover, is an implicit acknowledgement of their immense power, for good or ill. As the inevitable gateway between inner experience and the outer world, the senses provide a potentially slippery avenue for either sinful extravagance or devout adoration. By the same token, they are closely tied to the dynamic emotions that can be stirred and manipulated through them. By means of the senses, devotion shifts from abstract concept to urgent sensation. The senses provide physiological access to the otherwise inaccessible quandaries of religion.

Deliberately juxtaposing essays by medievalists and early modernists, this volume challenges the persistent idea that the Middle Ages denied the senses while the Renaissance celebrated them.[2] It is refreshing to see the continuum between the Middle Ages and the Renaissance explored with such scrutiny, and the changes and continuities recorded with such nuance and rigour. By demonstrating sensuous engagement on the part of a wide range of writers and practices, the volume also confronts the prevalent perception that certain denominations are far more involved than others in matters relating to the senses. The essays presented here implicitly dispute the widely accepted claim that 'Protestant meditation did not stimulate the senses'.[3] While it may have worked differently, and at times emphasised different senses from Catholic practices, Protestant meditation and devotion did not fail to engage the senses. Indeed, a leading Puritan preacher, Stephen Egerton, published a book entitled *The Boring of the Eare* (1623), depicting in detail the processes by which one must ready oneself in order to hear a sermon properly. While the title inadvertently advertises the effect many Puritan sermons must have had on their hearers, it also indicates the critical importance of an active sense of hearing to allow divine messages to penetrate to the core of the believer. To 'heare then', Egerton argues, 'is to attend with the eare, to receiue with the heart'; the biggest impediment to proper hearing is 'carnall Securitie, Impenitence, Worldliness, Uncleannesse of life, etc., which things altogether draw men away from hearing, or else make them heare with a deaf eare, or a dead heart'.[4] Hearing well is for Egerton a profoundly ethical action.

In a poem called 'The Invitation', the Conformist George Herbert (a poet invoked frequently in this collection) cleverly exploits the fact that the Eucharistic feast entails the primal activities of eating and drinking. This meal, Herbert suggests, can be imagined as the epitome of epicurean sensuous experience, fulfilling rather than repudiating terrestrial appetite. Herbert tells those who have sought pleasure in their lives that this feast will finally give them exactly what they have always wanted. The poem extends a gracious invitation to those whose 'taste / Is your waste', those 'whom wine / Doth define' and those 'whose love / Is your dove'.[5] 'Here is joy', the speaker announces (l. 22), suggesting that the carnal satisfactions of the Eucharistic meal in fact embody various sensuous indulgences frequently rendered as sinful.[6] The Puritan John Milton is so fully invested in the religious centrality of the senses and the appetites that his *Paradise Lost* emphasises that angels possess 'every lower faculty / Of sense, whereby they hear, see, smell, touch, taste'.[7] As we see, his angels even eat earthly food with relish. Both Conformists and Puritans regularly address the importance of the senses in the effort to exhort an audience to their religious persuasion.

This admirably interdisciplinary volume does a splendid job of addressing what John Arnold, in the opening essay, terms 'the inherent complexities and tensions within the senses'. The essays reveal fascinating accounts of unanticipated but fruitful intersections of sense and spirit. The essay by Richard Newhauser analyses the anxious processes by which Peraldus imagined that the volatile senses could be properly steered toward heaven. The essays by Erin Lambert and Emilie Murphy, on the other hand, provide engaging analyses of the rich soundscapes produced by choirs and churchbells – sounds that must have suffused everyday religious experience. C. M. Woolgar's essay asks a fascinating question – by what sensuous processes might something be made holy? – while Joe Moshenska and Abigail Shinn both offer absorbing accounts of the critical role of the senses in the conscientious act of religious conversion. Several essays attest to something that is frequently forgotten: the subtle ways in which language is itself a profoundly sensory phenomenon, invariably entering consciousness through the eyes and ears and even touch. Robin Macdonald's essay reminds us that the very material on which something is written affects both the way it is composed, and the way it is read. Subha Mukherji explores how these complex interactions of matter, spirit, and sense translate to some luminous and troubling moments on the Elizabethan stage, while Bronwyn Wallace offers an edgy analysis of Robert Southwell's interpretation of Mary Magdalen's inevitably frustrated longing to touch the resurrected Jesus. In the final essay, Elizabeth Swann investigates the surprising phenomena of works that imagine God's sensory experience. Together, these essays develop a powerful case for the critical importance of the senses to any study of religion.

Almost every essay in this wonderful collection emphasises the Janus-faced nature of the senses – the crucial role they can play in devotional attention, and the myriad ways in which they can distract from the divine subject. It is telling that when we think of the proper bodily disposition for prayer, we imagine closed eyes, and hands touching each other, as if to seal off our sensory engagements with the outside world as much as possible from the powerful but distracting senses of sight and touch. But other senses are more difficult to shut down; we have no flaps to cover our ears and keep out distracting sounds. In a sermon, John Donne (another writer who makes several appearances in this collection) describes with some exasperation how easily the senses can distract the devout worshipper from appropriate attention to the divine:

> I throw my selfe downe in my Chamber, and I call in, and invite God, and his Angels thither, and when they are there, I neglect God and his Angels, for the noise of a Flie, for the ratling of a Coach, for the whining of a doore; I talke on, in the same posture of praying,; Eyes lifted up; knees bowed downe; as though I prayed to God; and, if God, or his Angels should aske me, when I thought last of God in that prayer, I cannot tell: Sometimes I finde that I had forgot what I was about, but when I began to forget it, I cannot tell. A memory of yesterdays pleasures, a feare of to morrows dangers, a straw under my knee, a noise in mine eare, a light in mine eye, an any thing, a nothing, a fancy, a Chimera in my braine, troubles me in my prayer.[8]

As Donne knew all too well, the senses could be a hindrance to devotion, allowing irrelevant aural, tactile, and visual phenomena to invade a consciousness that aspires to be turned exclusively to God.

But Donne, a popular and immensely talented preacher, also knew that properly concentrated senses were an essential element of true religious experience. In a sermon on the Annunciation, that joyous but perplexing moment when the Word truly was made flesh and dwelt among us, Donne offers a stunning description of the pleasurable sensations one can receive from the well-chosen words of another:

> a man may upon the hearing of something that strikes him, that affects him, feel this springing, this exultation, this melting, and colliquation of the inwardest bowels of his soule; a new affection, a new passion, beyond the joy ordinarily conceived upon earthly happinesses.[9]

The Incarnation occasions Donne's fulsome praise of the deeply sensuous experience of being moved to joy, in the innermost core of our being, by another's words. For Donne, this involves an exhilaration that is at once profoundly intellectual and deeply visceral. And it starts with the thoroughly sensuous act of hearing.

One can begin to make sense of religion, then, by exploring the myriad ways in which the senses are oriented toward sacred subjects. The senses were unavoidable, even indispensable, thresholds linking the external world to the inner recesses of the individual. In various religious texts, materials, and practices, we can see that the senses, when properly engaged, were imagined to offer a conduit to spiritual matters. A full history of religious experience would be incomprehensible without careful and rigorous attention to the role of the senses. The essays in this collection allow us to explore the rich and complex relationship between earlier sensory worlds and our own. While the senses have probably not changed that much over the centuries, what they apprehend, and how they construe sensation, certainly has.

When Bottom wakes from his dream in Shakespeare's *Midsummer Night's Dream*, as Mukherji's essay suggests, he amusingly bungles the quotation from Paul in 1 Corinthians 2.9 in fascinating ways: 'The eye of man hath not heard, the ear of man hath not seen, man's hand is not able to taste, his tongue to conceive, nor his heart to report what my dream was'.[10] His unintentionally nullified synesthesia about the 'vision' he has just had, which was 'past the wit of man', gently mocks Paul's suggestion that faith is infinitely superior to the senses in religious devotion. Yet even the Pauline letters can when necessary argue that the sacred is not so much a renunciation of this world as an intensification of its sensations and experiences. When Paul wants to describe the invariably partial nature of human apprehension of the sacred, he writes: 'For now we see through a glass, darkly; but then face to face' (1 Corinthians 13.12 AV). And in the letter to the Hebrews, the author (probably not Paul) remarks: 'For the word of God is quick, and powerful, and sharper than any two-edged sword, piercing even to the dividing asunder of soul and spirit, and of the joints and marrow, and is a discerner of the thoughts and intents of the heart' (Hebrews 4:12 AV). Like Donne's account of piercing eloquence, this riveting passage describes no 'common sense', but rather the vivid, visceral experience of a fully engaged worshiper responding to religion's ability to percolate through the senses into the innermost recesses of the body. In such moments, the ineffable material of religion is rendered palpable and dynamic, wrenching humans out of the everyday and into a realm of intensified sensation that may be as close as we can get in this life to something approaching the sacred.

Notes

1 For exemplary accounts of the importance of the sensation of suffering in early modern Christianity, see, for example Jan Frans Van Dijkhuizen, *Pain and Compassion in Early Modern English Literature and Culture* (London: D. S. Brewer, 2012); the essays collected in *The Sense of Suffering: Constructions of Physical Pain in Early Modern Culture*, ed. Van Dijkhuizen and Karl Van Enenkel (Leiden: Brill, 2009); and Mitchell B. Merback, *The Thief, the Cross, and the Wheel: Pain and the Spectacle of Punishment Medieval and Renaissance Europe* (Chicago, IL: University of Chicago Press, 1998).

2 This seductive historical fiction continues to surface in some otherwise essential works, such as Stephen Greenblatt's *The Swerve: How the World Became*

Modern (New York: W.W. Norton, 2011), and Richard Strier's *The Unrepentant Renaissance: From Petrarch to Shakespeare to Milton* (Chicago, IL: University of Chicago Press, 2012).

3   Barbara Kiefer Lewalski, *Protestant Poetics and the Seventeenth-Century Religious Lyric* (Princeton, NJ: Princeton University Press, 1979) 150.

4   Stephen Egerton, *The Boring of the Eare* (1623), A4.

5   George Herbert, 'The Invitation', in Helen Wilcox, ed., *The English Poems of George Herbert* (Cambridge: Cambridge University Press, 2007), 624–25.

6   See my essay, 'Herbert and Pleasure', *George Herbert Journal*, 38 (2014/2015): 145–57.

7   John Milton, *Paradise Lost*, in Stephen Orgel and Jonathan Goldberg, eds., *The Major Works*, Oxford World's Classics (Oxford: Oxford University Press, 2003), 5.410-11.

8   John Donne, *The Sermons*, ed. George R. Potter and Evelyn M. Simpson, 10 vols. (Berkeley: University of California Press, 1953–62), 7: 264–65.

9   Donne, *Sermons*, 4: 159.

10   William Shakespeare, *A Midsummer Night's Dream*, The Arden Shakespeare, ed. Sukanta Chaudhuri (London: Bloomsbury Arden Shakespeare, 2017) 4.1, 205–9.

Index